Lois C. Heming
Univ. of Natal,
1976.

P9-CAS-336

MY GEMS
William M. Harnett
National Gallery of Art, Washington, D.C.
Gift of the Avalon Foundation

THE GREAT CONDUCTO

HAROLD C. SCHONBERG

The
Great Conductors

LONDON
VICTOR GOLLANCZ LTD
1973

COPYRIGHT © 1967 BY HAROLD C. SCHONBERG
ISBN 0 575 00029 5

First published February 1968
Second impression May 1973

Quotation on pages 18-19, reprinted from The New York Review of Books, *is copyright © 1966 by Igor Stravinsky.*

PRINTED IN GREAT BRITAIN BY
LOWE AND BRYDONE (PRINTERS) LTD., THETFORD, NORFOLK

For many reasons, to *The New York Times*

Contents

List of Illustrations

Preface

BASICALLY THIS BOOK is a study in style, an attempt to present, in continuous evolution, the musical attitudes and techniques of the great conductors. Very little has been written in English on this fascinating and extremely important subject. In general, I have followed the style of my previous book, *The Great Pianists* (1963). To my surprise, I discovered, on starting the research, that there was even less available information on conductors and conducting than there had been on pianists and piano playing. Indeed, the standard source, Georg Schünemann's *Geschichte des Dirigierens*, was published as long ago as 1914, and never has been translated. Therefore, more than the usual amount of grubbing in old books, magazines and newspapers had to be done.

The opinions in the following pages are not necessarily guesswork. When musicians discuss other musicians, a comprehensive and fairly consistent pattern emerges; and the great conductors from Lully to the present have been thoroughly discussed by their own colleagues. The more important the figure, the greater the amount of information that can be unearthed about him. Letters, criticisms, conversations, analyses, biography, anecdotes—all can be sifted to arrive at a conclusion that, I am confident, gives an accurate estimate of the conductor and his place in history. The greater the conductor, the more original and strong-minded he was, the greater the impact he made on his contemporaries. This kind of impact is relatively easy to describe, for originality always arouses admiration (or envy, as the case may be), with a consequent spate of the written word attempting to evaluate (pro or con) and explain that originality. As one goes through the literature connected with any of the great conductors, it is amazing to see the consistency of thought with which an age presented that figure. Even the adverse criticisms—indeed, as often as not, *especially* the adverse criticisms—are invaluable in fixing a subject's place in history. Davison's attack on Wagner in 1855 serves to show, as few sources can, the power of Wagner's conducting and his ability to drive the conservative mind to a frenzy. Yes, the essential traits of the great conductors can be resurrected with accuracy. Richter *was* stolid; Bülow *was* mannered; Nikisch *was* hypnotic; Mendelssohn *was* fast; Mahler *was* intense.

The legacy of early orchestral recordings must be approached with caution. While the phonograph was from the beginning kind to the human voice, and while even the earliest piano recording can be reproduced on modern instruments with surprising success, it was not until 1925 and the advent of electrical recordings that an orchestra and its conductor could be heard with a fair idea of what they actually represented. Conductors who recorded acoustically had to make do with a considerably curtailed group working under conditions that resembled high comedy. Schubert's *Unfinished* was recorded with an orchestra that had only six violins and two violas; there were no double basses or timpani. Herbert Ridout, advertising manager of the Columbia Record Company in England in the early days, has described some of the techniques: "The French horns, having to direct the bells of their instruments towards the recording horn, would turn their backs on it and were provided with mirrors in which they would watch the conductor. The tuba was positioned right back, away from the horn, and his bell turned away from it; he also watched in a mirror. The big drum never entered a recording room." Obviously such conditions were not conducive to music, much less realism, and it is just as well that most early orchestral recordings are devoted to light material. Not until the middle 1920s did orchestras begin to achieve results that can be trusted.

With all that, something can be deduced from the conductor's work on acoustic records: his tempos, his phrasings, rhythms and accentuations. In the case of Nikisch and a few others, the acoustic discs are the only surviving aural documents and, as such, invaluable. Nikisch, at least, did leave us a complete symphony (the Beethoven Fifth) and other important music. In that he was unique at the time.

This book is a study that necessarily has had to be selective, else it would have degenerated into mere listings of names. For the most part, discussion has been given only to those who have made a permanent impression on the art. Biography is incidental. The focus is on what the individual represented, not on details of his life, except those that help explain his work. Birth and death dates of conductors mentioned in the text are supplied in the index.

I wish to make special acknowledgment of two books that are invaluable to anybody working in the field of early orchestras: Adam Carse's *The Orchestra in the XVIII Century* and *The Orchestra from Beethoven to Berlioz.* To Ward Botsford and Dr. A. F. R. Lawrence I am in debt for the time they unhesitatingly gave me to browse in their spectacular collections of early orchestral recordings. Henry Pleasants read the manuscript and offered many constructive suggestions. Henry Simon, my editor at Simon and Schuster, helped with reminiscences of his own long life in music and did some skillful operating on the manuscript. Eric Schaal put at my disposal his great musical iconography. My wife, Rosalyn, painstakingly read copy, corrected my excesses, and unearthed many of the illustrations.

HAROLD C. SCHONBERG

New York, 1967

The Genus

Oh! to be a conductor, to weld a hundred men into one singing giant, to build up the most gorgeous arabesques of sound,
to wave a hand and make the clamoring strings sink to a
mutter, to wave again, and hear the brass crashing out in
triumph, to throw up a finger, then another and another, and
to know that with every one the orchestra would bound forward into a still more ecstatic surge and sweep, to fling
oneself forward and for a moment or so keep everything
still, frozen, in the hollow of one's hand, and then to set
them all singing and soaring in one final sweep, with the
cymbals clashing at every flicker of one's eyelid, to sound the
grand Amen.

—J. B. PRIESTLEY

You conductors who are so proud of your power! When a
new man faces the orchestra—from the way he walks up the
steps to the podium and opens his score—before he even
picks up his baton—we know whether he is the master or we.

—FRANZ STRAUSS (father of
Richard, and a famous horn
player)

HE IS OF commanding presence, infinite dignity, fabulous memory,
vast experience, high temperament and serene wisdom. He has been

tempered in the crucible but he is still molten and he glows with a fierce inner light. He is many things: musician, administrator, executive, minister, psychologist, technician, philosopher and dispenser of wrath. Like many great men, he has come from humble stock; and, like many great men in the public eye, he is instinctively an actor. As such, he is an egoist. He has to be. Without infinite belief in himself and his capabilities, he is as nothing.

Above all, he is a leader of men. His subjects look to him for guidance. He is at once a father image, the great provider, the fount of inspiration, the Teacher who knows all. To call him a great moral force might not be an overstatement. Perhaps he is half divine; certainly he works under the shadow of divinity (or so a certain school of romantic idealism would have us believe). He has to be a strong man; and the stronger he is, the more dictatorial he is called by those he governs. He has but to stretch out his hand and he is obeyed. He tolerates no opposition. His will, his word, his very glance, are law.

Sometimes his name is Wilhelm Furtwängler, sometimes Arturo Toscanini, sometimes Fritz Reiner, Leonard Bernstein, Arthur Nikisch or Otto Klemperer. It makes no difference. Whatever his name, he stands in front of a group of musicians as their conductor. He is there because somebody has to be the controlling force. Somebody has to set the tempo, maintain the rhythm, see to it that proper ensemble and balances are kept, try to get out of the score what the composer put into it. From his baton, from the tips of his fingers, from his very psyche, flows some sort of electric surcharge that shocks a hundred-odd prima donnas into bending their individual wills into a collective effort. His ears have a hundred-odd invisible tentacles, each one plugged, switchboard-like, into the very subconscious of each player under his command. Let one of those men play a faulty phrase or a wrong note, and that particular tentacle twitches. Immediate wrath then descends.

He plays on those hundred-odd men, and gets his results in a variety of ways. Conductors like Fritz Reiner and Arturo Toscanini were the instrumentalities of fear. One malevolent glance from those slitted Reiner eyes, and musicians would be turned to whimpering blobs of protoplasm. Bruno Walter had a completely different method. He expressed such desolation, such sorrow and disillusion, that musicians were ready to break down and cry, swearing to sin no more. "Gentlemen, *gentlemen*," Walter would say, with Christlike reproach, "to play the D on an open string. What would Mozart say?" Leonard Bernstein does it with a hearty, hail-fellow-well-met camaraderie, something like a football coach between halves. "Now, fellows, let's get together on that phrase. Let's have the strings come in exactly on the beat. Ready? One and two *and* . . ." Leopold Stokowski, at rehearsals, speaks in a monotone and is strictly business. "Three measures before letter D the A flat should be A natural, play it mezzo-forte and accelerate poco a poco to the double bar, ready, let's go, all together now."

Through his orchestra the conductor translates musical symbols into meaningful sound. Each conductor reads the symbols differently, for each is a different human being. "How far is up?" asks the child. "How fast is fast?" To the conductor, these are far from childish questions. How fast *is* fast? When Mozart writes "allegro," is it a pace, a trot or a gallop? Each conductor has his own ideas. All he can do is follow his instincts, based on years of thought and study.

With his orchestra the conductor is, or should be, as one. If he has the knowledge and the inner power, he can bend it entirely to his wishes. This cannot happen overnight, unless the conductor is a Nikisch or a Reiner. It may take years before each is attuned to the other's idiosyncrasies. But the conductor has to be good to begin with. It ordinarily takes about fifteen minutes for an orchestra faced with a new conductor to determine whether he is a poseur, a phony, a routinier, a good musician or a great one, a negative personality or a forceful one who *will* impress his ideas over any kind of opposition. The musicians may test him in a hundred cruel ways, ignoring his directions, questioning his beat, inserting wrong notes into the score, playing correct notes an octave up or an octave down, creating wrong balances. If the conductor calls them sharply to heel, they will respect him. But if the slips pass unnoticed, they *know*. And having lost respect they can make life miserable for the man in front of them. They tell the story of one poor wretch, with more money than talent, who got in front of an orchestra and proceeded to mess things up to a point where the percussionist gave a resounding wallop to the drum and threw his stick away in disgust. The conductor looked around. He suspected something was wrong. "Who *did* that?" he wanted to know. Money has been known to buy an orchestra for a conductor, but money has never been known to win its respect.

Between the orchestra and the conductor must at least lie mutual respect and understanding. Not love; that would be asking too much. The players tend to look on the conductor as a disciplinarian (and sometimes a heartless or even sadistic one); the conductor tends to look on the players as a group of undisciplined children who are threatening to develop into juvenile delinquents. Both may be right.

Years ago, a Boston Symphony man was near death, and Serge Koussevitzky paid him a visit. The player, freed from all earthly responsibilities, took the opportunity of telling Koussevitzky exactly what he and the orchestra thought of him. Koussevitzky, he said, was a bully, a dictator, a tyrant, an autocrat, and a selfish, inconsiderate seven-letter word. These opinions delivered, the player sank back on his pillow refreshed, prepared to die happy. He had achieved the goal of every orchestra musician. Koussevitzky was honestly bewildered. "But I never mean it," he said. "You should know that. I am your father. You are my children." It so happened that the player, to his great embarrassment, did not die after all. He returned to the orchestra. Koussevitzky never forgave him. And Koussevitzky furthermore happened to be right in his statement. In many curious parallels the conductor *is* the father, the players *are* his children.

To convey his instructions, the conductor generally uses a sliver of tapered wood with a cork handle, seven to fifteen inches long, weighing less than an ounce. This is called a baton, and the conductor waves it in stern rhythm. Some conductors of the past, such as Richard Strauss or Karl Muck, stood motionless, moving the tip of the baton in tiny gestures. But Koussevitzky and Dimitri Mitropoulos, who did not even use the baton, twitched, jittered and jutted; and as for Furtwängler, his beat was the despair of musicians the first time they encountered it, so inexplicable was it. Some conductors, such as Bernstein or Leon Barzin, flail the air with near-infinite amplitude, hips and legs in motion as well as arms and shoulders. Conductors like these sometimes actually leave the ground in direct defiance of the laws of gravity, and they hover in the air in a sheer *raptus* of creation and physical involvement. This has come to be known as the choreographic school of conducting; and of it Igor Stravinsky in *The New York Review of Books* has delivered himself of a few tart remarks:

The performance of performance has developed to such an extent in recent years that it challenges the music itself and will soon threaten it with relegation. I have seen performances (of a performance) as fully worked-out as a sonata, as neatly contrived as a fugue. The new conductor, X., for example, controls every stage of the operation as thoroughly as a cradle-to-grave social welfare plan, from a first entrance that exudes just the right amount of artistic mystique, to a final few dozen exhausted bows. I will not attempt to describe the performance that X. employs with the actual music except to say that its most winning features are a crucifixion, the extended arms motionless and the hands limp in frozen passion; a pelvic thrust co-ordinated with a throwing back of the head, used at climaxes; and a turning of the profile not just toward the first violins but beyond them and out to the audience. Most of the other repertory is composed of stock mirror-the-music "expression movements" (Lorenz's term for the same thing in geese ethnology), but another innovation has been promised before the show reaches Broadway and according to rumor it will be handstands during inverted counterpoint. Still, the high point is none of these but the after-performance performance. It begins with a tableau of moribundity modeled on the Descent from the Cross. The arms are lifeless, the knees are bent, the head (hair artfully disarrayed) is low, and the whole corpse is bathed in perspiration (warm water, one suspects, squirted from hidden atomizers). The first step down from the podium just fails to conceal a totter, but in spite of that the miracle-worker somehow manages to reappear forty-six times. It *is* a great performance, though, and could be topped as an advertisement only by skywriting. Even a musician could be swept away by it.

Toscanini made circular motions, left hand pressed against his heart. Eugene Ormandy and Leopold Stokowski, sans baton (though of late Ormandy has again been using the stick after a lapse of some thirty years), have wrist and finger motions that make their hands disembodied and intelligent entities. George Szell, with baton, has almost textbook clarity, and so has Erich Leinsdorf. Klemperer beats with a fist of a size that would terrify a heavyweight prize fighter. As for women conductors, a musician knows when the upbeat starts, because that is when the slip starts to show.

Reiner handled the baton daintily, between the thumb and the third finger, and he described minuscule motions. It is said that one of his players, short of eyesight and desperate because he could not see his master's beat, came to rehearsal with a brass telescope, which he applied to the supreme figure before him. It is further related that Reiner, whose eyesight was as sharp as that of a hawk circling for the kill, noticed the player peering through the glass and discharged him on the spot; but this story is doubtless apocryphal.

It is at rehearsals that most of the work is done. There, as Reynaldo Hahn once observed, the batteries are charged. Some conductors are notorious for painstakingly working out details of interpretation at rehearsals, and then—stimulated by the audience (which acts as an aphrodisiac on some performers), or feeling different, or merely forgetful—throwing new concepts, new beats, new tempos to the orchestra at the actual concert. This can make orchestra players, and especially a soloist, most unhappy. For the most part, though, what a conductor does at rehearsal is what he does at the concert, only with added gestures that secretly amuse the orchestra no end. With certain conductors, an act accompanies their white tie and tails, and they add new meaning to the vocabulary of movement.

If nothing amuses an orchestra more than the conductor who is out to slay an audience rather than to make music, nothing irritates an orchestra more than a rehearsal philosopher. Some conductors, especially the German or German-oriented ones, are talkers and analysts. Willem Mengelberg is still considered the all-time champion in this respect, although Otto Klemperer was at one time considered a rival. This is a dangerous practice, and few can emerge unscathed. The better the orchestra, the better the musicians; the better the musicians, the more they resent lectures. And so ringing down the ages will resound the story about Klemperer, who gazes upon the world from an altitude of six feet, four inches, and Bruno Labate, the globular oboist who stood erect at perhaps five feet, two inches. Klemperer started a New York Philharmonic rehearsal with an exegesis of a Beethoven symphony: its meaning, its symbolism, its position in time and space, its *Zeitgeist* and the importance here of *Zusammenspiel*. Time crawled until the historic moment when Labate stretched to his full height and rudely interrupted. "Klemp, you talka too much," he said. Ensued a *scandale*. The standard orchestra story about this type of conductor has the concertmaster breaking into his speech. "Look," says the concertmaster, "just tell us whether you want us to play soft or loud."

Conductors are colorful, strong-willed people, and around them stories naturally gravitate. There are Toscanini stories, Beecham stories, Koussevitzky stories, stories about every man who ever lifted a baton. Some of those stories may even be true. More often they are the invention of public relations people, and soon the anecdote enters public domain, to be related of this conductor or that. *Tableau*: the conductor screams at a player, casts doubt upon his ancestry, flays him before the orchestra. "Nuts to you," the player snarls, picking up his instrument and walking out. The conductor almost relents on hearing these words, then becomes firm again. "It's too late to apologize." This is a very good story, and it is told about Toscanini, Koussevitzky, and probably can be traced back to Homer, just as the famous query by the tenor in *Lohengrin*—"When does the next swan leave?"—can be traced back far before Melchior and Slezak. Indeed, it can be traced back to Tichatschek, Wagner's first important tenor.

One thing that conductors can look forward to is a healthy statistical hope of practicing their art for many years. There is something in the practice—constant exercise? the triumph of will? getting rid of aggressions on a captive orchestra?—that seems to provide a salubrious, invigorating climate. Toscanini, Pierre Monteux, Bruno Walter, Tullio Serafin, Carl Schuricht, Sir Thomas Beecham, Stokowski, Ernest Ansermet, Klemperer—all were or are (at the point of writing) active in their eighties and, in the opinion of many, better than ever. Yet they lived through a fearsome regimen and discipline. A conductor's job, like any musician's, is basically complicated enough, but the conductor has extra responsibilities that add even more to his mental and physical strain. In addition to presiding over some five-score players (many of whom are convinced they could do a better job) and welding them into a precision instrument, the conductor must play several instruments well and have a working knowledge of every instrument in the orchestra; must be able to read the entries in a full score as easily as an accountant reads the entries in a ledger; must, while reading a score, assimilate its structure and meaning, decide what the composer wanted and then stimulate his men into achieving the vision; must have stocked in his mind, ready for instant use, all of the standard works in the repertoire and a good deal non-standard besides; must have the technique and memory that can break down and assimilate a contemporary new work; must have the kind of ear that can spot one wrong note in a welter of orchestral noise; must have absolute pitch (most great conductors have had this ability to hear a note or combination of notes and instantly rattle them off); must be able to compose, orchestrate and analyze; must keep track of musicological research, especially that pertaining to performance practice;

must have the knack of assembling programs that will advance the cause of art without permanently alienating the public; and above all must have—in addition to an elephant-like constitution—the mysterious thing known as projection: the ability to beam his physical and musical personality directly forward into the orchestra and directly backward into the lap of every listener in the audience. All great conductors have a remarkable power of projection. Without it, a conductor's music making tends to be negative. The audience must be enveloped in white-hot belief, and a conductor is great in direct ratio to his powers of communication. And yet there are those naïve enough to think it is easy. Why, all they do is stand up there and wave a stick. Bruno Walter loved to tell the story of an orchestra player who conducted a concert for the first time. After this experience he ran into the great Hans Richter. "How did it go?" asked Richter. "Very well indeed," said the musician. "And do you know, Herr Hofkapellmeister, this business of conducting is really very simple." From behind a shielding hand Richter whispered back: "I beg you, don't give us away."

There have been experiments with conductorless orchestras. New York had one in the late 1920s; the concertmaster was Paul Stassevitch. All it proved, wrote the music critic Robert A. Simon, was that an orchestra of able musicians could do better *without* a conductor than *with* a bad one. Possibly the most famous conductorless orchestra was Persimfans, founded in Moscow in 1922. The theory was that the members of the orchestra should have an equal degree of freedom and responsibility. But even in those early, idealistic days of communistic brotherhood it was found out that some players were more equal than others. It was noticed that at the beginning of a piece, all eyes would turn to the concertmaster, just as in a string quartet—as close as music can come to a republic of equals—the three other strings are constantly glancing at the first violin for cues. As things turned out, the Persimfans concertmaster ended up conductor in all but name. Somebody has to take the lead; somebody has to assume responsibility; somebody has to hold things together. And so, in a way, the old analogy is true. The conductor is a soloist and the orchestra is his instrument. How he plays it depends upon his technique, imagination, resource, sensitivity.

The conductor as he stands today is the result of several centuries of experimentation and development, but he emerged only a little over a century ago and came to full flower a still shorter time ago, around the last quarter of the nineteenth century. Even at that time musicians gazed upon the phenomenon with disbelief, unable to comprehend why he had suddenly reached such heights. As early as 1836 Robert Schumann was issuing warnings in the *Neue Zeitschrift für Musik* against "the vanity and self-importance of the conductors who do not want to relinquish the baton, partly because they want to be constantly before the audience, partly to hide the fact that a competent orchestra can take care of itself without their leadership." Schumann's doubts were echoed many years later by Pablo Sarasate, the great Spanish violinist. Sarasate ran into Enrique Granados. "Enrique," he said, "do you know what is happening today? I mean these conductors, with their little sticks. They don't play, you know. They stand in front of the orchestra waving their little sticks. And they get paid for this, get paid well, too. Now suppose, Enrique, suppose there were no orchestra and they stood there alone. Would they pay them just the same—them and their little sticks?" And then we jump still further, to that admirable violinist, Carl Flesch, who played under all the great conductors until his death in 1944. Flesch called the mentality of conductors "a dark, abysmal chapter." Conducting, he said seriously, tends to spoil the character. In addition, "when all is said and done, it is the only musical activity in which a dash of charlatanism is not only harmless but absolutely necessary."

Nevertheless, no matter what Schumann said, or Sarasate, or Flesch, or anybody, there has been no holding back the conductors. These autocrats, these didacts, these flamboyant figures, took over the musical world. All of a sudden the cult of the virtuoso conductor had come to stay. He and his kind became the kings of music, before whom even star sopranos trembled. Adored by the public, scorned by many musicians, distrusted by many composers, the conductor nevertheless emerged as the one figure who represented music *in toto,* the one whose musicianship surrounded and drew together the individual arts of the pianist, singer, violinist, orchestra player, even of the composer. It was the conductor who, for better or worse, represented an all-embracing musical culture in the eyes of the public. Today the conductor, more than any one musical figure, shapes our musical life and thought. That may not be how things *should* be, but it is the way they are. In a future, fully automated age, it may be that the conductor, along with all performing musicians, will be obsolete. Musical creators are working toward that day, assembling electronic scores that, once put on tape, never vary. Which may make the creator happy. But until that unfortunate day is here, let us be thankful that there still remain interpretive musicians to synthesize the product of the composer. For without the interplay between the minds of the creator and interpreter, music is not only stale, flat and unprofitable. It is meaningless. Imagine the *Eroica* Symphony, *Le Nozze di Figaro*, the Verdi Requiem, *Le Sacre du Printemps,* sounding exactly the same at every performance! But fortunately there is no danger of that. Musical notation is an inexact art, no matter how composers sweat and strive to perfect it. Symbols and instructions on the printed page are subject to various interpretations, not to one interpretation. Hence the function of the interpreter, and especially of the conductor, who stands over many individual interpreters and makes them refract the ideas of the composer through his own mind.

· II ·

From Elias Salomon
to Divided Leadership

TODAY THE PRIME FUNCTION of the conductor is interpretive. But that is a recent phenomenon, one that did not start until the nineteenth century was well under way. Before that, the conductor served primarily as a beating machine, as a kind of human metronome who would keep things steadily in motion. Very little research has been done on the history of conducting, and nobody knows much about its very beginnings. It is clear, though, that where music was, rhythm was. Rhythm creates an emphatic response. The listener, child or adult, primitive or sophisticated, taps his foot, or swings his body, or waves his arms to the rhythm. And when a group got together to play or sing, somebody had to be in charge to start things off. This held true even in groups as small in numbers as five or six, the norm for Italian or Elizabethan madrigals (and madrigal music could be very complicated rhythmically). There are allusions in ancient times to some kind of time beating. Horace asks the maidens and youths to pay attention to the Sapphic step and the snap of his fingers. Thus Horace was, in a way, a conductor, marking the rhythms of his songs by foot and hand.

One of the earliest descriptions of a conductor's duties derives from the *Tracatus de musica* by Elias Salomon. It dates from the late thirteenth century. The conductor, writes Salomon, should be one of the singers and "has to know everything about the music to be sung. He beats time with his hand on the book and gives the cues and rests to the singers. If one of them sings incorrectly, he whispers into his ear, 'You are too loud, too soft, your tones are wrong,' as the case may be, but so that the others do not hear it. Sometimes he must support them with his own voice if he sees that they are lost."

In the fifteenth century it was the custom for somebody in command of the Sistine Choir to beat time with a roll of paper or even a short stick. This instrument was called a "sol-fa." But if no sol-fa specialist was around, a singer would take charge. Ornithoparcus, the

NEW YORK PUBLIC LIBRARY

A fourteenth-century drawing entitled "The Poet Frauenlob." Seated above his forces, Frauenlob appears to be conducting with a long baton.

author of *Musicae activae micrologus* (Leipzig, 1516), describes motions made by the hands of the chief singer, "according to the nature of the marks [notes], which directs a song according to measure." In 1583 Vincenzo Galilei, father of the astronomer, mentions in his *Dialogo* that the ancient Greeks did not beat time "as is customary now." We would like to know a great deal more about the nature of

"Die Musik," from Gregor Reisch's *Margarita Philosophica* (1503), showing musicians and singers led by a conductor with a very long baton.

the beat Galilei was accustomed to, but his words are clear evidence that somebody pretty close to a conductor was beating time. The same was true in England. Thomas Morley, in his *Plaine and Easie Introduction to Practicall Musicke* (1597), writes a provocative bit of dialogue:

PHILOMETHUS. What is a stroke?
MAGISTER. It is a successive motion of the hand, directing the quality of every note and rest in the song, with equal measure, according to the variety of signs and proportions.

These early time beaters probably did no more than establish the right tempo and then hold a pulse. The practice seems to have been universal up to at least the first part of the eighteenth century. There is a painting, dated 1710, believed to be of Johann Kuhnau, Bach's predecessor at the Church of St. Thomas in Leipzig. The painting shows a periwigged musician wielding a roll of paper before an instrumental and choral group. In 1719 John Bähr wrote about one man conducting with his fist, another with the head, still another with the hand, some with both hands, some with a roll of paper, some even with a stick.

But with the evolution of the orchestra, this type of conducting disappeared, not to show up again for another hundred years or so. It was a strange progression. First the conductor disappeared. Then, as the orchestra grew more and more complex, along with it grew that equally complex figure known as the orchestra conductor. Those interested can refer to the two major books on the subject—Adam Carse's *The Orchestra in the XVIII Century* and *The Orchestra from Beethoven to Berlioz*. Most of the following information has been drawn liberally from the two Carse books.

Broadly speaking, the evolution of the orchestra shows two periods, the first ending soon after the middle of the eighteenth century with the deaths of Bach and Handel, and the rise of the modern orchestra beginning with Haydn and Mozart. Until Haydn and Mozart came along—and, indeed, for many years later outside of the big European cities—the orchestra was altogether a flexible affair. The "conductor" was almost always the composer, and as often as not he wrote for specific groups in Mannheim, Paris, Salzburg, Leipzig. Under those circumstances the composer's orchestration depended upon the groups involved. Orchestration would be adapted to fit the needs of individual players. The period from Bach through the appearance of Haydn and Mozart was also the era of baroque music and the figured bass—that set of numbers from which the continuo player at the keyboard could instantly "realize" and supply a solid harmonic underpinning. Textures were largely polyphonic, though the period did see the rise of suite, overture, oratorio and opera. By the end of the seventeenth century, the four-part string orchestra—violins, violas, cellos and basses—which is the basis of the modern orchestra, had become stabilized. In Bach's time the normal orchestra consisted of two flutes (or recorders), two oboes, one or two bassoons, a trumpet, drums and four string parts of which the bass was generally "realized" by cellos (or gambas), basses, keyboard instruments and lute. Bach's orchestra at Leipzig numbered eighteen to twenty players. Of these, about ten were wind instruments, leaving only two or three strings to each part. Even then there was no set procedure. Often Bach, like most other composers of the time, did not specify instrumentation, and he would use whatever was at hand. Wind players would interchange, with the trumpeter being called upon to play horn parts. Bach composed for whatever he had at his disposal for the specific occasion, constantly complaining about the paucity of his forces and their low ability. Never in his career did Bach get what he wanted in the way of orchestral resource, though goodness knows he tried. A large part of his correspondence has to do with squabbles with the ecclesiastical authorities, and his constant complaining did not help make him a popular figure in Leipzig.

The polyphonic and baroque school gave way around mid-century to a monodic style of writing. Violins and the violin family replaced the gamba family, the transverse flute replaced the recorder, the oboe replaced the shawm and bombard, and the orchestral horn nudged out the hunting horn. And, most important, the figured bass disappeared. Around 1790, clarinets were in general use. A little after that, trombones. During the first half of the nineteenth century valved instruments were perfected. These were easier to play and were much more reliable in pitch. The divisions of the orchestra became established: woodwind, brass, percussion, strings. At Beethoven's death the orchestra was substantially as we know it today, though instruments were constantly being improved or added.

There was no revolution accompanying the change from baroque to classic. It was a smooth, steady shift that had been anticipated by such composers as Alessandro Scarlatti, Telemann, Gluck, Carl Philipp Emanuel Bach, Rameau and, in some cases, J. S. Bach himself. All of these composers brought, among other things, a new concept of the orchestra: the concept of instruments within the orchestra accompanying other instruments. Thus some instruments had a purely melodic function, others a purely harmonic one. This meant that melodic elements would stand out prominently, against a block of harmonies. It also meant that composers began to think in terms of tonal color, using specific instruments for specific effects. Composers began to pay special attention to strings, using double notes, pizzicatos, arpeggios, tremolos. The violin itself underwent changes. Its neck was lengthened, its bridge and fingerboard raised. It was even played differently, being brought up under the chin where previously it had rested on the shoulder. But all instruments in addition to the violin were beginning to be improved. Gluck was one of the first to feel the new colors, and he became one of the pioneers of orchestration, enlarging the percussion section with bass drums, cymbals, side drums and triangle, using the harp for special effects and liberating the viola.

This led directly to the Mozart orchestra, as represented by the ensembles of Mannheim, Dresden, Leipzig, Berlin and Paris. The Mannheim Orchestra, which so excited and stimulated Mozart, was considered the finest in Europe, and was famous for its precise ensemble, its crescendo and diminuendo effects, its general polish. But orchestras of Mozart's time produced a sound that would fall strangely upon today's ears. Balances were different, especially in the proportions of winds to strings. Few orchestras then had more than twenty strings, but they all had from three to six oboes, three to six bassoons, three or four flutes and four horns. Here is the constitution of the Mannheim Orchestra in 1782: eighteen violins, three violas, four cellos, three basses, four flutes, three oboes, three clarinets, four bassoons, four horns, trumpets and timpani. The orchestras in Dresden, Vienna and Berlin had almost as many players, in much the same ratio. Almost to the end of the eighteenth century this preponderance of winds to strings was common. Indeed, as late as 1841 the Berlin Opera's orchestra consisted of twenty-eight violins, eight violas, ten cellos, eight basses, and four each of flute, oboe, clarinet, bassoon, horn, trumpets and trombones. Johann Joachim Quantz, in his *Versuch einer Anweisung die Flöte Traversière zu spielen* (1752), gave specifications on what he considered ideal orchestral balance. For twelve violins he recommended three violas, four cellos, two basses, four flutes, four oboes, three bassoons, two cembalos and theorbo. It would be most interesting today to hear baroque music with that combination, or to hear a Mozart or Haydn symphony played by a group duplicating the Mannheim forces. With all of the present-day insistence on "getting back to the composer," no conductor has as yet made the attempt.

Where did the conductor fit into the baroque or early classic scheme of things? Strictly speaking, he didn't, not if we equate eighteenth-century leadership with the function of the modern conductor. What developed in the eighteenth century was a divided leadership. It may have started in France. At least, it has been suggested that the French, always having been a most logical people, had figured out that because half to two-thirds of the orchestra consisted of strings, it would be the logical thing to put the orchestra in charge of a string player. The idea swept Europe; and, as far as Paris was concerned, there was no necessity for ever changing. Virtually all French conductors until the middle of the nineteenth century were string players, and almost all of *them* were violinists. Berlioz was the big exception. Conducting with the bow hung on in Paris as late as 1878. Édouard Deldevez used it at the Opéra. He said, defiantly—one imagines an old man with a white beard, wearing clothes long out of fashion— *"Le violon est l'instrument naturel du chef d'orchestre."*

With the violinist was a co-conductor, the player who officiated at the keyboard instrument. This man was called the "conductor," while the violinist was called the "leader." The former supplied the rhythmic function, the latter took care of ensemble. Carl Philipp Emanuel Bach, in his famous *Versuch*—the *Essay on the True Art of Playing Keyboard Instruments* (Part I in 1753; Part II in 1762)—explains the duties of the conductor:

The keyboard, entrusted by our fathers with full command, is in the best position to assist not only the other bass instruments, but the entire ensemble in maintaining a uniform pace. . . . The tone of the keyboard which, correctly placed, stands in the center of the ensemble, can be heard clearly by all. And I know that even diffuse, elaborate compositions, played by impromptu, average performers, can be held together simply by its tone. If the first violinist stands near the keyboard, as he should, disorder cannot easily spread. . . . Should someone hasten or drag, he can most readily be corrected by the keyboard player. . . . In addition, those performers located in front or beside the keyboard will find in the simultaneous motion of both hands an inescapable, visual portrayal of the beat.

C. P. E. Bach does not pursue the topic further, and he does not make clear exactly what he means by the simultaneous motion of both hands. Does this refer merely to the mechanics of playing? Or to an actual in-the-air beat? There is every indication that the clavier player cued the orchestra and beat the time when both hands were not occupied with filling in the harmony or giving soloists a helping hand by playing the melodic material. Every orchestra during most of the eighteenth century had one or more keyboard instruments in it. It was the clavierist who filled in the bass, gave cues to soloists, kept entries orderly (and rectified mistakes if soloists made a wrong entry), set tempos and maintained them by strong accents. The theory was that once the work had been set in motion by the clavierist, then the violinist leader would take direct charge of the ensemble. He too would beat time when not occupied in playing. Just as C. P. E. Bach had explained the role of the keyboard player (generally a harpsichordist; the piano did not take over until the last quarter of the century), so Thomas Busby outlined the role of the leader. In his *Dictionary of Music* (London, 1813) we can learn that

The leader, after the conductor, holds the most important station in the orchestra. It is to him that the other performers look for direction in the execution of the music; and it is on his steadiness, skill and judgment, and the attention of the band to his motion, manner and expression, that the concinnity, truth and force of effect do in a great measure depend.

But it would be a mistake to look upon these two figures—leader and conductor—as interpretive musicians in the modern sense. Basically their function was to correct rather than to initiate. Almost always they played along with the orchestra, beating time only when things started to get out of hand. (Of course, this might well have been more often than not.) Then the clavierist would hit the right chords, or play the melody; the leader would pick up from there, and both would strive to restore order. If perchance leader and conductor had different ideas about the music, so much the worse for the music. Audiences were not particularly demanding in any case. That was how things were done in orchestras from, roughly, early in the eighteenth century to the third decade of the nineteenth and even beyond. But there were exceptions.

· III ·

Bach and Handel

DIVIDED LEADERSHIP or not, there were many times when the control of any large-scale performance—symphony, ballet, opera—was vested in one man. That would always have happened when the composer was in charge of a performance of his music. And until the 1850s, with the appearance of musicians who specialized in playing other men's music, composer, player and conductor were generally the same man. Naturally he would superintend all aspects of the performance, and it was expected that he participate as clavierist or leader (the latter especially in Italy, which created modern violin playing in such figures as Corelli, Vivaldi and the other great violinist-composers). In those cases the composer would have been the dominant force. The stronger the composer, the stronger the force he would have exerted. Regrettably little, for example, is known about Claudio Monteverdi's conducting, but we do know that as maestro di cappella of San Marco in Venice he had absolute control over some thirty singers and twenty instrumentalists; and it is also well known that Monteverdi, the father of the opera, greatly expanded the resources of the orchestra by introducing the tremolo and pizzicato for bowed instruments. It is said that the violinists of the orchestra were so horrified that they at first refused to make such ugly, anti-musical sounds. A string player himself, Monteverdi made the strings the backbone of his orchestra. The group he used for *Orfeo*, by the way, was extremely large for its day. Admittedly it was assembled for a special occasion: two gravicembali (claviers), two double basses, ten viole da braccio (predecessor of the viola), one double harp, two violini piccoli alla Francese (small violins, a minor third higher than the violin), two chitarroni (a type of lute), two organi di legno (small organs with wooden pipes), three bassi di gamba, four trombones, one regal (organ with reed pipes), two horns, one piccolo, one clarino

ENGRAVING BY F. M. DE LA CAVE, 1725

Three early composer-conductors: Antonio Vivaldi (above), Jean Baptiste Lully (lower left) and Claudio Monteverdi. Monteverdi cut is posthumous engraving from the title page of *Fiori Poetici*, published in 1664.

(predecessor of the clarinet), three muted trumpets, one harp, one ceteroni (large zither), one small flute.

While Monteverdi did not wave a stick, he was nevertheless a conductor. His *Orfeo* was given in Mantua in 1607, his *Il Combattimento di Tancredi e di Clorinda* and *L'Incoronazione di Poppea* in Venice in 1624 and 1642 respectively, and it takes little imagination to see the composer working with his forces, demanding certain tempos and balances, working with the singers, inspiring everybody by his presence. The same can be said of the despotic Jean Baptiste Lully, the leader of Louis XIV's band, *les petits-violons*. Lully, indeed, actually did use a baton—a long rod, or cane, that he struck on the ground to give the beat. He would have had a clavier player helping along, but if we know anything at all about this arrogant, scheming, ambitious, obsequious, brilliant, energetic man, it is that he alone would have dominated any performance in which he was involved. A forceful disciplinarian, he seems to have been the very first orchestra director to impose uniform bowing on his string players. This was unheard of in those freewheeling times. Lully's development of what became known as the *premier coup d'archet* (first stroke of the bow) was the talk of musical Europe, and remained one of the identifying marks of French orchestral playing for many years. Up came the bows and down they came as one instrument. Everybody marveled. (Many years later Mozart on his visit to Paris wrote to his father saying that he had composed a symphony for Paris. "I have been careful not to neglect *le premier coup d'archet*—and that is quite sufficient. What a fuss the oxen here make of this trick! The devil take me if I can see any difference. They all begin together, just as they do in other places. It is really too much of a joke.")

Lully's orchestra became the model on which the modern orchestra developed, especially the opera orchestra, with singers on the stage, the orchestra below, both led by a conductor on a podium. This we owe to Lully. Musicians from all over Europe went to Paris to study Lully's orchestral technique. They also learned from Lully what temperament could be. Lully was a Toscanini-like prima donna who would, in a fury, grab a violin from the hands of an offender and smash it to pieces. But results are what count. Lully created the world's best orchestra at the time, and has a legitimate claim to being called the first of the great conductors. The circumstances of his death in 1687 are famous. Carried away—whether in the throes of rage or inspiration or excitement nobody knows—he accidentally rammed his staff against his foot. It must have been a colossal blow, and history does not tell of the equally colossal scream of pain that must have followed. Obviously he broke the skin, and the cane may have gone clear through his foot. An abscess developed, then gangrene, and Lully died.

Any of the great composer-performers would have been equally dominating personalities when directing an ensemble. All of the history books talk about divided leadership in the eighteenth century; but how could there be divided leadership with musicians as powerful as Bach, Handel, Haydn, Mozart or the young Beethoven in an orchestra? It may be technically true that they shared conducting responsibilities with a first violinist or clavierist. Practically speaking, though, they must have been the only guiding force in any orchestra in which they sat. The same would be true of any orchestra in which an outstanding musician appeared as violinist or clavierist. That goes for Alessandro Scarlatti and Arcangelo Corelli, both of whom extended the potentialities of the strings in the orchestra; for Heinrich Schütz, who returned to Germany from Italy and introduced to the orchestra the ways of the Italian innovators; for Johann Mattheson, who tidied up the opera in Hamburg; for Georg Muffat, who carried Lully's way of conducting to Germany; for Johann Sigismund Kusser, who brought many of Lully's ideas to, of all places, Dublin, in 1706. Kusser (also known as Cousser) was almost a career conductor. From 1682 until his death in 1727 he was a court composer and conductor all over Europe. He took his conducting so seriously that he would invite members of his orchestra to come to his home, where he would play, sing and explain every note of the score. Mattheson, in his *Volkommenen Kapellmeister* (1739), was impressed enough to write: "He had a gift that could not be bettered."

There was Vivaldi in Venice, taking the orphan girls of the Pietà and making of them an admired orchestra. "What precision!" Charles de Brosses wrote of them. "Only there is heard the crisp orchestral attack so falsely boasted of at the Paris Opéra." In his biography of Vivaldi, Marc Pincherle suggests that the orchestra was indeed very fine; and that, furthermore, Vivaldi had in it a veritable musical laboratory. "It is easy to imagine the responsiveness of such a group, dominated not by more or less blasé or hypercritical performers, but by young students abounding in enthusiasm and curiosity. This was the group over which Vivaldi's personality was to have complete ascendancy. In this respect he was even more favored than J. S. Bach at the court of Cöthen, or Joseph Haydn at Esterház. He could experiment and study at his leisure the best way to apportion the orchestra; he could attack various comprehensive or detailed problems without being at the mercy of the clock . . ."

It turned out—as it had to turn out, by every law of psychology, of life, of psychic transmission—that the stronger the creator, the stronger his ability to take charge of an orchestra. Naturally a Bach would be infinitely superior to a run-of-the-mill musician. Bach, Handel, Mozart, even the sweet-tempered Haydn—they all were domineering people who had to have their own way when it came to music. Bach's temper was legendary. As a youth he got into trouble with a fellow student, one Geyerbach, calling him a *Zippelfaggotist*—a nanny-goat bassoonist. Words passed, and Bach actually drew his dagger before they were separated. Even at that time, in Arnstadt (1705), Bach had the reputation of being arrogant, of not getting along with his fellow students. The chances are that he held a low opinion of them; and, indeed, probably with good reason. One of the titanic figures in musical history, his powers already must have been stupendous, and he would have been to nonentities like Geyerbach as an oak among matchsticks. Anyway, his reputation was bad. He was thought sullen and rebellious, and was officially reproved for his standoffishness. "For," says one report, "if he considers it no disgrace to be connected with the Church and to accept his salary, he must also not be ashamed to make music with the students assigned to do so." But Bach was incorrigible, and to the end of his life was in constant hot water with the authorities. It would appear that musicians were as frightened of him as they later were of Toscanini. When in charge of an orchestra he would rage at inferior musicians, and once he tore off his wig and hurled it at an offender. "You should have been a shoemaker!"

Quite possibly, though, musicians admired Bach as much as they feared him, for his musicianship was transcendent. He could immediately reduce a score from parts laid side by side, was an unparalleled sight reader, was a good singer, was the greatest harpsichordist and organist in Europe, and probably could play every instrument. Everything musical was easy for him, and he became extremely impatient when it was not equally easy for everybody else. (His poor children!) As Johann Adolf Scheibe pointed out in 1737: "Since he judges according to his own fingers, his pieces are extremely difficult to play, for he demands that singers and instrumentalists should be able to

Frontispiece of J. G. Walther's *Musikalisches Lexicon* (Leipzig, 1732), showing leader with a roll of paper (or wooden baton?) in each hand.

do with their throats and instruments whatever he can play on the clavier. But," Scheibe reasonably says, "that is impossible."

Even if the good people of Leipzig accepted him as second best—they had wanted Telemann as cantor of St. Thomas—Bach simply awed the professional musicians who came into contact with him. Their reports also make clear that Bach at the head of an orchestra was a conductor very much as we understand the term today. The only missing thing was the baton, for Bach officiated at the clavier or from the concertmaster's chair. But he had the entire performance under his direct control, whether conducting services at church or leading an orchestra at a public concert. There were public concerts during Bach's time in Leipzig, and he participated in the weekly Friday evening events at Zimmermann's coffeehouse in the Katherstrasse. The musicians were chiefly students, and things were run quite loosely. "Any musician," runs a 1736 announcement, "is permitted to make himself publicly heard at these musical concerts, and most often, too, there are such listeners as know how to judge the qualities of an able musician." The description of Bach supplied by Johann Matthias Gesner in 1738 gives us the picture of a musician who is doing no more or no less than any conductor in front of an orchestra has ever done. Gesner, in fine classical style, wrote an epistle to Marcus Fabius Quintilianus, mentioning the Greek cithara players and aulists (tibia, or reed, players). He then goes on to describe Bach playing the clavier, an instrument that "is many citharas in one"; and then says:

If you could see him, I say, doing what many of your cithara players and six hundred of your tibia players together could not do, not only . . . singing and playing at the same time his own parts, but presiding over thirty or forty musicians all at once, controlling this one with a nod, another by a stamp of the foot, a third with a warning finger, keeping time and tune, giving a high note to one, a low note to another, and notes in between to some. This one man, standing alone in the midst of loud sounds, having the hardest task of all, can discern at every moment if anyone goes astray, and can keep all the musicians in order, restore any waverer to certainty and prevent him from going wrong. Rhythm is in his every limb, he takes in all the harmonies by his subtle ear and utters all the different parts through the medium of his own voice. Great admirer as I am of antiquity in other respects, I yet deem this Bach of mine to comprise in himself many Orpheuses and twenty Arions.

Johann Sebastian Bach (left), from a pastel drawing done in 1736 by his cousin, Gottlob Friedrich Bach.

George Frideric Handel (below), in the famous portrait by T. Hudson, London, 1749.

This happens to be a compendium of any twentieth-century conductor's functions. An obituary notice, probably by C. P. E. Bach and Johann Friedrich Agricola, helps fill out the picture of Bach as a conductor. A glance sufficed for Bach to condense even the most complicated full score. His ear was so accurate that the tiniest slip of any musician was noticed. "It is a pity," Bach-Agricola write, "that it was only seldom that he had the good fortune of finding a body of such performers as could have spared him from unpleasant discoveries of this nature [wrong notes; inferior playing]. In conducting he was very accurate, and in tempo, which he generally took very lively, uncommonly sure." It was not only seldom, as C. P. E. Bach writes, that Bach had an orchestra close to his heart's desire. It could very well be that he never found such a group. In Leipzig Bach was constantly battling with the authorities about his players, complaining of their weakness and the small size of the ensembles. In 1730 he submitted a memorandum to the town council, saying that for a double chorus motet a minimum of thirty-six singers was needed; and that the orchestra should have at least eighteen players. But, wrote Bach, he had only eight.

Some twenty years after Bach's death, in 1774, C. P. E. Bach was to supply some additional information on his father as a conductor. Johann Nikolaus Forkel was preparing the first biography of the composer, and his son told Forkel that "the exact tuning of his instruments, as well as of the whole orchestra, had his greatest attention. No one could tune and quill his instruments to please him. He did everything himself. The placing of an orchestra he understood perfectly. He made good use of any space. He grasped at the first glance the acoustic properties of any place. . . . As the greatest expert and judge of harmony, he liked best to play the viola, with appropriate loudness and softness. In his youth, and until the approach of old age, he played on the violin cleanly and penetratingly, and this kept the orchestra in better order than he could have done with the harpsichord. . . . He had a good penetrating voice of wide range and a good manner of singing." (It is interesting to note that C. P. E. Bach felt the violinist—in his father's case, anyway—to be a stronger force than the harpsichordist. In actual practice, the stronger musical personality always took the lead in divided responsibility.)

Thus is seen Bach, the complete musician presiding over his orchestra at the harpsichord as conductor, or with a violin as leader, singing along, particular about tempo and intonation, strong and secure in his mighty musicianship, completely modern in his approach to the problems of conducting.

Nor was the approach of Handel dissimilar. Like Bach, Handel was a handy musician to have around. Famous as harpsichordist and organist, he could play quite a few other instruments. And, like Bach, he could be testy and impatient, and he refused to be pushed around. In Hamburg he was a close friend of Mattheson, but when Mattheson tried to dislodge Handel from the harpsichord during an opera performance, there was real trouble. Mattheson had composed *Cleopatra*, a success, and he also sang a leading role in it. Handel was in the orchestra, acting as conductor, which meant presiding over the harpsichord. When Mattheson finished on stage, he ordered Handel away. Handel refused. There was an argument, and the two hotheaded young men marched grimly to the Goosemarket and drew their swords. Handel almost lost his life. Mattheson lunged, and his sword snapped against a metal button on his opponent's coat. A quarter of an inch in any other direction . . . The two made up and remained friends.

As a young man in Italy, Handel attended a rehearsal of his Overture to *Il Trionfo del Tempo*, at which none other than the great Corelli himself came to grief in a passage where the violin part went high up, into the seventh position. Handel, no respecter of his elders, grabbed the fiddle from Corelli and demonstrated how the passage should be played. Corelli, who seldom played or composed beyond the third position (his music calls for an occasional fourth position and a very rare fifth), did not appear to be perturbed by the composer's rudeness. "My dear Saxon," he is reported as saying, "this music is in the French style, which I do not understand." Handel, big and burly, the toast of the continent, always had to have his own way. His most famous encounter with the vagaries of musicians came when the soprano Cuzzoni, at a rehearsal of his *Ottone* in London, refused to sing *Falsa immagine* as written. Handel went into one of his rages. According to Sir John Hawkins, he grabbed Cuzzoni and made as if to throw her out of the window, bellowing meanwhile in his bad French: *"Oh! Madame, je sçais bien que vous êtes une veritable Diablesse; mais je vous ferai sçavoir, moi, que je suis Beelzebub, le Chef des Diables."* Cuzzoni, they say, was so terrified she gave in. Still another story of Handel's impatience and sarcasm concerns the fine violinist Matthew Dubourg, who got lost during a violin solo. Poor Dubourg had to improvise until he found the right key, at which moment Handel said very loudly, to the vast amusement of orchestra and audience, "Welcome home, Mr. Dubourg."

Romain Rolland's study of Handel contains an accurate description of Handel presiding over an orchestra, seated before a harpsichord or small organ:

He is surrounded by the violoncellist (placed at his right-hand side), two violins and two flutes which are placed in front of him, under his eye. The solo singers are also near him, on his left, quite close to the clavier. The rest of the instruments are behind him, out of his sight. Thus his directions and glances would control the *concertino* [the solo instruments], who would transmit in their turn the chief conductor's wishes to the *concerto grosso* [the rest of the orchestra]. . . . In place of the quasi-military discipline of modern orchestras, controlled under the baton of the chief conductor, the different bodies of the Handelian orchestra governed one another with elasticity, and it was the incisive rhythm of the little clavier that put the whole group into motion. Such a method avoided the mechanical stiffness of our performances. The danger was rather a certain wobbling without the presence of the powerful and infectious mind of a chief such as Handel, and without the close sympathy of thought established between him and his capable subconductors of the *concertino* and the *grosso*.

Handel, a composer-conductor constantly before the public, interested in turning a financial profit from his operas and oratorios, was much more of a showman than Bach, and undoubtedly had a more colorful approach to his music making. If his scores are any indication, he must have been far ahead of anybody in his day in demanding subtleties of light and shade. Bach's scores, for instance, are extremely sparing in dynamic indications (though that of course does not mean that Bach played or conducted without nuance), whereas in Handel are found such directions as *pp, p, mp, mf, un poco più forte, forte,* and *ff.* Those new extremes of texture and dynamic markings were in the air, and they soon became common property with the development of the Mannheim school. In any case it is clear that Handel, like Bach, was an imperious force who, when he took over an orchestra, was its conductor in fact, operating much the same way modern conductors do, asking for and getting much the same thing.

· IV ·

Haydn, Mozart and Beethoven

WITH THE DISAPPEARANCE of the baroque style and the emergence of the modern orchestra came new concepts of conducting. The Mannheim Orchestra, with its perfect (for those days) ensemble, its large size (about forty-five in 1756; it was larger in later years), its uniform bowing, its delicacy and force, its dynamic innovations (the "Mannheim crescendo" was emulated all over Europe), its accuracy in phrasing—all these helped spark an entire new school of composers and conductors. Johann Stamitz was the one who brought the orchestra to its peak, and when Charles Burney heard him conduct it, he called the group "an army of generals." Stamitz did his pioneer work from the first violin desk, and in 1757 was succeeded by Christian Cannabich, who enlarged and further polished the brilliant organization. Cannabich, like Stamitz, was a violinist. All contemporaries hailed his prowess as an orchestral technician. Even the supercilious, hard-to-please Mozart praised him as the best conductor he had met. Christian Schubart, the composer and critic, went into lyric raptures describing the Mannheim Orchestra under Cannabich. "Here the forte is thunder, the crescendo a cataract, the diminuendo a crystal streamlet bubbling away in the far distance, the piano a breeze of spring." All musicians who heard it (and even many who didn't) were inevitably influenced by the Mannheim virtuosity. Some scholars point out that the Italian composer-conductor Niccolò Jommelli might have anticipated the Mannheim school. When Jommelli was appointed court composer in Württemberg in 1753, he built up a superb orchestra that specialized, among other things, in the crescendo. But whether Jommelli influenced the Mannheimers, or whether he was influenced by them, it was the Mannheim style that carried all before it. Burney was but echoing the opinion of his age when he wrote that "the variety, taste, spirit and new effects produced by contrast and the use of crescendo and diminuendo in these [performances of Mannheim] symphonies, had been of more service to instrumental music in a few years than all the dull and servile imitations in the styles of Corelli, Geminiani and Handel had been in half a century." In 1763 Leopold Mozart and his famous seven-year-old son visited Mannheim for the first time. The elder Mozart was tremendously impressed. "The orchestra," he wrote, "is undeniably the best in Europe. It consists altogether of people who are young and of good character, not drunkards, gamblers, or dissolute fellows, so that both their behavior and their playing are admirable." This is most interesting. What kind of personnel did other orchestras have in those days?

Among the offshoots of the Mannheim style was a realization in European musical circles that a symphony orchestra was a delicately assembled unit, one that needed top players and alert direction. Very few courts or cities at that time had the money, personnel or desire to emulate Mannheim. Nevertheless, the Mannheim Orchestra was there to show what could be done. A few strong-minded musicians tried to get similar results. Mannheim's influence was especially felt in Paris; and Gluck, who was busy reforming opera, brought the orchestra into his orbit. A perfectionist, a rude, demanding, arrogant, quarrelsome man, as so many conductors have been, he would have his players repeat a passage twenty or thirty times until it was done to his satisfaction. So cruel was he in Vienna that often the Emperor himself had to intercede. It was common gossip that when Gluck was preparing a performance of one of his operas, he had to bribe musicians to play in his orchestra by offering them double rates. He had as low an opinion of them as they had of him, and he said that if he received twenty livres for composing an opera, he should be paid twenty thousand for rehearsing it. It is related of Gluck that he once crept under his desk and pinched the calf of an errant double-bass player "so that he gave a yell and came to earth along with his instrument." Gluck was asking for, and determined to achieve, things that not many orchestras at that time were prepared to give. He wanted all kinds of nuance, and well knew that no other conductor around could achieve them. He also knew, thanks to Mannheim, that they could be achieved. An indication of his approach can be found in a letter to Friedrich Gottlieb Klopstock, dated May 10, 1780: "About

PAINTING BY J. S. DUPLESIS (PARIS, 1775)

Christoph Willibald Gluck, the famous composer and the terror of orchestra musicians. Hardly any orchestra could meet his novel, uncompromising demands.

Christian Cannabich, conductor of the Mannheim Orchestra. He brought it to its height, and Mozart thought it by far the best group he had ever heard.

ENGRAVING BY EGIDE VERHELST (MANNHEIM, 1779)

the accompaniment [of *Alceste*], where the instruments require so many directions, nothing can be done unless I am there in person. Some notes must be drawn out, others pushed out, some at half volume, others louder or softer, not to mention the tempo. A little slower or faster destroys the whole piece." This almost sounds like Wagner talking about conducting; and, indeed, there is a certain resemblance between the two men in more ways than one.

Even before Gluck's death in 1787 the Mannheim influence bore fruit in Paris with the creation of the Concerts des Amateurs, also known as the Concerts de la Loge Olympique. François Gossec founded the series in 1770, and he was to the Parisian orchestral scene what Stamitz had been to Mannheim. Gossec believed in discipline and was also a showman. He made his players wear periwigs and brocade coats, lace ruffles, plumed hats and swords. They were permitted to remove the swords when they played. Haydn composed six symphonies for this group. As for Haydn, there is no evidence that he ever heard the Mannheim Orchestra, though without any doubt he had examined scores of the Mannheim school, and Stamitz was a strong influence on his development. Haydn of course would have heard stories about the glories of the orchestra, glories that he with his slender forces at Esterház never had the remotest chance of duplicating. At most, Haydn had twenty-four players.

In 1761 Haydn had entered the service of Prince Esterházy as second Kapellmeister, and was appointed Kapellmeister in 1766. The thirty-year-old composer found himself engaged in the duties that all conscientious Kapellmeisters were expected to supply. At Esterház, in addition to taking charge of the orchestra, he had to compose, do a great deal of administrative work, select the programs and rehearse the concerts. His music-loving Prince demanded two weekly concerts, Tuesdays and Saturdays, from two to four in the afternoon. Prince Nicholas, who had succeeded his brother Paul Anton in 1762, took great personal interest in his orchestra and supervised his Kapellmeister very closely. Often he insisted on certain kinds of music (an order of 1765 tells Haydn to compose more "and especially to write such pieces as can be played on the gamba"), and he knew enough about music to expect the best from his Kapellmeister. He played the baryton, a now obsolete instrument related to the viola da gamba; hence his request to Haydn to compose gamba music.

Haydn obliged. He also composed much music of every description.

The little orchestra at Esterház was considered one of the finest in Europe. As a conductor, Haydn was forceful and demanding. Naturally he had a precise ear, and he was the equal of Gluck in demanding unheard-of nuances. His players probably considered him a slave driver. He would not tolerate sloppiness and—within the framework of the period, of course—demanded precise adherence to the notes. As early as 1768 he was writing instructions about the kind of performance he expected of one of his cantatas. He asks that strict tempo be observed, that care be taken to make orchestral entrances on time, that the singer's text be allowed to come through intelligibly, and "that the fortes and pianos are written correctly throughout and should be exactly observed; for there is a very great difference between piano and pianissimo, forte and fortissimo, between crescendo and sforzando, and so forth." He gives explicit instructions about bowings, and he asks that ties be observed. The mind of a careful, sensitive musician is revealed in these instructions.

Haydn's life revolved around his orchestra. Much of his correspondence to the Prince and his administrators is concerned with new players, new instruments, working conditions. He fought for his men, constantly asking for uniforms, better salaries, better living quarters. It was Haydn who arranged the contracts of the musicians. It was Haydn who was in charge of copyists, the music library, and dealings with publishers. In addition, of course, there was his own music; and as Haydn became famous, his negotiations with the outside world multiplied. He was especially concerned with printing problems. Printing those days was generally inaccurate, and the well-organized Haydn was all but driven out of his mind by the necessity for constant correction. He complained bitterly to the famous firm of Artaria: "It is always painful to me that not a single work of mine you have published is free from errors."

Yes, Haydn worked terribly hard. But his life had its compensations. He was respected, lived in one of the showplaces of Europe, had a maid, a coachman, carriage and horses, had freedom to audition and select the best singers and players who came his way. Opera was just as important as orchestral music at Esterház. The place also boasted the most elaborate marionette theatre in Europe, for which Haydn had to compose music. But most of his time was occupied with opera. In 1786 seventeen operas, including eight premieres, were given a total of 125 performances. H. C. Robbins Landon estimates that in

This painting is believed to be the final scene of Haydn's other, though glancing at the small orchestra at the left. opera *L'Incontro improviso*. Note musicians facing each Haydn, with white wig, is directing from the harpsichord.

the course of one ten-year period, from 1780 to 1790, Haydn conducted 1,026 performances of Italian opera, not to mention the marionette operas and incidental music for plays. He was sick to death of them. He reorchestrated, he cut, he changed, he recomposed. His patron expected no less. But that all was part of the job, and Haydn well knew that his position was ideal. He told his biographer, G. A. Griesinger:

My Prince was satisfied with all my endeavors; I was applauded; as chief of the orchestra I could make experiments, observe what improved the general impression and what weakened it; and so I could correct, add, cut out; and I could be daring. I was isolated from the world and there was nobody near me to torment me or make me unsure of myself; and so I had to become original.

In the course of his long life Haydn lived to see the disappearance of the baroque orchestra and the emergence of a symphonic ensemble quite close to the modern kind. Of course he was one of its prime molders. As he began to go around Europe, preparing his own symphonies and choral works, he quite naturally would take over the function of the clavierist, with the concertmaster deferring to him. Almost always he conducted his music from the clavier. By the 1790s his reputation was such that he would have been the dominant figure in any orchestra. At his famous concerts in London, 1791 and 1794, the impresario Johann Peter Salomon, who had brought him to England, was the leader of the orchestra, with the composer officiating at the piano. (By that time the harpsichord was passé.) Salomon put himself out to do justice to the distinguished visitor, assembling for him an orchestra of forty in 1791 and a really tremendous one of sixty in 1794. At the 1791 concerts in the Hanover Square Rooms (95 feet by 35) the group was the largest Haydn had ever conducted. Perhaps he was not used to such luxury. In any event, there was some trouble at the first rehearsal. The violins sounded too loud, and Haydn had them play the phrase over and over again, without being satisfied. Finally he borrowed Salomon's violin, demonstrated the bowing he wanted, and there was no more trouble.

Haydn was active as a conductor nearly his entire life. And, as with any brilliant musician, there was no doubt about who was running the show. A critic for the *Allgemeine musikalische Zeitung* in 1799 gives us one of the rare pictures of Haydn in action: "Haydn's gestures were most interesting to me. With their aid he conveyed to the numerous executants the spirit in which his work was composed and should be performed. In all his motions, though they were anything but exaggerated, one saw very clearly what he thought and felt at each passage." Haydn's last appearance as a conductor was in 1803, in his cantata *Seven Last Words of Christ*.

Of Haydn's great contemporary, Wolfgang Amadeus Mozart, a much fuller picture can be drawn. Mozart's letters are full of information about his musical philosophy and practice. In addition, his contemporaries described him in such detail that it is not difficult to present a reasonably accurate estimate of him as a conductor. But first a few words about his general musicianship.

We know that he was born with a perfect ear, that he was the most brilliant musical prodigy history has known, that he developed into a patrician, all-encompassing creator. He was the classicist supreme, abhorring empty show; and the professional supreme, working on the kind of lofty level to which none, not even Haydn, could aspire. His concepts as a performing musician, and hence as a conductor, were governed by the eighteenth-century concept of "taste." Taste in those days meant something quite different from what it does today. When we say that a present-day musician has taste, we take it to mean that he follows the notes, keeps his own personality to a minimum, tries to reproduce the ideas of the composer as diligently and honestly as possible. But taste in the eighteenth century involved precisely the opposite: the ability of the performing musician to embellish or even improve the ideas of the composer. The notes were the ground plan, and they only served to stimulate the ideas of the performer. If the performer made of those notes something grand, logical, imaginative, he had good taste. If he indulged in vapid display work, or in other ways displayed a conventional and commonplace mind, his taste was suspect.

Mozart is constantly referring to taste. To his sister, about his piano sonatas: "Play them with plenty of expression, taste and fire." Of the violinist Regina Strinasacchi: "She has a good deal of taste and feeling in her playing." Of the pianist Georg Richter: ". . . too rough and labored, and entirely devoid of taste." And so on. In addition to taste, Mozart demanded rhythm ("the chief requisite in music"), clarity, feeling, precision and, above all, smoothness. That did not exclude spirit and fire. Mozart often used the words "fire" or "fiery." He objected to several singers in his *Idomeneo* because "Raaff and Dal Prato spoil the recitative by singing it without any spirit or fire." As an instrumentalist, Mozart also insisted on legato phrasing. One of his favorite, most-repeated expressions is "it should flow like oil," in reference to legato playing. Mozart was anti-bluff, anti-fakery. He could have no higher praise for a fellow musician—and Mozart was not at all generous with his praise—than to say he was completely in charge of the mechanical elements that went into music. This does not necessarily mean virtuosity, though Mozart was the last one in . the world to turn up his nose at instrumental brilliance. It means perfect control and command over whatever specific problem is at hand. Thus, about the violinist Ignaz Fränzl (concertmaster of the Mannheim Orchestra): "I like his playing very much. You know that I am no great lover of difficulties. He plays difficult things, but his hearers are not aware they are difficult; they think they could do the same thing themselves. That is real playing."

As for Mozart's attitude toward the printed note, he expected adherence to the composer's intent, within the freedom allowed by the age. He took it for granted that musicians would ornament and embellish —that showed their taste—but not at the expense of the composer. He had nothing but contempt for the kind of musicianship represented by Abt Vogler, who "generally played the bass differently from the way it was written, inventing now and then quite another harmony and melody." Anything unnatural bothered him; it was impure and anti-musical. Thus he complained about the singing of Joseph Meisner, who had

the habit of making his voice tremble at times, turning a note that should be sustained into distinct quarter or even eighth notes, and this I could never endure in him. And really it is a detestable habit and one which is quite contrary to nature. The human voice vibrates naturally—but in its own way—and only to such a degree that the effect is beautiful. Such is the nature of the voice; and people imitate it not only on wind instruments, but on string instruments too, and even the clavier. But the moment the proper limit is overstepped, it is no longer beautiful—because it is contrary to nature.

Proportion, freedom, discipline, flexible rhythm, taste, plenty of fire and spirit—all that is what Mozart looked for. His own prescrip-

Wolfgang Amadeus Mozart. Detail from the unfinished painting by Josef Lange, 1782.

Joseph Haydn, who conducted orchestras all his life. Wax bust was made by Thaller in 1790.

tion: ". . . playing the piece in the tempo it ought to be played, and playing all the notes, appoggiaturas and so forth, exactly as they are written, with the appropriate expression and taste." Naturally those attributes would be present in his conducting. And conducting was one of Mozart's outstanding gifts. He was taking charge of orchestras from the age of twelve and even before, and was active as a conductor his entire life. Generally he conducted from the clavier, though in his youth he was a violin-conductor. Mozart was an expert violinist; indeed, his father, who was completely objective and unsentimental when it came to his son's musicianship (and who himself was one of Europe's most respected violin teachers), always said that had Mozart stuck to it, he would have developed into the first violinist of Europe.

Mozart did not especially like the instrument, though up through his Paris days he was never far from it. It was while in Paris that he attended a rehearsal of a symphony (K. 297) that he had composed for the Concert Spirituel. He went through a few unhappy days and described his experiences in a letter to his father (July 3, 1778), a letter that gives a vivid picture of orchestral conditions at the time:

I was very nervous at the rehearsal, for never in my life have I heard a worse performance. You have no idea of how they twice scraped and scrambled through it. I was really in a terrible way and would gladly have had it rehearsed again, but as there was so much else to rehearse, there was no time left. So I had to go to bed with an aching heart and in a discontented and angry frame of mind. I decided next morning not to go to the concert at all; but in the evening, the weather being fine, I at last made up my mind to go, determined that if my symphony went as badly as it did at the rehearsal, I would certainly make my way into the orchestra, snatch the fiddle out of the hands of [Pierre] Lahoussaye, the first violin, and conduct myself!

Fortunately the performance came off better than Mozart had expected; the symphony made a grand success, and Lahoussaye was saved.

It was also in Paris that Mozart wrote his declaration of independence from the violin. Although his father kept insisting that he should conduct with the bow, and although the violin-conductor was more important than the clavierist in many European orchestras, Mozart rightly felt that his abilities and inclinations were much too strongly centered on the piano. So he stuck out his chin and—from a safe distance—penned a letter from Paris to Salzburg in which he told his father that he was not too happy about the way matters were going. And, "there is one more thing I must settle about Salzburg, and that is I shall not be kept to the violin, as I used to be. I will no longer be a fiddler. I want to direct at the clavier." Mozart was then twenty-two years old, and for the rest of his short life he held to his purpose.

Working with all kinds of orchestras and in all kinds of opera houses, Mozart must have developed into the best conductor in Europe. He knew his powers. As early as 1778 he let his father know that if the Archbishop of Salzburg "would only trust me, I should soon make his orchestra famous; of this there can be no doubt." Mozart was not bragging; he was a brilliant musician and would have been a sheer idiot had he not himself realized the fact. The technical parts of conducting came easily to him. Score reading, sight reading, transposing, all were as child's play. The conductor Joseph Weigl (who took over from Mozart the direction of *Le Nozze di Figaro* and *Don Giovanni* in Vienna) tells of Mozart in action: "Those who never saw Mozart play Handel scores of sixteen or more staves, with inimitable dexterity, and at the same time heard him sing and correct the singers' faults, do not know him thoroughly, for he was as great there as he was in his compositions. One always heard a whole orchestra." Fluent score reading is of course expected of any good conductor, though Mozart must have been phenomenal. But he was more than a technician. He developed into a good practical psychologist, able to work with orchestral musicians, knowing just how much to prod them and when to leave them alone. At a concert in Leipzig in 1789 he took the tempo of one of his symphonies so fast that the orchestra got all mixed up. Mozart stopped, explained what he wanted, and started again at the same tempo, stamping his foot to keep the players together. Mozart was reported as explaining why he used this tempo: "It was not caprice, but I saw at once that most of the players were old. There would have been no end to the dragging if I hadn't got them angry at me so that they did their best out of spite."

Occasionally he hàd the chance of working with big orchestras. Like any composer, Mozart was never so much delighted as when a really big group played one of his symphonies. The nineteenth century had a tendency to look on Mozart as a rococo composer whose sonorities were dainty and who must be approached with a mincing step, little finger in air. Today we know differently. We know that there was a demon in the man; that his music, especially his later music, can be passionate, intense and powerful. It also can take considerable sound. But it has to be a textured sound, with the balances and inner voices clearly maintained. One of Mozart's letters, from Vienna, dated April 11, 1781, gleefully describes a performance of (probably) the C major Symphony (K. 338): "It went *magnifique* and had the greatest success. There were forty violins, *the wind instruments were all doubled,* there were ten violas, ten double basses, eight cellos and *six bassoons.*" (Italics added.) An orchestra of over seventy is not inconsiderable, even by today's standards; but observe the proportions, with six bassoons and doubled winds counterbalancing the weight of the strings. No orchestra today, even when conductors are so anxious to be "authentic," observes those proportions.

Mozart could be testy and temperamental, and despite his diminutive size could exercise immense authority. When things did not go to his satisfaction, he would stamp his foot with impatience. At those times he cared for the feelings of neither the orchestra nor the audience. At a performance of his *Entführung aus dem Serail* the tempo got out of hand, and Mozart yelled at his players to bring them back into line. Michael Kelly, the Irish tenor who sang in the world premiere of *Le Nozze di Figaro,* writes that Mozart "was as touchy as gunpowder." But when things were going well, he was transformed; and Kelly talks about "his little animated countenance . . . it is as impossible to describe it, as it would be to paint sunbeams." At *Figaro* rehearsals, Mozart was all over the place, giving instructions, jumping from stage to orchestra, seeing to it that tempos were observed, working closely with the singers. He would have conducted from the piano.

But did he always do so? In the literature of the time there are some tantalizing references to Mozart's beating time, with no mention of the piano. Thus in Forkel's *Musikalischer Almanach für Deutschland,* in the 1789 volume, there is an entry dated from Vienna, February 26, 1788. It discusses a cantata by C. P. E. Bach played by an orchestra of eighty-six, and states that the "Kapellmeister Herr Mozart beat time and had the score," and that the other Kapellmeister, Umlauf, was at the keyboard. *Beat time and had the score!* And somebody else at the clavier! That Mozart did indeed beat time, and probably very much in the modern manner, we know. At the first *Zauberflöte* performance, the composer Johann Schenck had a place in the orchestra; and, unable to contain his delight, "crept to the conductor's stand, seized Mozart's hand and kissed it. Mozart, still beating time with his right hand, looked at him with a smile . . ." Both accounts—the Forkel and the Schenck—make one pause. It might be that the orchestras had two keyboard instruments (though that was not too common so late in the century), and Mozart was presiding over one. It could also be that Mozart was standing up and conducting—one, two, three, four. Schenck specifically mentions a "conductor's stand," not a piano. Still another possibility was that Mozart was seated before a clavier purely for form's sake. By the 1780s the old functions of the violinist-clavierist were beginning to disappear. Toward the end of the century it would appear that the piano player did very little playing, devoting his efforts toward maintenance of ensemble. In the *Jahrbuch der Tonkunst* of 1796 is an observation that "the concertmaster is in the position, as it were, of the front-rank man to whom the whole orchestra looks for guidance. But the Kapellmeister at the piano must sometimes stop playing to cut the air with both hands." It is quite likely, too, that the violinist beat time with his bow as often as he played. Certainly Forkel and Schenck strongly indicate that Mozart was accustomed to beating time and even working from the full score at the concert. This would make him the first of the great conductors, in the modern sense of the word.

There is considerable evidence that Beethoven also cut the air with both hands. But from all accounts, Beethoven seems to have been one of the worst conductors in history. Stubborn, defiant, he refused to bow to his deafness and often insisted on conducting first performances of his works. The result was inevitably a tragicomedy, though with much more tragedy than comedy: a handicapped giant in awesome throes, fighting to do that which could not be done. On top of that, he never could get along with people even before his deafness, and was constantly antagonizing every orchestra with which he was associated. Yet he stubbornly kept on. Even when the orchestra refused to play under his direction, as happened in 1808 at the premiere of his Fifth and Sixth Symphonies, he stormed to the podium after sulking in an anteroom during rehearsals. He should not have. Johann Friedrich Reichardt, in the audience, wrote that "many a failure in the performance vexed our patience in the highest degree." One of the things that happened was that Beethoven, playing the piano part of his *Choral Fantasy* (also on the gargantuan program), forgot about some repeats he had told the orchestra to disregard. He went back, the orchestra continued on, and the performance had to drag to a dismal stop. In the meantime Beethoven, noticing that something was wrong, was yelling, "Stop! Stop! Wrong! That will not do! Again! Again!" Some of the musicians were insulted and wanted to walk out. It was a typical mess. In Vienna, orchestral musicians hoped and prayed that Beethoven would stay away from them. If he did turn up, they hoped and prayed even more strongly that he would merely observe, not participate. When Ferdinand Ries played the C minor Concerto, Beethoven conducted but, to everybody's immense relief, only turned the pages. "Never," Ries slyly says, "was a concerto more beautifully accompanied."

Nevertheless, Beethoven as a conductor is a fascinating figure: a solid, even prophetic, link between divided leadership and the tyrannical, choreographic, virtuoso conductors who were to follow not much later. During his lifetime the baton came into use, but there is no real evidence Beethoven ever used one. And as late as the premiere of the Ninth Symphony, in 1824, several conductors shared the per-

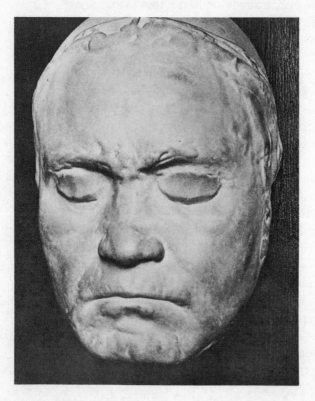

Ludwig van Beethoven, in life mask by Franz Klein, 1812. He was not a great conductor, but in many ways was a prototype of the great ones to come.

formance. But Beethoven insisted on making his presence felt, as he always had done. From the moment he arrived in Vienna he threw his weight around. His first benefit concert in Vienna—at which Beethoven conducted only his own music—took place on April 2, 1800, and the program was typical of the time: a Mozart symphony, an aria from Haydn's *Creation,* an improvisation by Beethoven, a Beethoven concerto with the composer as soloist, the Beethoven Septet, a duet from the *Creation,* another improvisation by Beethoven, and finally his C major Symphony. The critic of the *Allgemeine musikalische Zeitung* has a few things to say about the affair: "First, quarrels about who should conduct [the concerto]. Beethoven thought quite rightly that he could entrust the conducting not to Herr Conti but to Herr Wranitzky. The gentlemen refused to play under him." That must have gotten things off to a fine start, and one can guess—knowing Beethoven's hair-trigger temper—at the uproar that followed. The musicians undoubtedly took it out on the composer. "When they were accompanying, the players did not bother to pay any attention to the soloist. As a result there was no delicacy at all to the accompaniments, and no response to the musical feeling of the solo player. In the second part of the symphony they became so lax that despite all efforts on the part of the conductor, no fire whatsoever could be gotten out of them."

Music seems to have acted upon Beethoven as a drug. He literally seems to have lost control as sheer sound seized him. We can imagine him seated at the piano, conducting one of his orchestral works. As the music progressed, he would quite forget the purpose of his job. He would rise, be carried away, make motions that might be understood today but were the equivalent of gibberish then. Every musician spoke of Beethoven's conducting motions with amazement and disbelief. Ludwig Spohr, the important violinist-composer-conductor, played in the orchestra when Beethoven conducted the premieres of his *Wellington's Victory* and Seventh Symphony in 1814. Spohr discussed the composer's "extraordinary" motions. "Whenever a sforzando occurred, he tore apart his arms, which he had previously crossed on his breast, with great vehemence. At a soft passage he bent himself down, and the softer he wished to have it, the lower he bent." The reverse happened, says Spohr, as the music grew louder; and "to increase the forte yet more he would sometimes, also, join in with a shout to the orchestra without being aware of it." Ignaz von Seyfried has left us a famous and unforgettable description of Beethoven as a conductor:

Our master need not be presented as a model in respect of conducting, and the orchestra always had to take care in order not to be led astray by its mentor; for he had ears only for his own works and was ceaselessly occupied by manifold gesticulations to indicate the desired expression. He often made a downbeat for an accent in the wrong place. He used to suggest a diminuendo by crouching down more and more, and at a pianissimo he would almost creep under the desk. When the volume of sound grew, he rose up also as if out of a stage trap; and with the entrance of the full power of his orchestra he would stand on the tips of his toes almost as big as a giant and waving his arms seemed to soar upwards to the skies. Everything about him was active, not a bit of his body idle, and the man was like a *perpetuum mobile*. He did not belong to those capricious composers whom no orchestra in the world would satisfy. At times, indeed, he was altogether too considerate and did not even repeat passages that went badly at rehearsal. "It will go better next time," he would say. He was very particular about expression, the delicate nuances, the equable distribution of light and shade as well as an effective tempo rubato, and without displaying vexation would discuss them with the individual players. When he observed that the players would follow his intentions and play together with increasing ardor . . . his face would be transfigured with joy, all his features beamed with pleasure, a pleased smile would play around his lips, and a thundering *"Bravi, tutti!"* would reward the successful achievement.

That is one side of Beethoven as a conductor. The other shows temperament, storms, tears and destruction. Beethoven's friends were ashamed of his extravagant podium motions and were constantly making apologies, ascribing Beethoven's eccentricities quite properly to his deafness. "At the time when his hearing was still perfect," says Schindler, "he seldom had occasion to come into contact with the orchestra, and especially to acquire practice in conducting." As Beethoven's symphonies grew bigger and bigger, their conducting problems grew correspondingly greater and greater; and with the deaf Beethoven on hand to muddle things, history relates one terrible story after another. Musicians trembled when they heard Beethoven was going to participate in a performance. People like Seyfried would run around, telling the sullen musicians to ignore Beethoven and concentrate on the leader. But nothing seemed to help, even when conductors corrected Beethoven behind his back. In addition, Beethoven's memory was unreliable; he was extremely absent-minded. Seyfried told Spohr about the time Beethoven was playing a concerto and forgot he was the soloist. Springing up, he began to direct in his usual way, and at the first loud chords threw out his arms so violently that he knocked both lights off the piano.

No; nothing helped. Spohr gives a harrowing account of the 1814 premiere of the Seventh Symphony:

The performance was absolutely masterly, despite Beethoven's uncertain and often ridiculous conducting. It was quite plain that the poor, deaf master could no longer hear the softer passages of his music. This became particularly apparent during a rehearsal in the second part of the first movement, where there are two successive holds, the second of them pianissimo [presumably measures 299 and 300]. Beethoven apparently overlooked this, as he began to beat the time before the orchestra had even attacked the second hold. Thus, all unknowingly, he was ten or twelve measures ahead of the orchestra when the latter began, and piano at that. In order to indicate the piano, Beethoven had practically crawled under the desk. With the oncoming crescendo he became visible again, rising higher and higher and leaping into the air at that moment when, according to his calculations, the forte should have been reached. When the forte failed to materialize, he looked around in amazement, then stared incredulously at the orchestra, which was still playing piano. He got his bearings with the arrival of the forte, something that he could hear.

Pity and terror; and it rises to its height at the 1822 revival of *Fidelio*. Beethoven got the rehearsals into an irretrievable mess, and nobody had the courage to tell him. Things finally came to a stop, and Schindler passed a note to Beethoven: "Please do not continue; more at home." Beethoven, realizing the situation, fled the theatre. In the role of Leonore was Wilhelmine Schröder-Devrient, and she has left an account of the performance. She says that during rehearsals Beethoven "sat in the orchestra and waved his baton over everybody's heads," throwing everybody off. Waved his *baton*? But Schröder-Devrient was writing many years after the event, and memory may have played her false. Yet Beethoven may have used a stick; by that time the baton was not that rare in Vienna.

Two years later, at the premiere of the Ninth Symphony, Beethoven did relatively little interfering. He was conducting as a symbol; all the players' eyes were either on the concertmaster, Ignaz Umlauf—who had told the orchestra not to pay any attention to Beethoven—or on Conradin Kreutzer at the piano. Yes, the piano. It is not scored in the symphony, but was used at all early performances. Kreutzer would have been beating time to one or another segment of the orchestra, or to the chorus, using the piano only when things were getting out of control. (As late as the 1840s, English magazines were describing conductors "presiding at the pianoforte"; and in some European orchestras the piano held on until the 1870s.)

The Ninth Symphony caused unprecedented problems. As closely as can be figured out, Umlauf was in charge of the entire project, beating time with his bow. He had sub-conductors. In addition to Kreutzer at the piano, Ignaz Schuppanzigh led the violins. The symphony was played from manuscript after only two rehearsals. One shudders to think of what it sounded like. It evoked an audience reaction, however. At one point—accounts vary; some say after the scherzo, others after the finale—Caroline Unger, the contralto soloist, plucked Beethoven by the sleeve and directed his attention to the audience's applause. Beethoven had been lost in his own world, staring at the score and beating time. Probably not until 1843 did Vienna hear an adequate performance of the Ninth, when Otto Nicolai directed it, after thirteen rehearsals, with his newly formed Vienna Philharmonic.

If Beethoven's ideas as a conductor paralleled his ideas as a pianist —and, of course, they would have—he would have called for a great deal of freedom in phrase and rhythm. Rubato effects would be included. And if Anton Schindler is accurate—his testimony, despite his notorious inaccuracy about dates, seems to be as good as any; he was, after all, one of Beethoven's few pupils—Beethoven's ideas about orchestra performance involved a kind of fluctuation in tempo that would be inadmissible today. (All music until well after the beginning of the twentieth century was performed with a degree of freedom that would horrify modern purists.) Schindler makes the point that orchestral music does not admit of such frequent tempo changes as does music in smaller forms. "But," he continues, "it is equally well known that in orchestral performances the greatest and most unexpected effects can be produced by even slight variations of tempo."

He goes on to discuss the Second Symphony. In twenty-one measures of the second movement, Schindler indicates about seven tempo
changes. He wants several poco accelerandos, crescendos and the like:

Elsewhere in the discussion of the symphonies, Schindler is constantly referring to "little breaks of the tempo." Again, if one trusts

Schindler's accuracy (though it should be pointed out that many scholars do not), his remarks should be an eye-opener to present-day conductors. In the Fifth Symphony, for instance, he claims that Beethoven wanted measures 22 to 24 to be played slower than the first two measures. "Fate again knocks at the door, only more slowly" —an unforgettable line. Later on, when the "fate" motto turns up again, Schindler requests the same retardation. Beethoven, says Schindler, wanted the motto emphasized. Presumably the rest of the symphony goes in tempo. At least, Schindler says that "respecting any essential changes of tempo in the other three movements of the symphony, I received no information from Beethoven."

It is hard to imagine Schindler inventing all this out of thin air. And there is enough information about performance practice of the time to indicate that considerable leeway in tempo was granted the performing musician. It would, of course, be easy to take Schindler too literally and conduct Beethoven in a burlesque manner. But what Beethoven, through Schindler, was aiming at can be stated in one word: expressivity. Beethoven did not want his music played in a metronomic fashion. He certainly would not have wanted a broken or distorted musical line, but he would have welcomed devices that added to the tension. Any conductor of taste and imagination can easily understand what Schindler is talking about. By the same token, it is easy to see what Beethoven as a conductor stood for. He wanted to take the orchestra in his two hands and mold it. His was a constant search for expressivity, and he would have achieved it on the podium as he had achieved it on the piano had not his deafness intervened. Through all his epic struggles with the orchestra, through those grotesque but meaningful physical movements, we see the first of the modern conductors, the one who wanted to shape sound, in a personal, romantic manner, according to his inner vision. He never achieved that vision; his handicap was too great. But as a conductor Beethoven was, as in so many things, the pioneer, the prototype.

· V ·

Orchestras, Tuning and Audiences

By BEETHOVEN'S DEATH the orchestra, thanks to him, was almost in its present form. But work remained to be done, especially technical work. Before the invention of keyed wind and brass instruments, all orchestras were plagued by intonation problems. Back in 1725 Alessandro Scarlatti had taken it for granted that wind instruments would make intolerable noises ("They are never in tune"), and there was no great improvement during the century. Even the great Mannheim Orchestra could bother sensitive ears. Burney's complaint was typical. Naturally he was swept away the first time he heard the orchestra. But, "I found, however, an imperfection in this band, common to all others that I have ever yet heard but which I was in hopes would be removed by men so attentive and so able; the defect, I mean, in the want of truth in the wind instruments. I know it is natural for these instruments to be out of tune, but some of that art and diligence . . . would surely be well employed in correcting this leaven, which so much corrupts all harmony." Up to the first quarter of the nineteenth century such reliable musicians as Spohr and Moscheles were complaining that the horns were always false; and Henry Chorley, the British critic, who went to hear his first *Freischütz* in Berlin with great anticipation, came away disillusioned. The horns were "lazy and false."

But poor intonation was not necessarily the fault of the player. An idea of how an orchestra of Handel's day might have sounded is provided in a recording of Handel's *Fireworks Music* (Vox 500750), played by some of the best musicians in Boston and New York in an orchestra consisting of valveless horns, valveless trumpets, a cavalry serpent, oboes and bassoons. Some of the dissonances are excruciating, though after a while the ear accommodates and there

E

is something actually bracing in the sharp harmonic bite. The valve-less instruments could produce tones only in the natural harmonic series, and some of those pitches are well off the corresponding pitches in our tempered scale. For example, the thirteenth harmonic of an instrument in C is flat for an A, sharp for an A flat; and yet it has to serve for both notes. The horn players on this record, all from the Boston Symphony Orchestra, state that contrary to common conception, it is impossible to "lip" those tones into tempered-scale tones. Out-of-tune playing in the eighteenth century was a fact of musical life and nothing much could be done about it. Audiences took it for granted, complaining only when the dissonances were worse than usual. As long as composers stuck to keys in which the instruments were comfortable, the troubles were minimized.

Bach had established the equal-tempered scale in the forty-eight Preludes and Fugues of the *Well-Tempered Clavier,* but most in-struments of the day were tuned in mean-tone temperament, in which, as Friedrich Wilhelm Marpurg put it in 1779, "three scales were made ugly in order to make one scale beautiful." Bach's tuning, which we use today, was a compromise. In the words of Percy Scholes, "It is not possible to tune any keyed instrument *perfectly* for more than one key; if you tune it correctly for key C, the moment you play in another key some of the notes will be out of tune. On the mean-tone system just a single key was perfect, but, by a com-promise, a certain number of keys were made near enough perfect for the ear to tolerate them, the rest being left outside the pale." The six practicable keys were C, G, D, A, F and B flat; the three practi-cable minor keys were A, D and G. Thus composers before the adoption of the well-tempered scale had a limited choice of key. What Bach did was make a compromise. No *one* key was perfect, as it was in mean-tone intonation, but there were slight imperfections in *all* keys, the imperfections so small that the ear could tolerate them. Scholes, in his biography of Dr. Burney, estimates that most British organs and pianos did not adopt equal-tempered scales until nearly the middle of the nineteenth century. He cites Samuel Wesley's performance of the *Well-Tempered Clavier* on the piano and organ in the early 1800s, and ends his discussion of temperament with a pertinent question:

It would seem that the whole question of keys in use before the intro-duction of Equal Temperament needs study. Handel (to take one instance) sometimes used certain keys that we should not expect to find him using. Nevertheless it remains true that there were keys that no composer would have thought of using before the days of Equal Temperament. Burney, it will be noted, leaves eight unused—four major and four minor —and certainly it would seem that those eight, on a mean-toned instrument, would produce a very bad effect. Yet they must have been used in playing the "48"—unless Wesley transposed certain of Bach's preludes and fugues, and we hear nothing of that.

It looks as though, in asking the simple question, "How did Wesley play Bach's '48' on Burney's piano?" one is challenging the acousticians and scientific musical historians to a little fresh consideration of a subject on which they have so far pronounced rather too dogmatically and without sufficiently checking their statements by an examination of the actual musical repertoire of the eighteenth century.

But as for the keyed instruments of the orchestra, the first half of the nineteenth century did set out to do something about intonation problems and facilitation of playing. Such instrument makers as Theobald Böhm and Apollon Barret perfected, by ingenious mechanisms, the flute and oboe respectively. Iwan Müller and Hyacinthe Klosé perfected the clarinet. Adolphe Sax worked out a piston mechanism for the trumpet and invented a whole family of "saxhorns," of which the tuba was one. Valve horns started coming out by 1835. By 1850 the orchestra was pretty much stabilized.

With the newly improved wind instruments, an increased number of strings also came into the orchestra. The violins were "improved," with a longer neck and a higher, rounder bridge. Where Beethoven in his early days in Vienna used to plead for not fewer than four first violins and four seconds for his symphonies, the orchestras of the 1830s had many more. They were necessary. Long gone were the days when pundits seriously suggested, as did one writer for Cramer's *Magazin der Musik* in 1783, that symphonies should be played by no more than seventeen performers. Beethoven toward the end was demanding sixty and sometimes got even more. Wind instruments began to be so powerful that they swamped the strings, and Fétis in 1828 took note of the situation, having in mind the oncoming romantic music. As the number of strings "has not yet been augmented in the theatres of the chief towns of Europe," he wrote in *The Harmonicon*, "the consequence is that the stringed instruments are overpowered by flutes, oboes, clarinets, bassoons, horns, trumpets, trombones, ophicleides, timpani, drums and cymbals. At the Opéra in Paris, where the violins and basses are very numerous, this defect is not so striking. But it is already perceptible at the Théâtre-Italien; in the provincial theatres it is worse. In a word, in increasing the masses of sound, it is not always possible to preserve a just proportion. The scarcity of artists and the want of space present important obstacles."

A few European orchestras, however, were very large even as early as the first quarter of the nineteenth century. In Munich there were forty-eight strings. The Paris Opéra, to which Fétis referred, had fifty-nine—fifteen first violins, sixteen seconds, eight violas, twelve cellos, eight basses. (The New York Philharmonic in 1967 had seventeen, seventeen, twelve, twelve, nine—sixty-seven altogether.) The composers, of course, spurred orchestras to increasingly greater sizes and technical feats. Weber, Schubert, Berlioz, Wagner—all asked for more and more in the way of color effects, sonorities and new technical demands. And so to Mahler, Strauss and the gargantuan orchestra of Schoenberg's *Gurrelieder*. For the most part, the strings in a typical good orchestra of the last quarter of the nineteenth century averaged fifty-five.

The change in the orchestral situation during the first half of the nineteenth century was but one expression of the changes sweeping Europe. Everything was in flux. The middle class was exerting itself. The Industrial Revolution had brought factories and railroads; had brought new manufacturing techniques (including techniques in book and music publishing). The arts were no more the province of clergy or aristocracy. Now the *nouveau riche* and even the common man wanted to participate in the musical experience. For a while, though, they had nowhere to go. As late as the 1830s there was no decent concert hall in Paris, and there were very few in Europe. Salons, hotel rooms, riding academies—everything was pressed into service for music. Soon halls began to be built. And conservatories began springing up—in Paris in 1795; Milan and Naples in 1808; Prague in 1811; Vienna in 1817; London in 1822; Brussels in 1832; Leipzig in 1843; Munich in 1846. Major orchestras could be found in those cities, though there were almost no orchestras that were "symphony orchestras." The opera house was their natural habitat, and symphonic work was extracurricular. Touring artists had to make do with what they found, and in the provinces they found precious little. Moscheles in 1825 had to content himself in Liverpool with eight strings and "four halting wind instruments." That was his accompaniment for a concerto. At least in the big cities could be found the London Philharmonic (founded 1813), the Paris Conservatory Orchestra (1828) and the Vienna Philharmonic (1842).

The institution of public concerts was a long time getting under way, and not until the 1840s and 1850s did they become prevalent. Previously there had been sporadic attempts. As early as 1672 John Banister, an English violinist, conceived the idea of charging admittance to concerts at "a shilling a head, and call for what you please." His first advertisement appeared in the London *Gazette* of December 30, 1672:

These are to give notice that at Mr. John Banister's house, now called the Musick-School, over against the George Tavern in White Friars, the present Monday, will be musick performed by excellent masters beginning precisely at four of the clock in the afternoon, and every afternoon in the future, precisely at the same hour.

These Banister concerts continued through 1678. Later in London were John Britton's concerts, those of the Academy of Antient Music (founded 1710), the Castle Society (1724) and various series by such entrepreneurs as Salomon. In Paris, Anne Philidor (a man, despite his feminine first name) founded the famous Concert Spirituel—often incorrectly referred to as Concerts Spirituels—in 1725. These continued for sixty years and were one of the most important musical institutions in Europe. Philidor also had a hand in the formation of the Concert Français in the Tuileries, twice weekly (Saturday and Sunday) in winter, once a week in the summer. These went on from 1727 to 1730, during which time over a hundred concerts were presented. Leipzig began its famous concerts in 1743, and these concerts were moved to the Gewandhaus in 1781. The Music Exercising Society in Berlin started in 1749; the Tonkünstler Societät in Vienna was in existence by 1772 and the Felix Meritas concerts in Amsterdam by 1777. But even in the enlightened musical centers, actual events were very few in the course of a year. When Beethoven came to Vienna at the end of 1792 there were plenty of solo concerts but only four scheduled annual symphonic concerts. These were given at the Burgtheater—two at Christmas and two at Easter.

Mary's Chappel   Five at Night

H. Hogarth Inv.   Jane Ireland

ERIC SCHAAL COLLECTION

This Hogarth engraving, entitled "Five at Night," is an actual concert
ticket for St. Mary's Chapel in 1799. Note the conductor, at far right,
wildly gesticulating—without a baton—in an altogether modern fashion.

Programs invariably were of the variety type, in which the orchestra was supplemented by vocal and instrumental soloists and
some kind of novelty. Often the orchestra would be a pick-up group,
largely amateurs belonging to the town's music club, enthusiastically
out of tune and seldom together. Movements of a symphony would
not be played in succession. The sponsors of a concert obviously felt
that such extraordinarily concentrated intellectual effort as listening
to three consecutive movements of a symphony would give the audience brain fever. Programs ran terribly long, even if the content was
thin: two or more symphonies, two overtures, vocal and instrumental
numbers, duets, a concerto. Over three hours was the norm, and

many musicians complained. "It is a mistake," Moscheles wrote in 1830, "to give at every [London] Philharmonic concert two symphonies and two overtures, two grand instrumental and four vocal pieces. I can never enjoy more than half." As late as 1855 Wagner screamed at the length of the Philharmonic programs in London. (He had to conduct them.) If nothing else, however, a large amount of the music on those programs was new. Today's audiences look for the old, but in the early 1800s they were interested primarily in the very latest products. Adam Carse went through programs of early organizations and came up with some impressive statistics. Between 1830 and 1839 the Paris Conservatory concerts presented seventeen symphonies by eighteenth-century composers as against ninety-five by nineteenth-century ones. There were no eighteenth-century concertos at all, and fifteen composed after 1800. At Leipzig during the same decade the ratio of eighteenth-century symphonies to nineteenth-century ones was 51 to 154; overtures, 21 to 258; concertos, 6 to 148. This proportion was much the same everywhere.

But outside of Paris, London, Berlin and one or two other cities, the standards of execution must have been very low, especially in the early years of the nineteenth century. On this all experts are unanimous. Adam Carse flatly states that "the standard of performance in the eighteenth-century orchestras was such as would hardly be tolerated at the present time." Without any trouble at all, reference after reference to inadequate orchestral playing can be dug up from qualified commentators of the time, and of the first half of the nineteenth century, too. Adolphe Adam attended a performance at Covent Garden in 1833. The orchestra was at its worst on Saturday night, he says, because the members were paid on Saturday and promptly got drunk. He describes the startling noises made at the start of the overture. The oboe went *couak*, followed by an even more prodigious *couak* from the clarinet. The bassoon produced a series of frightful snores. The flute continued to make increasing *turlututus*. The trumpet put the bell of his instrument in a neighbor's pocket and blew through the clothing. The bass drum banged away like mad. In the meantime, conductor and singers carried on as though nothing unusual was happening. The performance of *Don Giovanni* that Vincent Novello heard in Vienna in 1829 was not on the Covent Garden order, but the orchestra played without consideration for the singers, the singers in self-defense had to yell, and the result was "a coarse, noisy and violent effect."

In the United States during the first half of the nineteenth century performances must have been indescribable. Max Maretzek attended a performance of *Il Barbiere di Siviglia* at the Astor Place Opera House in New York. The orchestra was about thirty-six weak. "They had a leader, Signor Lietti, who did not apparently consider it necessary to indicate the movement by beating the time." Not Signor Lietti; he was too busy playing the violin, completely unconscious of the other instruments in the orchestra. He loudly stamped on the floor and made faces. The other violinists "exerted themselves with a purely musical ferocity which you have never seen equalled. . . . After the first eighty bars of the allegro movement, you would, had you been there, upon shutting your eyes, have undoubtedly believed that you were surrounded by a series of saw-mills in vigorous operation." Maretzek, appalled, spends pages in a description of this mess; and even allowing for exaggeration and Maretzek's natural ebullience, it clearly was a performance to be missed.

All musicians were agreed that Italian orchestras were the worst in the world. Spohr noted that "nuances of piano and forte are unknown to them. Even with this, however, one can make do. But each one [player] makes his own embellishments according to his own dictates, with the result that the sound resembles that of an orchestra tuning up rather than a coordinated performance." In addition, Spohr wrote, violinists not only played what came into their heads, but "used double stops on almost every note." There is the testimony of George Sievers. He was a scholar and the correspondent of several German publications who lived in Italy during the 1820s and '30s. His account of Italian orchestras is long, but it is not well known and is worth quoting as an all too graphic picture of musical manners in Italy:

The Italian orchestras are in a far from admirable condition. Lack of precision, of unity and cooperation, even lack of technical skill are noticeable everywhere. Passages that are not at all difficult are botched and mangled; indeed, the player often breaks down completely. . . . The orchestras are requested to accompany singers with full, healthy voices requiring powerful support so that the singers can let them out to the fullest extent. The weak, forceless and savorless fiddling customary with German orchestras—and to a great extent also with the French—is foreign to the Italian bands. Everybody fiddles and blows with all his might and main! It would be absolutely unthinkable for a singer to ask for a softer accompaniment; the orchestra would immediately think he was incapable. The orchestra plays everything at the inspiration of the moment; nothing is thought through. . . . Since there are no public concerts they have no experience in performing so-called symphonies. . . . Even more striking is the carelessness, negligence and total lack of enthusiasm on the part of the players. While in the Paris orchestra every member is on the alert to catch every indication of the conductor, in the Italian orchestras it is a matter of every man for himself. They tune their instruments while the singer is singing a bravura passage, talk while they are playing, put their instruments down when the notion strikes them to rest or scratch their heads. Altogether they act as if the whole business was not serious. They have as little enthusiasm as technical discipline. . . . When the violinist-leader gives the sign to begin, he strikes the brass candleholder of his desk several times with all his might, without giving the musicians the slightest hint. He then immediately draws his bow for the first stroke of the work, quite unconcerned whether all the rest, or only a few, or in fact anybody at all, begins with him at the same time. These heartrending blows on the candleholder are repeated many times before each number, first by the cembalist, who accompanies the simple recitatives on the piano, and later by the first violin. During the recitatives the other players creep under the seats of the orchestra to chat with one another, take a grain of snuff, or even play a practical joke on one of their colleagues. When the leader bangs on the candleholder they rush out in all directions, two-thirds of them usually too late, because in their haste one has knocked over a stand, another a candleholder, another the music, or has stepped on a colleague's corn and stops to have an argument with him. In Paris the players are not allowed to leave their seats except in cases of the utmost necessity. The Italian musicians, who take good care of their heads, all wear red caps, which makes them look like the French revolutionaries of 1790.

Berlioz and Mendelssohn fully back up Sievers' description. Berlioz wrote of "the wretched blowing and scraping, as indifferent to what is being shouted on the stage as to what is being buzzed in the boxes and parterre, and possessed of but one thought—that of earning their supper. The assemblage of these poor creatures constitutes what is called an orchestra." And Mendelssohn in 1831 was greatly struck by the way the leaders beat against the candleholder. Yet "in spite of that the voices are never together."

Just as most orchestras were in what the twentieth century would regard as a primitive state, so the approach toward music itself was entirely different. There was, for instance, no concept of adherence to the printed note. During almost the entire nineteenth century there was a carryover from the eighteenth-century practice of embellishment and improvisation. Musicians, even the purest and noblest, had not the least hesitation changing things to suit themselves. No such thing as scholarship or musicology existed. After 1750 early compositions were modernized as a matter of course (see Mozart's orchestration of Handel's *Messiah*) or completely rewritten. As a practical musician of the day, Mozart himself knew that his operas and other works were never going to be performed after his death exactly as he wrote them. Or even during his lifetime, for that matter. He knew, for instance, that few orchestras in Europe had clarinets or English horns. In a letter to Sebastian Winter, written in 1786, he referred to the scoring of the Piano Concerto in A (K. 488) and its two clarinets. Should no clarinets be around, said Mozart, "a competent copyist might transpose the parts into the suitable keys, in which case the first clarinet should be played by a violin and the second by a viola." This is what was bound to happen. At Salzburg performances of the *Entführung aus dem Serail* the clarinet and English horn were played by the violas. But Mozart would have been appalled to discover what happened to his operas after his death. *Die Zauberflöte* in Paris, 1801, was given under the title of *Les Mystères d'Isis*, with the text changed, harmonies altered, solos and duets made into trios, sections of *Don Giovanni, Figaro* and *Clemenza di Tito* inserted, and even with parts of Haydn symphonies introduced into the opera. In England, popular songs of the day were put into the Mozart operas, and this kind of pastiche was on the boards until 1820 (Spohr mentions it with great indignation). Rossini's *Barbiere di Siviglia* came out in Covent Garden in 1818 as follows:

The Overture and Music (complete) to the Comic Opera called the Barber of Seville, as performed at the Theatre Royal, Covent Garden, partly selected from Paisiello and Rossini's highly celebrated operas, Il Barbiere di Siviglia, partly composed, and the whole arranged, altered and adapted to the English stage, by Henry R. Bishop.

Bishop, among other things, discarded Rossini's overture and wrote one of his own. And Rossini was very much alive at the time!

As often as not, alterations were made not because the arranger thought the original composer was not very good. Quite the contrary:

because in all humility the arranger wanted to help a great man. Thus Mendelssohn honestly believed he was doing Bach a favor by cutting and revising the St. *Matthew Passion* so that Berlin audiences would find the work more palatable. Vincent Novello was only echoing contemporary feeling when he made additions to Handel's scoring because of "the profound veneration I feel for the memory of the most sublime of all composers. . . . I have carefully selected only such additional instruments to enrich my new edition of the orchestral score, as to the best of my judgment, I think that Handel would *himself* have chosen if these had been at his command when he first wrote these oratorios." So even in the middle of the nineteenth century we have the argument: "If Handel [or Bach, or anybody] were alive today . . ." that Leopold Stokowski and the other arrangers were to use in the twentieth. In 1837 Moscheles introduced a Bach cantata to England, providing it with new accompaniments written by himself "with great taste and ready appreciation of the character of the music." It also was Moscheles, one of the really fine musical minds of the first half of the century, who added organ accompaniments to the chorus in the Beethoven Ninth Symphony and, while he was about it, rewrote some of the vocal parts.

Wagner complained bitterly about alterations made by conductors who interpolated or changed material. He was the one to complain! He "improved" Gluck's *Iphigenie in Aulis,* linking passages together, composing the connecting links, introducing his own recitatives and, he tells us in his autobiography, "Throughout the work I revised the whole instrumentation more or less thoroughly." It is very hard for us in the last third of the twentieth century to put ourselves in the place of people like Wagner and Mendelssohn, who were only trying to do their best for the earlier composers. What today strikes us as vandalism or sacrilege was then an act of the deepest homage when done with restraint and integrity. Hans von Bülow summarizes the philosophy in a letter he wrote in 1850. He is discussing Wagner's conducting of *Don Giovanni* in Zurich, before "a most dull, stupid and thankless public." Wagner, writes Bülow,

had taken exceptional trouble and we all had been several days and nights correcting errors in the orchestral parts, replacing instruments that were lacking, such as trombones, by others—deep trumpets, etc. He had had the Italian recitatives translated into good German dialogue, some even

COOPER UNION MUSEUM

A performance at Castle Garden, New York, around the middle of the last century. The conductor, with his back to orchestra and audience, leads his singers from a position directly behind the prompter's box. Such positioning was quite common in the first half of the nineteenth century.

A rehearsal of the famous Leipzig Orchestra, around 1850. Julius Reitz is the conductor, and the concertmaster is Ferdinand David. All of the musicians except the cellists play from a standing position. Until almost the turn of the century, many orchestras made their players stand.

admitted in their original form; he had also simplified the scenery, and had cleverly reduced the everlasting scene-changing to a single one in the middle of the first act; and further he had arranged that the last aria of Donna Anna, which is usually sung in a room, should be given in the churchyard, to which she goes with Don Ottavio, for whom a little recitative, composed by Wagner, precedes the aria as a sort of introduction to it. Thus a sensible consistency was given to the entire dramatic action, which, alas! is almost always lacking in a performance. It has driven me almost wild when I remember how Wagner used to be accused in Dresden of conducting Mozart's operas badly on purpose. The warm and loving artistic feeling of reverence for Mozart, shown by this disinterested act, will not be brought to light by any of the so-called Mozart specialists. It is clear that *Don Giovanni,* as given everywhere up to now, does not give the pleasure or make the effect that it can and ought to do; there is need for ample reform in this matter.

It is safe to say that not until the twentieth century was any baroque or classic composition played in seventeenth or eighteenth century style. It is also safe to say that all scores, including those of Beethoven, were touched up even by the conductors of greatest integrity, such as Wagner and Habeneck. Daniel Türk, the conductor at Halle in the early years of the nineteenth century, used to omit the introduction of the last movement of Beethoven's First Symphony; he thought the audience would laugh at those ascending scales, and he obviously did not realize their meaning.

Yes; they ordered things differently in those days. That also pertained to the orchestral musician himself. He was underpaid, overworked and, early in the century, was considered an undesirable member of society. To add to his indignity he had to stand, in many European orchestras, during performances. The physical discomfort must have led to even worse playing. It is not generally realized, but it was an almost universal custom for all musicians except cellists to stand. At the first concert of the New York Philharmonic in 1842 the instrumentalists stood, in approved Leipzig Gewandhaus manner, and eleven years later a writer was wondering why they played standing up when they would be so much more comfortable seated. Not until 1905 did the players at the Gewandhaus rest their weary feet.

Bad as was the behavior of many musicians and orchestras, free as was the approach to the printed note, the behavior of audiences until the first half of the nineteenth century could be even worse. Throughout the eighteenth century, many concerts were likely to be given in the salons of royalty, as background to card games and conversation. More than once Spohr refused to play under those circumstances. Musicians like him, Moscheles, Liszt and Mendelssohn demanded respect and helped make the artist a glamorous, divinity-touched figure to whom even royalty had to pay respect (Liszt once told off the Czar of all the Russias in no uncertain terms). But when the middle and lower classes began to go to concerts, and especially to the opera, they had to be educated. At the beginning they talked so much it was hard to hear the music. Haydn on his first visit to London went to Covent Garden and made an entry in his diary:

The theatre is very dark and dirty, and is almost as large as the Vienna Court Theatre. The common people in the galleries of all the theatres are very impertinent; they set the fashion with all their unrestrained impetuosity, and whether something is encored or not is determined by their yells. The parterre and all the boxes sometimes have to applaud a great deal to have something good encored. That was what happened this evening, with the duet in the third act, which was very beautiful; and the pro's and contra's went on for nearly a quarter of an hour, till finally the parterre and boxes won and they repeated the duet. Both the performers stood on the stage, quite terrified, first retiring, then again coming forward.

The bad behavior of Covent Garden audiences was notorious. Moscheles reports that Carl Maria von Weber in 1826 conducted one of his overtures amid screams and hubbub from the galleries. Then Moscheles himself had to come forth and play a work for piano and orchestra. "At the opening bars of the introduction the roughs in the gallery made themselves heard by whistling, hissing, shouting and calling out 'Are you comfortable, Jack?' accompanying the question with volleys of orange peel." Moscheles was followed by a Miss Paton, who tried to sing, had to stop three times because of the noise, and then retired in tears. Moscheles, in writing about this episode, does not sound particularly shocked or even surprised. The English tradition always was one of uninhibited self-expression. In 1775 Jean Monnet brought a dance company to Drury Lane. Because the audiences did not like the show, and because in addition anti-French sentiment was running high, the audience demonstrated its feeling at one performance by demolishing the house. Glass was broken, benches torn up and thrown on the stage, walls defaced. Drury Lane had to be closed several months to repair the damage.

Paris could have its moments, too. Burney, at the opera in 1770, heard a work "that was as thoroughly damned as ever piece was in England. I used to imagine that a French audience durst not hiss to the degree I found they did on this occasion. Indeed quite as much, mixt with horse-laughs, as ever I heard at Drury-Lane or Covent-Garden. In short, it was condemned in all the English forms, except breaking of the benches or the actors' heads, and the incessant sound of *hish* instead of *hiss*." And, of course, there was, some eighty years later, the famous demonstration that the Jockey Club put on against Wagner's *Tannhäuser* at the Opéra. German and Austrian audiences seemed to have been much more disciplined, and their disapproval, while often weighty and expressed vocally, did not take physical forms of expression.

· VI ·

The Arrival of the Stick

AROUND THE last quarter of the eighteenth century, when the figured bass had just about passed into history, divided leadership clung on only by force of habit. The *maestro al cembalo* was no longer needed to realize those mysterious digits below a bass line; and as orchestras and operatic groups grew bigger, as scores got more complicated, a single controlling force was obviously needed. A Vivaldi concerto can almost run by itself; the *Eroica* Symphony or *Fidelio* can not. It also turned out that there were all kinds of trouble with divided leadership. Spohr, early in the nineteenth century, looked upon the situation and found it not good. He poked fun at the then current procedures. The "conductor," he said, sits at the piano and plays from the full score, but in actuality gives neither the beat nor the tempo. This is supposed to be done by the "leader," but as that worthy has only the first violin part before him he cannot be of much help to the orchestra. "So he contents himself with emphasizing his own part and letting the orchestra keep with him as best it can." Moscheles agreed that the man at the piano was an anachronism. "He sits there and turns the leaves of his score, but after all he cannot, with his marshall's staff, the baton, lead his musical army. The leader [concertmaster] does this, and the 'conductor' remains a nullity." Moscheles wanted the *maestro al cembalo* to dispense with the piano, get up and beat time like a man.

Paganini added his voice to those who were dubious about divided leadership. The great violinist did some conducting and seems to have been remarkably good at it; and he threw up his hands when he thought of the mess in which Italian orchestras found themselves. The pianist, he said, could act only as a chronometer, the violinist has enough to do without worrying about the rest of the orchestra, and the chief responsibility (pleaded Paganini) should be vested in a conductor who should be a real master. "He should have composed music and have had the practical experience that gives the freedom so necessary to good conducting."

When the composer was not at hand, and when neither the violinist nor the pianist could dominate, there was likely to be all kinds of trouble—rivalry, jealousy, pettiness. Each felt that *he* was the important force in the orchestra (and, as a by-product, both would join forces to resist the appearance of a third dictator, the man with the baton). The *Musical World* of March 29, 1840, has an amusing piece on the new arrangement (in England, as elsewhere on the continent, the violin-leader and pianist were retained even after the batonist appeared):

Down goes the conductor's *baton*, ditto the heel of the leader's boot— perhaps simultaneously, perhaps not, as the case may be—*"piano!"* vociferates the conductor; "S-s-s-sh!" responds the leader—that is, if he thinks *piano;* he may, perhaps, think *forte* and act accordingly, whereupon, as a matter of course, wind and strings follow suit . . .

Only a few years later the *Musical World* commiserated with a poor soloist who had to work under the "discordant batons of no less than three different individuals." These were Sir George Smart, the batonist; Mr. Loder, the leader; and Mr. T. Cooke, a violinist who had decided notions about how the performance should go. "These gentlemen were all beating different times, and the consequence was, that the band was bewildered." As well it might be.

Even in 1847, when Mendelssohn conducted his *Elijah* in London, the *Times* complained that Mr. Perry, the leader, was constantly beating time with his "fiddlestick" in such a manner as to obstruct the view of the conductor and to confuse the attention of the instrumentalists. Conducting, up to the 1830s and even much later, was apt to be as distracting aurally as it was visually. Sometimes the various leaders had to resort to drastic measures to get things under control. In Vienna, before Nicolai took over, the foot stamping of the violinist made a bigger racket than the orchestra did. Or the leader might loudly clap his hands to keep things together. Whatever the means used, it was noisy. An article in the January 1830 issue of *Harmonicon* contrasts the Berlin orchestra with the London Phil-harmonic, to the detriment of the latter. For in Berlin "our ears are not excruciated by two distinct beats, intended to represent the same time—one being clapped by the hands of the conductor [the man at the piano], the other being stamped, sometimes furiously, by the foot of the first violinist or leader." Dionys Weber, in Prague, wore a deep groove in his music stand by constantly hammering on it with his baton. Berlioz, at the San Carlo Opera in 1832, grudgingly conceded that the performance was at least meritorious. But "the noise made by the conductor tapping his desk bothered me greatly. I was gravely assured, however, that without this support the musicians could not possibly keep in time." The custom—in Italy, at any rate—held on for a remarkably long time. C. Adby-Williams, writing in the October 1895 issue of the *Musical Times,* describes one aspect of Rossini's *Barbiere* in Pisa: "The conductor had to beat time on his desk so often in order to keep his forces together, that he had a small sheet of copper fastened on it to save wearing it out . . . He struck this at the first beat of every bar in the opera."

The advantages of a single supreme figure were obvious, but it took a long time for the batonist to make his way. There had been pioneers. From here and there come suggestive accounts of people who must have been early batonists—men who beat time with a stick but whose innovation was not pursued. In 1709 the Abbé Raguenet published a pamphlet, immediately translated into English as "A Comparison between the French and Italian Musick and Operas." On page 142 is a footnote:

Some years since, the Master of the Musique in the Opera at Paris had an Elboe chair and Desk plac'd on the Stage, where, with the Score in one Hand and a Stick in the other, he beat Time on a Table put there for that purpose, so loud, that he made a greater Noise than the whole Band, on purpose to be heard by the Performer. . . . The same was observ'd in London six or seven years ago; but since the *Italian* masters are come among us, and the Operas have been introduced, they have put a stop to that ridiculous Custom, which was Founded more upon ill habit than any Necessity there was for it, as doing more harm than good.

Similarly in Germany there was a man who gave an audible beat. He was called a *Taktschläger* (literally, time beater). The Paris

Opéra may have dispensed with the noisy table beater, but by 1802 had come up with something else. George Smart watched a performance there, a performance that used a huge orchestra of ninety, and he specifically mentions *"a maître d'orchestre* with a small roll of wood,"* standing in the middle of the orchestra with the score before him and answering "the purpose of the prompter at our opera house." Often the leading violinist would stop playing and actually beat time with his bow. Gluck did this often. In Paris, the home and last retreat of the violin-conductor, they came up with an extra time beater, a *batteur de mesure,* who recalled the days of Lully by loudly rapping the floor with a wooden staff of some kind. Jean Baptiste Roy was probably the last of the *batteurs de mesure.* He was succeeded at the Opéra in 1810 by Louis Loc Loiseau (what a liquid name!) who had been a violinist in the orchestra since 1793. Loiseau conducted with his bow when not actually playing. Rodolphe Kreutzer, the well-known violinist, conducted the Opéra orchestra from 1817 to 1824; and the greatest French conductor of the period, François Antoine Habeneck, continued the French tradition, leading with bow rather than baton.

But elsewhere there were a few eighteenth-century batonists. Guillaume-Alexis Paris, the Belgian composer-conductor, is said to have directed performances of French opera in Hamburg with a foot-long baton in 1794. Other musicians used a roll of paper, but used it very much like a baton. In Berlin, the influential and capable Bernhard Anselm Weber wielded a roll of leather stuffed with calf's hair, and pounded it so vigorously against his desk that dust and calf's hair flew in every direction. It is not known when Johann Friedrich Reichardt adopted the baton, but when he was appointed Kapellmeister in Berlin in 1776 he rearranged the orchestra, abolished the piano, and directed orchestra and singers from a separate desk placed close to the footlights in the center of the orchestra. Reichardt is one of the most important of the early innovators.

So is Ludwig Spohr, the leading classical violinist of his day, an important composer and one of the very first of the batonists. Spohr was influential in introducing the baton all over Europe. A musician of the old school, he at first had used his violin bow, like everybody else. Then he graduated to a roll of paper. In 1810 this alone was considered quite daring, not to say avant-garde. One of the major things noticed about this new method was that it seemed to make

Ludwig Spohr, one of the first of the modern conductors, who was using the baton by 1820. Photograph dates from c. 1855.

Caricature of an old-fashioned conductor beating time with a roll of paper and also marking rhythms by stamping his foot.

conducting easier; and another aspect, about which contemporaries marveled, was that it was silent. Conducting without noise! No rappings, stampings, clappings! "Herr Spohr's conducting with a roll of paper," a critic wrote, "without the least noise and without the slightest distortion of countenance, might be called a graceful conducting if that word were sufficient to express the precision and influence of his movements upon the entire ensemble . . ." In 1817 Spohr finally took the last step. It was that year in Hamburg that he "directed in the French style, with a baton," as he puts it in his autobiography. (Spohr's use of the expression "French style" indicated that musicians of his day believed the new system had originated in Paris. He was probably referring to the violinists who waved the bow and did almost no playing any more.)

So great was Spohr's reputation, so strong his influence, that many musicians followed his lead, all the more so in that the virtues of the baton were immediately apparent. There was resistance in conservative circles, of course. Spohr's own account of his adventures with the London Philharmonic is deservedly famous. He went to London in 1820 at the invitation of Beethoven's pupil, Ferdinand Ries. The idea was that Spohr play solos and concertos, and also conduct from the violin section. As he tells the story:

It was at that time still the custom that when symphonies and overtures were performed, the pianist had the score before him, not exactly to conduct from it, but only . . . to play along with the orchestra at pleasure, which when it was heard had a very bad effect. The real conductor was the first violinist, who gave the tempi, and now and then gave the beat with the bow of his violin. So numerous a personnel, sitting so far apart from each other as that of the Philharmonic, could not possibly play precisely together; and in spite of the excellence of the individual members, the ensemble was much worse than we are accustomed to in Germany. I had therefore resolved, when my turn came to conduct, to remedy this defective situation. Fortunately at the morning rehearsal on the day I was to conduct the concert, Mr. Ries took his place at the piano, and he readily agreed to surrender the score to me and to remain wholly excluded from participation in the performance. I then took my position with the score at a separate music desk in front of the orchestra, drew from my pocket my directing baton, and gave the signal to begin. Quite alarmed at such a novel procedure, some of the directors would have protested against it;

but when I pleaded with them to grant me at least one trial, they became pacified. . . . I could, therefore, not only give the tempi in a very decisive manner, but also indicated the entries to all the wind instruments and horns, which ensured them a confidence they had not known before. I also took the liberty, when the execution did not satisfy me, to stop and in a very polite but earnest manner to comment on the manner of execution. . . . Incited thereby to more than usual attention, and conducted with certainty by the *visible* manner of beating time, they played with a spirit and correctness as until then they had never been heard. Surprised and inspired by the result, the orchestra immediately after the first movement of the symphony expressed aloud its unanimous assent to the new way of conducting, and thereby overruled all further opposition on the part of the directors. . . . The result in the evening was still more brilliant than I could have hoped for. It is true that the audience was at first startled by the novelty and was seen whispering together. But when the music began, and the orchestra executed the well-known symphony with unusual power and precision, the general approval was shown immediately after the first movement by long-sustained applause. The triumph of the baton as a time-giver was decisive.

Myles Birket Foster, the historian of the Philharmonic Society, gives April 10, 1820, as the epochal date on which Spohr faced down the frightened musicians of the orchestra with a sliver of wood. Adam Carse says May 8, 1820. But the English critic Arthur Jacobs, curious about the discrepancy of dates, went to the programs and newspapers and could not find any reference to Spohr's use of the baton. What probably happened, says Jacobs, is that only at the rehearsal of the third concert, on April 10, did Spohr use the baton. Spohr wrote his autobiography in 1847 and got mixed up on some of the chronology. Writers those days were notoriously inaccurate. Often the last rehearsal was equivalent to the concert; public and critics attended, and as far as Jacobs can determine, Spohr did not use the baton at the actual concert. But whether or not Spohr's memory was playing him tricks in 1847, there is no doubt that he was using the baton extensively in the 1820s. In that, he was one of the pioneers.

Still another contribution to the art of conducting was made by Spohr. It is a contribution far less publicized than his baton work, but it is of great importance and greater convenience. Spohr seems to have been the first to introduce reference numbers or letters into the score and parts. Now conductors could say "Two measures before Letter M," or "Four bars after Number Nine." Previously the conductor had no easy way to isolate a specific measure. He would know it was, say, the third bar on page 14 of his score, but that was of no help to the clarinetist, or to the violin section. Thus there would have to be long halts while a conductor and orchestra counted measures. By his simple and satisfactory solution, Spohr made life easier for generations of musicians to come.

He died old and full of honors, spending the last thirty-one years of his life as a conductor in Kassel. There he composed steadily and took up Wagner's cause—a most surprising action from a conservative, classically oriented musician. But there always had been a dichotomy in Spohr's life. His own tastes as a violinist looked back to the purity of Mozart's style, and in his maturity he did not understand the music of the late Beethoven. He also actively disliked romantic opera as represented by Weber. Yet as a young man he composed music that contained some remarkable anticipations of the romantic movement; and toward the end of his life he espoused the cause of that madman Wagner, conducting *Tannhäuser* at Kassel in 1853 against the united opposition of the court. Spohr called Wagner the greatest of all living dramatic composers, and he was correct.

It was thanks to men like Reichardt and Spohr that the new art of conducting came into being. Naturally there was a great deal of experimentation and trial and error. Even the physical location of the conductor was not immediately determined. Jean Jacques Grasset, who conducted at the Paris Opéra the first quarter of the nineteenth century, stationed himself at the end of the orchestra, his left side toward the stage. Other conductors at the Opéra felt more secure alongside the prompter's box, with their back to the orchestra. Carl Maria von Weber occasionally conducted while facing the audience, a custom that seems to have been fairly prevalent at the time. It was also common for conductors to station themselves next to the prompter's box, wheeling from stage to orchestra as the occasion demanded. Berlioz indicated as much in his essay on conducting: "If the conductor has his back turned to the orchestra, as is customary in theatres . . ." In Russia, facing the audience was the regular practice of conductors until Wagner visited Moscow in 1865. This we have on the authority of Rimsky-Korsakoff. Well into the nineteenth century Felix Mottl, in Munich, used to conduct Mozart seated at a piano next to the stage. He would play the recitatives, then pick up the baton and—still facing the stage—conduct the singers. The orchestra, behind him, followed his beat. Nikolai Malko, who describes this, says that contact with the orchestra suffered from such an arrangement, "but in former days the singers on stage needed the conductor more."

The beat had to be stabilized, and it took some time before the basics were established: up and down for duple time; the triangle for triple time; the *one* down, *two* left, *three* right and *four* up for common time. Then there was the question of the baton itself. Spontini in Berlin used something like a marshal's baton, made of ebony, long and thick, with a large ivory knob on either end. He grabbed it in the middle with his fist. Louis Antoine Jullien, the unparalleled showman, had a jeweled baton, 22 inches long, of maple, with chased gold circlets, entwined with two golden serpents, each with a diamond in its head. Further additions to this spectacular musical instrument included a big gold circlet set with seven diamonds topped by a brilliant. On the other hand, Spohr's stick must have been short and simple, for he drew it from his coat pocket. Berlioz later recommended a thin wand 22 inches long. But that is not what he used in 1843, when his famous exchange of batons with Mendelssohn took place. The meeting of the immortals occurred in Leipzig, while Berlioz was on tour. He asked Mendelssohn for his baton. "By all means," Mendelssohn gallantly said, "if I may have yours instead." Berlioz was even more gallant. "It will be bronze for gold; still, you shall have it." Berlioz' baton was, according to Sebastian Henschel, "a cudgel of lime tree with the bark on." Berlioz himself called it "a heavy oaken staff." Mendelssohn's baton was delivered the next day, and Berlioz obviously got the better of the trade. Mendelssohn's baton was, like Mendelssohn himself, elegant: a light stick of whalebone covered with white leather to match Mendelssohn's white gloves. (All conductors in England, and most conductors elsewhere, wore white gloves while conducting: a habit that ran well into the century. In Russia, Czar Alexander II kindly allowed the conductor to remove his left glove because it was hard to turn pages with a glove on.) Berlioz, who like most European romantics had gone through a James Fenimore Cooper binge, sent Mendelssohn a note with his baton, a note "which I hope would not have disgraced the Last of the Mohicans":

Great Chief! To exchange our tomahawks is our word given. Common is mine, plain is yours. Squaws and Palefaces alone love ornate weapons. May we be brethren, so that, when the Great Spirit calls us to the happy hunting grounds, our warriors may hang our tomahawks side by side in the doorway of the Long House.

Dear Berlioz.

At least one revolutionary did not use a baton at all. Tiny, bushy-browed Cipriani Potter, the friend of Beethoven ("He seems to be a good man and has talent for composition," Beethoven said of the tiny Englishman), went back to London and used only his hands. Potter was alone in this; his innovation never took hold, even though many years later, in 1906, Vassily Safonoff was loudly proclaiming, "Mark my words: in ten or fifteen years there will be no batons in orchestras."

There also was, in the early days of conducting, a great deal of discussion as to how much the conductor actually should conduct, and what his deportment should be. Should he be violent, like Daniel Türk in Halle, who as early as 1810 was demonstrating a kind of footwork not normally seen until well over a hundred years later? Türk used his baton with such energy that he would sometimes strike the chandelier above his head, showering himself with broken glass. Many musicians deplored this kind of activity. There was a feeling that it was somehow improper and perhaps even indecent for a conductor to assert himself too greatly. Many early conductors conceived their function as more rhythmic than interpretive, and did not even beat time all the way through. Carl Maria von Weber, in Dresden, was so confident about his orchestra that he would drop his arms and let it go on by itself for long stretches. Schumann tells of Mendelssohn putting his baton down and standing motionless. Many years later, Hans Richter was to do the same in the 5/4 movement of Tchaikovsky's *Pathétique,* but that was in the nature of a stunt, whereas many early conductors stopped beating time because they thought it proper to do so. As Eduard Devrient, Mendelssohn's friend, outlined the duties of a conductor: "The continued beating throughout a movement, which must necessarily become mechanical, vexed me and does so still. . . . It always appeared to me that the conductor ought to beat time only when the difficulty of certain passages, or unsteadiness of the performers, rendered it necessary. Surely the aim of every conductor should be to influence without obtruding himself."

But by this time the institution of the conductor was firmly established. Where the new arrival was going, nobody could guess (though the work of Spontini in Berlin and Weber all over Europe must have given a strong clue). But that he was there for good there could be no doubt after the middle 1820s. In the early 1840s Schumann, in one of his essays in the *Neue Zeitschrift für Musik* (that storehouse of information about musicians of the time) gives a run-through of important orchestras and conductors. It is a roll-call of the day. Schumann mentions

Ries in Frankfurt, Chélard in Augsburg, L. Schuberth in Königsberg, Spontini in Berlin, Spohr in Kassel, Hummel in Weimar, Mendelssohn in Leipzig, Reissiger in Dresden, Schneider in Dessau, Marschner in Hannover, Lindpaintner in Stuttgart, Seyfried in Vienna, Lachner in Munich, D. Weber in Prague, Elsner in Warsaw, Loewe in Stettin, Kalliwoda in Donaueschingen, Weyse in Copenhagen, Mosewius in Breslau, Riem in Bremen, Guhr in Frankfurt, Strauss in Karlsruhe, Dorn in Riga.

Some of these names are famous, most are long forgotten. All of these conductors were composers, and very well known as such in their time. It is interesting that the more important they were as composers, the more important they also happened to be as conductors. The most important ones of Europe up to mid-century were Weber, Spontini, Nicolai, Berlioz, Mendelssohn and Wagner. There was but one exception to the rule—Habeneck in Paris. As in the eighteenth century, the creator and the performer were one. It remained for the last half of the nineteenth century to produce a new crop of performing musicians who regarded themselves as interpreters rather than creators.

· VII ·

Weber and Spontini

OF THE EARLY FIGURES of the baton, the most important and in some respects the most modern was Carl Maria von Weber, a genius who died too young to accomplish all that was in him. As it was, he founded the romantic opera, created a new keyboard style, was one of the first of the traveling piano virtuosos, and was a brilliant, resourceful, imaginative conductor. Very few musicians in history have had his natural gifts, and even fewer (only Mozart, perhaps) managed to pack such intense activity into so few years. Weber was forty when he died.

A thin, taut, constantly ailing man, he operated under extreme tension all his fearfully overworked career. His prodigy days behind him, his greatest music still to come, he started conducting in Breslau in 1804, at the age of eighteen. He immediately ran into opposition, finding everybody and everything against him. He was too young to be taken seriously, this child who was going to take over an orchestra of veteran musicians. In Prussian Breslau his name also was a handicap. The descendant of a once noble family, he was distrusted by the middle class and scorned by the aristocracy. When Weber came to Breslau, the first violinist of the orchestra promptly resigned, and the young man found himself faced with a revolution.

Nevertheless he immediately took charge, reorganizing the opera company (throughout his career, nearly all of Weber's conducting was in the opera house) and reseating the orchestra. One of the first to adopt a modern seating plan, Weber put the winds in the rear and distributed the violins much as they are today. Naturally there was tremendous opposition. Musicians, then as now, tend to be extremely conservative, resisting change. What with one thing and another, including his terrible accident—he gulped down a glass of nitric acid, mistaking it for wine, and nearly died—Weber resigned in 1806.

His next few years were spent as a touring piano virtuoso and guest conductor. In those days he led an orchestra with a roll of paper, and a Berlin critic in 1812 described his conducting as "firm and noiseless." By this time Weber was a thorough professional, one who knew every short cut and could work with speed and efficiency. The Intendant of the Berlin opera company watched him closely. "When he conducted his opera *Silvana* here," that gentleman reported, "I had the opportunity of observing his great gifts as a conductor. Whereas most conductors would have required six or seven rehearsals to prepare the difficult music, Weber did it in three." In 1813 he took a position with the Prague Opera and again found himself faced with difficulties, as does any conductor who has new ideas and the determination to put them into effect. He describes the situation in a letter to Gottfried Weber (no relation; a close friend):

The orchestra is in complete rebellion, and in the midst of this worry I have to correspond with all the new members to be engaged, to draw up their contracts, to bring the confused library into order and compile a catalogue, to correct scores, to prepare the scenarios of the operas first to be produced, to describe scenery to the painters, costumes to the costumers. And one is never left a peaceful moment because of the influx of people. . . . I get up at 6 o'clock and am often at work until midnight.

In Prague, Weber led off on September 9, 1813, with Spontini's *Fernand Cortez,* fighting the hostility of the orchestra. The members would insult him in Czech, a language he did not know. But that lasted just so long; for Weber, a fast study in everything and a natural linguist, readily learned the language. Soon he was able to report his ascendancy: "The members of the orchestra are gradually submitting to my iron scepter and knuckling under to me." And, a few months later, after he had conducted seventeen more operas, "Your heart would beat with joy if you could hear my orchestra now. They have such energy, force and delicacy, I am very much pleased with them."

Dresden, in 1817, was Weber's next port of call. He immediately laid down the law to orchestra and singers: "I expect implicit obedience. I shall be just, but pitilessly severe with all who need severity—

myself included." Weber found, as usual, that he had to exert every bit of authority he owned. He reorganized the administration from top to bottom, systematized the rehearsals, and instituted sweeping changes in policy and operation. Dresden did not give him too much of an orchestra with which to work. George Smart heard Weber conduct *Der Freischütz* with only sixteen strings—ten violins, and only two each of violas, cellos and basses. It was at Dresden that Weber began using a baton, and the orchestra did not like it a bit. Another thing they did not like was Weber's sole authority on the podium; they were accustomed to divided leadership. When Weber tried to get rid of old or inefficient players, open warfare was declared.

The orchestra found Weber a modernist who made them discard all eighteenth-century habits. He conducted his first opera—Méhul's *Joseph in Egypt*—on January 20, 1817, and the bass singer ignored Weber's directions. Instead he inserted his usual eighteenth-century ornaments and embellishments. Weber, who in musical matters was tough and uncompromising, gave the offender a verbal hiding he never forgot. On the podium Weber was quiet and restrained, undemonstrative, keeping physical movement to a minimum. Often he would follow practice of the day in merely beating a few bars and then letting the orchestra go it alone until it needed guidance. Of course, this only proved that Weber had done his work during rehearsals. Alert, efficient, possessed of an infallible ear, firm and exacting, yet considerate to his players, Weber was a musician's musician. He needed no violent gestures to convey his wishes; a sharp glance was enough. In a letter to the pianist Ferdinand Praeger he had some illuminating things to say about the functions of a conductor:

The beat must not be like a tyrannical hammer, impeding or urging on, but must be to the music what the pulse-beat is to the life of man. There is no slow tempo that does not contain passages which demand a quicker motion, so as to obviate the impression of dragging. Conversely there is no presto that does not in many places need a slower delivery, so as not to throw away the chance of expressiveness by hurrying. . . . Neither the quickening nor the slowing of tempo should ever give the impression of being spasmodic or violent. Changes, to have a musical and poetic significance, must come in an orderly way, in periods and phrases, conditioned by the varying warmth of the expression. We have in music no signs for all this. They exist only in the sentient human soul. If they are not there then there is no help to be had from the metronome—which corrects only the grosser errors—nor from these extremely imperfect precepts of mine.

Only a sensitive, thoughtful, creative musical mind could have written these sentences. From them it is clear that Weber was far from being a mere time beater. He looked upon a piece of music in its unity; he demanded flexibility; he had imagination; he abhorred sectionalizing and chopping up a series of phrases. Shape and phrase structure obviously meant a great deal to him. In many respects his strictures are startlingly reminiscent of Wagner's; certainly his remarks about tempo parallel Wagner's ideas about tempo fluctuation (a concept that was to govern much nineteenth-century conducting). Not so many years after Weber's departure, Wagner was at Dresden, and it is not difficult to believe that he picked up many of Weber's ideas without, as was his way, giving credit to the original. The full story of Weber's influence on Wagner—not as a composer, for that has been thoroughly examined, but as a conductor—is yet to be told. Weber was a prophetic figure, and he has a good claim to be called the first of the modern batonists. Certainly he thought and worked along lines that were not to be pursued again until the prime of Wagner.

Standing at a directly opposed polarity to the quiet, efficient Weber was the flamboyant and arrogant Gasparo (born Luigi Pacifico) Spontini, star of the Berlin Opera from 1820 to 1841. How good a conductor Spontini really was is hard to determine. For the most part he led only his own operas, which were highly regarded in their day (Berlioz had a lifelong love affair with *La Vestale* and *Fernand Cortez*), with occasional excursions into Mozart (*Don Giovanni*) and Gluck (*Armide*). When Spontini conducted the symphonic repertoire, which he seldom did, it offended serious musicians. At least, Mendelssohn was scarcely impressed by the way Spontini led the Beethoven Seventh: "atrociously . . . the coarseness and recklessness of the playing were such as I never heard anywhere."

Nevertheless, Spontini as a conductor was of great importance to the oncoming generation, and even Mendelssohn was forced to admit that in the opera house he was unparalleled. Berlioz thought so too, and when Wagner heard Spontini conduct *Fernand Cortez* in 1836 he flatly said that it was one of the overwhelming artistic experiences of his life. The spirit of the conducting, he said, "astonished me more than anything I had heard before. . . . The exceptional precision,

LITHOGRAPH BY MAURIN

ERIC SCHAAL COLLECTION

Left: Luigi Spontini, the Napoleon of the orchestra, one of the first of the virtuoso conductors. At the Berlin Opera he ran things with an iron hand. Wagner was greatly influenced by his spectacular conducting.

Right: Carl Maria von Weber, in many respects the first of the modern conductors as the term is understood today. He insisted on a thorough reorganization of the symphony orchestra, and led directly into Wagner.

Below: Three views of Weber conducting a concert performance of *Der Freischütz* at Covent Garden, 1826. Here he uses a roll of paper rather than a wooden baton. Behind him can be seen several of the soloists.

LITHOGRAPH BY HULLMANN, AFTER J. HAYTER

fire and richly organized rendering of the whole was new to me. I gained a fresh insight into the peculiar dignity of big theatrical representations which, in their several parts, could by well-accented rhythm be made to attain the highest pinnacle of art."

Spontini, born in Italy, went to Paris in 1803. It was there that he composed his best-known operas, *La Vestale* and *Fernand Cortez*. In 1810 he became conductor of the Italian opera in Paris. Friedrich Wilhelm III of Prussia called him to Berlin in 1819 to reorganize the opera and also compose two works a year for the company. Contemporary evidence suggests that Spontini was a clumsy conductor, one with a rather low musical culture and technique, ill at ease in recitatives, very slow and stiff at rehearsals. But, thanks to Friedrich Wilhelm, rehearsals were what Spontini got many of—as many as eighty for a new production. Thus Spontini could keep rehearsing until everything was letter-perfect. By the time the premiere came around, every musician and singer had his part by heart. Then would the great Spontini make his entrance, tall and aristocratic-looking, dressed in the dark, moss-green jacket he invariably wore, his orders and decorations on prominent display, clutching a baton that really was a baton: his famous knobbed marshal's staff. This he grasped in the middle. It must have been an imposing sight. (Berlioz inherited one of those batons. When he conducted excerpts from *La Vestale* in England in 1852, Spontini's widow sent one of the Italian's batons to him with a note: "It cannot be entrusted to better hands than yours.")

It was not only this kind of baton that led Spontini to be known as The Napoleon of the Orchestra. Spontini, who did have a Napoleonic complex, would even use martial, Napoleon-like exhortations during rehearsals, encouraging his men with great cries of *"Allez! En avant! Martelez!"* And, when the last rehearsal was satisfactory, Spontini would conclude, *"Au revoir au champ de bataille!"* Generally his speech was a jumble of Italian, French and German, and might go something like: *"Mein Erren! Il faut remarquer, dass il forte doit être . . ."* Vain, haughty, supercilious, he took himself very seriously and demanded complete obedience. He was the first of the famous baton egocentrics, and when Clara Novello visited him in 1837 she noted that "His house was a gallery of portraits of himself, alternating with sonnets in his praise, busts of himself, etc., all the way to his own sort of throne room, where he sat on a raised dais in an armchair with his portraits, busts, medals and sonnets all around him." It followed that he had to be the center of everything. At a party he told the soprano Schröder-Devrient, who had interrupted him by laughing at something someone had whispered, *"Je ne veux pas que l'on rie devant moi; je ne rie jamais moi, j'aime le sérieux."* Wagner, who was at the party and tells the story, was impressed by Spontini's "marvelous teeth," with which he crushed enormous lumps of sugar. (How did they remain so marvelous?)

It also followed that Spontini, who was so pompous and took himself so seriously, made many enemies and was fair game for ridicule. But nobody ridiculed the effort he put into his productions—his search for the ultimate fusion of voice, orchestra and stagecraft. The man had real flair. Not since the great days of the Mannheim Orchestra had there been such finesse, such exciting dynamic extremes. Musicians who played under him testified to the great care with which Spontini sought variations of "light and shade." He apparently had a mesmerizing effect on the orchestra, and a Berlin musician named Moritz Hanemann has described the way Spontini "like a king . . . strode into the orchestra and, taking up his field-marshal's position, he looked all around with his piercing eyes, fixing them on the heavy artillery—that is what he called the cellos and basses—and then gave the signal to begin." Hanemann says that Spontini stood "like a bronze statue, moving only the lower part of his arm."

To Wagner, who was so much influenced by Spontini, we owe the most graphic account of the Italian composer-conductor. Spontini came to Dresden in 1844 to produce and conduct *La Vestale,* and Wagner quizzed him at length. Spontini, Wagner said, had the manner of a Spanish grandee. The first thing Spontini wanted to know was the kind of baton available. Wagner described it, and Spontini said it would not do. So one of his famous beknobbed staffs had to be made, in ebony and ivory. It turned out that Spontini used this not for beating time, but to command. Indeed, Spontini told Wagner, he really needed no baton at all; that he did most of his conducting with his eyes. "My left eye is the first violins, my right eye the second violins, and if the eye is to have power, one must not wear glasses, as so many bad conductors do, even if one is shortsighted." Which Spontini was. He confided to Wagner that he could not see twelve inches ahead of him. "But all the same I can make them play as I want, merely by fixing them with my eye."

For *La Vestale* Spontini wanted a string body consisting of twelve first violins, twelve seconds, ten violas, eight or ten cellos and six or seven basses. He wanted the first violins at his left, the seconds at his right. This he insisted upon. "For the complete separation of the strings on one side, and the winds and brass on the other, results in two distinct orchestras." In this, Spontini was quite modern, and the only peculiarity Wagner noted was Spontini's habit—from his old Paris days—of placing two oboists directly behind him. Otherwise Wagner highly approved of Spontini's seating arrangements. Spontini also spread the wind and brass throughout the orchestra; and, wrote Wagner, "this further assisted in preventing the brass and percussion instruments from culminating in one point, and drowning each other, by dividing them on both sides, and by placing the more delicate wind instruments at a judicious distance from each other, thus forming a chain between the violins." Wagner followed Spontini's placements, for the most part, in his own orchestra.

It may be that Spontini was a limited conductor, with a limited repertoire and a concentration on the less expressive, more superficial aspects of music, on technical and orchestral polish over structure and content. And certainly he was a musician of the old school who despised the new romantic opera. Wagner cannot resist getting in a dig: "With such childish stuff [as romantic opera] so serious a man would have nothing to do; *he* had exhausted serious art. What nation could produce the composer who could surpass *him*?" But Spontini must have been electrifying when he conducted his own operas; and he and his Napoleonic complex were responsible for a new attitude toward the conductor. The new figures—Mendelssohn, Wagner, Berlioz—were quick to profit from his example. Now the conductor was king, the undisputed ruler of any and every aspect of a performance. Upon him and him alone would a performance devolve. The autocrat had arrived.

Spontini lived a stormy life. In Berlin he got into argument after argument with the authorities. These culminated in a clash with the king himself, and Spontini narrowly missed being jailed for *lèse-majesté*. His conceit and despotic manners had, in the meantime, alienated him from Berlin audiences. Retired on a full pension, he did very little after 1841. Berlioz saw him on his deathbed, and the following colloquy is supposed to have taken place:

SPONTINI: I do not want to die! I do not want to die! I do not want to die!
BERLIOZ: How can you think about dying, you who are immortal?
SPONTINI (angrily): Don't make bad jokes!

· VIII ·

François-Antoine Habeneck

WHILE SPONTINI was revolutionizing operatic performances in Berlin, François-Antoine Habeneck was doing the same for the symphonic literature in Paris. Even though he was a direct offshoot of the old violin-leader type of conductor, directing with the bow, he was one of the first to approach symphonic music with the attitude of the modern conductor, and he occupies a supremely important place in the history of conducting. He also created, at the Conservatoire, the first of the great modern orchestras, raising it to a point where it was considered the marvel of Europe. All musicians were agreed that not only did Habeneck have the best orchestra anywhere, but that its Beethoven was by far the best. To Mendelssohn in 1832 it was "the best orchestra I have ever heard." He admired its unanimity, the large number of strings "and how they start with exactly the same bowing, the same style, the same deliberation and ardor." Chorley came from England to hear Habeneck's Conservatoire Orchestra and was overwhelmed by its precision. "What brilliancy there is in its violins! . . . What a clearness and body of support, and pertinency of answer and sensitivity of expression in the violoncellos!" Chorley went on to catalogue all of the choirs, concluding that the orchestra "is a machine, in short, in perfect order, and under the guidance of experience and intellect;—for these, as regards French music, are thoroughly personified in M. Habeneck." Berlioz, no admirer of Habeneck, nevertheless had to praise the string section of his orchestra; and Wagner went him one better by stating that no orchestra in Germany could match the power and capacity of the French strings. Even crusty old Anton Schindler had good words to say. Schindler had become a bore on the subject of his teacher and *ami*, Beethoven, and would keep saying that nobody any longer had the faintest idea of how Beethoven should be played; but when Schindler heard the Conservatoire Orchestra in 1841 he, like everybody else, admitted Habeneck's supremacy as an interpreter of Beethoven. Habeneck, said Schindler, did not rush the tempos, as they did in Germany.

That the strings of the Conservatoire Orchestra should have been singled out for special praise was inevitable, for the orchestra had been brought together by a fine violinist. Habeneck had been a pupil at the Conservatoire, graduating in 1800 as a student of Baillot. He went on to teach violin at the Conservatoire, holding that position from 1825 until his death in 1849. He also was a musical director at the Opéra from 1821 to 1824, superseding Rodolphe Kreutzer (the Kreutzer of Beethoven's sonata). All during those years, Habeneck had admired and studied the Beethoven symphonies, then generally unknown in Paris. As early as 1807 he had directed a performance of Beethoven's First Symphony, and even tried a public performance of the *Eroica* Symphony in 1811. It met with little success.

On November 22, 1826, Habeneck invited a large group of musicians to lunch, telling them to bring their instruments. After lunch there was a surprise. Habeneck seated the players in front of stands that contained the parts of the *Eroica*. His enthusiasm carried them along, and they became as excited about the music as he. For over a year Habeneck and his dedicated group continued to meet and play the *Eroica*. Finally, in 1828, Habeneck asked Luigi Cherubini, the head of the Conservatoire, for permission to give concerts there. Cherubini not only agreed but got a grant of 2,000 francs toward expenses. Thus started the famous Société des Concerts du Conservatoire. The first, on March 9, 1828, naturally had the *Eroica* on the program. Habeneck, of course, was the conductor, and until his last concert on April 16, 1848, the orchestra had no other leader. By that time he had directed 148 concerts.

At that first concert Parisians saw a young orchestra, one with an average age of thirty. All were Conservatoire products. It was a large group, with eighty-six players—fifteen first violins, sixteen seconds, twelve cellos, twelve basses, four flutes, three oboes, four clarinets, and full winds, brass and percussion. Later on, the average size of the orchestra was sixty. The season consisted of six concerts, plus one or two special events; and Beethoven was the backbone of the repertoire. In the first ten years of its existence, the Conservatoire Orchestra gave

ERIC SCHAAL COLLECTION

François Habeneck, first of
the modern French conduc-
tors. He founded the Paris
Conservatory Orchestra.

A contemporary drawing of
Habeneck leading orchestra
with his violin bow. He
specialized in Beethoven.

DRAWING BY DANTAN

sixty-eight performances of Beethoven symphonies, seven of Haydn symphonies, five of Mozart symphonies, four of George Onslow's, and four of others. The period of 1838 to 1847 saw a similar ratio: ninety performances of Beethoven symphonies, twenty-three of Haydn's, fifteen of Mozart's, five of Mendelssohn's and ten of others. The programs followed the style of the day. They were long, containing an overture, one or two symphonies, one or two vocal solos or duets, a concerto or a group of instrumental solos, and one or two choral pieces.

Thanks to unlimited rehearsal and a discipline that, among other things, imposed uniform bowing, the Paris Conservatoire Orchestra actually made some listeners uncomfortable by its perfection. Chorley discussed "the phalanx of bows plying up and down," and found the orchestra almost inhuman: "No unfortunate flute there chirps half a note before its time—no plethoric bassoon drops one of its thick, Satyr-like tones in the midst of a pause—no horn totters on the edge of a coarse and mail-coach falseness . . ." Chorley was irked by such elegance, but his remarks do give an idea of what the norm was elsewhere.

When the stocky, quiet, bespectacled Habeneck took over, he still represented the old school. It is true that he had no clavierist, but he would often play along with his orchestra, beating time with his bow when he felt the necessity. In the early years of the orchestra he would have done more playing than conducting. Toward the end, when his players knew their parts virtually by heart, he played hardly at all. In front of him would be only the first violin part, with entries of other instruments marked by a cross. Thus the question has come up: How good a conductor can Habeneck have been if he did not conduct with score? But the question is a niggling one. Habeneck obviously had the scores of all the Beethoven symphonies committed to memory. Constant rehearsal alone would have insured that. The *Eroica* had had almost a year and a half of rehearsals. Wagner wrote that the Ninth had had three winters of rehearsals before Habeneck decided it was ready. The Ninth Symphony had first been conducted by Habeneck in 1831. It proved a puzzle for orchestra and audience, and after that it was presented movement by movement. Not until 1837 was the Ninth restored to the repertoire as a unit, and by that time the orchestra had had plenty of exposure to the music. (In 1824, Beethoven had received only two rehearsals at the Kaerntnertor Theatre, though he pleaded for three.) Wagner attended a rehearsal of the Ninth in 1839. He came away even more amazed than when he had heard Spontini's orchestra, and was unstinting not only in his praise but in his description of the impact that Habeneck and the music made on him:

The scales fell from my eyes. I came to understand the value of *correct* execution and the secret of a good performance. The orchestra had learned to look for Beethoven's *melody* in every bar—that melody which the worthy Leipzig musicians had failed to discover, and the orchestra *sang* that melody. *This was the secret.* Habeneck, who solved the difficulty, and to whom the great credit of this performance is due, was not a conductor of special genius. While rehearsing the symphony during an entire winter season, he had felt it to be incomprehensible and ineffective (would German conductors have confessed as much?), but he persisted throughout a second and third season until Beethoven's new *melos* was understood and correctly rendered by every member of the orchestra. Habeneck was a conductor of the old school; *he* was the master, and everybody obeyed him. I cannot attempt to describe the beauty of this performance.

Another thing that struck Wagner was the fact that the orchestra played the Ninth exactly as written. That seems to have been perhaps the most distinguishing feature of Habeneck's approach, and it was unprecedented in its day. Habeneck, as Wagner indicates, may not have been the most imaginative of conductors, but he was scrupulously honest, conscientious and self-effacing. He felt himself to be the servant of the composer, and tried with all his musicianship to deliver the music as accurately as possible, keeping himself out of it. Constant rehearsal gave the orchestra a gloss and an authority that were not to be common in Europe until some forty or fifty years later. Also of great help was the fact that the young and excellent players all had the same Conservatoire background. Adam Carse's summary appears definitive:

The Conservatory players studied a work as a soloist studies his piece before playing at a concert, or as a string quartet works at a piece till each member knows the whole work from every angle, not only his own part, but the work as a whole. Habeneck did not put the parts of a new and unfamiliar piece before his orchestra in the morning and then play it in public on the afternoon of the same day. He was, as Wagner said, no inspired conductor, but he knew the business of orchestral playing from start to finish, and knew that a correct rendering of every note and the observance of every mark of expression in each part was not enough. Each player had to grow into his part until he knew exactly what he was contributing to the whole. . . . There was no short cut. It took time; so Habeneck gave them time, and he was fortunate to be able to do so.

Occasionally dictatorial as he could be, Habeneck nevertheless instilled into his orchestra a tremendous *esprit de corps*. John Ella, the British violinist-impresario, tells a charming story that illustrates the spirit of the orchestra. It seems that the principal second violinist had died. Habeneck addressed the first violins—that elite of the orchestra —and said: "*Mes enfants,* you see that a most important place is vacant. Who will do me the honor of being my second?" Instantly, says Ella, the young Jean-Delphin Alard, pupil of Habeneck and considered the best violinist in Paris, "rushed across the orchestra to the vacant desk, amidst the cheers of the whole band."

It is one of the ironies of musical history that this dignified, admirable musician should be remembered in musical history chiefly as the object of Berlioz' satire. Berlioz never had too high an opinion of Habeneck as a creative musician, and that is understandable. Habeneck represented the music of the past, Berlioz the music of the future. Things came to a head at the first performance of the Berlioz Requiem. The year was 1837. Habeneck was the conductor; and as Berlioz tells the story:

The day of the performance arrived, in the Church of the Invalides, before all the princes, peers and deputies, the French press, the correspondents of foreign papers, and an immense crowd. It was absolutely essential for me to have a great success; a moderate one would have been fatal, and a failure would have annihilated me altogether.

Now listen attentively.

The various groups of instruments in the orchestra were tolerably widely separated, especially the four brass bands introduced in the *Tuba mirum,* each of which occupied a corner of the entire orchestra and chorus. There is no pause between the *Dies Irae* and the *Tuba mirum,* but the pace in the latter movement is reduced to half of what it was before. At this point the entire brass enters, first all together, and then in passages that challenge and answer each other—each entry being a third higher than the last.

It is obvious that it is of the greatest importance that the four beats of the new tempo should be distinctly marked, or else the terrible explosion, which I had so carefully prepared, with combinations and proportions never attempted before or since, and which, rightly performed, gives such a picture of the Last Judgment as I believe is destined to live, would be merely a hideous pandemonium.

With my habitual distrust, I had stationed myself behind Habeneck and, turning my back on him, kept an eye on the group of kettledrums, which he could not see, when the moment approached for them to take part in the general mêlée. There are, perhaps, a thousand bars in my Requiem. Precisely in that section, when the movement broadens out and the brass burst in with their terrible fanfare, in fact, in just the *one* bar where the conductor's direction is absolutely indispensable, Habeneck *puts down his baton, quietly takes out his snuff box and proceeds to take a pinch of snuff*. I had never taken my eyes off him. Instantly I turned rapidly on one heel and, springing forward before him, I stretched out my arm and marked the four great beats. The musicians followed me, I conducted the piece to the end, and my long-dreamed-of effect was a magnificent triumph. When, at the last words of the chorus, Habeneck saw that the *Tuba mirum* was saved, he said: "What a cold perspiration I have been in! Without you we would have been lost."

"Yes, we would," I answered, eyeing him steadily.

Berlioz wondered if Habeneck, in alliance with Cherubini, had planned that "dastardly stroke" to ruin him. "I do not like to think so, yet I have not the slightest doubt that this is true. God forgive me if I wrong them."

Some scholars, Ernest Newman included, have wondered whether or not Berlioz' imagination was running away with him in his description of this incident. Newman, indeed, seriously suggests that Berlioz may have dreamed it all in his later years while under the influence of opium. It is known, however, that Habeneck did not always beat time. Like most conductors of the day, he would lay down his bow when things were going well. Habeneck, who did not particularly respond to the new music, could very well have been confused by Berlioz' complicated, thunderous score, putting down his bow in the wrong place. There is no evidence that he was engaged in any kind of plot against Berlioz. Charles Hallé, the pianist and founder of the orchestra that bears his name, does, however, back up some of

Berlioz' story. Hallé was present at the performance of the Requiem and did see Habeneck put down his bow. Hallé thought Habeneck did so from force of habit, pointing out that Habeneck often would drop his arms "and listen complacently to the performance of his orchestra." To Hallé's vast surprise, and presumably to the great surprise of everybody in the audience, he "suddenly saw Berlioz standing in Habeneck's place and wielding the baton to the end of the movement." Hallé did not believe that Habeneck was trying to sabotage the performance.

But there is plenty of evidence that Habeneck did not understand or like the music of Berlioz. The composer describes still another encounter with the conductor, this one concerned with *Benvenuto Cellini*. Habeneck had constant trouble with the quick tempo of the saltarello. The dancers complained about his dragging tempo in this Italian dance. Berlioz tried to push Habeneck along. In a rage, Habeneck hit the desk and broke his bow. Years later Berlioz conducted the *Roman Carnival* Overture, in which this very saltarello is used. The piece went perfectly and was encored. After the performance Berlioz ran into Habeneck and threw a few words over his shoulder: "That's how it goes." Habeneck, says Berlioz, did not reply.

Once more did Berlioz have fun with Habeneck. In *Evenings with the Orchestra*—the tenth "evening"—Berlioz goes into great detail about Habeneck's habit of tapping the top of the prompter's box with his bow. Berlioz invented a prompter named Moreau. This man was driven to distraction by the Chinese torture of Habeneck's steady rapping. So he has the top of his box padded. Habeneck strikes. There is no noise. "What is this?" So Habeneck raps the *side* of Moreau's box. The wood promptly gives out a *tack!* more distinct, sharper, and more triumphant than the previous tap had done—a *tack!* all the more dreadful for the prompter because it falls right against his ear. Habeneck, with a Mephistophelean smile, redoubles his *tack!* during the evening.

So Moreau goes into a decline and dies.

Hector Berlioz

NASTY AS Berlioz was to poor Habeneck, he at least had a right to his criticisms in that he was the first of the modern French conductors, quite possibly the greatest, and one who knew infinitely more about the orchestra and its potentialities than Habeneck ever did. Berlioz, Mendelssohn and Wagner—that is the trinity upon which all modern conducting is based. All previous pioneers, from Lully to Habeneck, had led to those three: the three contemporaries who thought as modern conductors, acted as modern conductors and—in the cases of Berlioz and Wagner—actually wrote essays about the problems of their art.

Berlioz came to conducting at a somewhat later age than did Mendelssohn or Wagner. (It is interesting to note that Berlioz, like Wagner, was neither pianist nor violinist: the first maestros in history who lacked those supposedly basic requirements.) Several things prompted Berlioz' ascent to the podium. After his friend Girard had messed up *Harold in Italy* in 1834, Berlioz "resolved in the future to conduct myself and not allow anybody else to communicate my ideas to the performers." Berlioz had to do this. His music for those days posed the unprecedented kind of difficulties that the music of Boulez posed for orchestras of the 1950s. Nobody but the composer could bring an orchestra and such radically new music together. Another thing that bothered Berlioz was the abuse given to so many masterpieces, together with the prevalent sloppiness of orchestra playing. These Berlioz was determined to rectify.

For while the modern orchestra was beginning to come into being, there were few conductors to ride herd over musicians. And unless musicians are prodded, they will not respond. In his essay on conducting, Berlioz cites some of the bad habits found in almost all European orchestras—"habits that reduced composers to despair and whose prompt elimination is the duty of conductors." He gives as examples string players who will not produce a proper tremolo. "The rapid motion of the arm necessary for the real tremolo is doubtless too great an effort for them. This laziness is intolerable." He castigates double-bass players for constantly simplifying their parts "either out of indolence or from fear of being unable to master certain difficulties. This system of simplification, generally accepted for the past forty years"—these words were published in 1856—"can no longer be tolerated." Berlioz goes down the list: flutists who transpose an octave up; musicians who cannot count; instrumentalists who cannot tune up; clarinetists who stick to a B flat clarinet when one in D or A is specifically called for.

And so the fiery young Berlioz set out to correct those abuses, conducting all over Europe and England, specializing in his own music but also presenting that of Mozart, Beethoven and others. He was constantly on the move, traveling with five hundred pounds of his own music, paying not only his own traveling expenses but also the wages of whatever musicians were needed to fill out the orchestras he led. In his own music he must have been a sensational conductor, and he certainly influenced Wagner's ideas about conducting. The three who helped form Wagner's style were Spontini, Habeneck and Berlioz. While Wagner thought very little of Berlioz, on the whole, he was unstinting in his praise of the Frenchman when he heard him lead *Romeo and Juliet* in the winter of 1839. It was:

. . . quite a new world to me . . . At first the grandeur and masterly execution of the orchestral part almost overwhelmed me. It was beyond everything I could have conceived. The fantastic daring, the sharp precision with which the boldest combinations—almost tangible in their clarity—impressed me, drove back my own ideas about the poetry of music with brutal violence into the very depths of my soul. I was simply all ears for things of which I had never dreamed until then, and which I felt I must try to realize.

Wagner was not the only musician to become excited after an encounter with Berlioz' conducting. The volatile Frenchman, in constant motion on the podium, exuding electricity, carrying the players

along with him, made an enormous impression on everybody. Anton
Seidl described him to Cosima Wagner: "Now he was up in the air,
then under the music desk; now he turned uneasily to the big drummer, then he was coaxing the flutist." Seidl must have been very
young when he saw Berlioz conduct, but his description tallies with
most others. Hallé, the close friend of Berlioz and later the protagonist of his music, talks about Berlioz at the head of an orchestra "with
his eagle face, his bristling hair, his air of command, and glowing
with enthusiasm. He was the most perfect conductor I had ever set
eyes upon, one who held absolute sway over his troops and played on
them as a pianist upon the keyboard." Though Berlioz had a tendency
to gyrate upon the podium, his beat seems always to have been in-
telligible. "Simple, clear, beautiful," said Rimsky-Korsakoff.

Not that Berlioz was always able to get the results he was after.
Orchestras were often not up to his standard, much less his vision.
"Berlioz in his younger days," Saint-Saëns has written, "demanded
from orchestras far inferior to those of today efforts that were truly
superhuman. If there are some difficulties impossible to avoid in all
new and original music, there are others that can be spared the performer without detriment to his work. But Berlioz did not concern
himself with these practical details. I have seen him conduct twenty,
even thirty, rehearsals for a single work, tearing his hair, smashing
batons and music stands without accomplishing the desired results."
Yet as often as not Berlioz was presented with a set of handicaps that
nobody could overcome. When he first visited England in 1847 he
found a good orchestra. But the impresario took the best players on
tour. "We have to be content with the leavings," Berlioz disgustedly
wrote, "and get along somehow." The substitution system was then
in vogue, and Berlioz found that he was never able to have a single
rehearsal with the complete orchestra. "These gentlemen come when
they please and go away on their business, some in the middle, others
a quarter way through the rehearsal. The first day I hadn't any horns
at all; the second I had three; the third I had two who left after the
fourth piece." Such were the hazards of conducting orchestras in those
days.

How good Berlioz was at the beginning of his career as a conductor
we do not know. Obviously he had leadership, confidence and one
of the sharpest ears of his day. He learned as he went along, and
developed into a most experienced hand, one whom nothing could faze.

Hallé once had to play the Beethoven G major Piano Concerto with Berlioz. At the end of the rehearsal Berlioz struck his head. "I have forgotten the overture!" The overture was his own *Roman Carnival*, to be done that evening for the first time. Berlioz decided to take a chance without the rehearsal. Hallé never got over it:

Musicians who know the work, with its complicated rhythms and all its intricacies, will easily understand how bold the venture was, and will wonder that it could be successful. But to see Berlioz during that performance was a sight never to be forgotten. He watched over every single member of the huge band; his beat was so decisive, his indications of all the nuances so clear and so unmistakable, that the overture went smoothly, and no uninitiated person could guess at the absence of a rehearsal.

By the time he got around to writing his essay on conducting, there was nothing Berlioz did not know about the orchestra and the psychology of the orchestral player. It is fascinating to read his treatise along with Wagner's. Berlioz is almost entirely practical, technical, pragmatic; Wagner full of imagery, metaphysics, complications. Berlioz starts right out with a discussion of good and bad conductors. The good one must communicate to the players the feeling that he understands, is moved. Then his emotion will communicate itself. "His inner fire warms them, his enthusiasm carries them away, he radiates musical energy." The bad conductor, on the other hand, is cold, phlegmatic, indifferent, paralyzing everything around him. Berlioz goes into the matter of rehearsals and how to handle them. "The economical use of time is one of the most imperative requisites of the conductor's skill." He suggests the use of a metronome to determine the initial tempo of a piece, but warns against a beat of metronomic rigidity "which would give the music thus executed an icy frigidity." The conductor must of course know how to beat time, and this is not so easy as it sounds. Few persons, writes Berlioz, possess that ability, especially the knowledge of a subdivided beat. The conductor must have a clear idea of the principal points of a work, and of its character as a whole. The conductor also must insist that the men watch the baton, for "an orchestra that does not watch the baton has no conductor."

His treatise contains diagrams of basic beats. All of his suggestions are modern, wise and practical; and conductors today would do well

Hector Berlioz, about 1855. He brought the orchestra, and conducting, to unprecedented heights.

The mammoth orchestras favored by Berlioz were natural game for caricaturists. Here Berlioz is depicted using a cannon as one of his instruments and driving his deafened audience out of the hall.

NEW YORK PUBLIC LIBRARY

to ponder them, especially the remarks about the swing of the beat. "It is important that the conductor use his arm as little as possible for these movements, and consequently does not let the baton cover too much space." For if the arc is too wide, Berlioz warns, it will cause "a retardation of the intended tempo and an unpleasant heaviness in the orchestral performance." (How many times has one seen a young conductor widen his beat as the music gets faster, instead of shortening it, ending up by throwing a baffled orchestra completely off.) Rhythmic problems are of great interest and concern to Berlioz, and he spends a great deal of his space in his treatise in discussions of how to handle eccentric meters, syncopations and other such problems.

Ever of the avant-garde, ever looking ahead, Berlioz even gets himself involved in a full description of Verbrugghen's electric metronome, invented in 1848. He suggests using it to bring backstage music in on time. (Verbrugghen devised an instrument in which copper wires led to a voltaic pile. When the conductor pressed a button it made a marker oscillate. Berlioz had used one in Brussels, to his great satisfaction. He was as interested in new gadgets as Stokowski was to be some hundred years later.) In the treatise is a demand that conductors work from full score, not the violin part; that the orchestra placement should have (mounted on five different levels) violins on the left and right, violas in the middle, winds and brass behind the first violins, cellos and basses behind the winds, drums and other percussion behind the brass, and the conductor with his back to the audience, standing near the violins. He also makes a strong plea for section rehearsals. There is one oddity in the Berlioz essay. He insists that tuning be done backstage. "The conductor . . . must take great care that the musicians tune accurately. But this should not be done in the presence of the audience. Any kind of instrumental noise or of preluding during intermissions offends the ears of all refined listeners."

This essay on conducting comes at the end of the treatise on instrumentation. There Berlioz suggests 119 players as a normal orchestra (today the big orchestras have 106). Berlioz always was fascinated by size, and during his lifetime he had an occasional chance to conduct mammoth groups. In 1866 he led his *Damnation of Faust* at the Redoutensaal in Vienna using an orchestra of 150, a chorus of 300. Earlier in Paris he had engaged even larger forces. In his autobiography he is amusing on the subject of his famous 1840 concert (of Gluck, Handel and some of his own music). He says that he had hired

600 performers (it was really 450, but Berlioz is sometimes a little exuberant in his *Memoirs*) and spent days going from the Opéra to the Théâtre-Italien to the Conservatoire. "In the foyer of the Opéra I took the string instruments from 8 to 12 and the winds from 12 to 4. My throat was on fire, my voice gone, my right arm almost paralyzed." Berlioz lost (he says) a great deal of money on the project. "I organized the most tremendous concert Paris had ever seen and I was 350 francs out of pocket for my pains. I was likely to grow rich!" Four years later, in the Tuileries, he conducted a group consisting of 1,200 singers and players. For this seven sub-conductors were needed.

Never did Berlioz encounter the orchestra of his dreams, the one he wrote about in his treatise on instrumentation. Berlioz was always hypnotized by sheer sound; his scores alone are ample testimony. He fought, he struggled, and he as much as, or more than, anybody else made the orchestra what it is today. No composer before him, and in all likelihood none after, not even Mahler, had such a vision of pure sound and how to go about obtaining it. He reveled in new tonal combinations, in the potentiality of every instrument, in a kind of super-music played by a super-orchestra. And it indeed was a super-orchestra that he outlined as the group of his dreams:

120 violins (four divisions)
40 violas (ten able to play viola d'amore)
45 cellos
18 double basses (tuned G-D-A)
15 other basses (tuned E-A-D-G)
4 octobasses (invented by Vuillaume in 1849; 13 feet high, with three strings)
6 flutes
4 flutes in E flat
2 piccolos
2 piccolos in D flat
6 oboes
6 English horns
5 saxophones

4 quint bassoons (a small bassoon pitched a fifth higher than standard bassoons)
12 bassoons
4 clarinets in E flat
8 clarinets in B flat or A
3 bass clarinets
16 French horns
8 trumpets
6 cornets
4 alto trombones
6 tenor trombones
2 bass trombones
1 ophicleide in C (now extinct; the predecessor of the tuba)
1 ophicleide in B
2 bass tubas

30 harps
30 pianos
1 organ
8 timpani
6 small drums
3 large drums
4 pairs of cymbals
6 triangles
6 glockenspiels

12 cymbals (in addition to the four pairs listed above)
2 large bells
2 tam-tams
4 half-moons (a belled noise-maker, originally Turkish, used in military bands of the time)

The total, which Berlioz reckons at 465 (discounting some duplications) would have been supplemented by a chorus of 360. There would be, he says, "a million possible combinations with this gigantic group, in richness of harmony, variety of sounds, multitude of contrasts, comparable to nothing yet achieved in any art." Berlioz lets his romantic imagination run wild. There would be

a hurricane in the tropics or the explosive roar of a volcano. There would be the mysterious rustle of primeval forests, the lamentations, the triumphant mournful song of the soulful, loving and emotional nations. The silence would make one tremble by its solemnity. The crescendo would cause even an unresponsive nature to shiver. It would grow like an immense fire that eventually sets the whole sky aflame.

But, and this is integral to Berlioz' thinking, he was not interested only in climax, in noise. "Vulgar prejudice calls large orchestras noisy, but if they are well balanced, well trained and well led, and if they perform true music, they should rather be called powerful." Berlioz always was as much interested in meaning as he was in effect.

As a conductor, Berlioz must have exhibited classic French traits. His beat, from all accounts, was of admirable clarity, and his personality was of the kind to act as an inspiration to his players. Like all French musicians, he had steady but supple rhythm. Not for him were the tempo fluctuations of Wagner's German school. Rhythmic steadiness, with an avoidance of metronomic regularity, was what he sought. Logic, proportion, an ability to balance choirs to optimum result, a good measure of literalism—all these were what Berlioz represented. He was to the German school what, some hundred years later, a Monteux or a Munch would be to a Klemperer or Walter. Never ponderous, never inflated, Berlioz' conducting must have been full of clarity and grace, more interested in outline and in pure sound than in musical metaphysics.

Thus it was inevitable that he and Wagner, the Wagner who stood for the *melos*, whose rhythm was in eternal fluctuation, who dreamed great programs of storm and strife into the Beethoven symphonies, who carried into his music the tag ends of Hegelian, Schopenhauerian and Schillerian thought—it was inevitable that Berlioz and Wagner should not have seen eye to eye. They simply did not speak the same language; they were the antithesis of each other. There is only one known Berlioz comment about Wagner's conducting. Wagner, he said, "conducts in free style, as Klindworth plays the piano. . . . Such a style is like dancing on a slack wire, *sempre tempo rubato*." The very thought of Wagner's eternal rubato would have been distasteful to Berlioz' straightforward musical mind.

Wagner, on the other hand, had a good deal to say about Berlioz' conducting. Both appeared in London in 1855 and had a chance to hear each other. The German was set back at Berlioz' performance of the Mozart G minor Symphony. "I . . . was amazed to find a conductor who was so energetic in the performance of his own compositions sink into the commonest rut of the vulgar time beater." The two great men and strong personalities came together. Wagner was the host, and in his autobiography he goes into detail about the evening they had in London. One can visualize the picture: the voluble, metaphysical German who took himself so seriously; full of theories; everything settled to his own satisfaction in his own mind; and the witty, urbane, logical, sharp-minded, practical Frenchman: both geniuses, both as far apart as human beings can be. Wagner went into a long-winded exposition of his ideas about the secrets of creation, re-creation, and the artistic conception:

I tried to include the action of external experiences, which hold us captive in their own way, on the inner consciousness; how we escape from their influence purely by the development of our most intimate creative powers and that they are in no way called forth by such expressions but merely raised from their deep slumber, so that artistic creations are not in the smallest degree the outcome of external experiences, but on the contrary a liberation from them.

And so on, and so on, at great, ponderous, earnest, egocentric length. One wonders if Berlioz ever got a word in. Thus did Wagner entertain his colleague in London. Berlioz seems to have politely agreed with everything, probably pulling Wagner's leg in dead-pan manner. Wagner ended up deciding that Berlioz was immensely fluent and glib of tongue. A real Frenchman, he concluded. Which Berlioz was. They represented different concepts, different emotional and national attitudes. If nothing else, there was a strong streak of classicism in Berlioz' emotional make-up, his 465-piece orchestra notwithstanding. Wagner had little classicism in him; he was a romantic through and through, incapable of responding to the classicism that has never been entirely absent from the French interpretive school. Wagner called Berlioz' interpretation of the Mozart G minor nothing but time beating. The irony is that Berlioz' style in that work, if one may hazard a guess, would have been much closer to our taste than the surging, inflated dynamics and romanticisms Wagner brought to it.

· X ·

Mendelssohn
and the German School

In Germany the first dominating podium force was that perfect
musician, Felix Mendelssohn. A prodigy on the level of a Mozart, he
developed into an adult to whom all forms of music seemed to come
with exquisite ease and freedom. His ear and memory were legendary,
and Hallé was quite convinced that Mendelssohn knew every bar of
music ever written and, what was more, could reproduce it immediately. It is hard to think of a musician in history with the natural
endowments of this man. Born into a wealthy and cultured family,
he was fortunate in that his gifts were carefully nurtured: there was
no exploitation here, as there had been with Mozart, Beethoven and
Weber. His parents encouraged the development of the young genius,
even to the extent of providing a little orchestra for him. Some children have toy soldiers and dolls; Mendelssohn had a chamber orchestra. He conducted it at home from 1821 to 1824—he was twelve years
old in 1821—and from the very beginning he used a baton. He became
a patrician, all-encompassing musician, a musician *sans peur et sans
reproche*, one with a classic bent and integrity, one who was determined to raise standards, to play only the finest music, to combat
musical cheapness and hypocrisy.

His tastes showed up early and were brought to the fore with his
famous revival of Bach's *St. Matthew Passion* on March 11, 1829.
The score had been forgotten, and Mendelssohn reintroduced it to
Europe, thus giving impetus to the Bach renaissance (though it is a
mistake to believe that Bach was unknown until then; the fact is that
he never had been forgotten and was the bread and butter of every
musician from 1750 to the great nineteenth-century revival). About

117

Mendelssohn's resurrection of the score: if it illustrated that he had the purest and noblest of musical instincts, it also illustrated the fact that he was a child of his age. Like all musicians of the day, he had no hesitation about modernizing older music; and he thoroughly modernized the St. *Matthew Passion* to make it more palatable for his audiences. He chopped, recomposed, edited, romanticized and introduced special effects, such as in the recitative *Und der Vorhang im Tempel zerreiss,* where a lightning flash of sound ran through the orchestra. Mendelssohn used a chorus of 400 and a greatly augmented orchestra.

Apparently there was some resentment that a youth of twenty, and a Jew at that, should be in charge of so imposing a force in so "Christian" a work. But the performance turned out to be a triumph. It was repeated on March 21 and again in Holy Week. Mendelssohn's friend, Eduard Devrient, described one aspect of Mendelssohn's conducting that many were to note in later years: "Many whole sections were often beaten through, but Felix . . . as soon as large segments were running smoothly, dropped his baton and listened with seraphic transport, occasionally beckoning with eye or hand." Naturally he had the score by heart; and, indeed, he had conducted all the rehearsals from memory. Those days it was considered impolite, and a disrespect to the composer, to play or conduct from memory; and so at the actual performance Mendelssohn used a score. If Hallé's anecdote is true, the wrong score was put on Mendelssohn's desk at the first concert. Mendelssohn gravely turned the pages, so as not to upset anybody.

Greatly in demand as composer, teacher, pianist, organist and conductor, Mendelssohn was constantly on the move. Often he encountered opposition because of his new-fangled ways. Despite Spohr's historic innovation in London in 1820, the players did not take kindly to the baton, and when Mendelssohn conducted there in 1832 he found himself confronted with a violin-leader and a clavier-leader. Neither of those two worthies was happy when Mendelssohn drew his baton; they hated to give up any of their power. Mendelssohn, affable as always, was willing to retire rather than offend those two fine gentlemen, but was talked out of it by Michael Costa, John Ella and Giacomo Meyerbeer. Ella was at the concert and long remembered the sour faces and "the frowns of the fiddlers whose authority Mendelssohn's baton had so completely usurped."

Genius or not, Mendelssohn went through a conductorial apprenticeship. He had learned a great deal on his own, he had picked up even more by guest-conducting appearances in his youth, and in 1833 he became musical director of the Düsseldorf Orchestra. There he won his spurs. He immediately reorganized the orchestra, he revived church music by Palestrina, Lotti and Leo (Düsseldorf was a Catholic area), and in concerts he emphasized Handel, Gluck, Beethoven, Weber and Cherubini. He also, after twenty rehearsals, came forth with a production of *Don Giovanni*—one of the few times in his life he conducted opera. Mendelssohn was not very happy at Düsseldorf. The orchestra players would get drunk and beat each other up. Discipline was wretched; and even the easygoing, handsome, aristocratic, small-boned Mendelssohn often lost his temper, ripping up scores and screaming at the orchestra. From Düsseldorf Mendelssohn went, in 1835, to the Lower Rhine Music Festival at Cologne; and, the same year, to Leipzig. He had been offered the Munich Opera, but refused. Mendelssohn was never happy with opera; he was a symphony and choral man.

It was at Leipzig that most of Mendelssohn's activities were centered the rest of his short life. Leipzig had a tremendous musical reputation—it was, after all, the city of Bach—and the St. Thomas Choir was flourishing, as were the Gewandhaus concerts, the Singakademie, the Euterpe Society and the opera. But the city needed a vitalizing force. Christian August Pohlenz was conductor of the Gewandhaus concerts and he was a nullity of the old school. Wagner had heard him in the 1831–32 season and had been shocked. Pohlenz, he wrote, "belonged to the type of fat and pleasant musical director and was a great favorite with the Leipzig public. He used to come on the platform with a very important blue baton in his hand." Wagner goes on to describe a performance of the Beethoven Ninth by Pohlenz. The first three movements were like a Haydn symphony, and the playing was so catastrophic that Wagner began to think Beethoven had written nonsense. The performance was in a complete mess until a double-bass player "in rather coarse and energetic language," told Pohlenz to stop conducting. Then things went better.

Mendelssohn's first steps on replacing Pohlenz were to weed out the inferior players, raise the strength from forty to fifty and bring in Ferdinand David as concertmaster. David was one of the best violinists in Europe. Then Mendelssohn demanded, and got, a pension for every player in the orchestra. He immediately discarded the sleazy old repertoire of Ries, Reissiger, Neukomm and other such mediocrities, replacing them with the best composers of past and present. His very first program, on October 4, 1835, contained his own *Calm Sea and Prosperous Journey* Overture, an aria from *Der Freischütz*, the Spohr Violin Concerto No. 8, Cherubini's Overture and Introduction to *Ali Baba* and the Beethoven Fourth Symphony. This was not a typical Mendelssohn program. Later he evolved a formula, and his ideas about program format were soon largely adopted all over Europe: an overture or classical symphony; an aria; a concerto; a vocal ensemble (from quartet to full chorus) from an opera; and, after intermission, a smaller symphony or overture; an aria; followed by a lengthy piece for orchestra, often with soloists and chorus.

He was just the man Leipzig needed. A musician of his brilliance could not but be an inspirational force; and all of a sudden the orchestra found itself one with an international reputation rather than a sleepy provincial ensemble. Schumann describes its new-found enthusiasm: how it developed an *esprit de corps,* how it began to work together with enthusiasm under Mendelssohn's urgings. The musicians, wrote Schumann, "see each other and practice together daily; they are always the same, so they are able to play a Beethoven symphony without the music in front of them. Added to this a concertmaster who can conduct such scores from memory, a director who knows and reveres those scores, and the crown is complete."

Though his work was centered in Leipzig, especially after he founded the famous conservatory there, Mendelssohn managed to fill many guest-conducting engagements. His contract called for six free months and he made the most of them. As the most popular composer of the day, he was well written up, and plenty of documentary evidence can be found for an accurate description of his podium approach and musical ideas. The dominant impression one gets is of classicism. Mendelssohn's conducting was like his own music and like his own personality: elegant and polished, never overstated, objective, proportioned. His was not an extroverted temperament, and he shrank from any excess—in his conducting, in his own music, in his private life. On the podium he was a restrained figure, sparing of gesture. Schumann liked this. "It was a joy to watch, and note how with his eye he anticipated and communicated every meaningful turn and nuance, from the most delicate to the most robust, an inspired leader plunging ahead—in contrast to those conductors who threaten with their scepters to thrash the score, the orchestra and even the audience." Joachim backs Schumann up, describing Mendelssohn's "almost unnoticeable but extremely lively gestures . . . through which it was possible to transmit the spirit of his personality to chorus and orchestra, to correct little errors with a flick of his finger."

It is clear that Mendelssohn preferred the velvet glove, using the iron hand only when necessary. Everybody attests to his sweet disposition, his friendly air before any orchestra he conducted. Berlioz, himself apt to be quick-tempered, never ceased to marvel at Mendelssohn's patience and politeness. "His every remark is calm and pleasant, and his attitude is the more appreciated by those who, like myself, know how rare such patience is." Mendelssohn strove for a community of equals, united in love of making music. But he would not let anybody take advantage of him. The Berlin orchestra had the reputation of being a terror when the despotic Spontini was away: children out of school. Mendelssohn faced them in 1841 and described his experience to David:

At the first rehearsal the orchestra was disposed to behave badly. Disorder and arrogance prevailed, and I could not believe my eyes and ears. At the second rehearsal, however, I turned the tables. It was my turn to be rude. I punished [fined] half a dozen of them, and now they regard me as another Spontini. Since then there has been no sulking. As soon as they see me, they are attentive and they do their best. Instead of being haughty, they are now obsequious, they bow and scrape. . . .

Mendelssohn had been summoned to Berlin when Friedrich Wilhelm IV became King of Prussia, and was connected with the orchestra until 1844.

As a conservative, Mendelssohn was suspicious of the new music of Berlioz, Wagner and Liszt. "He loves the dead too much," Berlioz gibed. His repertoire extended through Beethoven, Schubert and Schumann. Mendelssohn conducted the world premiere of the Schubert C major Symphony in 1839, and he also introduced two of Schumann's. His programming could be very imaginative. He would give Bach-Handel evenings (Schumann maintained that Mendelssohn knew Bach and Handel much better than any musician alive); or a Beethoven program in which reposed the *Fidelio* and the three *Leonore* overtures. When he conducted "new" music it was in the direction of such contemporary but conservatively oriented composers as Hiller or Lachner. From all accounts his conducting was precise, lively and suave, with emphasis on rhythm and control; he was especially impatient with players who had poor rhythm. Another thing upon which all commentators agreed—with one exception—was Mendelssohn's penchant for fast tempos. The sole exception was Schumann, who complained about Mendelssohn's poky tempos in the *Eroica*. Possibly Schumann caught Mendelssohn on a bad night. Certainly the overwhelming weight of evidence suggests that Mendelssohn's tempos would create a great deal of discussion today. *"Nur flott, frisch, immer vorwärts!"* he would cry. And Joachim simply says: "Mendelssohn loved lively tempos." It was primarily on matters of tempo that Wagner fulminated against Mendelssohn, whom he thought completely superficial. Wagner heard Mendelssohn conduct a rehearsal of the Beethoven Eighth:

I noticed he would pick out a detail here and there—almost at random—and polish it up with a certain insistence until he got it clear. This was of such excellent service to the detail that I wondered why he did not pay the same attention to other nuances. And so this incomparably buoyant symphony flowed in a vastly tame and chatty manner. As to conducting, he personally informed me once or twice that too slow a tempo was the devil, and he would rather choose to take things too fast; that a really good performance was a rarity at any time. With a little care, however, one might gloss things over, and this could never be done by dawdling but by covering ground at a good, stiff pace.

In short, Wagner was accusing Mendelssohn of bluffing, of covering up inadequacies by fast tempos, especially in the third movement of the Beethoven Eighth. "A perverse piece of negligence," asserted Wagner. But how much can he be trusted? He could work only with people he could dominate, and Mendelssohn was not easily dominated. Wagner had a notorious inability to see any other view but his own; and, in addition, Mendelssohn was a Jew. Yet Hans von Bülow, almost as rabid an anti-Semite as Wagner, raved about Mendelssohn's "elastic sensitivity," "the magnetic eloquence of his ges-

LITHOGRAPH BY JOSEPF KRIEHUBER (VIENNA, 1847)

Felix Mendelssohn, whose conducting dominated the musical life of Germany and England for some 20 years. His interpretations were strongly classic.

Otto Nicolai, conductor and composer, and first director of the Vienna Philharmonic, which he founded in 1842. Nicolai unfortunately died young.

tures," the "wonderful nuances of color," and so on. Joachim took issue with Wagner. Mendelssohn, he claimed, "was far removed from the superficialities . . . that Richard Wagner attributed to him, and he had an inimitable freedom of rhythm." Indeed, Wagner's is the only major dissenting viewpoint about Mendelssohn's ability as a conductor, and that alone makes it suspect.

Mendelssohn worked himself to death. He was very tired toward the end, yet he maintained his full schedule of teaching, composing, conducting, editing, playing the piano and organ, running the Leipzig Conservatory, maintaining a tremendous correspondence. "Playing and conducting," he wrote to Karl Klingemann in 1846, the year before he died, "in fact any and every official appearance in public has grown intensely distasteful to me, so that each time I make up my mind to do it only with the greatest reluctance and unwillingness." The unexpected death of his beloved sister Fanny was the final blow. Mendelssohn never recovered from the shock. But in his thirty-eight years he had done much, and he inaugurated a school of conducting that, while it may later have been eclipsed by the subjective ardors of Wagner and his school, has never been entirely submerged and still comes to light in the person of those conductors who represent grace, lucidity, intelligence, objectivity and profound musicianship.

In any case the period of conducting from 1830 to 1850, before the Wagner band took over, was dominated by Mendelssohn. Otto Nicolai, almost Mendelssohn's exact contemporary (1810–1849), was of the Mendelssohn school. He lives today primarily as the composer of the *Merry Wives of Windsor,* but he also was a brilliant conductor, one of the first of the modernists, a man who enlivened music every time he lifted his baton. In 1837 he was Kapellmeister of the Kaerntnertor Theatre in Vienna, and from 1841 to 1847 first Kapellmeister. In 1842 he founded the Vienna Philharmonic, conducting the first concert on March 28, 1842. Strict, a disciplinarian, careful of detail, he resembled Mendelssohn in his determination to present only the best music. Berlioz called him one of the best orchestra leaders he had ever met:

He possesses three qualities indispensable for a finished conductor. He is a learned composer, skilled and enthusiastic; he has a strong feeling for rhythm; and his method of conducting is perfectly clear and exact. In short, he is an ingenious and indefatigable organizer, grudging neither time nor trouble at rehearsals; one who knows what he is doing because he does only what he knows.

Another conductor much admired by Berlioz was the greatly respected Peter Joseph von Lindpaintner of Stuttgart. And not only by Berlioz. Mendelssohn in 1831 flatly called Lindpaintner the best conductor in Germany. Unlike many of his German contemporaries, Lindpaintner had the mind and technique to take care of modern music. Berlioz could not get over the orchestra that Lindpaintner had trained: "Young, fiery, enthusiastic . . . Intrepid readers, too. Nothing upset, nothing disconcerted them, and they never missed a single expression mark either. . . . I was astonished, for with two rehearsals the whole thing was done." The "thing" in question happened to be the *Symphonie Fantastique*: a mighty handful of notes even for an orchestra today, and much more so in the 1840s. And in two rehearsals to satisfy the finicky Berlioz! Berlioz also had good words to say about the Dresden orchestra and its conductor, Karl Gottlieb Reissiger. This man had the reputation of being the sort of easygoing conductor all orchestras love. He would look at his watch during a performance and if necessary would hurry the tempos so that he could be home when he promised his wife he would be.

Among the other important conductors of the Mendelssohn era was the arch anti-Wagnerian, Heinrich Dorn, active in Riga (where he succeeded Wagner in 1839), Cologne and Berlin. He is reputed to have been a precisionist with a keen ear and an infallible memory. (Dorn anticipated Wagner in at least one respect. He composed an opera on the Nibelung saga in 1854. Has anybody ever looked at it?) Carl Wilhelm Ferdinand Guhr, active in Frankfurt, was a conductor of an older generation and a little outside the general run. One of the first showmen-conductors, he went in for sensational effects. In a performance of Haydn's *Creation*, at the words "Let there be light," he had several military bands join the orchestra in a great chord; and at the word "light" all the gas jets of the house were suddenly turned up. Guhr was dyspeptic and despotic, and of him Berlioz dryly said, "It is plain that he will never err through overindulgence at the head of his orchestra." More important was Franz Lachner of Munich: never inspired ("more understanding than poetry," was Clara Schumann's impression) but capable, painstaking, thorough, a fine musician who built the orchestra that soon was going to play the premieres of *Tristan und Isolde* and *Die Meistersinger* under Bülow in the 1860s.

The long career of Karl August Krebs saw him conducting in Hamburg as early as 1827 (he was head of the opera there for twenty-three years) and in Dresden as late as 1871. He had the reputation of being severe, cold, correct and unimaginative; and the same was said of the brusque Julius Rietz, who was active for many years in Leipzig before succeeding Reissiger at the Dresden Opera in 1860. Wagner dismissed him as "an orthodox Mendelssohnian. . . . A very good leader who is capable of keeping an orchestra together, but he is entirely unable to penetrate a dramatic work, which demands something far more than a good orchestra." Nevertheless, Rietz for a long time was one of the most influential musicians in Germany, the archetype of the dry, pedantic, learned but very efficient conductor.

There was Ferdinand Hiller of Cologne, friend of Chopin, friend of Mendelssohn, friend of Liszt, friend of Wagner, friend of everybody. Thus he was respected and lived a full, active life. He was not a very good conductor. Wagner, for one, called him careless and indifferent. At a Leipzig performance he took the *Hallelujah* Chorus at such a slow tempo that Ferdinand David said they might be finished in time to begin next year's festival. Hiller wrote an essay on conducting. He said that virtuosity and personality had no place in this art. The only one who had praise for his slow tempos was old Anton Schindler, who scurried about telling all who would listen that while Mendelssohn's tempos in Beethoven were too fast, Hiller's were exactly right.

Not much can be said in praise of Robert Schumann's conducting. The great composer was impossible on the podium. He could not hold an orchestra or chorus together, and his personality impressed musicians as weak and negative. There is something heartrending about poor Schumann's epochal inefficiency as a conductor. He was pushed into it by his wife, who always had rose-colored vision when it came to her Robert. And so we find him conducting his own *Faust* in Dresden, 1849:

Inattention on the part of the players brought about confusion and even chaos, and constant but necessary repetition served only to increase the despair of all who were present. When in spite of frequent repetitions a sour note from the horn broke in on the quiet of a placid soft passage, annoyance and irritation gave place to amazement when, with inexhaustible patience, Schumann would lay down his baton, excitedly rub his hands together, and then, in the most polite and friendly manner, ask the orchestra to play the whole passage once again.

Things were even worse in Düsseldorf, where Schumann ran the orchestra and chorus into the ground. He seems to have made only one contribution to conducting. After much thought, he attached his baton to his wrist with a string, so that he would not drop it. Schumann was very proud of the idea.

Richard Wagner

BEETHOVEN MAY HAVE BEEN the prototype, Weber the pioneer, Mendelssohn and Berlioz the first of the modern conductors, but the giant of his time, the strongest conducting force of the century, was Richard Wagner. Associated with orchestras from the very beginning of his career, Wagner was the one who more than anybody else launched the cult of the conductor: that divine figure who was all-wise, all-seeing, omnipotent, supreme in law, word and deed. And more, he wrote voluminously about conducting, his technical ideas shaped the oncoming generation of baton wielders, his philosophy shaped their ideas about music, his protégé Hans von Bülow spread the gospel, and his theatre at Bayreuth sent forth into the world many of the great conductors of the last half of the century—men like Richter, Levi, Mottl, Seidl.

One of the few conductors not a child prodigy, Wagner fought his way to the top despite certain handicaps that would have proved fatal to anybody else. He played no instrument, for example, and thus was an indifferent score reader, a fact about which he made no bones. In 1854 Bülow sent him some scores for appraisal. Wagner honestly admitted he had trouble. "In the first place, how am I to get any clear idea of the things? You know how abominably I play the piano, and that I cannot master anything by that means unless I can get a clear conception beforehand. What I get from a simple reading is not enough (compared with what I expect) to arrive at an idea of a composition." What Wagner did have was a blazing, passionate love for music. That, plus an awesome confidence in the infallibility of his taste and knowledge. Where others think they are right, the fortunate Wagner always *knew* he was right. His ideas were formed early, and they changed very little throughout his career.

In his autobiography he tells of his early musical experiences—of the impression that *Der Freischütz* made on him; of how he got a score of the Beethoven Ninth, copied it out and made a piano reduction. The Ninth "became the mystical goal of all my strange thoughts and desires about music . . . the spiritual keynote of my life." He was seventeen years old at the time. It was the following year that he heard Pohlenz ruin the Ninth in Dresden. Conducting exerted a strong pull on him, and with his usual confidence he stepped before an orchestra in 1834, at the age of twenty-one. The occasion was nothing less than *Don Giovanni*, at Lauchstädt. A year later, Wagner says, he had succeeded in obtaining "perfect confidence" in conducting an orchestra.

His career as a conductor followed the classic European pattern that exists to this day: working up from microscopic positions in opera houses, advancing at every step. The year 1833 saw him as chorusmaster at Würzburg. In 1835 he was at Magdeburg, in 1836 at Königsberg, and from 1837 to 1839 he had those stormy years at the opera house in Riga. There he had an orchestra of twenty-four—he disgustedly called it "one calculated for a string quartet"—with only two first and two second violins, two violas and one cello. The ambitious Wagner could not be satisfied with such a state of things. He tried to turn the opera house upside down, proposing plans for a subscription season of six concerts in addition to the opera season, and carefully figured everything out:

Not only would the prospect of uplifting musical experiences be offered to the connoisseur, but the rest of the public should be given an opportunity for meeting and talking, which could take place freely during the long intermission between the first and second part of the concert. A Swiss bakery, for instance, could be given charge of a buffet, whereby refreshments could be offered during the intermission. In a word, everything would have to be done to combine the concerts with pleasant evenings of entertainment for the greater part of the public, since everybody knows quite well art alone is not what the majority of the people want.

The plan was never carried out. After a quick look, Riga discovered that Wagner's lengthy memorandum called for an entire reconstruction of the opera, orchestra and concert life of the city.

There were great quarrels. Wagner's dogmatism and refusal to compromise made enemies, and he was dismissed in 1839. His *Wanderjahre* took him to Paris, where he heard Habeneck and his great orchestra. He managed to keep alive by hack work. His next major step was Dresden, in 1843, where he shared conducting duties with the stout, easygoing, comfortable Reissiger. Reissiger could live with conditions there; but the young visionary, fire-eating, dedicated, radical Wagner could not. He threw the orchestra into rebellion with his demands: for sectional rehearsals, for full rehearsals, for better players. There were screams from the orchestra when its old routine was shaken up. "No," the players would say, with meaningful shakes of the head, "there's never been anything like this before. As if our cello and bass players haven't learned long before this what to do!" Wagner went complaining to Reissiger, who attempted to comfort him with a bland statement to the effect that this was the inevitable fate of a conductor. "Thereupon," Wagner says, "he proudly smote his stomach and hoped that I might soon have one as round as his own." Another thing that bothered Wagner was the seating arrangement of the orchestra, which was placed in a semicircle around the chorus during concerts. Reissiger assured Wagner that this stemmed from the time of the late conductor, Francesco Morlacchi, and that therefore there could be no change.

It was during his six years at Dresden, however, that Wagner sharpened himself and developed into the greatest conductor in Europe. His inflexible will prevailed over the orchestra, though he was constantly getting in trouble. But he did learn to make a certain amount of compromise. The first thing he tried to do on arriving in Dresden was to break the seniority system. Players had what amounted to civil-service tenure, no matter how bad they were. When Wagner tried to import a player from Darmstadt he had what amounted to a strike on his hands, and he had to back down. He also tried to fight the old divided leadership. Karl Joseph Lipinski, the leader of the violins, was a violent opponent of the young conductor and did everything he could to sabotage him. Lipinski thought a great deal of himself and his playing, and Wagner noted that he "came in a little before the other violins; he was a leader in a double sense, as he was always ahead." To make things even more difficult, Wagner's ideas about music and its interpretation were strange to the orchestra and the public. In a letter to Baron von Lüttschau, the Intendant of

PENCIL DRAWING BY E. B. KIETZ

Richard Wagner in 1842. At that time he was doing hack work in Paris.

Wagner, 1865. This photo was taken in Munich not long after the premiere of *Tristan und Isolde*.

the theatre, Wagner promised "to alter nothing in the hitherto accepted interpretation of tempo, etc., when conducting older operas, even when it goes against my artistic judgment, leaving me nevertheless free, when studying newer operas, to exercise my best judgment toward the object of getting as perfect an interpretation as possible." One can see Wagner's sour face writing this letter; his nose was being rubbed in the dirt. Those were stormy days in Dresden. Wagner was constantly submitting propositions, recommendations, reports and memoranda on how to improve the orchestra. All of his recommendations made good sense. As Ernest Newman says, they carry their own justification and conviction; they are "the work of an idealist indeed but not of a visionary," and are the quintessence of practicality. Wagner saw none of his suggestions taken up. His unpopularity did not help. He was considered vain, overbearing, pretentious and expensive. Often he was in receipt of official reprimands.

But he began to present deep, intense, highly personal interpretations that were unique in Europe. And the orchestra, little by little, began to see things his way. The flutist of the Dresden Orchestra many years later told Felix Weingartner that when Wagner conducted, "the players had no feeling of being led. Each believed himself to be expressing himself freely, yet they all worked together in perfect ensemble." The members of the orchestra may have resisted Wagner's sectional rehearsals, but when he finally got around to doing a Beethoven symphony they burst into an involuntary cheer after the full rehearsal. They had never come across a conductor who could draw such an even volume of tone at every dynamic. Wagner asked for, and insisted upon, all kinds of nuances and dynamic subtleties, down to the smallest point—the poco crescendo, for instance, "which, alas! is well-nigh unknown to our players" and which must be differentiated from a più crescendo. (How many conductors today would bother to observe the difference between two tiny shades of crescendo?) Wagner was constantly concerning himself with this kind of detail (and also writing about it, as he was constantly writing about everything; and his long and explicit treatises on acting, singing, stage management and the entire *Gesamtkunstwerk* eventually were to be put into practice in Bayreuth). No detail was too small. "Nothing is so worth the utmost study as the attempt to clarify the meaning of a phrase, a bar, nay more, a single note."

In 1846 he finally conducted the Beethoven Ninth. It was typical of the times that he felt it necessary to draw up a program for the score, drawing heavily on Goethe's *Faust*. (The romantics had a sheer mania for reading things into music, and even such intellectual stalwarts as Schumann, Joachim and Bülow saw in any piece of music a "message" far beyond the printed note. Joachim, for instance, was convinced that the finale of the Brahms Third Symphony represented Hero and Leander. Clara Schumann, on the other hand, called the symphony "a forest idyll" and sketched out a complete program for it.) In this performance of the Ninth, Wagner aimed for "as expressive a rendering as possible." But, much as he adored Beethoven, Wagner was not the one to let the composer have the final say:

I never carried my piety to the extent of taking directions absolutely literally. Rather than sacrifice the effect intended by the master to the erroneous indications given, I made the strings play only moderately loudly instead of real fortissimo, up to the point where they alternate with the wind instruments in taking up the continuation of the new theme. Thus the motive, rendered as it was as loudly as possible by a double set of wind instruments, was, I believe, heard with real distinctness for the first time since the symphony was composed.

Wagner is referring to the spot in the second movement where the strings carry a rhythmical accompaniment against the woodwind theme. The point is that already we have the papa-knows-best attitude represented by Wagner and his school. They were not worried much about the letter of the score; they were always more interested in its spirit. Thus, when Wagner conducted Gluck's *Iphigénie en Aulide* in 1847, he sent to Paris for the original edition. That was merely the point of departure. He proceeded to cut some of the plot, recomposed, composed and thoroughly revised the work. This he did "only with the object of making the existing version produce the effect I desired." Not what Gluck desired; what *I* desired. But that was part of the rules of romanticism, and Wagner was one of the arch-romantics. In romanticism the ego was all-important, the performer on the level of the creator, and one's aspirations were much more important than any such vague thing as scholarship or fidelity to the printed note. Nobody in the nineteenth century thought about "fidelity"; he thought about self-expression. When it came to music of a previous century, it was the avowed aim of the romantics to modernize the older composers, thus making them more palatable for audiences: this in the name of homage. When Liszt edited the piano music of Schubert he was very proud of his wholesale alterations. "Several passages and the whole of the C major Fantasy I have re-written in modern piano form, and I flatter myself that Schubert would not be displeased with it." In adapting Gluck and Beethoven, Wagner was doing no less than any musician of the day was doing. The middle twentieth century may disagree with the concept; but it is always dangerous to judge a previous age by later standards. If the situation could be reversed, the nineteenth century would have quite a few disparaging remarks to make about *our* standards.

Came the Revolution of 1849, in which Wagner was on the wrong side, and he fled to Switzerland. At Zurich he also proposed a complete revision of the orchestra and of concert life. Among his suggestions were: an orchestra to be engaged on an eight-month basis (five months of opera, three of concerts); the formation of a society to present subscription concerts; three rehearsals for each concert; a drive for funds among the music lovers of the city; a minimum of thirty-two players for the opera and forty-six for the concerts. All of this made sense, and all was discarded by the authorities. Wagner busied himself conducting the Zurich opera in 1850 and 1851. In his repertoire were *Der Freischütz, Norma, La Dame Blanche, Die Zauberflöte* and *Fidelio.* There also was *Don Giovanni,* as altered by Wagner and prepared with the help of Bülow and Karl Ritter, his two assistants. Also in Zurich were the Music Society concerts, of which Wagner conducted twenty-two between 1851 and 1855.

His theories of conducting and interpretation were certainly solidi-fied in his mind by the middle 1850s, and were set forth in his 1869 essay on conducting. Basic to an understanding of what Wagner was after is his concept of the *melos,* or song (in its transfigured sense), of a musical work. To Wagner, tempo was the all-important consideration, but only a correct conception of the *melos* could supply the proper tempo. "The two are indivisible; one conditions the other." Most conductors, Wagner maintained, knew nothing about proper tempo because they knew nothing about song. How is the *melos* to be achieved? The conductor must study theme and figuration, and he can determine the correct tempo only by the special character of the phrase. He accuses conductors of approaching any adagio by hunting for some figuration or other and then adjusting their tempo

Four caricatures of Wagner as a conductor. They date from 1863 to 1877. As the greatest and most controversial conductor of his day, Wagner was constantly being caricatured. His ideas about conducting featured much fluctuation in tempo, absolute domination over the orchestra, a beat that moved in phrases rather than bars, and a great deal of expression. It was a highly personal, romantic kind of conducting, quite different from the more reserved, classic approach of Berlioz and Mendelssohn.

to the hypothetical speed of that figuration. "Perhaps I am the only conductor who has dared to take the adagio proper of the third movement of the Ninth Symphony at a tempo in strict accordance with its character." But correct tempo is only part of the story. Even more important is modification of tempo—"a thing not merely quite unknown to our conductors, but doltishly proscribed by them." Wagner calls modification of tempo "a positive life principle of all our music."

By this he means the necessity of modifying a basic tempo for expressive reasons. From Wagner's writings, it would appear that virtually all conductors of the period up to 1850 or so relied exclusively on a metronomic, bar-line beat, a beat with little nuance or flexibility. Wagner looked far beyond that in his concept of tempo modification (which he may have got from the piano playing and conducting of Liszt, as he got so many other things from Liszt). The concept is more than rubato; it is a rise and fall, slowing and speeding, variation of tempo, with the use of ritards to link contrasting passages, always in evidence but under strict control. Wagner illustrates this through a section of his *Meistersinger* Prelude. When the lyric theme in E major enters, "the pace must necessarily be a little slackened" in order "to preserve the theme's chief characteristic, that of tenderness." To bring this imperceptibly about (that is, without effacing the fundamental character of the overall tempo), a few bars of poco rallentando introduce the phrase. Then, as the theme is developed more and more restlessly, "it was easy for me to lead the tempo back to its original swifter motion." What Wagner is driving at is amazingly similar to what Schindler had said in his description of how the Beethoven symphonies should go (see page 63). And when Wagner gets into a discussion of how to conduct the Beethoven symphonies, he calls for the same kind of freedom that Schindler had claimed as the composer's own interpretations. Could Wagner have been familiar with Schindler's exegeses? At any rate, Wagner makes it clear that he is not pleading for random changes in tempo. He was aware of the dangers. "It certainly is a valid argument that nothing could do more harm to the pieces I have instanced than a willful introduction of random nuances of tempo, which must at once throw open wide the door to the fantastic whim of every empty or conceited time beater aiming at effect, and would in time make our classical literature completely unrecognizable." But, at the same time, "all attempts at modification of tempo in behalf of the rendering of classical music, and particularly that of Beethoven, have been received with displeasure by the conductors' guild of our time."

Now all this about *melos* and tempo modification is rather vague; and it does indeed throw open the door to a kind of interpretive anarchy. Wagner was trying to arrive at a general rule underlying interpretation, but his writing is muddy and his thought processes not very clear. In any case, he was trying to define the indefinable, to draw universal rules from what basically were his own intuitions. Any interpretive act is a process of refraction, the interpreter being a prism through which the composer's thought is refracted. No matter how much Wagner pontificates, interpretation remains a personal matter based on knowledge plus intuition. Wagner's knowledge and intuition were of a superior order, but they could not be transmitted to anybody else, and his desperate efforts at an esthetic of interpretation had to fail.

But his theories remain of interest, and his remarks on Beethoven of special importance, for Wagner was the Beethoven conductor whose ideas led directly to the highly personal interpretations of such conductors as Nikisch, Mengelberg and Furtwängler. Beethoven from the beginning had occupied a special part of Wagner's life. He saw in the nine symphonies a mythos and an ethos. Influenced by Schopenhauer, he extended that philosopher's ideas about music, which to Wagner provided "a state of ecstasy with which no other [art] can compare; in it the will perceives itself the almighty will of all things." And Beethoven's music "must positively appear to us a revelation from another world." Naturally the Ninth Symphony transcended all the others, and it laid its spell on Wagner as it later did on Mahler and Bruckner. "The last symphony of Beethoven is the redemption of music from out of her peculiar element into the realm of universal art. It is the human evangel of the art of the future. Beyond it no forward step is possible, for upon it the perfect art work of the future alone can follow: the universal drama for which Beethoven has forged the key." These lines were written in 1849. Later Wagner called the Beethoven symphonies "veritable poems in which it is sought to bring a real subject to representation. The obstacle to their comprehension lies in the difficulty of finding with certainty the subject that is represented. . . . The poetic subject of a tone piece by Beethoven is thus only to be divined by a tone poet." Naturally the tone poet would be Wagner himself.

When Wagner writes about bringing "a real subject to representation" in the Beethoven symphonies, he means just that. In his analysis of the *Eroica* he talks about "the lovable glad man" of the third movement, whereas the fourth movement represents the man whole, harmoniously at one with self. Then woman enters, and the symphony ends as the overwhelming power of Love. "Once more the heartstrings quiver, and tears of pure humanity well forth; yet from out the very quick of sadness there bursts the jubilant cry of force—that force which lately led itself to Love, and—helped by that—the whole, the total man now shouts to us in avowal of his godhead." Drivel? Bosh? Yet one can read beneath this romantic nonsense to the symbolism that makes the *Eroica* a manifestation of mighty forces, and that is not drivel at all. In his discussion of the Fifth Symphony, Wagner imagines Beethoven himself talking:

My pauses must be long and serious ones. Hold them firmly, terribly. I did not write them in jest or because I was at a loss how to proceed. I indulge in the fullest, the most sustained tone to express emotions in my adagio. . . . The very lifeblood of the tone is to be extracted to the last drop. I arrest the waves of the ocean, and the depth must not be visible; or I stem the clouds, disperse the mist, and slow the pure blue ether and the radiant eye of the sun. For this I put fermatas—sudden, long, sustained notes—into my allegros. Ponder them here in the first announcement of my theme. Hold the long E flats firmly after the three short tempestuous quarter notes, and learn what the same thing means when it occurs later in the work.

A man who could write these words would obviously make a dramatic, pulsating thing of the Fifth Symphony. We can discard most of Wagner's verbiage, and when his ideas are peeled down to essentials, a very clear picture emerges. We get a conductor of remarkable force and imagination, one who attempted to *create* in his interpretations. We get a man possessed of a thorough knowledge of the orchestra (his remarks about phrasing, instrumental short cuts and modifications in the Ninth Symphony can still be read with profit). We get a man who regarded music as an ethical force, a man who took nothing for granted but absorbed a score until it was part of him. We get a conductor who *listened;* one who was particular about balances, about how to make the melody sing out so that it would never be obscured by a clumsy bit of orchestration (and, if the orchestration happened to be inept, to change it as tactfully as possible). We get an interpreter with very free ideas, one who looked for rhythmic nuance and plasticity, *basing his accentuations on the phrase and not the bar line* (which may well have been Wagner's greatest single contribution). We get an original mind that was sure to shake up the Establishment. We get a man of supreme confidence, not to say arrogance, who insisted on perfection. We get a supreme subjectivist, one whose interpretations were as expressive of self as of the composer. We get an approach to rhythm and tempo that demands perpetual fluctuation, a kind of super rubato, in which changes of idea and mood are connected and linked by shifts in speed and dynamics.

Wagner probably was not a very good baton technician. A conductor like Nikisch could face any strange orchestra and get tremendous results from one rehearsal. Not Wagner, who had to work very hard. Complicating the situation was the novelty of his ideas—ideas that were to become common practice the following generation. Observers are agreed that it took Wagner much time to make an orchestra respond. Anton Seidl testified that early rehearsals went badly "because the master was impatient and expected everything to be perfect at once. The strange and significant movements of his long baton bewildered the players and put them out until they began to understand that it was not the bar line that ruled here, but the phrase, or the melody, or the expression." Francis Hueffer saw Wagner at rehearsals in sheer desperation, storming, hissing, stamping his feet. (Years later, George Bernard Shaw, writing about the 1877 Wagner Festival in London, describes Wagner as stamping when he wanted more emphasis. Shaw also refers to Wagner's "tense neurologic glare.") Wagner did not have a firm beat, Hueffer says, nor was he of much help assisting an orchestra through the intricacies of a new work. But once the orchestra got the idea, "he would make them do things which a humdrum conductor would never think of." Felix Weingartner called this trait of Wagner's "a faculty of immediate communication."

To musicians trained in an earlier school, Wagner's beat was incomprehensible. Older conductors went up and down with the bar line. Not Wagner, who conducted in phrases; and the esteemed James William Davison, one of the leading music critics in England, complained that Wagner beat "up" and "down" indiscriminately. "At least, *we* could not, with the best intentions, distinguish his 'ups' from his 'downs,' and if the members of the band are down to his 'ups' and up to his 'downs' by the end of the season, we.shall be ready to present each of them with a quill toothpick as a forfeit for our own lack of discernment." Davison was considered quite a pretty stylist, and this is a good example of the exquisite delicacy of his wit.

By 1855 Wagner was one of the most famous and controversial musical figures in Europe, and when he was invited to conduct the London Philharmonic Society concerts, there was a great flurry in the English capital. The Philharmonic wanted a major name to offset that of Berlioz, then conducting the "New" Philharmonic concerts. Lindpaintner of Stuttgart was the first choice, but he refused. Wagner agreed to conduct eight concerts for a fee of £200. He arrived in London on March 4 and promptly proceeded to hate the city and everything concerned with it. "I live here like a damned soul in hell. . . . The abominable London air paralyzes mind and body. Besides, there is the unbearable coal vapor, which cannot be avoided either in the house or in the street. Every moment one has hands like a chimney sweep and I have to wash once every hour." Tactless as always, he aired his complaints in the dressing room of the theatre, loudly saying that he regretted having come to London, that his esthetic sense was offended, and so on. The newspapers picked this up, and the resulting stories did not help Wagner's popularity. He was unhappy when he found he could have but one rehearsal a concert. When he conducted the rehearsal for the first concert, his worst fears were confirmed. To his horror, he found the orchestra full of the Mendelssohn tradition. Wagner smelled Mendelssohn (who had been eight years dead) and Jews everywhere. "Mendelssohn had conducted that band for a considerable period," Wagner later wrote, inaccurately (Mendelssohn had led it only five times in his life), "and the Mendelssohnian type of performance had confessedly been raised to a tradition." Wagner continues:

In fact, it so well suited the customs and peculiarities of this society's concerts that it almost seemed as if Mendelssohn had derived his mode of performance from them. As a huge amount of music was consumed at these concerts, but only one rehearsal allowed for each performance, I myself was often obliged to leave the orchestra to its tradition, and thereby made acquaintance with a style of execution that forcibly reminded me at any rate of Mendelssohn's dictum to myself. [Wagner is referring to Mendelssohn's statement that "too slow a tempo was the devil."] The thing flowed on like water from a public fountain. To attempt to check it was out of the question, and every allegro ended as an indisputable presto. . . . The orchestra never played anything else but a mezzo forte; neither a genuine forte nor a true piano came out. In important cases, as far as possible, I at least insisted on the interpretation that I myself thought right, and also the correct tempo. The good fellows had nothing against it and expressed real delight, and to the public it clearly seemed right; but the critics flew into a rage and so alarmed the committee that I once was actually asked to be so good as to scurry through the second movement of Mozart's E flat Symphony again, as one had always been accustomed to and as Mendelssohn himself had done.

Wagner showed his contempt. It was the custom in London to come out wearing white gloves and then remove them. But at one concert Wagner kept his gloves on for Mendelssohn's *Italian* Symphony, taking them off for the other pieces on the program. Wagner seems to have interested the orchestra as much as he infuriated the press. At the first rehearsal he conducted the *Eroica* without a score, at that time an almost unprecedented feat of memory. After the rehearsal the orchestra burst into a storm of applause. But the critics slaughtered Wagner. Davison's blast was typical: "No foreign conductor ever came with such extraordinary pretensions and produced so unfavorable an impression. . . . The result has been a series of performances unparalleled for inefficiency. . . . Another such set of concerts would go far to annihilate the Philharmonic Society." The only critic who suported Wagner was George Hogarth in the *Daily News*. All the other critics responded in bewilderment to Wagner's ideas. Perhaps some chauvinism was involved, for before Wagner's arrival there had been agitation for a British conductor to take over the concerts. There seems, however, to have been honest disagreement with Wagner's nuances and especially his tempos, with his strong contrasts between the powerful and lyric elements of a score (masculine and feminine) and his habit of slowing down at the approach of second subjects. Wagner was accused of taking liberties with the music. Henry Smart's reaction was typical, and Smart was a good musician. He did not like Wagner's habit of taking quick movements faster than anybody else, and slow movements slower;

and he especially did not like the way Wagner "prefaces the entry of an important point, or the return of a theme—especially in a slow movement—by an exaggerated ritardando; and . . . he reduces the speed of an allegro—say in an overture or the first part of a symphony —fully one-third immediately on the entrance of a cantabile phrase." Wagner read reviews like this and shrugged his shoulders. He was convinced that the entire press was in the pay of the Jew Meyerbeer.

Could Smart have been exaggerating *that* much? Obviously Wagner changed tempos to bring out and emphasize lyric elements. We have this in his own words. But the wild kind of distortion indicated by Smart is hard to believe. Yet Wagner's constant ebb and flow of phrase kept bothering musicians and critics on those occasions he conducted after 1855. That London season was Wagner's last as a guest conductor of the standard repertoire. From that year he concentrated more and more on writing his own music, though he made guest appearances here and there to fill his pockets. In 1860 he conducted in Paris and Brussels; in 1862, Leipzig; in 1863, Prague, St. Petersburg and Moscow. In 1864 he met Ludwig II of Bavaria, and his needs were taken care of thereafter. For special occasions, though, Wagner would make appearances, and Hanslick listened to Wagner conducting the *Eroica* in Vienna in 1872. Hanslick's review, a thoughtful one, provides a good image of Wagner's style and the problems it caused listeners oriented to a less personal approach:

The novel element in Wagner's interpretations consists, to put it briefly, in frequent modifications of the tempo within a single movement. . . . After a very fast beginning of the first movement, for example, he takes the second theme (forty-fifth measure) conspicuously slower, thus disturbing the listener's hardly confirmed establishment of the fundamental mood of the movement and diverting the "heroic" character of the symphony toward the sentimental. He takes the scherzo uncommonly fast, almost presto—a hazardous undertaking even with a virtuoso orchestra. . . . Were Wagner's principles of conducting universally adopted, his tempo changes would open the door to intolerable arbitrariness, and we should soon be having symphonies "freely adapted from Beethoven" instead of "by Beethoven." . . . Wagner approaches conducting as he approaches composing. What suits his individuality and his utterly exceptional talent must be accepted as the one and only universal, true and exclusively authorized artistic law.

And César Cui, the Russian composer, was equally bothered. "I much prefer Berlioz to Richard Wagner as a conductor of Beethoven. Despite all of his excellent qualities, Wagner often shows affectation, and introduces accelerandos of doubtful sentimentality." Just how much Wagner exaggerated we shall never know. The chances are that his tremendous personality applied to a Beethoven symphony would be unpalatable to a stricter age, or to an age that regards the letter more important than the spirit. But it is also true that *no* nineteenth-century conductor (Berlioz perhaps excepted) could satisfy an audience of the latter half of the twentieth century. As it stands, Richard Wagner was the right man in the right place at the right time, and he shaped a generation of conductors just as he shaped a generation of composers.

· XII ·

The Scene in England

In ENGLAND the right man at the right time was Michael Costa, whose long career as a conductor—from 1833 to the year of his death in 1884—saw order and discipline replacing anarchy. It *was* anarchy, for the most part. Until Costa took charge, England had no orchestra to come near the fine ones that dotted Europe. Divided leadership was still the rule, and so was the deputy system, in which an orchestral musician could send a substitute if a more lucrative engagement came along. Costa, a small, perky, determined man of Spanish descent, but Italian by birth and education, was a well-equipped musician—singer, pianist, composer—who could browbeat the English musicians and bend them to his will because he knew more than all of them and they knew he knew more than all of them. He had come to England in 1829 as a singer, became *maestro al cembalo* at the King's Theatre in 1830 and took over the orchestra in 1833. By the end of that decade he had taken a ragtag group of indifferent musicians and made them a well-drilled group of seventy-seven players. Then he left for Covent Garden, taking along some of the best players of King's. He also conducted the Philharmonic Society concerts, the Sacred Harmonic Society and the Birmingham Festival. For many years he was the big man in British music and, until mid-century, certainly the only conductor of importance.

Costa brought authority to the scene. Spohr and Mendelssohn had shown what a strong-willed leader could do, but they were guest conductors and made little permanent impact on London orchestras, which were loath to give up the old ways. The orchestra expected divided leadership and resented any kind of discipline. The members were prima donnas to whom the concept of ensemble—of pooling personality for the common musical good—was unknown. Each player, and there were some good ones, was more interested in showing off his ability as a soloist; and, from all accounts, pre-Costa performances were a sort of saturnalia, each player trying to outdo the other. The conductor was considered little more than a lackey. Singers would tell *him* what tempos to take, where to cut, when to throttle down.

Costa came in with a new broom. When he took over the Philharmonic Society, he found himself plagued by absentee musicians. He started distributing fines with a lavish hand. That did no good. So, as John Ella tells the story, he called the orchestra together. "Gentlemen, I am happy to tell you that I have abolished fines for absentees." Great applause. "But any one absent from rehearsals without my permission forfeits his engagement." Murmurs, sotto voce. Costa made his decision stick, and those who did not like it got out of his orchestra. He watched over his players like a schoolmarm over a class of juvenile delinquents; and although fines for absenteeism were abolished, as there was no absenteeism any more, there were plenty of other fines. Costa saw to it that the levy was exacted. On payday he would sit on the stage while the players passed him in review. One time a young violinist arrived with mud on his boots, wearing a frock coat. Costa asked him how he dared appear in such a condition. The man explained that he had just arrived from out of town and had not had time to make his toilet. "Go home instantly," ordered Costa, "and come back with clean boots and in evening dress." By the time the poor fellow returned, the second act was nearly over, and he ended up being fined for missing two-thirds of a performance.

Costa was considered better in opera than in symphony. As an operatic director he was held in great respect by Rossini and Mendelssohn, and Meyerbeer went so far as to say he was the greatest in the world. It does seem clear that compared with Costa the other British conductors of the day—Bishop, Smart, Parry, Balfe and Benedict were the best known—were little more than good-natured, agreeable dilettantes. When Costa was in charge, there were discipline and accuracy. He may not have had much imagination, but he was a craftsman, and every critic and musician agreed that nobody in England at the time, and very few in Europe, had better control over an orchestra. Part of this control came from a good stick technique, and part came from pure psychic domination. Great surly musicians

ENGRAVING BY D. J. POUND FROM PHOTOGRAPH BY MAYALL

Michael Costa, around 1850, the most important conductor active in England. He was a good musician and a stern but fair disciplinarian.

Costa in 1872, conducting opera from the piano. Note the tassel swinging from the bottom of his baton.

CARICATURE BY SPY IN VANITY FAIR

would suddenly become meek when Costa glanced at them. His temper was legendary. As late as 1879 he had a tremendous fight with the famous tenor Angelo Masini, one result of which was Masini's refusal to sing in England at all. As often as not, Costa was tilting with singers. Once a prima donna about to make her debut in England sent him a £100 note, the idea being that he take care of her wishes, including never cutting off any of her high notes. She did not realize it, but her action was equivalent to tipping the Prince of Wales. Costa refused to conduct for her.

Probably he was a pedantic conductor. The music had to go just so; there never was a feeling of improvisation when Costa was in charge. The impresario Henry Mapleson writes that Costa was born with the spirit of discipline within him:

His love of order, punctuality, regularity in everything stood him in good stead. At many operatic theatres the performance begins some five or ten minutes after the time announced; at no theatre where Sir Michael conducted did it ever begin a minute late. The model orchestral chief arrived with a chronometer in each of his waistcoat pockets; and when, after consulting his timepieces, he saw that the moment for beginning had arrived, he raised his baton and the performance began. He did not even take the trouble to see that the musicians were in their places. He knew that, with the discipline he maintained, they must be there.

As with every conductor of the day, Costa's work would sound strange to modern ears. His rhythms were rather metronomic and his tempos, especially in symphonic music, were fast. William Sterndale Bennett wrote to James Davison in 1836: "Is it true that Costa will conduct the Philharmonic concerts next year? I hope not: the only advantage would be that we might have the whole of Beethoven's symphonies in one night and still have time for supper." In addition Costa, again like every conductor of the time, was constantly retouching, rescoring and rewriting, and this appalled such pure musicians as Berlioz. Costa went about it wholesale, more so than even the liberal dictates of the day permitted. Berlioz heard him conduct operas by Mozart and Rossini, and could not believe his ears. "Mr. Costa has for a long time seen fit to give them lessons in orchestration, and I say with regret that Balfe has followed his example." Berlioz contemplated the score of *Don Giovanni,* in which Balfe, imitating Costa, had inserted three trombones, an ophicleide, a piccolo, a bass drum and cymbals. Berlioz was especially intrigued with the ophicleide. "The bovine snorts of the instrument disfigure the delicate instrumentation of Mozart as would mortar flung on a painting by Raphael." Costa liked the combination of drum, cymbal, trombones and ophicleide, and it was almost his trademark. "They are stuck in everywhere," said Berlioz.

But the man nevertheless had stature, and was the most important single influence on conducting in England until Hans Richter appeared. George Bernard Shaw in 1877 called Costa the one "who has secured the foremost place in the very thin ranks of our conductors. His place is indisputed." Shaw went on to say that Costa was the only one in England under whose baton orchestras displayed good training; that in his orchestras refinement and precision were cultivated. Shaw did not consider him one of the immortals. "That highest faculty of a conductor, which consists in the establishment of a magnetic influence under which an orchestra becomes as amenable to the baton as a pianoforte to the fingers, we do not give Sir Michael credit for. Instead, he has the common power of making himself obeyed, and is the aristocrat rather than the artist."

Costa was a prolific composer, but none of his music has remained in the repertory. Rossini, that noted gourmet, passed judgment on Costa's music in 1856. "Good old Costa has sent me an oratorio score and a Stilton cheese. The cheese was very fine."

Almost an exact contemporary of Costa was Charles Hallé, but where Costa had been the dominant figure in British conducting from the 1830s, the German-born Hallé did not settle in England until 1848, and did not found his monument—the Hallé Orchestra in Manchester—until 1857. He was an important musician, a friend of Chopin and Berlioz, one of the best and most honest pianists of the period. (He was the first pianist in history to play the cycle of the thirty-two Beethoven sonatas.) Hallé's entire life was that of a devout musician, and a phenomenally busy one. "During the greater part of the year," said Hermann Klein, "he used to spend his mornings practicing the piano, rehearsing his orchestra and planning tours; his afternoons giving recitals; his evenings conducting concerts; his nights sleeping in a hotel bed or a railway carriage." Eventually Hallé built the best orchestra in England, and Shaw was willing to stack the Manchester group against that of the great Hans Richter, the Wagner disciple who held forth in London before eventually taking over the very orchestra that Hallé had built.

Lesser figures included Carl Rosa, really more of an impresario and businessman, whose mission was to bring opera in English to the multitude; Luigi Arditi, whose mission was to bring opera in Italian to the multitude (and who lives today through his popular vocal waltz *Il Bacio*); August Manns, a German who settled in London and whose mission was to bring symphonic music to the multitude. Manns took over the popular concerts at the Crystal Palace and developed a fine orchestra. He was the progenitor of the Proms, and his low-priced concerts introduced good music to many who would otherwise never have heard a note in their life. Harold Bauer always maintained that Manns never received the recognition due him for his pioneer work in doing for symphony what Rosa and Arditi did for opera. George Henschel, composer, singer and pianist (and probably better in those three fields than as a conductor), also presented low-priced concerts for many years. He was the first conductor of the Boston Symphony, and his lack of expertise led to a critical gust that blew him from the scene.

But the conductor active in England who achieved the most popularity, the most publicity, who made the most unforgettable impact, was the French-born Louis Antoine Jullien, the first of the important virtuoso-showman kind of conductor, the originator of the line that was to lead to men like Leopold Stokowski and Leonard Bernstein. As a musical mentality, Jullien may not rate high in history, but as a force, as the first of the great popularizers, and as a showman unexcelled before or since, he occupies a unique place.

He was in England from 1841 to 1859, and it was there that his particular genius flowered. In his own country his career had not been particularly distinguished. He had been graduated from the Conservatoire as an indifferent student, and 1836 saw him at the Jardin Turc, where he conducted dance and popular music. There Jullien undoubtedly picked up ideas from Philippe Musard, who gave tremendously popular promenade concerts. "Napoléon Musard," or "The Great Musard," he was called, this untidy, unkempt little man, always dressed in black, with a pockmarked face. People came to watch him smash chairs, or fire pistols into the air, or throw away his baton. Berlioz had some comments to make in 1835. "At present we sit dumb under the triumph of Musard, who, puffed up by the success of his dancing-den concerts, looks upon himself as a superior Mozart. Mozart never composed anything like the *Pistol-Shot Quadrille*, consequently Mozart died of want." Musard died a very rich man.

Jullien plagiarized many of Musard's tricks and went him considerably better in dress. He was a dandy. George Augustus Sala, the British journalist and traveler, once found himself in a railroad compartment in Germany with "a magnificent Incarnation, all ringleted, oiled, scented, dress-coated, and watered-silk faced, braided, frogged, ringed, jeweled, patent-leathered, amber-headed sticked, and straw-coloured kid-gloved." The apparition, of course, was Jullien, the idol of England, and one can see why he made such an impact. In his biography of Jullien, Adam Carse makes the not inconsiderable claim that Musard in Paris, Jullien in England and the elder Strauss in Vienna "were the first conductors who by their own skill and personality were able to draw audiences to the concerts at which they were conducting quite independently of any other attractions that were offered or of any other influences that were in operation. . . . People did not go to see Habeneck or Costa conduct, although they would go to hear the music they conducted; but many went to see Musard or Jullien conduct, quite regardless of what music they heard."

In most respects Jullien had charlatan writ large over him, but he was a musician. Before the public from the age of six (when he could sing a repertoire of nearly a hundred French and Italian songs), he grew up to be a natural musician who could play all instruments. His promenade concerts in Paris became popular, but Jullien could not make much headway against Musard, and around 1840 he left Paris for London—one step ahead of the sheriff. He was not the first to give promenade concerts in the English capital. London already had a long tradition, and Vauxhall, Marylebone and Ranelagh gardens were equivalent to the Jardin Turc in Paris or the Augarten and Belvedere in Vienna. But from 1840 to 1860 the Jullien prom concerts offered something new—light music played by a precision orchestra in programs where the names of Mozart and Beethoven occasionally appeared. Goodness knows how Beethoven must have sounded under the gilded Jullien baton. As early as 1841 he had been reproached for too much tinkering with the Beethoven scores, and Punch printed an unforgettable couplet with one of the more delirious rhymes in the history of poetry:

ERIC SCHAAL COLLECTION

Louis Antoine Jullien, the greatest showman-conductor of the nineteenth century. At lower left is an etching made from his last photograph. The caricature at upper left appeared in *Le Charivari*. At lower right is a caricature by an unknown English artist. Underneath the drawing is a scribble: "Victory is proclaimed as the conqueror enters the city. Nov. 21, 1856." Off to the right of this drawing is a parenthetical remark that looks something like "Fee Gee Just," whatever that may mean.

ERIC SCHAAL COLLECTION

Why did you leave your stew-pans and meat-oven
To make a fricassee of the great Beeth-oven?

Jullien's first step was to take over the Concerts d'Été at Drury Lane. There he reveled with an orchestra of a hundred plus some two-score vocalists. One of the high spots there was a performance of the Beethoven *Pastorale,* with Jullien helping nature and Beethoven along by rattling a tin box of dried peas to imitate falling hailstones in the storm sequence. (When Jullien conducted Beethoven his reverence was such that he wore special white gloves and used a jeweled baton presented to him on a silver platter. This was only for Beethoven.) He gave low-priced concerts at Covent Garden, at Drury Lane and elsewhere. Now and then he went bankrupt but always managed to recoup. One resounding failure was a season of opera in English, for which Berlioz was brought over.

Most professional musicians could not stand this weasel in the musical henhouse. Jullien asked Joachim to appear as soloist at one of the concerts, and the famous violinist huffily refused. He said he did not care to associate himself with an "undisguised charlatan," and he also said, primly pulling up his skirts and stepping daintily away, "What relations can remain sacred to me in life if I cheapen my art by active association with a mountebank?" Little did Jullien care. He prospered. And as he became more secure his programs began shifting to a point where about half were devoted to classical music, including complete symphonies and concertos. He gave his audiences quite a show. He conducted from the middle of the orchestra, and his podium was fitted with a big gilded easy chair, in which he would rest between numbers. His music stand was made of gold, and his baton studded with precious jewels. The bigger the orchestra, the happier was Jullien. At special events in the Royal Surrey Gardens, or for his Congrès Musicale in Exeter Hall in 1849, he had an orchestra of between 300 and 400 players; and in 1856 he brought together an orchestra and chorus of 1,000 for popular oratorios. Exotic and outsized instruments were his special joy. His orchestra had a double bass that was almost fifteen feet high—the colossal octobass, brought from Paris in 1850. He had a monster drum, a double-bass saxophone, and such bastard instruments as the serpentcleide, bombardon and clavicor. At each of his concerts the main feature was some sort of monster quadrille, in which his own orchestra might be beefed up by as many as six full military bands. Behold Jullien disposing of these forces: Jullien with his big shock of black hair, his coat carelessly thrown open to reveal a dazzling white silk shirt, embroidered weskit, enormous embroidered wristbands turned over his cuffs! Behold him standing erect, cueing in his players with the imperious gesture of a Louis XIV summoning a courtier! Behold him adjusting his profile so that the audience should glory in his finest aspect! Behold him riding the thunders as the cannon went off, the chorus yelled, the audience squealed!

Many observers of the day felt that Jullien was something more than a mere entertainer. The fact that a decent percentage of good music found its way into his programs made a big impression. The middle class faithfully attended, and so did some of the lower classes. As the *Illustrated London News* said:

His earliest concerts were not what they afterwards became. They consisted almost entirely of showy and brilliant dance music, quadrilles, waltzes, polkas, etc., things calculated to catch the most uncultivated ear. But he began to mingle this familiar music with things of a higher order: movements (short at first) from the symphonies of Haydn, Mozart or Beethoven, and a few vocal pieces from the finest Italian or German operas. But these innovations, cautiously as they were made, were not immediately successful. They were often received by the denizens of the promenade not merely with impatient attention but with loud (and sometimes riotous) disapprobation. But still Jullien went on, gradually increasing the wholesome doses, till his treatment of the patient (the public) at length prevailed; and he has left behind a name which will live in our musical annals as the name of a distinguished man, who has done as much as ever has been done by any single individual in promoting the progress of his art in this country.

Having conquered England, Jullien looked for new worlds to conquer, and thus inevitably went to the New World, bringing along a nucleus of about two dozen of his players. He made his New York debut in 1853, and the American press went wild. Some reporters had a lot of fun, including the one who wrote about Jullien's much-publicized monster drum: "a wonderful *E pluribus unum,* made up of a vast number of all sorts of drums, including *snare* drums, *side* drums, *bass* drums, humdrums and doldrums." The report of the New

York *Courier and Enquirer* on the debut concert is a prime example of American journalistic style of the day:

. . . Exactly in the middle of the vast orchestra was a crimson platform edged with gold, and upon this was a music stand formed by a fantastic gilt figure supporting a desk, and behind the stand a carved arm chair decorated in white and gold, and tapestried crimson velvet, a sort of throne for the musical monarch. He steps forward, and we see those ambrosial whiskers and moustaches which Punch has immortalized; we gaze on that immaculate waistcoat, that transcendant shirt front, that inimitable cravat which will be read about hereafter; the monarch graciously and gratefully accepts the tumultuous homage of the assembled thousands. . . .

Naturally he had to give his monster quadrilles. Most talked-about was the *Fireman's Quadrille,* during which flames burst from the ceiling, the clang of fire bells was heard from outside, and three companies of firemen rushed in to extinguish the blaze. Through all this the orchestra was playing, women in the audience were screaming and ushers were running around reassuring the audience that this was all part of the show. The New York *Tribune* approved, in fine-chopped logic: "If he plays a quadrille, it is because a man of genius can put his genius into a quadrille as well as into a mass or symphony, and a good quadrille has more merit than a mediocre mass or symphony; or, in other words, such is the quality of genius, that the soul may shine in the narrowest limits, and show itself to be divine. We claim all this for M. Jullien." The divine Jullien did have competition in New York, that center of culture, and grandly rode over it, as witness the report of the *Sunday Dispatch*:

Yes, Jullien! The whole city is alive with Jullien! What a week we have had! What with a *Turnverein* Festival, a whole week's Temperance Convention, a Women's Rights Convention, a Women's Total Abstinence Society meeting, followed upon the heels of a Graham bread and gold water spree, Socialist and Fourierite meetings, Military and Firemen's visits, opening of theatres, gas-light exhibitions at the Crystal Palace—yet above all these men, women and Bloomers, these Maine Law Advocates, Social Disorganizers, Abolitionists, White and Black Niggers, politicians, Fourierites, Hypocrites, Grahamites, Men-women and Miss-

Nancy-men, Soldiers, Turners and Firemen, Jullien floated triumphantly on top.

Jullien was in America for nearly two years, touring as far South as New Orleans and Mobile. His impact on nearly everybody was hysterical. Toward the end of 1854 he returned to London and resumed his concerts. In 1860, the last year of his life, he went mad. Berlioz saw him toward the end and had to listen while Jullien excitedly explained his new, extraordinary discovery in acoustics. "Putting a finger to each ear," Berlioz wrote, "he listened to the dull sound thus produced in his head by the blood passing through the arteries, and firmly believed it was a colossal A produced by the globe revolving in space. Then whistling a D, or an E flat, or an F, he would exclaim enthusiastically: 'It is the A, the real A, the A of the spheres, the Diapason of eternity.'" Then Jullien saw God in a blue cloud. He conceived the idea of setting the Lord's Prayer to music. Jullien said it would provide him with a grand title page, as indeed it would have:

THE LORD'S PRAYER

Words by
JESUS CHRIST

Music by
JULLIEN

XIII

Franz Liszt

ON THE CONTINENT it was the Wagnerian school of conducting that was to be the dominant force for over fifty years: the school of *melos,* of freedom, of inspiration. Its first two great exponents were Franz Liszt and Hans von Bülow, though with Liszt it is often difficult to decide whether he took from Wagner or gave to Wagner. Both, probably: the two men were constantly stimulating each other, and Wagner often admitted how much he owed to his father-in-law. (Wagner, two years younger than Liszt, had married Liszt's daughter Cosima, who previously had been married to Bülow; and Wagner often called Liszt "Papa.") Liszt was one of the most astoundingly original musical minds in history, and without him a good deal of modern music would be inconceivable. Even the most important chords of the nineteenth century—the ones that open *Tristan und Isolde*—

had previously occurred, almost note for note, in Liszt's song, *Ich möchte hingehn,* composed in 1845, more than ten years before Wagner "composed" the *Tristan* opening. The chords in Liszt's song are:

Liszt, of course, started as a pianist and did not concentrate on conducting until 1848, just after retiring from the concert stage. At that time he was not an entire stranger to the baton. He had occasionally conducted, and Berlioz, who had heard him lead the Beethoven Fifth in 1845 at the Beethoven Festival in Bonn, was ecstatic, especially about the third movement, which Liszt "gave just as Beethoven wrote it—not cutting out the double basses at the beginning, as was done so long at the Paris Conservatory, and playing the finale with the repeat indicated by Beethoven—a repeat that is still audaciously left out even today at the concerts of the said Conservatory." (Berlioz raises an interesting point. Today all repeats are generally, and even slavishly, followed. But there is every indication that after 1820 the repeat signs were written in as a matter of convention. Very few romantic performers observed repeats; and the chances are that in most cases during the nineteenth century not even the composer expected repeats to be observed, leaving the matter entirely to the performer. Very little research has been done on this important subject.) After Liszt settled in Weimar, where he raised the flag of The Music of the Future, he found it necessary, as the leader of the movement, to direct many performances himself. He had misgivings. He knew that he was nowhere near as good a conductor as he was a pianist, and he diligently set about improving his baton technique. The chances are that he never developed into a good baton technician. But where his technique failed, his marvelous musical mind and instinct could see him through.

At Weimar he made the little town the center of contemporary music, attracting the most brilliant talent in Europe. It was Liszt's aim to foster "a rebirth of the art of music." Among his projects was the presentation of at least one new opera a year by a German composer. But the forces at Liszt's disposal were not imposing. He had a small opera house and an orchestra of thirty-seven players, a chorus of

twenty-three and a ballet of four. The orchestra he inherited was a
joke. Berlioz had heard it in 1843 and described it as "a lot of wretches
squalling out of tune and out of time." Liszt had to redo the entire
orchestra, which he did, bringing in the famous Joachim as concertmaster and Bernhard Cossmann, one of Germany's finest players, as
first cellist. Liszt promptly kept his promise of introducing new music:
Schumann, Berlioz, Weber, Smetana, Schubert, Raff. Early along he
became interested in Wagner, first staging *Tannhäuser* in 1849 and
giving the world premiere of *Lohengrin* on August 28, 1850. This
performance of *Lohengrin* was done with thirty-eight players; the
valiant band of thirty-seven had been augmented by a tuba. It must
have been a wretched and grossly inadequate performance, and in
later years Liszt admitted so.

Liszt had first met Wagner in 1840, in Paris, but not until 1848
did the two men become friendly. They got to know each other at
the famous evening spent with Schumann in Dresden. Wagner found
a fellow soul. When Liszt conducted *Tannhäuser* at Weimar, Wagner
was greatly impressed (and he was a merciless critic when it involved
his own music). He pointed out that Liszt's conducting, "though
mainly concerned with the musical rather than the dramatic side,
filled me for the first time with the flattering warmth of emotion
roused by the consciousness of being understood by another mind in
full sympathy with my own. . . . I saw Liszt conduct a rehearsal of
Tannhäuser and was astonished at finding my second self in his
achievement. What I had felt in composing the music, he felt in
performing it; what I wanted to express in writing it down, he proclaimed in making it sound."

Liszt continued at Weimar until 1858, when there was a demonstration—much of it directed against him—at the world premiere of
Peter Cornelius' *Barber of Bagdad*. Liszt thereupon resigned. In any
case, there was a new era at Weimar. When Liszt had arrived in 1848,
the Grand Duke Charles Frederick had enthusiastically supported
him. But the Duke died in 1853, and his wife, the Grand Duchess
Maria Pavlovna, died shortly thereafter. Their successor, the Grand
Duke Charles Alexander, was not interested in music, and was appalled at the expense of Liszt's musical establishment. He did ask
Liszt to stay on, but without much fervor. The poor reception of the
Cornelius opera brought matters to a head. Liszt did not leave Weimar. He stayed on, dropping everything but his piano teaching. To

Franz Liszt and his daughter Cosima. She was married to Hans von Bülow but eloped with Wagner and later became his wife. Liszt brought many imaginative concepts to the podium.

Liszt as a conductor favored great leeway in tempo. Wagner may have learned much from his father-in-law.

LITHOGRAPH BY C. HOFFMANN

Weimar came many of his greatest pupils. But Liszt's eleven-year tenure as a conductor meant very much to the musical development of Europe, and those years were generously summed up by Bülow: "The sight of a living conductor . . . undertaking and successfully carrying through the work of a radical rejuvenation of opera, so far as such a thing is possible under present political and social conditions, may perhaps wake up the rising generation."

As a conductor Liszt brought to the podium many of the effects of his piano playing. He was far less interested in strict beat and literal interpretation than in color, flexibility, drama, effect. He must have been an inspirational figure on the podium. Young Bülow, hearing him for the first time, was carried away: "Admirable! Astounding!" Liszt himself had a few words to say about the art of conducting. He demanded that the baton "must be handled with more care, suppleness and knowledge of effects of coloring, rhythm and expression than hitherto has been customary in many orchestras." To achieve a more expressive beat, Liszt discarded the standard triangular or rectangular motions and substituted a beat that outlined the rise and fall of a phrase. (Furtwängler was to do this many years later.) Liszt pointed out that he, as a composer himself, gave as many detailed instructions as possible in his own scores. But, again speaking as a composer, he above all people knew how inexact the printed note can be. "It would be illusory to believe that one can put down in black and white everything that gives a performance character and beauty. The secret lies in the talent and inspiration of the conductor and of the players." Liszt knew very well that contemporary musicians and critics attacked his "insufficiencies" as a conductor, and suggested that was because they did not realize what he was trying to do. Liszt proudly pointed out that he represented progress "in the style of the execution itself"; that he looked for other things than "an imperturbable beating of the time." In a letter to Richard Pohl he explained his aims:

In many cases even the rough, literal maintenance of the time and of each continuous bar | 1, 2, 3, 4 | 1, 2, 3, 4 | clashes with the sense and expression. There, as elsewhere, *the letter killeth the spirit,* a thing to which I never will subscribe, however specious in their hypocritical impartiality may be the attacks to which I am exposed. . . . The old habits and routines of usual conductors no longer suffice, and are even contrary to the dignity and the sublime liberty of the art. . . . Whatever esteem, therefore, I may profess for many of my colleagues, and however gladly I may recognize the good services they have rendered and continue to render to art, I do not think myself on that account obliged to follow their example in every particular—either in the choice of works, or in the manner of conceiving and conducting them. I think I have already said to you that the real task of a conductor, in my opinion, consists of making himself *ostensibly* quasi-useless. We are pilots and not mechanics. . . .

Like Wagner, Liszt insisted on a subtlety of accent that often involved a complete disregard of the bar line. "It is not enough to beat down the life-nerve of a beautiful symphonic performance." Thus he pleaded with conductors not to mark regular accents by coming down heavily at the bar lines (which insensitive conductors always have done and will continue to do). Instead he wanted music to be conducted in phrases rather than bars, with emphasis on the thematic elements, with free declamation. All of this is very Wagnerian, complete to the *melos;* but, as has been said, the chronology is inexact and it could very well be that Liszt was the originator, Wagner the follower. Certainly Liszt's interpretive habits were fixed long before Wagner's; and the freedom characteristic of his piano playing—which involved going across the bar line—must have influenced Wagner's ideas about phrasing.

On the podium Liszt was a lively figure. A showman like him would not be expected to discard his tricks when he took baton in hand. George Smart commented on Liszt's choreography: "Plenty of twisting of the person." The conservative faction was outraged, especially those who were constantly battling with everything Liszt represented. Joachim, who soon broke away from the Liszt camp and entered Brahms's, wrote in great distaste of Liszt's mannerisms: "At the conductor's desk Liszt makes a parade of moods of despair and the stirrings of contrition . . . and mingles them with the most sickly sentimentality and such a martyr-like air that one can hear the lies in every note and see them in every movement. . . . I have suddenly realized that he is a cunning contriver of effects who has miscalculated." Clara Schumann, who received these words and who hated Liszt, must have read them with deep contentment.

Naturally, Liszt's new ideas and new kind of baton technique kicked up a storm. Not trained to the baton, Liszt had trouble explaining his approach to an orchestra, especially one he had never conducted. Even good musicians came away with the notion that Liszt was inefficient. Ferdinand Hiller wrote some biting words about Liszt as a conductor after the 1853 Karlsruhe Festival:

The unanimous opinion was that he was not fit to wield the baton, at any rate in music on a large scale. It is not merely that in general he does not mark the beat (in the simplest sense of the term, the way established by the great masters), but rather that by his baroque animation he continually, and sometimes dangerously, causes the orchestra to vacillate. He does nothing but keep changing the baton from one hand to the other—sometimes, indeed, laying it down altogether—giving signals in the air with this or that hand, or on occasion with both, having previously told the orchestra "not to keep too strictly to the beat" (his own words at a rehearsal) . . . Is it any wonder that . . . such gross errors were made, as in the finale of the Ninth Symphony, when Liszt, apprehensive that a breakdown was imminent—and with good reason—had to stop the orchestra and start the movement again from the beginning.

But Hiller, a musician of the old school and a pedantic pianist and conductor, entirely missed the points that made Liszt so modern: his very instruction to the orchestra not to keep so strictly to the beat; his use of both hands for cues; the flexibility he was trying to achieve. Hiller would have been comfortable with strongly marked, regular accents, where Liszt was much more interested in phrasal rise and fall. Liszt did reply to Hiller's attack, saying that the new kind of music posed new problems, and that conductors were not oarsmen but steersmen. That was something a later age was to realize. It may be that Liszt never was able fully to carry out his intentions on the podium; he was more pianist than conductor. But he did point the way to the future. Had he started as a conductor, he would have been the greatest of his day. As it was, he brought to the baton new ideas, new expression and new rhythmic concepts, and with Wagner he stands as the founder of the new German style, and hence as one of the founders of modern conducting.

XIV

Hans von Bülow

LISZT AND WAGNER were primarily composers, creative men. Conducting had to take a secondary role in their careers. The same might be said of most conductors before them, the sole exception being Habeneck (and even he had some pretensions as a composer). But with the emergence of Hans von Bülow something new came on the scene—the re-creative rather than the creative musician, the man whose destiny it is to interpret the works of other men. Today that is the norm. The great instrumentalists and conductors of the twentieth century are seldom important composers.

Bülow, great pianist, great conductor, nervous little man (it is surprising how many conductors have been diminutive; is some sort of Freudian compensation at work?), terrible-tempered, acid of tongue, sharply intelligent, autocratic, was a mighty figure in German music for about three decades. Closely allied at first to the Wagner-Liszt circle, then moving into the Brahms camp without dropping Wagner, he was a dominant figure in all worlds of German music. He was the *Tonkünstler* exemplified—the man of ideals who lived for nothing but music, knew little but music, was governed by the sounds that entered his infallible ear, who was in addition dictatorial, omniscient, chauvinistic and omnipotent.

Music seized him at an early age, though he had to overcome the objections of his mother. He started as a pianist (an activity he kept up throughout his life; he was one of the major ones) and worked under Louis Plaidy at the Leipzig Conservatory. He was fifteen years old at the time, and nearly killed himself trying to drill his fingers into obedience. A letter to his mother in 1845 gives an idea:

With regard to my piano playing, you may set your mind at ease. *"Je travaille comme un nègre,"* I can truly say. Every morning I play trill exercises, simple and chromatic scales of all kinds, exercises for throwing the hands (for these I use a study of Moscheles, one of Steibelt's, and a two-part fugue of Bach's, which I play with octaves in both hands . . .), toccatas of Czerny, which Herr Plaidy gave me, and Moscheles' and Chopin's études, so that I don't find any others of Bertini, Cramer or Clementi necessary. I have enough to do with the Chopin études, which fully take the place of all these others, and I hope you will think I am doing right. I finished Field's A major Concerto yesterday; I have only studied the first movement—Herr Plaidy thinks the others are not worth much—and at my next lesson I shall begin Mendelssohn's D minor Concerto. Besides these I am studying by myself Bach's fugues, Klengel's canons, Oberon's *Zauberhorn,* Hummel's fantasias, a Beethoven sonata (the *Pastorale,* in D major), and am keeping up my old pieces, such as Chopin's *Tarantella* and nocturnes, Henselt's variations and *Frühlingslied* and Hummel's B minor Concerto.

Another portrait of the artist as a young man, and a not uncommon one in music. The talented boy met Liszt in 1849, and there was interest on both sides. Bülow, swept off his feet, developed a hero-worshiping crush on the older man. But a few years were to elapse before Liszt took him as a piano student. What happened to Bülow was that his mother packed him off to the University of Berlin, where he was supposed to study law. Instead, of course, he spent most of his time in music, playing the piano, writing criticism, allying himself with the avant-garde school of Liszt and Wagner. His piano studies were as intense as ever, and were marked by a good deal of self-criticism:

After frequently hearing Liszt, I have now made a special study of what was particularly defective in my piano playing, namely, a certain amateurish uncertainty, a certain angular want of freedom in conception, of which I must completely cure myself. In modern pieces especially I must cultivate more *abandon,* and when I have conquered the technical difficulties of a piece I must *let myself go* to a greater degree, according to how I feel at the moment.

This is an interesting and revelatory piece of auto-analysis from a young man of twenty. It marked the psychic struggle of his whole life. For he never really was able to let himself go. He was primarily an intellectual with an analytic mind, a geometrist rather than a poet, a man who would have liked to be loved but was never capable of loving. Conducting, like any other means of expression, is the man; and as a man Bülow burned with a cold fire that was reflected in his work. Both as pianist and conductor he was renowned for his "passionate intellectuality," and there were those who found his music-making cold. Probably it was; and one reason why it was so overburdened with unconvincing expressive devices was that Bülow, who never did have any warmth to him, found it necessary to counterfeit a warmth he did not feel.

Bülow heard Liszt conduct *Lohengrin* at Weimar in 1850 and that was the turning point. He dropped any pretense at studying law and went to Liszt, making his debut as a pianist in 1853. Even at that time he had an unprecedented knack of making enemies. Never one to hold his tart tongue, he soon had the reputation of being a radical in both music and politics, and such conservative old musicians as Moscheles were scandalized. "My unpopularity is unbounded," Bülow wrote home, quite accurately. "I rejoice in it to the utmost, because it is a sort of filial unpopularity to that of Liszt; and the saying, *'qu'ils me haïssent, pourvu qu'ils craignent,'* is applicable here." In 1857 he married Liszt's daughter, Cosima. Seven years later he was summoned to Munich by Wagner. Bülow dropped everything to rush to King Ludwig's court and help his idol. On his arrival, in May 1864, he loudly announced: *"Ich bin nur der Taktstock Wagners,"* or "I am only Wagner's baton." Bülow's great assignment in Munich was directed toward the world premiere of *Tristan und Isolde,* which he conducted on June 10, 1865. What Bülow did not know was that his wife and Wagner were having quite an affair, and that Wagner had had more reasons than one for summoning him to Munich. When a daughter, Isolde, was born in April 1865, poor Bülow thought it was his. Wagner and Cosima ran off together in 1869, and Bülow divorced Cosima the following year. Throughout all this Liszt maintained a discreet silence. Considering *his* sexual exploits, who was he to act the heavy father, especially as Cosima was an illegitimate child to begin with?

Bülow had worked under Wagner almost fifteen years before Munich. His first association with him had been in Zurich in 1850. Wagner had recommended his protégé, Karl Ritter, as musical di-

ERIC SCHAAL COLLECTION

Hans von Bülow, from photograph about 1865. That was the year he led the world premiere of *Tristan und Isolde*. In cartoon below, Bülow follows at a respectful distance behind Wagner and Cosima. The caption says: "In the Maximilianstrasse after the *Tristan und Isolde* rehearsal. Drawn from life 1864 by M. Schultze." Bülow in 1864 was still married to Cosima.

rector of the theatre. It did not work out. Ritter was too inexperienced, not to mention untalented, and Bülow came in to share the podium with him. Bülow acted as Wagner's right-hand man, conducting rehearsals and preparing soloists. It was fine, heady experience, and he picked up a great deal from Wagner, including Wagner's pathological anti-Semitism. "This winter," Bülow wrote, "I hope to finish my bread-earning studies and become a good all-round conductor, for which Wagner says I possess the most decided talent, by the keenness of my ear, my quick perception, rapid reading and finished playing." He flung himself into his work. "Rehearsal upon rehearsal, looking through and correcting the orchestral parts, in which the most flagrant disorder, the crassest carelessness, reigns; composing couplets and that kind of stuff for farces, so that I have hardly a moment to myself." Through all this he was aiming at big things. When it came to music, Bülow always had his eyes fixed on the highest goals. "A drawing-room musician I cannot and may not be without doing violence to myself."

Musicians began to talk about Bülow's memory. All musicians must have good memories, but Bülow's was extraordinary, and he automatically learned everything by heart. Thus when he made his debut with *Il Barbiere di Siviglia* in 1850, "I myself had the score in my head, was thoroughly sure and master of it." Bülow strongly believed that a musician had to have things by heart. "I think it is only when one has gone so far as to know every note, every nuance, the exact place and significance of any instrument . . . that one is fit to get it by heart, which one can only do when one does not have to look at the score any more." Years later, Richard Strauss was the recipient of one of Bülow's most famous aphorisms: "You must have the score in your head and not your head in the score."

Bülow lasted only a few months in Zurich. He was too idealistic, too uncompromising; his tongue was too sharp and his temper too nasty. Finally the leading soprano took offense. Either she or Bülow must go, she announced. It was not she who left. Leading sopranos are harder to replace than young conductors. Bülow was forced to resign. He landed a job in Saint Gallen, got a few performances under his belt, and wrote home: "Wagner is right in saying that I have a great talent for conducting." But conditions in Saint Gallen could scarcely have satisfied him. The orchestra was composed of merchants, lawyers, government officials and a smattering of professionals. Bülow did not stay there very long. But here too he learned a great deal about the ABC's of conducting. *"Ten hours* of daily rehearsal! I am perfectly ruined and going to the dogs!" That was the way one learned conducting in those days.

For many years after 1864 and his association with Wagner in Munich, Bülow toured as a pianist. He conducted here and there, but not until 1878 did he concentrate on the baton. That year he became conductor of the Court Theatre at Hannover, and two years later became conductor of the Duke of Meiningen's orchestra. Duke Georg II and his wife, Helene von Heldburg, were connoisseurs and were fabulously wealthy. Quite willing to put up with the autocratic whims of a martinet like Bülow, they were happy to put their orchestra at his disposal. And Bülow for once was ideally situated, for his mind was attuned to symphonic rather than operatic music, and symphonic music was what the Duke and Duchess wanted. Bülow's intellectual organization was much more abstract than dramatic. According to Weingartner, Bülow paid much more attention to the orchestra than to the singers when he was conducting opera, and gave no more attention to the stage than was necessary to correct musical errors. "He conducted an opera as if it were a symphonic work in which the singers' voices were merely instruments."

During those six years, from 1880 to 1885, Bülow presided over what many considered the best-drilled, most disciplined orchestra in the world. It was not a large group, numbering only forty-eight players, but it made an enormous impact, just as the mature Bülow made an equal impact on the podium. He invariably conducted from memory and insisted that his orchestra play from memory. The players could not always do that, but they did have a good part of the standard repertoire by heart. Bülow also insisted that his orchestra play standing up, and drilled it until it was a precision instrument. In addition he himself put on quite a show, lecturing to his audiences, remonstrating with them, indulging in such mannerisms as putting on a pair of black gloves—in all seriousness—to conduct the *Funeral March* of the *Eroica* Symphony, or putting the Beethoven Ninth twice on the same program. "Baptizing the infidels with a fire hose," Hanslick said of that double Ninth.

Toward the end of his tenure at Meiningen he took the twenty-five-year-old Strauss as his assistant. Strauss has written fondly of those Meiningen days—of the daily (nine to twelve) rehearsals; of

Bülow, about 1885, toward the end of his career. He was the undisputed czar of music throughout Germany.

Bülow's strenuous mannerisms on the podium were the joy of contemporary cartoonists.

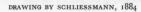

DRAWING BY SCHLIESSMANN, 1884

Bülow's moodiness, temper and autocracy; of advice that Bülow was constantly giving. "Learn to read the score of a Beethoven symphony *accurately*," he told Strauss, "and you will have found its interpretation." Strauss indicates that when Bülow was presiding over his orchestra nobody, not even His Royal Highness, dared interfere. There was the time Berlioz' *Harold in Italy* was being rehearsed,

when Duke Georg entered the theatre, followed by his adjutant, Herr von Kotze. Bülow immediately broke off and asked what were the Duke's wishes. The affable Duke only wanted to listen and asked what was being played. Berlioz' symphony, replied Bülow, but added that he was unable to play the work for the Duke because he had only just begun to rehearse it. The Duke replied: "Never mind. I'll just listen." Bülow: "I am very sorry, sir, the performance is not polished enough. I cannot play it for Your Highness." The Duke then said: "But Bülow, don't be funny. It does not matter how it is played. I shall be glad to listen." Bülow, bowing stiffly for the third time: "I am really sorry. At this stage we have reached with the symphony it would do at the most for Herr Kotze." On the stage the grinning orchestra; in the center Bülow, in impeccable court attitude; below them the Duke and the poor victim. It made a pretty picture.

Strauss tells another amusing story. Bülow learned that Brahms would be in the audience for a performance of his *Academic Festival* Overture and got the notion of playing the cymbals, while Strauss would bang the drums. But, writes Strauss:

It turned out that neither of us could count rests. During the rehearsal I lost count after the fourth bar and eventually helped myself by putting a full score on my stand. Bülow, on the other hand, whose attention constantly wandered from his part, which also consisted mainly of rests, invariably stopped after eight bars of steady counting and kept running to a trumpeter to ask: "To what letter have we got?" And then he would start afresh: "One, two, three, four." I do not think that a greater mess has ever been made of the percussion part than on the evening when the two conductors took a hand.

At Meiningen Bülow took up the cause of Brahms. He previously had been interested in Brahms's music and seems to have been the first pianist, aside from the composer, to play the D minor Concerto in public. Soon after settling in Meiningen, Bülow was visited by Brahms, who was bearing the manuscript of the Piano Concerto in B flat. The world premiere took place on October 27, 1881, Bülow conducting, Brahms at the piano. From that point, all of the dedication that Bülow had previously bestowed on Wagner was transferred to Brahms. He even arranged concert tours with the Meiningen Orchestra to make his friend's music better known, and those *Brahms-Abende* concerts did much to spread the new gospel. With Bülow there never were halfway measures. On the famous evening when he conducted the two performances of the Beethoven Ninth, Strauss and Alexander Ritter, the Lisztian, went backstage before the performance. Brahms was there. "You have come to hear the Ninth Symphony?" Bülow asked Strauss and Ritter. "Meet"—pointing to Brahms—"the composer of the Tenth." Brahms was embarrassed, Ritter furious.

In his way, Brahms could be as tactless as Bülow. Brahms conducted his Fourth Symphony in Frankfurt, just before the Meiningen Orchestra was due to arrive there with that very symphony. Bülow, who had had his heart set on conducting the Frankfurt premiere (he had shortly before conducted the world premiere at Meiningen), took Brahms's action as an insult. Even less touchy men might have felt the same. But Bülow, in one of his typical rages, resigned from the orchestra (to be succeeded by Fritz Steinbach, the famous Brahms interpreter; he was the composer's favorite and was greatly admired by such musicians as Arturo Toscanini and Fritz Busch).

Meiningen was Bülow's last permanent orchestral position, though he made many guest appearances all over Europe after 1885, including a much-publicized appearance with the Berlin Philharmonic during the 1891–92 season, the occasion of his fiftieth appearance with the orchestra. This concert achieved worldwide coverage. Bülow, who could be counted upon to make a speech almost every time he conducted, made an especially long one even for him, just before conducting the *Eroica* Symphony. "Ladies and gentlemen, once more I enjoy the privilege of using Section 27 of the Constitution and delivering an address to you . . ." He discussed Beethoven in general, then Beethoven and Napoleon in particular. He then turned from music to politics and derided "those words of insanity: *liberté, egalité, fraternité.*" Instead he offered as a substitute "cavalry, infantry, artillery." He dedicated this performance of the *Eroica* to "the brilliant star of Germany, the greatest man of his time, the Beethoven of politics—Prince Bismarck. *Er lebe hoch!"* The speech aroused consternation in the hall. Hisses were mingled with cheers. Bülow ended by taking out his handkerchief and wiping his shoes. Everybody in the audience knew what he meant. Kaiser Wilhelm had said, "If anybody doesn't like the way things are going in this country, let him shake the dust from his shoes." Bülow did exactly that. After his symbolic gesture he went off to Egypt, where he died in 1894.

Let us look at this man. He was diminutive, with a mandarin beard and burning, fanatical eyes. He was frail and sickly, nervous and high-strung, suffering from incessant headaches, always coming down with colds. At least five times he had what in those days was known as brain fever. He inspired fear in people. Brahms, who himself had a fearsomely sarcastic tongue, said of Bülow: "His praise smarts in the eyes like salt, so that the tears run"; and César Cui told him: "You don't shave, but you always have a razor in your mouth." His sarcasms made the rounds of Europe and America. He told one of Liszt's young ladies that she should be swept out of *Der Meister's* class not with a broom but with a broomstick. To another girl, who played Liszt's *Mazeppa*, the étude that describes the galloping of a horse, his compliment was that her only qualification for playing the piece was that she had the soul of a horse. He fought constantly with critics, and carried his fight to the audience, as in Vienna, where he was supposed to conduct the *Egmont* Overture. He came on stage and told the audience that since the critic of the *Fremdenblatt* had found fault with his previous performance of the *Egmont,* and as he would not like to wrong Beethoven again, he would instead conduct the Brahms *Academic Festival* Overture. To a tenor in *Lohengrin:* "You are not a knight of the swan [*Schwan*] but of the swine [*Schwein*]." To a man who came up to him in the street saying, "I'll bet you don't remember me," there was the curt answer: "You have won your bet." To a trombone player: "Your tone sounds like roast beef gravy running through a sewer." To a committee that gave him a laurel wreath: "I am not a vegetarian." From Bülow came the well-known aphorism: "A tenor is not a man but a disease." He was told of the venality of a music critic whose approval could be purchased through taking moderately priced lessons from him. "That's not too bad," Bülow said. "He charges such small fees you might almost call him incorruptible."

His part in the Wagner-Cosima triangle must have been traumatic, and might explain some of the pathologic tension and explosive temper of his later life. Certainly he must have picked up some of the gossip in Munich and elsewhere. And when the lovers eloped he—a man of such fierce pride—must have felt like the prize cuckold of all time. He concealed his hurt by constant work, and in 1882 he even remarried. Years later William Mason asked him about the touchy subject of his relations with Wagner after the elopement. Bülow tried to shrug it off. "What happened," Mason quotes him as saying, "was the most natural thing in the world. You know what a wonderful woman Cosima is—such intellect, such ambition, which she naturally inherits from her father. I was entirely too small a personality for her. She required a colossal genius like Wagner's, and he needed the sympathy and inspiration of an intellectual and artistic woman like Cosima. That they should have come together was inevitable." Sweet words, tempered by time; but it is hard to escape the notion that the wound never healed.

His mind was didactic, and so were his piano playing and conducting. To him music was a noble art, partaking of the divine, and had to be approached as such. Milo Benedict, a student in Berlin, wrote a description of Bülow that is amusing but that also presents the spirit of a Bülow concert. The conductor came out in short, rapid steps, "expanding his chest, which was well suited for the display of decorations." His air was lordly. "Everything was now serious. The people looked serious. The musicians on stage looked serious." Bülow's high, bald forehead and arched eyebrows "stood for intellectual austerity. He despised ease." Audiences were petrified. Musicians respected his knowledge, and more sensitive ones, such as Bruno Walter, respected even more what Walter called his "sublime artistic purity." Nobody ever disputed Bülow's musical integrity. But some found him lacking. Hiller described his Beethoven as "dull, dry, unfeeling, unimaginative"; and Hanslick, while hailing the precision of the Meiningen Orchestra, complained about the lack of anything resembling a sensuous quality.

Bülow was a musical chauvinist who responded only to German and Austrian music, and very little else was in his conducting repertoire. (His piano programs could be more catholic.) All other music was worthless, and in 1874 he threw Milan into an uproar by deriding Verdi and all Italian composers. He had been invited to the world premiere of the Verdi Requiem, and the newspapers quoted him as saying: "To fancy that *I* should go and compromise myself with a bunch of idiots who will flock with their long ears to St. Mark's!" It sounds like Bülow. (Later he changed his mind about the Requiem and apologized to Verdi.)

Two major conductors, and fine musical minds, have given detailed accounts of Bülow's conducting. Richard Strauss and Felix Weingartner came to rather different conclusions. Strauss says of Bülow that "the exactitude of his phrasing; his intellectual penetration, combined with almost pedantic observance of the score; his analysis of the phrase structure, and above all his understanding of the psychological content of Beethoven's symphonies and Wagner's preludes in particular, have been a shining example to me." Bülow's specialties were Beethoven and Wagner; and, says Strauss, "These works were performed with a clarity which to this day constitutes for me the zenith of perfection in the performance of orchestral music."

But Bülow, a child of Wagner and Liszt, must have indulged in a great deal of tempo modification, and even his idolator Strauss had to admit that in his own conducting he tried to achieve "a greater uniformity of tempo." In the Beethoven Seventh, for example, Bülow took the three repetitions of the scherzo faster each time, ending with a prestissimo. Such an effect, like many of the ones introduced by Wagner and Liszt, and followed by Bülow, was perfectly permissible by the standards that then prevailed. New winds, however, started blowing around the turn of the century, and twentieth-century ideas of interpretation started to come in. Strauss was bothered by some of Bülow's devices, and to Weingartner they were anathema. To Weingartner, musical sensationalism began with Bülow.

In his little brochure, *On Conducting,* Weingartner pays tribute to Bülow's skill and his ability to discipline an orchestra. After Bülow and Meiningen, Weingartner states, no orchestra could any longer afford to be sloppy. But Weingartner then proceeds to take Bülow apart. He objects to Bülow's pedagogic approach. He especially objects to Bülow's modification and exaggeration of tempo. As an example, Weingartner cites Bülow's performance of Beethoven's *Coriolanus* Overture, in which (swears Weingartner) Bülow started almost andante, increasing the speed to the fermata in the seventh bar, then going back to andante and accelerating the same way. In his last years, says Weingartner, Bülow's eccentricities were intolerable. His conducting was full of errors of taste, constant rubatos, shifts, misplaced emphases. What was worse, the great Bülow spawned a tribe of little Bülows who copied him in everything: "his nervous movements, his furious glances at the orchestra whenever anything disturbed him, his half-instinctive, half-demonstrative look around at some special nuance, and finally the nuances themselves."

But what Weingartner does not say is that the last years of Bülow's life certainly could not have represented him at anything near his best. His mind was giving way, and toward the end his conducting was a travesty. When Bülow conducted in Hamburg in 1887, the three regular conductors—Sucher, Field and Weingartner—had to take up positions in the wings to help the musicians with signs and cues, for Bülow, lost in his private world, never would turn his eyes to the players. Sometimes he was normal, sometimes he was in a deeply depressed state. He was committed to an asylum for a while, from which he wrote some pitiful words to his wife: "Hell, hell, with blue sky and golden sun, double hell. All by my fault—I know, I know." Surely Weingartner knew of Bülow's mental condition; there was no secret about it. The fact that he does not mention it in relation to Bülow's conducting does suggest personal bias. It can of course be conceded that Bülow's conducting could be eccentric, and that his interpretations could be exaggerated. But one wonders if his conducting was any more exaggerated than that of other musicians of his generation—than that of Liszt and Wagner, say. The earlier critics, far from condemning Bülow for waywardness, seemed to think that his faults if anything lay in an overabundance of intellect and an emotional frigidity. They thought that everything was too well organized. Nobody until the arrival of the twentieth century complained of Bülow's freedom with tempo. The conclusion seems inescapable. Weingartner was guilty of judging Bülow by a later set of standards, and that is an esthetic error. The fact is that Bülow conducted very much in the Wagner manner, but without the sensuous quality that Wagner brought to his interpretations. And it also is a fact that for many years Bülow was the most important conductor in Europe and the most powerful musical mind of his day.

· XV ·

The Wagner School
–Richter and Others

BÜLOW WAS THE FIRST to come out of the Wagner school of conducting. He was soon followed by many others. Wagner-trained conductors—with the exception of Arthur Nikisch; and he too had a heavy Wagnerian indoctrination as a young man—dominated the European scene in the last half of the nineteenth century. It was not that Europe lacked respected conductors. There was Otto Dessoff, in Vienna, Karlsruhe and Frankfurt: Dessoff, the great friend of Brahms who conducted the world premiere of the First Symphony in 1876, and who also was a choral specialist. There was the bearded, conservative Karl Reinecke, active in Leipzig for so many years. There was Ferdinand Löwe, a pillar in Vienna and Munich, who is best known to posterity for his "corrections" of the Bruckner scores. There was Max Fiedler of Hamburg and Berlin, who came to America to conduct the Boston Symphony for several years and who made several early recordings with the Berlin Philharmonic. Wilhelm Gericke of Vienna was another who had several years in Boston; he was a cold, precise disciplinarian. There was Johann Herbeck, the Schubert authority and one of the big guns of Vienna. There was Ferdinand Hiller of Cologne, he of the slow tempos, who held that virtuosity and personality had no place in conducting. There was the competent Josef Sucher of Leipzig, who so desperately wanted to be known as a great composer. Other names could be mentioned: Hans Pfitzner, Max von Schillings, Franz Schreker. All of these were fine, dedicated conductors. There even was Johannes Brahms himself, who could have been a great pianist or a great conductor but who settled for being a great composer. In his youth Brahms set his cap for the Hamburg Philharmonic, and the fact that he was passed over was one reason he settled in Vienna, where he took the position as conductor of the Singakademie in 1863. He kept it for a year. Eight years after that, he took over the New Philharmonic Society and conducted it for three seasons, presenting a full repertoire including much eighteenth-century music, in which he was an expert (and which he edited far less than any conductor of his time).

But none of these figures made the international impact created by the group coming out of the early days of Bayreuth—Hermann Levi, Felix Mottl, Anton Seidl and, especially, Hans Richter.

Richter, a Hungarian, had been hand-picked and trained by Wagner. The young man had come to Triebschen in 1866 at the age of twenty-three as Wagner's copyist and musical handyman. He was a big, blond, stolid giant, slow-moving and perhaps not very brilliant, but a natural musician who could play every instrument in the orchestra, several of them on a professional level. As a student he would pop up in the Vienna Conservatory Orchestra now playing trombone, now oboe or bassoon, filling in when trumpet or percussion was missing, sitting among the violins and holding his own, bowing the double bass. (He kept this up his entire life. The music critic of the London *Times* was invited to dinner by Richter. On approaching his house, strange noises were heard, and there was Richter practicing the double bassoon.) He also was an expert pianist and organist, and a singer good enough to take a solo role in a concert of the Vienna Conservatory Orchestra under the direction of the demanding Joseph Hellmesberger. After graduation, Richter became a horn player in the orchestra of the Court Opera. Wagner, always on the lookout for talent, especially hero-worshiping talent, did not make a mistake in selecting Richter. The young man was delirious with joy at being near the famous composer, "the greatest man of all time." Wagner, who expected no less in the way of adulation, made him a member of the family and was rewarded with doglike devotion. All through 1866 and 1867 Richter worked on the score of *Die Meistersinger*, which was to become one of his specialties.

When Bülow left Munich in 1869, Wagner saw to it that Richter was his replacement. But Richter's tenure there lasted only a few months. He resigned on the grounds that the forthcoming production of *Das Rheingold* could not do justice to Wagner. Everybody knew the story behind the story: that Richter, who was Wagner's creature, would not have resigned without the full approval of his master.

Ludwig II was furious at both of them. Franz Wüllner was brought in, and conducted not only *Rheingold* but also the world premiere of *Die Walküre* in 1870.

Richter and Wagner were never far apart. Although Richter secured a position for himself—the National Opera in Budapest, from 1871 to 1875—he was at Wagner's call and spent much of his time helping Wagner prepare the *Ring* score. Thus it was no surprise when it was Richter who conducted the entire *Ring des Nibelungen* at the first Bayreuth season in 1876. The following year he visited London with Wagner and made such a success that his career was henceforth divided between England and Vienna. In Vienna he was the conductor of the opera and the symphony concerts. In England he started the Richter Concerts in 1879, took over the Hallé Orchestra from 1900 to 1911, and directed the Birmingham Triennial Festival concerts. Naturally he was a regular conductor at Bayreuth until his retirement in 1911; and it was equally natural that he spend the remainder of his life in Bayreuth. It is interesting to note that his lifelong devotion to Wagner did not preclude interest in other music. No conductor in Vienna could ignore Brahms, and it was Richter who led the world premiere of the Second Symphony in 1877 and the Third in 1883. He also conducted the world premiere of the Bruckner Fourth Symphony in 1891, and the composer was so thrilled at the rehearsal that he gave the wealthy Richter an Austrian thaler. "Take this and drink my health with it in a mug of beer." Richter did indeed take it, and ever afterward wore the coin on his watch chain.

Few conductors of the day achieved such respect as the massive, dignified, heavily bearded Richter. But at the same time his deliberate qualities annoyed some musicians. It would seem that Richter, despite his natural gifts, was not abundantly blessed with sensitivity or imagination. Indeed, Wagner was not overjoyed with Richter's interpretation of the *Ring* of 1876. In Cosima Wagner's diaries—which, of course, reflect Wagner's views—there is an entry after the *Ring* to the effect that "Richter was not sure of a single tempo. . . . He sticks too close to his four-in-a-bar." And in 1878 Wagner wrote of being "horrified" that his conductor, Richter—"whom nevertheless I regard as the best I know"—often "could not maintain the right tempo even when it had been achieved, simply because he is incapable of understanding *why* it should be thus and not otherwise." Bülow found him ponderous, and in 1881 wrote to his daughter of "the

NEW YORK PUBLIC LIBRARY

Hans Richter, one of the most important conductors of the Wagner school. As a young man he worked closely with Wagner.

Richter's many activities are symbolized by the four arms. They are labeled Oper (Vienna Opera), Bayreuth, Philh. Konz. (Vienna Philharmonic), and London. Score, with sunburst, has Richard Wagner on cover.

beery complacency with which Herr Richter conducts *Die Meister-singer*." If Alexander Mackenzie is to be believed, Brahms ran out of his box during a Richter performance of the C minor Symphony, disturbed by the conductor's metronomic quality. Brahms later raised the roof about it.

In addition, Richter's repertoire was not very big. He said that there was no French music; showed very little interest in any development after Wagner and Brahms (with the sole exception of Elgar); disgustedly threw away the score of Delius' *Brigg Fair* with the comment, "This is no music"; was very uneasy when faced with a new score and botched up the world premiere of Elgar's *Dream of Geron-tius*. Sir Thomas Beecham, with typical exaggeration, was to go around saying that Richter could conduct only five works, no more. Definitely he was not a man with a light touch, and his Mozart was described as being as heavy as he himself was; and that would be a grievous weight.

And yet Hans Richter, heavy-handed or not, basically unimaginative as he might have been, square and unyielding in his tempos and rhythms, nevertheless had the power to stir audiences, to impress musicians and to be hailed by many knowledgeable observers as the best conductor of his time. In music that he knew and loved, Richter undoubtedly was an overwhelming force, conducting with bigness, security and a sort of cumulative propulsion, directing without frills, going straight to the heart of the matter with firm rhythm and massive strength.

Among his admirers was George Bernard Shaw, who was present at Richter's first performances in England in 1877. The orchestra, Shaw says, disliked Wagner very much, and very much liked Richter, who spoke their language. "He did not pose and gesticulate like a savage at a war dance." He was humble toward the music and thought more of it than of himself. This kind of humility lent dignity to the music, and the audience felt it. Later, when Richter had been invited to take over the Birmingham festivals, quite a tempest was kicked up. Many, including Sir Arthur Sullivan, clamored that the post should go to a native conductor. Shaw thought this preposterous. "Orchestras only need to be sworn at, and a German is consequently at an advantage with them, as English profanity, except in America, has not gone beyond a limited technology of perdition." Shaw was all out for Richter, whom he regarded as a conductor of genius, capable of "poetic creation in musical execution." The thing that impressed Shaw was Richter's instinct. "A conductor who takes the time from the metronome and gives it to the music is, for all conducting purposes, a public nuisance; a conductor who takes the time from the music and gives it to the band is, if he take and give it rightly, a good conductor. That is what Richter does." Shaw obviously had been reading up on his Wagner, *melos* and all.

In any case, Richter was insultingly superior to any conductor active in England at the time, and Shaw is very funny when he discusses the conditions that prevailed in the pre-Richter days. There was the Philharmonic directed by Sir William Cusins:

The usual thing is for Mr. Cusins, looking every inch a fine old English gentleman, to make astounding faces at the band, of which they are much too well bred to take the slightest notice. He is conscious that they are doing nothing right; and they are conscious that they are doing nothing wrong; and between the two one learns how it was that the Philharmonic so narrowly escaped coming to grief in Mr. Cusins' time, despite the rare degree of skill on both sides.

Shaw implies that British conductors got nothing but puffs and scrapes from the orchestra. Along came Richter, who illustrated the "power of the sustained tone."

Claude Debussy was no less impressed. He heard Richter in the early Bayreuth days ("At that time his hair and his beard were red-gold"), was bowled over, and saw no reason to change his mind when he again heard Richter some years later. To Debussy, Richter was the greatest of the Wagner conductors, and it was impossible to achieve greater perfection. "Now his hair has gone, but behind his gold spectacles his eyes still flash magnificently. They are the eyes of a prophet, and he is in fact a prophet. . . . If Richter looks like a prophet, when he conducts the orchestra he is Almighty God; and you may be sure that God Himself would have asked Richter for some hints before embarking on such an enterprise."

Debussy gives a picture of Richter in action. He used a small baton, and his left hand directed the performance of each player. "This left hand is undulating and diverse; its suppleness is unbelievable! Then, when it seems there is no possibility of attaining a greater wealth of sound, up go his two arms, and the whole orchestra leaps through the music with so furious an onset as to sweep the

SILHOUETTE BY DR. OTTO BÖHLER

Richter conducting a symphony by Anton Bruckner. The composer is shown in the bottom three sketches. The unsophisticated Bruckner once tipped Richter a thaler.

most stubborn indifference before it like a straw. Yet all this pantomime is unobtrusive, and never distracts the attention unpleasantly, or comes between the music and the audience."

All are agreed that Richter used very little physical motion. His tiny baton had a thick cork handle that he grasped firmly with the entire fist. His wrist was loose, backed by the elbow, and the swing of his baton had an imperious point. Seldom did he raise his arms above his shoulders. In the pit of the Vienna Opera House he sat on a comfortable wicker chair, beating clearly and directly. He and Gustav Mahler, his successor in Vienna, did not see eye to eye on music; the two men were too opposed, emotionally, intellectually and technically. Mahler, when he took over the Vienna Opera, complained that Richter—*Richter!*—had no idea about Wagnerian tempo. Reminded that Richter had prepared *Die Meistersinger* and the *Ring* under Wagner's own direction, and that presumably he therefore knew how the operas should go, Mahler merely said: "Maybe he knew the right tempos then. Since that time he has forgotten them." Richter, on the other hand, said that Mahler was too nervous and had no idea of the *Innigkeit* of the music.

Orchestral musicians invariably respected Richter, though he could be the kind they hate. Sir Adrian Boult got reports from old musicians who remembered Richter in his first London years as "a grumpy German, muttering in his beard, with a piercing eye that missed little. There seemed nothing about him that could endear him to anyone, and orchestras (a good deal tougher in those days) disliked him more and more." He never forgot a mistake; and if a player hit a wrong note the miscreant would be reminded of it next year, or five years thence, or whenever the piece was next played. "And remember, three bars after No. 32, E flat, not E natural." But one thing that made musicians admire him was the fact that when he himself made a mistake, he was the first to stop the orchestra and admit it, even to the audience. He knew his repertoire by heart (though he always had a score in front of him), was as solid as the pyramids, never lost his temper, never lectured, never changed his musical conceptions. He was a technician. Once he was asked what he thought of a new piece he was rehearsing. "I am not a critic. I conduct." His rhythm was utterly dependable. He would call rhythm the frame; the melody, the flesh. Never was there anything devious about Richter as man or interpreter. He was direct in everything he did. That included his beat, which one orchestral player said contained room enough for any number of notes. Richter never claimed any special gifts, presenting himself merely as a craftsman.

Orchestras would sit entranced waiting for the linguistic pearls that would fall through his beard. Richter and the English language were a legend. He would plead for "entoosum"; he would ask for the sound to "varnish" into the distance; he asked a railway clerk for two tickets, "vun vor me to come back und vun vor my vife not to come back." He looked at his orchestra, saw several vacant chairs, and announced: "I see several who is not here." Worried about the effects of liquor on one of his players, he took a friend into his confidence: "All the day he quaff und quaff, then when evening comes, he cannot."

Naturally a conductor of such fame would be invited to America. Henry Higginson wanted him for the Boston Symphony, and Richter all but signed the contract before balking. He did not look forward to the sea voyage, and he did not want to take up life in America, about which he had heard terrible things. In 1907 Oscar Hammerstein announced him for the Manhattan Opera House. Again Richter found excuses not to go.

But two great Wagnerians did. They were Anton Seidl, who settled in America, and Felix Mottl, whose American career was very short. Seidl studied in Leipzig and caught Richter's attention. Richter sent him off to Wagner, to whom he became secretary and assistant in 1872, making himself indispensable. "What would I do without my Seidl?" Wagner would ask. Later he conducted opera in Leipzig and Bremen before coming to the Metropolitan Opera in 1885. He was brought there to take over the German repertoire after the sudden death of Leopold Damrosch; and he introduced to America *Die Meistersinger*, *Tristan und Isolde*, *Das Rheingold*, *Siegfried* and *Götterdämmerung*. He knew this repertoire inside out. "If I forget a line," Jean de Reszke said, "I look at Seidl and read it on his lips." In 1891 he took over the New York Philharmonic. Apparently he was not too successful there; the feeling was that his forte was opera. "It may truthfully be said," James Huneker wrote, "that he conducted certain classic compositions for the first time in his career at the Philharmonic Society concerts. This is not surmise but fact." Seidl was, in addition, accused of tampering with the classics. The days when a conductor could get away with anything were drawing to a close. Seidl's chief accomplishment with the Philharmonic was the world premiere of Dvořák's *New World* Symphony. He died suddenly in 1898 at the age of forty-seven: a tremendous but not fully realized talent.

Mottl's experience in America was miserable. He came to the Metropolitan Opera in 1903 with high hopes, only to run into a situation that is still the norm there and, indeed, plagues conductors in most opera houses of the world—lack of rehearsal, lack of authority. After the first *Rheingold* he conducted he went to Heinrich Conried, the manager, complaining that a mezzo-soprano was singing a soprano part (one of the Rhine Maidens). "That will never do, Herr Director." Conried blandly turned to him. "You know that, my dear Mottl. I know that and so did the composer. But does the public know that?" Conried refused to make a change, and Mottl resigned himself to the inevitable. He was a very important conductor, but he made little impact on New York and never returned to America after 1904.

He had participated in the 1876 *Ring* cycle as stage conductor, being one of Wagner's three bright young men (Richter, Seidl, Mottl). Wagner, talking about his early Bayreuth conductors, said that Mottl's *Tristan* was by far the best, just as Richter was supreme in *Meistersinger*, and Levi in *Parsifal*. For years Mottl was a Bayreuth regular. Insiders thought him somewhat weak as a human being, too ready to compromise (his experience with Conried, and his capitulation, would bear this out), too anxious to please Cosima. After Wagner's death, the operation and artistic policy of Bayreuth devolved on Cosima, and she took it upon herself to tell the conductors how to conduct. She could not get very far with the immovable, imperturbable Richter, but she seemed to be able to bend Mottl to her will. The gossip was that she so befuddled him that the 1888 *Parsifal* he conducted was a mess. According to Weingartner, the amenable Mottl got *Parsifal* because Cosima simply had to get rid of Levi, a Jew and hence a corrupting influence. She succeeded. "They are very glad at Wahnfried to have got rid of Levi," Weingartner reported. "Now *Parsifal* for the first time will be in the right hands; it will be conducted Christianly and appear a new work." Weingartner wryly notes that Levi, who had studied the opera with Wagner, "was quite as much a Jew in 1882 as in 1888 [the year Mottl took over]." Under Mottl the tempos "were dragged and torn to bits. Every idea that had been hammered into orchestra and singers since

1882 was turned topsy-turvy." But Cosima was happy. "Mottl has the only correct tempos," she said, and declared in a speech that *Parsifal* was now sacred.

Mottl's major posts were Karlsruhe, where he built up one of Germany's best opera companies, and, from 1903 until his death in 1911, Munich. He also did a great deal of guest conducting and was as active in symphony as he was in opera. A heavy-set man, he was a conductor entirely without mannerism. To the critic of the Boston *Transcript* he represented "physical power. He settled himself sturdily into his place; he beamed professionally upon his audience and his orchestra; he moved his stick in sober and precise fashion; he made no effort to write the contour of the music upon the air with his left hand." He also is said to have favored slow tempos, and his conducting had thoroughness and authority. One of the few German conductors to take an interest in French music, he conducted a great deal of Berlioz, Franck and Chabrier, and also was one of the first Debussy conductors, presenting *Pelléas et Mélisande* in Munich.

Bruno Walter, who succeeded Mottl in Munich, always maintained that Mottl was one of the greatest conductors' of his period, one who was as imaginative in Mozart as he was in Wagner. "He had the instinct of the born musician in every branch of music." Shaw marveled at him. His "strictness, refinement and severe taste make the music go with the precision and elegance of a chronometer." Shaw in addition called him a forcible conductor, and "in spite of all that has been said about his slowness, a very fast conductor when the right tempo also happens to be fast. . . . His self-possession is completed instead of destroyed by excitement; and his speed and energy are those of a strong man on level ground, and not those of an ordinary man going downhill." To Shaw, Mottl's only possible rival was Richter. Mottl was a smooth, supple workman who had taste, simplicity, musical naturalness and also a perfect technique. "A look here, a nod there, the elevation or depression of a hand, were enough," wrote W. J. Henderson. "The men knew what he wanted."

In Munich there was a great deal of talk about Mottl's relations with singers. He liked women and, as one obituary notice delicately said (in reference to the fact that he left no disciples), Mottl cultivated women singers and not promising young conductors. His second marriage caused tongues to wag. He had been divorced from a singer named Henriette Standhartner and took up with a soprano named Sdenka Fassbender. She was the Isolde at his last performance. He

The first Bayreuth trinity: Hermann Levi (left), Felix Mottl (center) and Hans Richter. Levi, a Jew, was picked by Wagner for the premiere of *Parsifal*.

had a heart attack in the pit (Walter claimed that he was struck at the very moment Fassbender sang "Death-doomed head, death-doomed heart"). He turned white, gasped for breath, gave the concertmaster his baton, was helped to a room and then had another attack. He lived only for a few weeks and, literally on his deathbed, did the right thing by marrying his Sdenka.

Hermann Levi, the last of the first Bayreuth quadrumvirate, came in after Richter, Seidl and Mottl. Levi was a Jew whose father was a rabbi. He became a brilliant, masterful musician and a noble human being. His great days were at Munich from 1872 to 1896. A close friend of Brahms, he was at first an anti-Wagnerian. Then he swung to the Wagner faction, a move that Brahms could not understand. There was a big quarrel over the issue in 1875. Brahms refused to believe that a man could make such a radical change without some cynical motivation. He refused to speak to Levi, and after 1878 there was no contact between the two men.

Wagner admired Levi's conducting; and, in addition, Levi was court conductor in Munich, the capital of Ludwig II, whose money had helped build Bayreuth. There was no doubt in Wagner's mind that Levi was the ideal conductor for *Parsifal*, but he did not like the idea of his being a Jew. Wagner had the nerve to try to talk him into baptism, a suggestion that did not exactly enchant the son of a rabbi. Finally Wagner went so far as to show Levi an anonymous letter attacking him as a Jew, attacking Wagner for permitting Levi to conduct so Christian a work as *Parsifal*. This action did not sit well with Levi. He thought that Wagner should have kept the letter to himself. After brooding about it, Levi asked to be released from the opera. Wagner, however, never let his anti-Semitism interfere with his artistic judgment, and managed to patch things up.

Not as much has come down about Levi's conducting as one would like to know. He had the reputation of being highly sensitive, imaginative and introspective: an inspirational conductor, something like Mahler, who could take fire and leave earth far behind. And, like Mahler, he could be erratic. Such solid figures as Richter and Mottl were always dependable, but Levi, if not in the mood, might merely go through the motions. Bülow once lit into a performance of the Ninth Symphony that Levi conducted; but that was in 1897, after Levi had suffered a nervous breakdown and had left Munich; he was a dying man at the time. At his best, Levi probably was an incandescent conductor.

· XVI ·

America and Theodore Thomas

THE UNITED STATES, which never has had much of an operatic culture, is a nation of orchestras. Even though it is the youngest of the great countries of the world, it formed a permanent orchestra—the Philharmonic Society in New York—as early as 1842 (the year that also saw the creation of the Philharmonic in Vienna). There had been attempts to create American orchestras even before 1842. New Orleans, late in the eighteenth century, saw a great deal of musical activity (nobody has written a musical history of that city; the results might be surprising), and there were sporadic efforts in the Midwest at concentrated musical activity. In 1819 there was a Haydn Society in Cincinnati, and in 1838 a Musical Fund Society in Saint Louis. The Chicago Musical Society was founded in 1842 and a Philharmonic Society in 1850. Hans Balatka, a Moravian-born musician, was active in Chicago in the 1860s and conducted many concerts there. The predecessor of the Boston Symphony was the Harvard Musical Association, founded in 1865 and conducted by Carl Zerrahn. Many fine musicians came to the United States around the mid-century point; the various European revolutions sent them packing, and they settled all over the New World. As the country at that time had no musical schools of any importance, and little musical culture, those foreign musicians quickly made a valuable place for themselves. They provided the nucleus of many orchestras and conservatories, just as foreign-born settlers provided the nucleus of a knowledgeable and demanding audience. The chronology of the important American orchestras would take in the New York Philharmonic (1842), the New York Symphony (1878), the St. Louis Orchestra (1880), the Boston Symphony (1881), the Chicago Symphony (1891), the Pittsburgh Symphony (1896) and the Philadelphia Orchestra (1900).

In its early days the New York Philharmonic was held together by Ureli Hill, a New York-born violinist who had studied with Spohr. He conducted some concerts, as did Henry Christian Timm, Theodore Eisfeld, William Scharfenberg and Carl Bergmann. Each of those four was German-born, and each was a good musician. Good, but not great. The first of the great conductors active in America was the German-born Theodore Thomas, whose family came to New York from Hannover when he was ten years old. Thomas can thus legitimately be called an American product.

Even at that age the boy was a capable musician who added to the family income by playing the violin in theatres, saloons and dance bands. His father, a musician, had given him some training; otherwise Thomas was self-taught. While still in his teens he made a concert trip through the South, advertising himself as "Master T. T., the prodigy." He was his own manager, did his own advertising, would stand at the entrance to collect admissions, then rush backstage to get into concert dress and play. He could have turned into a trained monkey, but a musical impulse ran deep and pure in him. Thus he maintained his ideals while earning a living by taking whatever came his way, including a stint in Jullien's orchestra in 1853 (he was disgusted by Jullien's antics). From the beginning Thomas dedicated himself to the idea that good music was a necessity for the people, not a luxury. He also made up his mind that he was going to be the man to bring music to them.

Somebody had to do the job. Musical sophistication in America was all but nonexistent. Such pieces as *The Battle of Prague* or *The Skinner's Quickstep* were highly esteemed as the height of classical music. In 1852 the most notable attraction in New York was Master Marsh, The Infant Drummer. Master Marsh, said the throwaways, was four years old and could play on two drums at once. Boston around the same time was partial to *The Railroad Galop,* in which a miniature steam locomotive ran around the stage in a circle. There were no concert halls. In New York the early Philharmonic concerts took place in Apollo Hall, a ballroom on Broadway between Walker and Lispenard Streets. The hall had no chairs, and wooden benches were dragged in for the concerts. Those concerts were, in any event, little more than amateur affairs. The orchestra was generally incomplete, which meant that oboe or clarinet parts had to be played on the violin, or horn parts on the viola or cello.

At first there was no indication that Thomas would turn into a conductor. He seemed happy as an instrumentalist, playing in orchestras as a free-lance musician, or joining William Mason's group for chamber concerts. He got the conducting fever in 1860. According to the well-known story, a performance of *La Juive* was scheduled at the old Academy of Music and the conductor, Karl Anschütz, was suddenly taken ill. Thomas was asked to fill in, with no advance notice at all. As William Mason relates it, the orchestra was in place, the audience waiting, but there was no conductor. Thomas lived only two blocks away, and a delegation rushed to his apartment. Would he help? Thomas had never conducted an opera and did not know *La Juive*. But this was a big opportunity. He hurried over and led the performance. History does not relate how it turned out. One can guess, shuddering. Thomas ended up with Anschütz' job.

Two years later he conducted a symphony concert for the first time, and from that point permanently laid aside his violin. He created the Theodore Thomas Orchestra in 1864, giving "symphonic soirees" at Irving Hall; and he also started a series of outdoor summer concerts. For the most part his programs contained a great deal of the usual junk of the day, but Thomas invariably would sneak into them a Mozart symphony or a Beethoven overture. His public, and some critics, too, resented the specter of classical music at these soirees, and when Thomas programmed Mozart's *Sinfonia Concertante* for violin and viola, the *Tribune* critic put his foot down: "One would prefer death to the repetition of this production."

In 1867 Thomas was in Europe, listening and taking notes. In his autobiography he admits to having been influenced by the conducting of Karl Eckert, a man who specialized in opera and was active in Paris, Vienna, Karlsruhe and Berlin. On his return to New York, Thomas organized concerts at the Central Park Garden (not *in* the park), running them on the order of a German beer garden. At the beginning his orchestra consisted of forty players. Later it grew to almost sixty. Once a week he gave symphonic nights, and even in his light programs he managed to insert some heavier material. By 1870 he was exulting that he occasionally could get away with an entire symphony on a program, and by 1872 he was giving all-Wagner concerts. Later there were to be Brahms and Richard Strauss programs. It was not long before Thomas had the best orchestra in America and, indeed, one of the best in the world. At least, that is what Anton

Rubinstein said on his tour of America in 1871. Perhaps the great Russian pianist was being polite to the aborigines, but there is every evidence that Thomas had really created something exceptional. When Henry Mapleson brought an opera company from England to the United States in 1883, he had some experience with Thomas, and in his memoirs (published in 1888) had a few words to say:

While on the subject of American orchestras, I may add that their excellence is scarcely suspected by English amateurs. . . . The only English orchestra in which the conditions essential to a perfect ensemble are to be found is the Manchester orchestra conducted by Sir Charles Hallé. A larger and better orchestra than the excellent one of Sir Charles Hallé is that of M. Lamoureux.

Better even than the orchestra of M. Lamoureux is that of M. Colonne. But I have no hesitation in saying that M. Colonne's orchestra is surpassed in fineness and fullness of tone, as also in force and delicacy of expression, by the American orchestra of 150 [Mapleson exaggerates] players conducted by Mr. Theodore Thomas. The members of this orchestra are for the most part Germans, and the eminent conductor is himself, by race at least, a German. Putting aside, however, all questions of nationality, I simply say that the orchestra directed by Mr. Theodore Thomas is the best I am acquainted with.

Mapleson added another observation about American orchestras that he thought specially worthy of note:

Let me mention one remarkable peculiarity in connection with them. So penetrated are they with the spirit of equality that no one player in any orchestra is allowed to receive more than another; the first violin and the big drum are, in this respect, on precisely the same footing. In England we give so much to a first clarinet and something less to a second clarinet, and a leader [concertmaster] will always receive extra terms. In America one player is held to be, in a pecuniary point of view, as good as another.

Mapleson went into some detail about the Thomas orchestra, citing as the main reason for its excellence the fact that its personnel was permanent. Thomas was the first in America to guarantee a full year's employment to an orchestra. He kept his symphonic nights alive for ten years, and in all presided over 1,187 such events in addition to his concerts of lighter music. He also took the orchestra on tour, not disbanding it until 1888. Through the years, the orchestra was so constantly on the move that its itinerary became known as the Thomas Highway, reaching from New England to New Orleans and thence to the Pacific Coast. Concerts were given everywhere—in· parks, in railroad stations, in ballrooms, theatres, churches. Thomas preached music the way a traveling evangelist preaches religion.

In 1878 he took over the newly founded Cincinnati College of Music, returned to New York two years later to conduct the Philharmonic, got mixed up with the American Opera Company and went bankrupt. The American Opera Company was dedicated to the proposition that opera should be sung in English. As Thomas succinctly summed it up: "Good intentions, bad management, no money." But Thomas did not let bankruptcy slow him down, and was constantly on the move. Through the years until he organized the Chicago Symphony in 1891 he lent his presence to many cities, including Philadelphia, where he headed the Centennial Concerts in 1876. For the latter he commissioned a work, at a very high fee, from Wagner. It turned out to be the *Centennial March,* a piece of trash, and Thomas never forgave Wagner for the "insult."

New York was having a musical boom in the 1880s and '90s. Anton Seidl was giving symphonic concerts in Manhattan, Coney Island and the Brooklyn Academy of Music. Leopold Damrosch and his New York Symphony were competing with the Philharmonic. The Metropolitan Opera was giving Wagner with unforgettable casts, and great touring artists from Europe began to fill the new Carnegie Hall (built in 1891) to great acclaim. Perhaps Thomas felt that his work in New York was done. Perhaps he did not care to be overshadowed by Seidl and Damrosch. Perhaps he was still pursuing his dream. And he always was restless. Anyway, in 1890, Charles Norman Fay, a prominent Chicago businessman, asked Thomas: "Would you come to Chicago if we gave you a permanent orchestra?" Thomas jumped at the chance. "I would go to Hell if they gave me a permanent orchestra."

He moved to Chicago and conducted the first concert of the new orchestra on October 17, 1891. At the end of the first season he had worked up a fine orchestra and a tremendous deficit, and he also made every conceivable enemy that could be made. Patrons and the press started murmuring, and things came to a head during the World's Fair of 1892. Thomas was the musical director of the Fair, and found himself involved in an operetta kind of plot that all but cost him his job. The fuss was over pianos. Steinway (and some other Eastern manufacturers) did not exhibit. Pianists scheduled to play on the fairgrounds demanded a Steinway and were told that no piano not on exhibition could be played. But Paderewski had a Steinway smuggled in for his concert. Whereupon Thomas was put on the carpet and accused of taking bribes from Steinway. He was discharged as musical director but stayed on anyway. Thomas was a fighter. All hell broke loose. A strong faction, objecting to Thomas' autocratic behavior and uncompromising program policy with the Chicago Symphony, did its best to beat him back to New York. Most of the Chicago newspapers were anti-Thomas, and they called him terrible things. Newspapers could get away with almost anything in those days, when the libel laws were looser. Here is an example of the dainty prose style of the Chicago *Herald* of May 11, 1893:

Mr. Thomas should have been leader of a barrack band in a mountainous camp in North Germany.

He is a small despot by nature; a dull and self-opinionated man, who has had unbounded opportunity in the land of his adoption and has disappointed, year after year, the sanguine friends who have been sympathetically petitioned to hold him up. A constitutional want of generosity, an unscrupulous resistance to reasonable appeals from every quarter, and a thrift that has looked out for himself no matter who suffered in consequence . . . a pragmatic curmudgeon . . . totally without prestige . . . uncouth and rough-shod . . . with the hoof of a hussar he tried to ride down all that is opposed to his vanity, his selfishness and his caprices.

Papers all through America picked up the progress of the quarrel, and Thomas finally resigned from the Fair. But he did not leave the Chicago Symphony, even though he was offered the Boston Symphony by Higginson. Chicago newspapers kept constantly attacking him, and finally Thomas had enough, resigning in 1899. But the board refused to accept his resignation, and the newspapers then became *really* personal. It could not have been pleasant for Thomas to pick up the papers and, day after day, read the poisonous pieces directed against him. His last great act for Chicago was to head the

PHOTOGRAPH BY MAX PLATZ

Theodore Thomas, the first great conductor active in the United States, and one of the most important figures in the development of the country's orchestral culture. He is shown below in his last years, in Chicago.

CHICAGO SYMPHONY ORCHESTRA

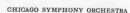

drive for the erection of Orchestra Hall. He bulldozed the city into building the auditorium, which cost $750,000 and was dedicated in 1904. Thomas died the following year, naming Frederick Stock as his successor. He had conducted only five concerts in the new hall.

In some respects the newspapers were right about Thomas. He *was* uncouth, he *was* autocratic, he *did* ride roughshod over everybody. But he also had a genuine nobility and a musical adventurousness far beyond that of any conductor active in America at the time. Nobody could swerve him from his mission. Why, he was asked, do you conduct Brahms when your audiences do not like the music? Down came the Thomas fist. "Then I will conduct him until they do!" He was not a tall man—he was only 5 feet, 5 inches tall, with a heroic head and torso, blue eyes, short legs—but he was burly and purposeful, and looked like a giant on stage. He scared orchestras. In middle age he began losing his hair and had a gray toupee made. He put it on, waited until his orchestra was seated, squared his shoulders and marched out. "Now laugh," he grimly said. "Once." He had none of the social graces and would brook no opposition. Fame and reputation of other musicians meant nothing to him. When Patti sang under his baton she wanted things her way; *she* was the prima donna, she said. Thomas corrected her. "Excuse me, madam. Here *I* am the prima donna." Thomas, said his old friend William Mason, was "born to command."

He was obsessed with efficiency and carried two of everything— two watches, two pencils, two keys to each lock. Two batons were always on his stand. He would arrive at railroad stations a half hour ahead of time. "Suppose my cab should break down? Suppose there should be a traffic jam?" One might have expected this tough, even flamboyant, person to have been a demonstrative conductor. The reverse was the case. Thomas' gestures were economical, and often he conducted only with his eyes. He may very well have been the least choreographic of the great conductors. Sidney Lanier, the poet-musician, effusively described Thomas in fine lisping prose:

To see Thomas lead is music itself. His baton is alive, full of grace, of symmetry; he maketh no gestures, he readeth his score almost without looking at it, he seeth everybody, heareth everything, warneth every man, encourageth every instrument, quietly, firmly, marvellously. Not the slightest shade of nonsense, not the faintest spark of affectation, not the minutest grain of effect is in him. He taketh the orchestra in his hand as if it were a pen, and writeth with it.

Thomas created a responsive and brilliant orchestra in Chicago. When Richard Strauss came there in 1902 to conduct *Also Sprach Zarathustra,* he was amazed at the virtuosity of the orchestra, and found that he did not need more than a single rehearsal. Of course, Thomas must have rehearsed the life out of the orchestra in *Zarathustra* prior to Strauss's arrival. He had the reputation of being a rigid drillmaster, and this time he outdid himself. But the point is that Strauss obviously agreed with Thomas' ideas about the score.

The importance of Theodore Thomas in the American scheme of things cannot be overestimated. More than any single person he raised the standards of orchestral playing and repertoire. Even a partial list of music he introduced to America is tremendous and imposing: two of the Bach suites; several major Beethoven works; Berlioz' *Harold in Italy;* Brahms's Second and Third Symphonies; Bruckner's Fourth and Seventh; a great deal of music by American composers; pieces by Dukas, Duparc, Dohnányi; a great deal of Dvořák, Liszt, Tchaikovsky and Mozart; pieces by Saint-Saëns, Goldmark and Rubinstein; the Sibelius Second Symphony and *En Saga;* Strauss's *Till Eulenspiegel, Don Quixote, Ein Heldenleben* and *Macbeth;* a great deal of Wagner in concert form. The man was protean and possessed of a high order of discrimination. He had daring, imagination and, above all, determination: a will that could not be bent, much less broken. It was he who, through his tours with the Theodore Thomas Orchestra, brought the sound of symphonic music for the first time to a large part of the United States. Pioneer, educator, organizer, scrapper, Theodore Thomas was in addition a brilliant and far-seeing conductor. Certainly his programs were, for their day, consistently far more interesting and exciting than any others to be found in their time (including Europe). And once he started, he never let down. He told George P. Upton: "I have been swinging the baton for fifteen years, and I do not see that people are any further ahead than when I started, but"—fist banging on the table—"I am going to keep on if it takes another fifteen years." Thomas did keep on, and lived to see the emergence of a great musical culture in his country. A substantial part of it was all his work.

· XVII ·

The Big Three in France

AFTER HABENECK, the three most important French conductors of the nineteenth century were Jules Pasdeloup, Édouard Colonne and Charles Lamoureux. Indeed, they were the *only* three French conductors of the time who made any great impression. Pasdeloup was especially important because he introduced so much new music to France. The curious thing was that he was not particularly interested in French music, though he did conduct the premieres of some important French compositions. His real love was the Austro-German school, especially Haydn, Mozart, Beethoven, Schumann and Wagner.

Like nearly all French conductors, he was a Conservatoire product (piano and composition), and in 1851 he founded the Société des Jeunes Artistes du Conservatoire, conducting its first concert on February 20. It is said that he turned to conducting because he had failed utterly as a composer. His orchestra was recruited from students at the Conservatoire, and Pasdeloup, apparently an old-fashioned type, led it with a violin bow. Later, with the creation of his Concerts Populaires at the Cirque d'Hiver in 1851, Pasdeloup headed a more professional group. It remained in existence until 1884, at which time it quietly expired with hardly anybody taking notice. Colonne and Lamoureux had by that time taken over the French orchestral scene. Pasdeloup moved to Monte Carlo and introduced his Concerts Populaires there. Then he returned to Paris in 1886 and attempted to revive his old series, but died a year later, without making much headway.

He was important, but he did not have the respect of the musical community. The fact was that he was not a very good conductor. He ruined Franck's *Symphonic Variations* by his inability to conduct the last section, and his obvious deficiencies caused a public scandal.

Bizet shuddered when he had to come into contact with him: "Pasdeloup is rehearsing a symphony of mine. What a dreary musician!" Nor did the composer Ernest Reyer have much more respect. "How well Pasdeloup is led by his orchestra," Reyer sarcastically observed. It was said in Paris that Reyer was the only man who could outyell Pasdeloup, who had a violent tongue and whose method of handling composers was: "If you think you can do any better, come take my place and I'll take yours." He tried that technique on Reyer, and nobody present ever forgot the shouting match that ensued. In 1860 Pasdeloup conducted the A minor Symphony by Saint-Saëns, and the composer thanked him. Pasdeloup's gracious reply was characteristic: "I only played it because it pleased me, and certainly not because I wanted to please you. I don't want your thanks." No wonder he had few friends. But he did pioneer work in introducing Schumann and, especially, Wagner to Paris. Pasdeloup was the first of the French Wagnerians.

Colonne, who had started his professional career as a player in Pasdeloup's orchestra, had much more talent. He was a violinist. It is surprising how many French conductors came up as string players, just as the majority of German conductors started as pianists. (In addition to Habeneck, Colonne and Lamoureux, one thinks of André Caplet, Walther Straram, Pierre Monteux and Charles Munch.) Colonne did a good deal of chamber music, in addition to playing in orchestras, before dropping everything in favor of the baton. In his early days he had a taste of conducting in the United States. Colonel James Fisk had formed an opéra-bouffe company in New York, and brought Colonne over as concertmaster. The enterprise did not flourish, but Colonne remained in New York as conductor of the orchestra in Niblo's Garden. He returned to Paris, established the Concerts du Grand Hôtel in 1871 and the Concert National in 1873. At that time he was little more than a beginner, learning as he went along, and some of the composers whose music he programmed had no cause to be grateful. He conducted the premiere of Franck's *Rédemption* in 1873 at his very first concert with the National; and Vincent d'Indy, who was in charge of the chorus, raged against the ruination of Franck's score:

The orchestra was execrable; it was only with difficulty that one could pick up the accompaniment in the vocal parts—if, indeed, one could get as far as that! But that was the fault of the conductor, who is totally inexperienced.

Colonne's life work came with the formation in 1874 of the Concerts du Châtelet (later named the Association Artistique des Concerts Colonne). Immediately he started competing with Pasdeloup, and, unlike the older conductor, went wholesale into French music of the new school—Massenet, Lalo, Dubois, some Franck (he did not understand or like Franck's music), Saint-Saëns and the others. Later he gave Berlioz concerts, and those put him on the map. From 1891 to 1893 he also conducted at the Opéra, where he led the first performance of *Die Walküre* in France. He left the opera house because the work was too hard. In addition to the Concerts Colonne, he organized a supplementary series at the Nouveau Théâtre, and made appearances as guest conductor throughout Europe and the United States. These he kept up until 1910, the year of his death.

Musicians felt that Colonne was far from being an expert technician. Pierre Monteux, who had many chances of seeing him in action, called Colonne a disagreeable person and an excellent musician, "but I could not admire the mechanics of his conducting; his arm was heavy, lacking the natural flexibility of the born conductor to convey every phase of the music to the ensemble. He had no facility with his arms and hands." At the same time, however, musicians agreed that Colonne had fire and temperament. Philip Hale, the eminent Ameriman music critic, once compared the two finest French conductors of the day. "As a student in Paris I heard the concerts led by Colonne and Lamoureux. Lamoureux' performances had greater finish; there was a finer sense of proportion in minute details; but they usually left the hearer cold. Colonne stirred the blood. When Saint-Saëns was asked which of the two he preferred, he answered: 'Both. Lamoureux is more precise; he is colder. Colonne is more elastic, more inspired.' "

Monteux did not tell tales out of school in calling Colonne a disagreeable person. There are plenty of attesting stories. Colonne had absolute power and his orchestra was quite literally his: he (like Lamoureux) managed his own concerts, engaged and paid the musicians and took the financial risks. Naturally, under those circumstances, he had the power to hold unlimited rehearsals. He would start at 9 A.M. and about noon would say: "Once more from the beginning, please." The work in question might be the *Damnation de Faust*,

Above, left: Édouard Colonne, the founder of the famous orchestra that for many years bore his name.

Above, right: Charles Lamoureux, one of the Big Three in France in the last part of the nineteenth century.

Jules Pasdeloup was the first important French conductor to emerge after the brilliant Habeneck and Berlioz era. ERIC SCHAAL COLLECTION

or something as grievously long. If one of the musicians grew restive, Colonne would pierce the man with a look and say: "Well, it seems you don't like music." The player would suddenly conceive a great love for music.

Lamoureux was the real technician of the three, and his orchestra displayed a clarity and precision unknown in France at that time. After a career as violinist in various orchestras, he formed the Société de l'Harmonie Sacrée in 1873, conducted the *St. Matthew Passion*, Handel's *Judas Maccabaeus* and *Messiah* and other large-scale choral works. These established him as an important conductor, and he was engaged by the Opéra-Comique, and then by the Opéra. His Concerts Lamoureux started in 1881, and the programs were avant-garde. Lamoureux not only succeeded Pasdeloup as the head of the Wagnerian movement in France (he conducted the Paris premiere of *Lohengrin* in 1887) but also was an early Straussian in addition to promoting the new French school.

He had more showmanship than Pasdeloup or Colonne. He even went one step further than Colonne as a conductor-impresario. Where the latter had engaged the players, Lamoureux not only did that but in addition supplied nearly all of the instruments. On his personal staff was a luthier to see that all instruments were in good shape. Before each concert, men in blue blouses would come out to inspect and polish the instruments, which were resting on chairs awaiting the musicians. At the end of the concert the blouses would reappear to remove the instruments and the music.

A fanatic about intonation, Lamoureux would have every string player come to his room and tune from his own fork. Pablo Casals tells the story of a player, one Brenoteau, who was called down by Lamoureux during a rehearsal for being out of tune. Brenoteau insisted he was not out of tune. "Well," said Lamoureux, "I'll tell you a story of what happened to me, when I went to see a sick friend in a miserable little room. Coming in I said, 'What a stink! How can you live here?' 'I can't smell anything,' said he. Brenoteau, do you know why my friend could not smell? Because he was used to it."

Carl Flesch, who played in the Lamoureux Orchestra, referred to him as "our almighty ruler . . . a thick-set, stout, energetic and hot-tempered gentleman." Flesch, who was to spend a great part of his life as an orchestral violinist, just did not like conductors as a species, and of Lamoureux he had a lower opinion than of most. Perhaps

Flesch was bothered by Lamoureux' rudeness, "a completely uncontrolled and unvarying lack of consideration." Insults followed in quick succession "until they ended in a choleric outburst of fury in which grown-up men, great artists among them, were treated like schoolboys." Threatened more than once, Lamoureux went around fearing reprisals, and at one rehearsal startled the orchestra by pulling out a gun and waving it around. "If I'm attacked, they'll find me ready!" he shouted.

On Lamoureux' death in 1899 he was succeeded by his son-in-law, Camille Chevillard, who became one of the first French conductors to investigate Russian music. Chevillard also conducted the world premiere of Debussy's *La Mer,* and carried on the family tradition by being loud-mouthed and arrogant. Désiré Inghelbrecht, the fine French conductor, knew Chevillard well and suggests that behind the fierce façade was a kind and even timid man who wore a bowler hat down low on his brow in order to conceal his failing eyesight and peering look. "A benevolent bully," says Inghelbrecht. Which may have been true; but every indication is that Chevillard was not a very accomplished conductor. His insecurity demonstrated itself in unfamiliar music. Debussy had no faith in him at all, and complained to Inghelbrecht that Chevillard was insensitive and had too many limitations. According to Debussy, Gabriel Pierné, the successor to the Concerts Colonne after the founder's death (Pierné held the post from 1910 to his retirement in 1932), was a much finer conductor. It seems that Chevillard was frightened at the complexities of *La Mer* and suggested that Debussy himself conduct it. Debussy was not a good conductor ("When I have to conduct I am sick before, during and after") and refused. At rehearsals of *La Mer,* Debussy would tell Chevillard: "I want this to be a little more deliberate, a sort of flowing." Chevillard did not understand this at all. "Slower?" he would ask. "No, more flowing . . ." "Faster?" "No, no . . . more flowing." Chevillard would turn to the orchestra. "Gentlemen, let's start again," and would repeat the passage without the slightest change.

· XVIII ·

Arthur Nikisch

MUSICALLY SPEAKING, one of the more significant events in history took place in 1877. Thomas Alva Edison invented the phonograph. At first he had no idea of its worth as a medium for preserving performance and performance practice. Had he been history-conscious, or even musical (which he was not; Edison's musical taste ran toward *Swanee River* or *Ma Curly Headed Babby*), he might have made an effort to preserve and even duplicate the cylinders made for him around 1890 by Josef Hofmann and Hans von Bülow, the first two important musicians in history to record. Edison machines were even brought into the new Carnegie Hall in 1891 and sections of Bülow conducting the *Eroica* Symphony were made—in stereo! Four machines were placed in different locations in the hall. And Lionel Mapleson had a cylinder machine backstage at the Metropolitan Opera from 1901 to 1903. He recorded sections of actual performances, and many of those cylinders have been preserved. By 1900 the flat disc, invented by Emile Berliner, was in general use, and suddenly the notion of making commercial recordings hit various entrepreneurs, Edison among them.

Most of the important early records are vocal, though pianists started recording around 1900 (Alfred Grünfeld of Vienna appears to have been the first). Violinists came on the scene around 1905 with Joachim and Sarasate, to be followed shortly afterwards by Ysaye, Kreisler and others. Orchestral recordings posed more problems and came a little later. A soloist could operate directly into the recording horn but an orchestra could not. The spread of the horn could not accommodate many players. Thus, before electrical recordings in 1925, most orchestral discs were played by groups numbering some twenty players (in the early days) to forty or so. Colonne made a group of recordings as early as 1907. Weingartner and Beecham began making records around 1910, but not until 1913 was the first complete symphony—the Beethoven Fifth—put on records. This was in Germany, and was followed, in February of 1914, by Nikisch and the Berlin Philharmonic in another performance of the Beethoven Fifth. Modest Altschuler and the Russian Symphony Orchestra were in the American catalogues by 1911; Ansermet and the Ballets Russes Orchestra in 1916; and then things really got under way. Stock and the Chicago Symphony; Muck and Boston; Stransky and the New York Philharmonic; Stokowski and Philadelphia; Bodanzky and the New Symphony Orchestra—all were in the American catalogues by 1920. In Europe pre-1920 conductors who made records included Coates, Pitt and Goossens. The period from 1920 to 1925 saw all of the great ones: Toscanini, Hertz, Wood, Harty, Mengelberg, Strauss, Max Fiedler.

Around 1923 there was a great outcry, sparked by the newly started *Gramophone* magazine in London, about mutilation of great music. There had been a sadly cut *Ring* cycle, abridged recordings of Dvořák's *New World* and the Beethoven Seventh, but the thing that really triggered the controversy was Sir Henry Wood's recording of the *Eroica*. Such a fuss was raised that the record companies actually took heed, with such results as a complete Brahms First by Weingartner, a Beethoven Fourth conducted by Landon Ronald, and a complete Berlioz *Fantastique* led by the Pasdeloup Orchestra under Rhené-Baton. In Germany, around 1924, Oskar Fried and the Berlin Philharmonic were responsible for an uncut Mahler Second Symphony on twenty-two sides. The acoustic catalogues are much richer in symphonic recordings than is generally realized.

But they were wiped off the map by electrical recordings. There had been experiments along that line. In 1920 engineers hung a microphone in Westminster Abbey during the Unknown Soldier ceremonies. This seems to have been the first electrical recording ever sold commercially, though it did not appear on a commercial label, being sold by the Dean of Westminster. The system actually used was developed in the United States by Bell Telephone Laboratories, which was experimenting with sound over long-line circuits, looking for a cyclic range that the telephone could handle. The story is too long and too complicated to go into here, but the first commercial electric record to be distributed by a record company came out toward the end of March 1925 on the American Columbia label. It was sung by the Associated Glee Clubs and contained *John Peel* and *Adeste Fidelis*. By the end of 1925 nearly all record companies everywhere (the major holdout was Edison) had adopted the electrical process and were recording everything in sight.

And long before sound on film—indeed, just before World War I— at least one film company was getting into the musical act. The Messter Film Company of Berlin got the idea of filming conductors. There were Weingartner in the *Egmont* Overture, Ernst von Schuch in the *Freischütz* Overture, Oskar Fried in the complete Berlioz *Fantastique*. "The purpose," explained Messter, "is to have these films reproduced before living orchestras, who follow the movements of the baton on the living screen." Weingartner came forth with an enthusiastic testimonial. "I consider that this discovery represents a new epoch, particularly as it is far removed from anything automatic in effect. The will of a great conductor can be exerted upon a living orchestra in far distant times." What, one wonders, has happened to those films?

It seems fitting that the earliest-born of the great conductors to record was Arthur Nikisch, the idol of his day, the conductor who was to his generation what Toscanini and Furtwängler were to the period after World War I. When we hear the old Nikisch recordings, and he made quite a few, we are listening to the work of a man born in 1855. (André Messager, born two years before Nikisch, also recorded; but Messager, an able operatic conductor, was not one of the great ones and lives today only by his charming stage works.) And when we listen to the Nikisch recordings we also are listening to the work of a man who achieved the respect and the admiration of virtually every musician who ever came into contact with him. Unlike so many great conductors, Nikisch was easygoing and understanding, and he had no enemies. Not an especially learned man— Carl Flesch called him "intellectually primitive"—he read nothing, cared only for music, cards, women and company. Nevertheless he was a good practical psychologist. His years as a violinist in many orchestras had given him an insight into the mental workings of orchestral players, and he automatically got on their right side. Orchestras loved him and would do anything for him. Nobody ever saw him lose his temper. His politeness never failed him, and his harshest words to an orchestra were "Excuse me, gentlemen, but . . ."

BOSTON SYMPHONY ORCHESTRA

The young Arthur Nikisch, perhaps the most celebrated conductor of his generation. He had the reputation of being a mesmerist who could hypnotize any
orchestra.

Silhouette of Nikisch, in dress uniform, complete
with high collar and enormous cuffs. Otherwise he
had few mannerisms. His conducting was quiet and
restrained.

or "Will you kindly . . ." The first time Lotte Lehmann sang under his baton, as Freia in *Das Rheingold,* she was nervous and let out a shriek. Nikisch called her to the footlights. "You're a beginner, I hear. But you musn't be so terribly frightened. Just take a good look at me. Do I look as bad as all that? Well, then, let's try again."

Fritz Busch at one time played in the Colonne Orchestra and Nikisch came as a guest conductor. At the first rehearsal, wrote Busch, he strode forth and beamed to the horns and winds on his way to the podium "with such charm that when he stepped up on the conductor's rostrum, the whole orchestra was already on its feet and had broken out into enthusiastic applause." Nikisch took his time. He removed his kid gloves. He said that it was the dream of his life to conduct this famous orchestra. (He said this to all orchestras.) Suddenly his eye lit on an old viola player. "Schulze, what are *you* doing here? I had no idea you had landed in this beautiful city. Do you remember how we played the *Bergsymphonie* under Liszt at Magdeburg?" Schulze indeed remembered, and immediately resolved that with *this* conductor he would use the whole length of his bow instead of the half he gave other conductors. By this time the orchestra would have died for Nikisch. Busch ended up calling him "the born guest conductor, an improviser of genius."

And in 1905 a member of the London Symphony Orchestra described the impact that Nikisch could make on musicians. The orchestra was in the midst of preparations for a festival and had been working nine hours a day. On this particular evening, it had had a morning rehearsal, an afternoon concert, and was scheduled for the first Nikisch rehearsal at seven. Tchaikovsky's Fifth Symphony (a Nikisch specialty) was the work, and the men were tired and sullen. But: "Before we had been playing five minutes we were deeply interested and, later, when we came to the big fortissimos we not only played like fiends but forgot we were tired." At the end of the first movement the orchestra rose and yelled its appreciation. "The weird part of it all was that we played the symphony through—with scarcely a word of direction from Herr Nikisch—quite differently from our several previous performances of the same work. He simply *looked* at us, often scarcely moving his baton, and we played as those possessed."

For many years Nikisch pondered the kind of men who played for him. He came to a conclusion that a player's psyche depended upon the kind of instrument he played. Clarinetists as a species, he maintained, are inclined to be sentimental and must be addressed with infinite gentleness. Violists or any of the higher brass instruments are calm and good-humored. Therefore with them a humorous or even slightly rude approach works best. Oboists and bassoonists are different. They have to blow into a narrow reed in such a manner that a great amount of air remains stored in the chest, to be released cautiously and gradually. This makes the blood rise to the brain and makes them so nervous they can be addressed only with the greatest tact. All these opinions Nikisch would expound with a straight face, but presumably with a twinkle in his own psyche.

A small man with a neatly trimmed, pointed beard, a dandy who affected an enormous mop of hair even before Paderewski floated through the skies with his aureole, a man who liked hand-made shirts with enormous collars and cuffs (these cuffs set off his tiny white hands and made them look even smaller), Nikisch seemed to have mesmeric powers over an orchestra. "Mesmeric" is the one word that crops up again and again in relation to Nikisch, and musicians all over Europe and America would go around telling everybody that they "felt unlike themselves" when Nikisch conducted. Apparently he had that trait from the beginning. He had started as a piano prodigy from Hungary who scared people with his natural aptitude for music. At the age of seven, for example, he heard the *William Tell* and *Barber of Seville* overtures for the first time, then went home and wrote them out from memory; and at eight he had made his debut as a pianist. (He kept up his piano technique all his life, and was fond of accompanying singers in concert, including the great Elena Gerhardt.) At the age of eleven he was in the Vienna Conservatory, and after graduating became a violinist in the Vienna Court Orchestra, where he played under such conductors as Brahms, Wagner, Herbeck and Dessoff. His own conducting career had an unusually rapid advancement. In 1878 he made his debut in Leipzig with an operetta named *Jeanne, Jeannette, Jeanetton*. A few months later, at the age of twenty-three, he was busy conducting *Die Walküre* and *Tannhäuser;* and at twenty-four, on the retirement of Josef Sucher, he became first conductor of the Leipzig Opera, where he remained for eleven years.

A good deal about the young Nikisch is learned from Angelo Neumann's *Personal Recollections of Wagner.* Neumann, an impresario from Leipzig, was preparing a company to tour with Wagner operas,

BOSTON SYMPHONY ORCHESTRA

Arthur Nikisch during his years as conductor of the Boston Symphony Orchestra. He was active there from 1889–1893. Below, an amusing silhouette of Nikisch and Emil von Sauer, the famous pupil of Liszt. Nikisch was as accomplished an accompanist as he was a conductor of symphony and opera.

and Nikisch was recommended to him. The young man got a job as chorus master for the preparation of *Das Rheingold* and *Die Walküre*, and Neumann was no end impressed:

From the first rehearsal I found this young friend invaluable. The assistance he gave us in our gigantic task called forth our amazement and delight. It often happened that an orchestra rehearsal was going on in the main hall with Sucher, while we were rehearsing some part of the chorus or the ensemble on the stage at the same time. Then it was that our new chorus leader, who took Sucher's place at the piano, often without opening the score, prompted the singers in each of their roles, word for word. When Sucher finally had so much to do that he could no longer conduct the solo ensemble work, it was a pleasure to see how eagerly all the artists demanded that the young fellow should take his place at the piano.

Later Neumann, away from Leipzig, received a telegram from the Intendant of the opera: "Orchestra refuses to play under Nikisch. Too young. What shall I do?" Neumann telegraphed back ordering a rehearsal, with instructions that the members of the orchestra could hand in their resignations if they did not like the conductor. Of course there were no resignations. All the players went mad for Nikisch. Even at the age of twenty-five he knew how to handle an orchestra with the utmost smoothness and suavity.

From that point Nikisch was associated only with the top opera houses and orchestras—the Boston Symphony from 1889 to 1893, director of the Budapest Opera from 1893 to 1895, the Leipzig Gewandhaus concerts from 1895 until his death in 1922 (he became director of the Leipzig Conservatory in 1902), permanent conductor of the Berlin Philharmonic, guest appearances with the Hamburg Philharmonic, London Philharmonic, London Symphony (with which he toured the United States in 1912), guest appearances everywhere.

He was much written about, more than any conductor of the day, including even Bülow. Everybody wondered how he got such effects with such a minimum of effort. Tchaikovsky heard him in Leipzig and noted that the orchestra was of first rank. But:

however faultless the orchestral performance appears under the direction of Reinecke, one only gains a true idea of the perfection to which an orchestra can attain under a talented conductor when one hears the difficult and complicated scores of Wagner played under the direction of so wonderful a master as Herr Nikisch. His conducting has nothing in common with the effective and in its way inimitable manner of Hans von Bülow. In the same proportion as the latter is full of movement, restless, effective in the sometimes very noticeable manner of his gestures, so is Herr Nikisch quiet, sparing of superfluous movements, and yet so extraordinarily commanding, powerful, full of self-control. . . . This conductor is small in stature, a very pale young man with splendid poetical eyes that really must possess mesmeric powers.

Some of his effects Nikisch achieved by evolving a new kind of baton technique. Nikisch probably was the first to guide the baton with fingers and wrist rather than fist and arm. This led to a more flexible beat and subtlety of expression. The baton seemed part of Nikisch's hand, an extension of his fingers. He used a long, thin, light stick and developed his left hand far more than any previous conductor had done. It was said of him that his left hand was never seen reflecting his right. When he wanted a legato, a horizontal, dragging motion of the baton was enough to do the job. Adrian Boult, who studied in Leipzig and was in constant attendance at the Nikisch rehearsals and performances, has written that Nikisch "made his stick say more than any other conductor that I have ever seen. His power of expression was so intense that one felt it would be quite impossible, for instance, to play staccato when Nikisch was showing a legato." Boult describes Nikisch as holding the baton with two fingers and thumb, the fingers separated by about a finger's width, the thumb exactly opposite the space between them. Among other innovations of Nikisch was the device of beating in advance, giving the note value a fraction of a second early. This was adopted by Furtwängler (as, indeed, he adopted many things from Nikisch). Nikisch almost always conducted from memory, although he invariably had a score before him. "I do not think you can conduct well," he said, "unless you know a work by heart or almost by heart."

No other conductor could get such a sound from an orchestra. When Harold Bauer played the Schumann Piano Concerto with Nikisch his heart sank, for "no soloist—I least of all—could hope to equal the beauty of sound that he conjured from the orchestra in the opening theme." Nikisch could get beauty of sound from any orchestra, even one he had never worked with before. When he conducted at La Scala he complimented Toscanini on the fine quality of the orchestra. Toscanini would have none of it. "My dear, I happen to know this orchestra very well. I am the conductor of this orchestra. It is a bad orchestra. You are a good conductor." Richard Strauss said that Nikisch had "the ability to get a sound out of the orchestra which we others do not possess." Furtwängler echoed Strauss: "Nikisch had precisely the capacity to make an orchestra sing." Nikisch would step in front of an orchestra, and the young Furtwängler would stay awake nights trying to figure out "why every orchestra sounded so changed under the simple beats of Arthur Nikisch; why the winds played without their usual exaggerated sforzati, the strings with a singing legato, and the sound of the brass fused with the other instruments, while the general tone of the orchestra acquired a warmth which it did not have with other conductors." Boult is another witness to Nikisch's apparent simplicity:

He always seemed to secure his results in the simplest way possible, with the slightest movement and the greatest beauty. I remember the most thrilling performance of the Brahms C minor Symphony I ever heard . . . and at the end, when the orchestra and audience had been worked up to a white heat and the movement had finished in a blaze of triumph, it occurred to me that Nikisch's hand had never been raised higher than the level of his face throughout the whole movement.

Nikisch always used a minuscule, even invisible, beat. When a slight accent or other effect was needed, he would indicate his desires by a slight movement of the baton. Orchestral players swore that he never made an unnecessary body movement; and, said one musician, "that, I believe, is the reason that when he does make a bigger beat than usual, or makes any sudden change of facial expression and gesture, it produces instant effect. . . . He can pull us up or send us along with a flash of his eye or the slightest motion of his baton." Nikisch himself could not or would not explain how he achieved his results. Perhaps he honestly did not know. "I do not pursue technical goals at all," he once wrote. "If one of my colleagues were to ask me after a concert how I achieved this or that particular effect, I would be incapable of answering him." Elsewhere he described himself as "a re-creator of the masterpieces according to my own ideas." A spiritual descendant of the conducting of Wagner and Liszt could say no more, or describe himself more accurately. Nikisch was a romantic conductor, in the best sense of the word. As Flesch said, Nikisch "impressionistically described in the air not simply the bare metrical structure, but above all the dynamic and agogical nuances as well as the mysterious feeling that lies *between* the notes; his beat was utterly personal and original. With Nikisch began a new era in the art of conducting." Nikisch, in short, beat phrases rather than bars; understood the *melos;* used considerable flexibility in tempo and rhythm.

And, of course, he aimed to go beyond the printed note even if that meant retouching the score. In an interview with a Berlin newspaper-man in 1907 he insisted on the necessity of revising the Beethoven symphonies. He pointed out (as Schumann, Wagner and many other musicians before him had done) that new instruments could do what Beethoven's "primitive" instruments could not. "In the same way the modern conductor is justified, nay, often compelled, to depart from Beethoven's instructions in regard to tempo and expression in order to bring out the real intentions of the master. If one were, for instance, to conduct the first movement of the Ninth Symphony exactly fol-lowing his instructions, then this glorious music would be made un-bearable."

There was always an improvisatory feeling about Nikisch's con-ducting, and this was noted again and again. Many musicians who played under him claimed that Nikisch did things on the spur of the moment; and they swore that he never conducted the same piece twice the same way. Performances could be quite different from rehearsals. Nikisch worked through intuition and emotion rather than planning or scholarship, and it may be that the type of freedom he represented would be unpalatable today, though his kind of conducting certainly lived on in Furtwängler. A representative Furtwängler performance (of the Schumann First Symphony, say) sounds exactly as one would imagine a Nikisch performance, complete with the romanti-cisms, the long ritards bridging various sections, the variations in tempo and dynamics. Nikisch's recordings cannot conceivably do justice to him, though his performance of the Fifth Symphony crackles with life and is very Furtwänglerian. Faded as they are, however, the Nikisch recordings are a fascinating document, representing the age as well as the man, linking up with Wagner in the middle of the nineteenth century and with Furtwängler in the middle of the twentieth. An interpretation like that of Nikisch in the *Egmont* Overture, with its slow lead-in, fiery tempo once the action really starts, and prolonged fermatas (how exciting they are!) puts us in the very world of the Wagner school of conducting. The *Freischütz* (with some remarkably bad horn playing) has immense drama and vitality. And the Beethoven Fifth is nowhere near as mannered as one m'ght imagine; nor is it old-fashioned even by current standards. There are, to be sure, several devices no longer in use, including a pronounced string portamento (characteristic of all orchestras playing at the turn of the century; listen to the first Weingartner and Beecham recordings), but as Nikisch handles them they are logical within his concept of the shape of the work. George Szell exaggerates when he writes about Nikisch's "wild, gypsy-like way of treating music." The records do not bear out that judgment. In any case, Szell says that Nikisch was "in the best sense hypnotic and magic. You could not extricate yourself from his spell."

The one criticism that was leveled against Nikisch was that he relied too much on his talent and that this led to laziness. Flesch described the way Nikisch could cut corners; that when he studied a new work (and he was an unparalleled score reader) he leaned too heavily on his facility; "and it was common knowledge that he often opened a new score at the first rehearsal." Artur Schnabel used to delight in telling the story that went around Berlin after Max Reger, at the first rehearsal of one of his new works, interrupted Nikisch and suggested trying the final fugue. Nikisch agreed, *ja, ja, ja,* and started thumbing through the score. He could not find the fugue. "Where is it? Where is it?" Reger growled: "There is none." But the chances are that the performance went exactly as Reger would have desired. One rehearsal was always enough to imprint the music in Nikisch's mind. The rest came naturally. As Franz Kneisel told his pupil Joseph Fuchs, Nikisch understood the language of the baton.

Karl Muck

QUITE DIFFERENT FROM the easygoing Nikisch was the saturnine and misanthropic Karl Muck, who aroused almost as much admiration as Nikisch in his day. Professionals were enthusiastic about his approach; they responded to the logic, finish and strong character of his work. Artur Schnabel, not a man to throw compliments around, called Muck "a very great master, whose reliability, maturity and unselfish dedication are not equaled by any living artist." And Muck's recordings—he was one of the earliest conductors active in the studios —bear this out. There is something fiercely organized about his interpretations, but it is not the kind of organization that usurps a feeling of spontaneity or poetry. What comes through these recordings, made from 1917 on, is a feeling of uncommon musical directness almost incredible considering that he was born in 1859, in the great days of the romantic approach. Somehow Muck managed to avoid the Wagnerian kind of romanticism. He kept his rhythms in order, refused to go in for fluctuations of tempo, took very few liberties, was concerned with shape as well as with emotion. Along with Weingartner, Strauss and Toscanini, he was one of the founders of the modern style, in which the printed note is the ultimate authority, and in which a kind of interpretive anonymity begins to appear. Where Liszt would say: "I am the servant of the public," Muck would say: "I am the servant of the score." Flamboyance gave way to sobriety and pure musicianship. Muck was one of the first to work along such lines. As such, he was the antithesis of conductors like Nikisch and Mahler.

He came late to conducting, first taking a Ph.D. in classical philology at Heidelberg. But there was music in his blood. He had studied the piano as a child, and after Heidelberg he went back to music, studying at the Leipzig Conservatory. Not until 1884 did he start conducting, and he followed the usual progression. In his case it was Zurich, Brno, Salzburg and Graz. His first major assignment was at the Landestheater in Prague, from 1886 to 1892. Then he took charge of the Royal Opera in Berlin, remaining there until 1912 but also including in his schedule Bayreuth, the Boston Symphony and the Vienna Philharmonic. He concentrated on the Boston Symphony from 1912 until a disastrous experience in 1917 with the American authorities. After returning to Europe he took guest assignments, then conducted the Hamburg Philharmonic until his retirement.

What happened in the United States was an outgrowth of the anti-German hysteria during World War I. Muck, born in Darmstadt, made no secret of being pro-German, and when the United States entered the war he offered to resign. His resignation was refused, and nobody made much of a point about his sympathies until an incident in Providence, where it was alleged that Muck refused to conduct *The Star Spangled Banner*. One story had it that when asked to conduct it, Muck said that a symphony orchestra was not a military band. Knowing Muck, it is easy to believe that he could have blurted out such a remark. But that story seems apocryphal. What did happen beyond any doubt was that various music societies, led by the Chaminade Club, had sent a telegram to C. A. Ellis, the manager of the orchestra, demanding that Muck conduct the national anthem in Providence. From that point the story is clouded, and the facts may never emerge. Irving Lowens, who has investigated the affair, writes that Ellis consulted with Henry Higginson, the orchestra's founder and sponsor, and both decided to ignore the telegram. When Muck did not conduct the anthem, Providence newspapers came out with a charge of treason, and the story was picked up from coast to coast, gaining violent momentum as it went along. Herbert Peyser, the knowledgeable musical journalist, believed that the whole affair started because the editor of a Providence newspaper had a grudge against Muck. The newspaper came out with a blast, charging that Muck was the Kaiser's favorite, a spy, a hater of America and things American. The charges caught Higginson by surprise. Off guard, he gave a statement to the press saying that there had not been enough rehearsal time for the national anthem: an asinine excuse. The following day, when Higginson had a chance to look into the situation, he learned that Muck had never heard of the request that *The Star Spangled Banner* be played. Geraldine Farrar, soloist at the Providence concert, confirmed the fact that Muck had never refused to conduct the anthem. As for the conductor, he had no qualms about leading the piece; and, indeed, he did open all subsequent concerts with it.

But the damage had been done. Everybody, whipped up by demagogues and the press, did in fact believe that Muck was a spy, supplying military information to the Germans. There were tales of lights mysteriously flashing in the night from Muck's window to lurking U-boats. Theodore Roosevelt headed a group demanding that Muck be sent back to Germany. Walter Damrosch joined the wolf pack. Muck was denounced at rallies, his figure was burned in effigy, his concerts were boycotted and one in Baltimore had to be canceled. On March 25, 1918, the United States government arrested him under the Alien Enemy Act, and he was taken to Fort Oglethorpe in Georgia, to be interned for the duration of the war. One of Muck's fellow internees was Ernst Kunwald, the Austrian-born conductor of the Cincinnati Symphony, also suspected of espionage activity. As Muck detested Kunwald as man and musician, there must have been seismic rumbles in Georgia. Muck was interned for six months, during which Higginson resigned in protest from the Boston Symphony and the orchestra nearly went under. When Muck left the United States, he was understandably bitter. He told the press, with his usual charm, that the United States was a country "controlled by sentiment which closely borders on mob rule."

He was a short, slim man with a prominent hooked nose (references were constantly being made to his "Mr. Punch profile"), a Mephistophelean expression and a fine collection of dueling scars he had picked up at Heidelberg. As a young man he resembled Wagner, and there were those who believed he was Wagner's illegitimate son. He smoked five packs of cigarettes a day, had a hair-trigger temper and a penchant for scatological expressions, even during a concert. Not many could cite a pleasant word ever coming from his lips. The story was told of a violinist coming to Muck with a pain in his arm: what to do? "Cut it off!" snarled Muck, walking away with vast indifference. Impatient, impulsive, explosive, nervous, he resembled Bülow in more ways than one. Reputations meant

BOSTON SYMPHONY ORCHESTRA

Karl Muck in 1882, at beginning of his career. He came to the podium rather late in life, but became an important conductor.

Muck at Bayreuth, about 1929, ever-present cigarette in hand. He smoked five packs a day.

nothing to him. When Paderewski was a little late in emerging from his dressing room, Muck sent a messenger. "Tell the King of Poland I am waiting for him." (Paderewski held no grudge, certainly not after the musical accompaniment Muck supplied. "He is an ideal accompanist," said Paderewski. "It was simply indescribable, the perfection of his accompaniment.") Muck also had wit. Somebody was trying to interest him in a new composer, "a self-made man." Muck was not impressed. "A self-made man? Where I come from, everybody has a father and a mother."

Behind Muck's sardonic exterior Bruno Walter claimed to have found a soft, serious and unmocking man who barricaded his vulnerability behind sharp words and cutting remarks. But nobody ever disputed the seriousness of Muck the musician. He was dedicated to his art, and he was even one of those conductors who led a great deal of music with which he was not in sympathy, simply because he thought it deserved a hearing. In Boston he conducted the American premiere of Schoenberg's *Five Pieces for Orchestra,* and made a typical remark: "I can't tell you whether we've played music, but I assure you we've played every one of Schoenberg's notes, just as they are written." Muck was a punctilious workman, and Weingartner said of him that he was without a doubt the most conscientious, hard-working conductor he ever had known, a conductor who took prodigious pains in his editing, preparation, corrections and rehearsals. With Muck, nothing was ever left to chance. He spent much time over his programs. They were always solid, and he tried to get the various pieces into correct (to him) relationship. "The classic and frankly romantic," he said, "should no more be thrown together than they should in a single room of an art museum." His tastes ran to Bruckner and Mahler, both of whom he was passionately fond of, but he conducted everything, including Tchaikovsky, a composer he didn't like very much. In his years in Boston he introduced much Sibelius (including the First and Fourth symphonies, the Violin Concerto and *Pohjola's Daughter*) and a good deal of Debussy. His very first two seasons in Boston, 1906 to 1908, saw forty-three pieces introduced to the orchestra, an astoundingly large number. He never conducted opera in the United States, which was a great pity. During his twenty years with the Berlin Opera he conducted 1,071 performances of 103 operas—what a repertoire!—of which thirty-five were novelties.

Muck had no podium mannerisms. His bearing was erect and quiet, his beat clear, his baton describing tiny, short arcs, his elbows moving only slightly. Like Strauss, Muck claimed that he never grew overheated while conducting. He never conducted without a score, saying that memorization was just a trick and that an orchestra was more at ease when a conductor had the music before him. One of the first of the anti-romantics, Muck was interested primarily in the architecture of a piece, in its shape and relationships. But all are agreed that if he sometimes could be pedantic, he was never heavy or stodgy. Herbert Peyser described his platform manner as "one of assured, concentrated but, withal, absolutely untheatrical domination." Yet Muck occasionally could show off. Or was it a carry-over of an old tradition from Mendelssohn through Richter? At any rate, Muck every now and then would drop his arms and stand like a statue, letting the orchestra play the scherzo of the *Eroica* without conducting at all. This used to irritate some critics, who thought it a bit of needless swank.

Active at Bayreuth for thirty years after 1901, Muck's specialty was *Parsifal*, and Peyser (America's outstanding Wagner specialist) thought Muck's interpretation of that opera the greatest he had ever heard: "the only and the ultimate *Parsifal*; the *Parsifal* in which every phrase was charged with infinities; the *Parsifal* which was neither of this age nor that age but of all time." Muck resigned from Bayreuth in 1931, sending a letter to Winifred Wagner saying that younger blood was needed. "For this sort of wheelwork I am no longer fit—I whose artistic standpoint and convictions, so far as Bayreuth is concerned, stem from the preceding century." Perhaps Muck at that time felt he was an anachronism. He even looked like one. When Frida Leider first ran across him in 1925 she was struck by his physical characteristics and dress. "He dressed in the style prevalent at the turn of the century and never departed from it as long as I knew him. A high stiff collar, a black tie with a jeweled stickpin given to him by the Emperor Wilhelm II, a plain, long black coat and stiff white cuffs with links to match the tiepin. One's first impression of him was of someone elegant, unapproachable and, in a way, belonging to a bygone age." Leider found his tempos in Wagner slower than any she and her colleagues had heard. This posed problems, for the singers had to work out new breath distribution and a different concept of word and phrase. Singers accustomed to the speedier twentieth-century tempos at Bayreuth were unhappy, and the venerable conductor found himself being pushed aside. His letter of resignation was noble and touching. But gossip had it that Muck resented the new ideas at Bayreuth; and it was no secret that he resented even more the figure of Arturo Toscanini, the new hero and a far greater drawing card. Muck felt that his *Parsifal* rehearsals in 1930 had been skimped in favor of the Italian conductor. His resignation was cheerfully accepted, and the old man crept sorrowfully from Bayreuth. No effort was made to keep him there.

Peyser was present at Muck's last concert. This was in Leipzig, early in 1933. The city was having a big Hitler demonstration. Muck came forth to conduct Wagner:

A gray shadow of himself, and practically hoisted up on the podium by two stalwart attendants, the musician nevertheless struck sparks again for a few brief moments. When they helped him off the podium he might well have said with Brünnhilde, *"Mein Auge dämmert, mein Licht verlischt."* Like a broken Wotan he passed from the public gaze and went off to seek the hospitality of some aloof and unpretentious Valhalla, there to await the dusk.

· XX ·

Gustav Mahler

Most of the great conductors after Wagner and Liszt were not composers. Nikisch, Bülow, Richter, Mottl, Seidl, Thomas, Levi—all were re-creative. They were men whose mission it was to interpret other men's thoughts. This was a sign of the times, and it was something new in music: conductors (and pianists and violinists) who were not themselves important creators. But with Gustav Mahler there was a throwback to the old days when the greatest conductors were also the greatest composers.

And with Mahler everything was intensified. Where all great conductors are autocratic, Mahler was despotically and almost maniacally so. Where all great conductors have faith in their ideas, Mahler's faith in what he was doing was messianic. Where all conductors do a certain amount of editing and changing, Mahler all but rescored. Where all great conductors indulge in a certain amount of tempo fluctuation, Mahler's rubatos, speedups and slowdowns fluctuated like a cork in a heavy sea. His interpretations would today be received with sheer incredulity. Mahler represented, more than any interpretive figure of his day except possibly Busoni, a kind of approach—some would call it arrogance—in which the conductor did thus and so because he knew that he knew more than the composer.

He was demonic, neurotic, demanding, selfish, noble, emotionally undisciplined, sarcastic, unpleasant, and a genius. His actions throughout his life strongly suggest those of a manic-depressive. Periods of gloom and silence alternated with periods of violence and vehemence. He was thin, sickly, subject to migraine headaches. His complicated inner life was a tortured one in which his Judaism fought with Christianity, and in which a large measure of a strange form of pantheistic mysticism contended with both. He felt that his mission in life was composition, but conductorial and administrative demands left him a minimum of time for creative work, and that was one of his great frustrations. He was determined and compulsive to a point where he could drive other people out of their minds. Hermann Klein met Mahler when he was trying to learn English. Mahler refused to speak in German. "He would rather spend five minutes in an effort to find the English word he wanted," said Klein, "than resort to his mother tongue or allow anyone else to supply the equivalent. Consequently a short chat with Mahler involved a liberal allowance of time." Mahler operated under a high tension that communicated itself to everybody, and he had a genius for making enemies. Only *he* knew how music should go; only *he* could set the composer to rights, the stage director to rights, the singers, the scenic artists, the producer. "One of the most strong-willed persons I ever knew," said Hans Pfitzner, something of an authority on strong wills. Mahler was constantly complaining, constantly arguing, constantly troublesome, and while he was in New York, Mrs. Charles Dana Gibson asked his wife: "How can a beautiful woman like you marry an old, ugly, impossible man like Mahler?" Orchestra players hated him. He was the kind of conductor who would go out of his way to pick on weak players, then make them stand and play solo. For this an orchestral musician would gladly cut a conductor's throat. The story goes that a double-bass player of the New York Philharmonic, ordered by Mahler to rise and shine, finally rebelled and asked the conductor why he didn't pick on the first-desk men. "Why don't you ask the first flute or the first oboe to play alone like this?" Said Mahler: "I'm afraid to take a chance on what I might hear." But Mahler treated even important fellow conductors with equal contempt. In Vienna, having prepared *Lohengrin* at the opera house, he had to turn it over to Franz Schalk, a conductor he did not particularly admire. Mahler called a rehearsal and sat on stage facing the podium. While Schalk conducted, he had to follow Mahler's beat and every nuance. This was a humiliating experience for Schalk, an experienced and respected conductor.

Mahler came out of Bohemia, attended the Vienna Conservatory, and by 1881 was conducting in Ljubljana. A series of appointments followed, and he then turned up in Leipzig, where he could not get along with Nikisch. The two quarreled, and Mahler was ousted in

1888. He went to the Budapest Opera, where he tried to do the sort of thing he later did in Vienna—take over all elements of a production in an effort to achieve his kind of *Gesamtkunstwerk*. One thing that did not make him popular in Budapest was the fact that he abolished the star system, getting rid of the great but egocentric figures, and substituting for them less imposing vocalists with superior musical intelligence. Mahler also insisted that all operas be sung in Hungarian. Popular or not, he made an impact. Strauss heard him and passed the word to Bülow: "I made a new, very attractive acquaintance in Herr Mahler, who appears to me a highly intelligent musician and conductor—one of the few modern conductors who knows about tempo modification; and he expressed splendid ideas in general, especially about Wagner's tempos (unlike certain presently accepted Wagner conductors)." Mahler remained in Budapest for two years and then, in 1891, moved to Hamburg, where he remained until 1897. It was in Hamburg that he attracted the attention of Europe. Bülow heard him and fully agreed with Strauss:

Hamburg has now secured a really excellent opera conductor in Gustav Mahler (a serious, energetic Jew from Budapest), who in my opinion equals the very best: Richter, Mottl, etc. I heard him do *Siegfried* recently. . . . I was filled with honest admiration for him, for he made—no, forced—the orchestra to pipe to his measure, without having had a rehearsal. In spite of various drawbacks and my nervous condition, I was able to hold out to the last note.

Everybody was talking about the young Mahler, and in 1897 he was summoned to Vienna as chief of the Staatsoper. The ten years he officiated there are now called the Vienna Opera's Golden Years. Of one thing everybody was sure during those ten years: there never was a dull moment. Irascible, impatient, full of exuberance, energy and new ideas, Mahler all but tore down the Vienna Opera and rebuilt it to the specifications of his inner vision. He ran it as a one-man show. The first thing he did was engage a new group of singers (often making mistakes; he would herald a new singer as a genius, only to learn after one or two performances that the genius had no voice and what was worse, in Mahler's view, no brains). Then he revitalized the orchestra, abolished the claque, did away with cuts in scores, refused leaves of absence to artists, insulted popular veteran singers, raged, stamped, swore, picked on musicians, lectured artists on their morals (Mahler appears to have been something of a prude), and insisted on obedience not only from his opera-house people but also from the audience. If there were a whisper or a noise in the house, Mahler would turn around and glare. Audiences were cowed. He became a legend in Vienna, and when cab drivers would see him walking down the street they would point him out and whisper to their fares: "Der Mahler!" His wife said that he was driven by demons, incapable of compromise. He kept seeking a perfection not to be obtained by mortals, and he demanded as much from himself as from others. At rehearsals and performances he would run up and down in his dressing room like a caged animal, sobs bursting from his lips.

The youth of Vienna, the young musicians and the gallery gods, loved and supported him. Conservatives growled at his name. Everything Mahler did was different from what had gone before. He strove for a complete blend of music and stage; he insisted on absolute clarity. When he presented Mozart he brought the music to the fore, with life and drama, trying to match the life of the characters on stage. All this was quite unlike the dry, or rococo, or quasi-elegant manner in which previous conductors had done the operas. When Mahler presented Tristan und Isolde with Alfred Roller's avant-garde set, there was a furor. The production anticipated expressionism, with its free forms and use of lighting effects. Also, Richter had conducted it as a symphony, whereas Mahler conducted it as an opera, in which the voices were featured as much as the orchestra, and in which the orchestral climaxes were all but hysterical when the mood and action demanded it. There was a heavy campaign against him, including virulent attacks from the powerful anti-Semitic forces in Vienna. Somehow Mahler survived.

He prepared and conducted every performance as a matter of life and death. An enemy of routine, he was constantly saying: "Tradition is laziness." (Toscanini was to say: "Tradition is the last bad performance.") The first performance in Vienna of Charpentier's Louise provides an example of his thoroughness and his quest for perfection. After having decided to stage the new opera, Mahler sent his stage director, régisseur and costumer to Paris to study the production. Then he invited Charpentier to attend the premiere. Charpentier turned up at a dress rehearsal and found fault with every-

NEW YORK PUBLIC LIBRARY

Gustav Mahler in 1907 (left), his last year in Vienna, and in 1911 (right). At that time he was the conductor of the N.Y. Philharmonic.

Mahler was a fierce perfectionist who demanded equal perfection from his players. He was not beloved in orchestral circles.

CARICATURE BY HANS BÖHLER

thing, including Mahler's conducting. Mahler promptly canceled the premiere, rescheduling it six weeks later. He ordered new scenery and costumes to Charpentier's specifications, and studied the score with him. When the premiere finally was given, Charpentier was (understandably) gratified, and praised it as superior to the Paris production.

Aiming as he did for a complete performance, Mahler was proud of the fact that when he conducted, the singers could be heard. This is the sign of an experienced opera conductor. Richard Aldrich, the critic of the New York *Times,* remarked on this when Mahler conducted Wagner at the Metropolitan Opera:

The voices were given rights of which it is certain that Wagner never intended them to be deprived. Chief of these is to be heard. . . . The orchestral part . . . did not drown the voices, and here, too, was an added beauty brought into prominence that has not always been heard in Wagnerian performances—that of the blending of voices with the orchestral tone.

Constantly striving for perfection, never finding it, Mahler tore himself apart. He never came across an orchestra that satisfied him, one that had his kind of dedication and musicianship. He wrote:

There are frightful habits, or rather inadequacies, which I have encountered in every orchestra. They cannot read the score markings, and thus sin against the holy law of dynamics and of the hidden inner rhythm of a work. When they see a crescendo they immediately play forte and speed up; at a diminuendo they become piano and retard the tempo. One looks in vain for gradations, for the mezzo-forte, forte, fortissimo, or the piano, pianissimo, pianississimo. And the sforzandos, forte pianos, shortening or extension of notes, are even less in evidence. And should one ask them to play something that is not written down—as is so necessary a hundred times when one accompanies singers in opera—then one is lost with every orchestra.

This is an old complaint, previously voiced by Haydn, Weber, Wagner and any good musician. The better the musical mind and the better the ear, the less happy is that man with mere mortals who play in orchestras. Theodore Spiering, Mahler's concertmaster, felt impelled to explain Mahler's stand and apologize for it: "As a conductor he attained an independence which at times proved almost fatal for the orchestra. He demanded initiative on the part of his men; he frequently forgot that a certain artistry, which not every orchestral player possesses, is essential to such initiative." At any rate, Mahler's statement about what he expected from an orchestra begins to give an idea of the kind of response and nuance he was looking for. He believed what every sensitive musician sooner or later realizes. In his own words: "What is best in music is not to be found in the notes."

In his earlier years Mahler was an energetic figure on the podium, wrapped in emanations of nervous energy. Max Graf, the Viennese critic, remembered Mahler as literally rushing to the podium. "His conducting was striking enough in his first years of activity in Vienna. He would let his baton shoot forward suddenly, like the tongue of a poisonous serpent. With his right hand, he seemed to pull the music out of the orchestra as out of the bottom of a chest of drawers. He would let his stinging glance loose on a musician who was seated far away from him, and the man would quail." Later Mahler was quieter, with a simple beat and a motionless body, his eyes darting here and there. Bruno Walter, who agreed that Mahler used violent motions in his early years, said that toward the end his conducting "presented a picture of almost uncanny quiet, although the intensity of expression did not suffer by it. I remember a performance of the *Sinfonia Domestica* by Strauss under Mahler's baton at which the contrast between the uproar of the orchestra and the immovable attitude of him who had unleashed it made a most eerie impression." Ernst Lert, the opera Intendant and stage director, who studied in Vienna during the Golden Years, confirms Walter's memory. Lert was "frightened and fascinated" by Mahler even before he attended the concert at which the composer conducted the premiere of his own Sixth Symphony. "His statuesque immobility before the huge orchestra, even when it exploded into an indescribable turmoil of temperament and despair, created the same uncanny impression, nay, an even more frightening one, because a single impulsive movement of his hand or head would have relieved the almost unbearable tension."

Mahler's interpretations must have been strikingly dramatic, full of contrast, highly mannered by today's standards. One of his mannerisms was to emphasize held notes, the way Wagner had done in

Mahler in action: silhouette by Dr. Otto Böhler. As a young conductor, Mahler indulged in extravagant gestures and podium mannerisms. Later his motions were reduced to a minimum, and he was almost stationary.

the Beethoven Fifth. In Vienna, Lert heard Mahler conduct the *Magic Flute* Overture, and "when Mahler finished the first chord, the ensuing pause was so long that I looked up from my score to find out why the conductor did not continue. Just then he attacked the second chord. Now came a pause that seemed still longer." And when the sequence was repeated toward the end of the overture, the pauses were yet more pronounced. Obviously Mahler's conducting had a great deal of rhetoric, complete with punctuation marks. Perhaps he was illustrating a program he had worked out in his own mind. Mahler once said that every symphony from Beethoven's on had in it some kind of implied program. And we know that all of the Mahler symphonies did: Fate, Nature, Destiny, God, the Abyss, Struggle, Resolution, Resignation—all in constant flux, coming together and breaking away.

Like every musician of the time, Mahler heavily edited the music he was conducting. "Of course the works of Beethoven need some editing," he said. Note the "of course." Bruno Walter, who idolized Mahler, attempted to explain his attitude. If Mahler did make changes in classical works, it was directed "against the letter and toward the spirit" of the composer. Mahler never hesitated to retouch, and was under constant attack for some particularly heavy modifications, as in the Schumann and Beethoven symphonies. Mahler answered his critics with the old—even in his day—if-Beethoven-were-alive argument. "The fanatical obedience to the score," Walter writes, "did not blind him to any contradiction existing between its instructions and the composer's actual intentions." But where is the line to be drawn? No matter how Walter or anybody else tries to justify them, or explain them away, Mahler's interpolations could be arbitrary and often actually opposed to the score. Schumann's *Manfred* Overture has always presented a problem because of its opening. The syncopation does not come through. Mahler's solution was to insert a great cymbal clash at the outset. This establishes the meter, but it is altogether anti-Schumann. Mahler also edited Tchaikovsky's *Francesca da Rimini* so that it came out eleven minutes long instead of its usual twenty-three. He used doubled woodwinds in the Beethoven Sixth; doubled oboes for the little cadenza in the first movement of the Beethoven Fifth. And so on. If Otto Klemperer is to be believed, Mahler had the same attitude toward his own music. Klemperer quotes Mahler as saying that if his Eighth Symphony did not sound well, anybody could "with an easy conscience" make changes in it.

After ten years, in 1907, Mahler resigned from the Vienna Opera. He had the public and most of the critics behind him by then, and was not forced out. Max Graf always believed that Mahler resigned more because his symphonies were not accepted rather than because of anti-Semitism or administrative troubles. Mahler's music—not his conducting—was under constant attack, and Graf's opinion was that Mahler handed in his resignation impulsively and on the spur of the moment, and later regretted it.

He went directly from Vienna to the Metropolitan Opera. At first he was happy. At the Metropolitan he had better voices to work with than he had in Vienna. Under his command were such as Caruso, Fremstad, Bonci, Scotti, Chaliapin, Gadski, Plançon, Stracciari, Van Rooy, Homer, Rappold, Sembrich, Farrar, Eames, Destinn and Burrian. What a roster! It also was noted that the tyrannical Mahler changed in New York. In Vienna he conducted all operas without cuts. In New York he not only used the standard cuts but even introduced new ones on top of the old. Sets that would have driven him into a rage in Vienna merely amused him in New York. Mahler worked hard in his first season, conducting *Tristan und Isolde, Die Walküre, Siegfried, Don Giovanni* and *Fidelio*. He returned for the 1908–09 season, and also was invited by Walter Damrosch to conduct the New York Symphony, with which he presented the American premiere of his Symphony No. 2. By this time Mahler was tired and ill, and he complained bitterly about everything. There were many facets of New York life he did not like. He preferred to be alone, but found he had to go to parties. Mahler, who had no small talk and was devoid of the social graces, loathed parties and society.

Adding to his troubles was the presence of Arturo Toscanini, who had come over for the 1908–09 season with the new manager, Giulio Gatti-Casazza. Toscanini demanded *Tristan und Isolde* as his first production. Mahler was resentful but had to give in, even though he already had rehearsed the orchestra. There was an inevitable clash between two such strong-willed persons. Toscanini soon became contemptuous of Mahler. Many years later Toscanini told his son that one reason he had come to the Metropolitan Opera was because so great a musician as Mahler was working there. But, said Toscanini, he soon saw that Mahler did not give everything he had, and was taking the easy way out. And, indeed, the Mahler of New York was quite different from the Mahler of Vienna. He himself apologized publicly for his poor showing. He said that men didn't come to rehearsals, that when they did come they didn't work hard enough, and that conducting in those circumstances was a farce. But Toscanini did not find it so.

Perhaps Mahler thought, when he came to New York, that the provincial Americans would not know if he tinkered with the score, or care even if they did realize it. Many European musicians of the day did come here with an honest belief that America was, by and large, a wilderness; that cowboys and Indians were on the other side of the Hudson River. Some of them still come to America with that attitude. It so happened that New York at the time had such critical sharpshooters as W. J. Henderson, Richard Aldrich, Henry Krehbiel, Henry T. Finck and James Huneker, as strong and knowledgeable a group of critics as ever worked together at one time. Some of them did not take kindly to Mahler's high-handed way, and his *Tristan* cuts especially caused a great deal of unfavorable criticism. The *Musical Courier,* then the most influential musical publication in the world, was one of the few willing to go along with Mahler. The *Courier* expressed itself on a frankly lowbrow basis:

Wagner's [operas] are too long—not for the pilgrims at Bayreuth but for busy New Yorkers who, after working hard all day, do not want to be kept in the opera house much more than three hours. By means of judicious excisions, Anton Seidl used to bring the Wagner operas within reasonable dimensions without sacrificing any of the best pages. Mr. Mahler is following his example. He has also promised to reduce the time of Mozart's *Don Giovanni* from three hours and a half to two hours and three quarters.

Instead of returning to the Metropolitan Opera, Mahler came back to New York as conductor of the New York Philharmonic. Mrs. Samuel Untermeyer and Mrs. George R. Sheldon decided that so great a conductor should have his own symphony orchestra. Mahler, who conducted two trial concerts, agreed, provided that he had complete control over orchestra, programs and personnel. In his first season he brought over his own concertmaster, Theodore Spiering, and replaced two-thirds of the orchestra. He immediately got into trouble with everybody—with the orchestra, the critics, the board of the symphony, the public. He loudly said that his mission was to educate the orchestra and the public. That did not sit very well with all concerned; and it was true that in 1909 there were very high standards in New York, which was as sophisticated musically as any of the European capitals.

About Mahler's qualifications there was no doubt. The better musicians responded. When Rachmaninoff played his D minor Concerto with Mahler, the pianist wrote that he was "the only conductor whom I considered worthy to be classed with Nikisch." Mahler really had studied the music, and Rachmaninoff was greatly impressed:

According to Mahler, every detail of the score was important—an attitude too rare amongst conductors. Though the rehearsal was scheduled to end at 12:30, we played and played, far beyond this hour; and when Mahler announced that the first movement was to be rehearsed again, I expected some protest or scene from the musicians, but I did not notice a single sign of annoyance.

Mahler's two seasons with the Philharmonic were stormy. Some critics could not stand him, objecting especially to his incessant editing and reorchestrating. If Mahler's orchestra did not like him, the feeling was reciprocal. He described the Philharmonic as "the true American orchestra—without talent and phlegmatic." He learned to distrust his orchestra and once, before starting the downbeat at a rehearsal of the *Lohengrin* Prelude, yelled at the players before a note had been sounded: "Too loud!" Shortly before the end of the season, Mahler was summoned before the board to defend himself against all kinds of charges. "It was a silly thing," the *Musical Courier* said, "to bring a supreme judge like Mahler from Europe and place him under the direction of a petticoat jury." Mahler had greatly displeased the ladies of the board. They did not like the way he had conducted the Tchaikovsky *Pathétique;* they did not like the scandal that followed when the pianist Josef Weiss walked out of a rehearsal and refused to play the concert; they did not like the way Mahler and Busoni delivered the *Emperor* Concerto. One of the ladies had the gall to say to those two great musicians, at the rehearsal, "No, this will never do." Then there was a deficit of $75,000. Nor was Mahler's programming to the good ladies' liking. Tensions mounted.

The orchestra claimed that Mahler had planted a spy among the second violins. (It was true.) All of this was brought against Mahler at the hearing. He might or might not have fought it out. But he became ill, and Spiering conducted the rest of the season. Mahler returned to Europe to recuperate, and his wife told the press what had happened: "You cannot imagine what Mr. Mahler has suffered. In Vienna my husband was all-powerful. Even the Emperor did not dictate to him, but in New York he had ten ladies ordering him around like a puppet . . ." A few months later, Mahler was dead. He did not live long enough to see his eventual triumph in the only thing that really mattered to him: his own music.

· XXI ·

Richard Strauss

IN MANY RESPECTS Richard Strauss continued the Mahler tradition. Like Mahler, he was a major composer and at one time was in charge of the Vienna Staatsoper, the house Mahler had raised so high. But musically and temperamentally no two conductors could have been more different. Strauss was in the Muck tradition: a musical literalist with a tiny beat and an anti-romantic approach. He did not start that way, though. As Bülow's protégé with the Meiningen Orchestra in 1884 he came for a while under the great man's influence, tempo modifications and all; and Max Graf, who heard Strauss in the early days, remembered the many accelerandos and ritardandos. It caused talk. People had been accustomed to the all-powerful, rolling, majestic breadth of Richter, and here was a young musician of the new school "who was not mighty and broad, but slender and nervous on the podium. . . . Most striking was the supple, delicate sense of sound, the nervous shading . . ."

That was at the beginning. Later Strauss, who was active on the podium one way or another all his long life, went out of his way to avoid excess and even emotion, developing into a thorough anti-romantic. As he grew older he became more and more suspicious of expressive effects. In 1933 he supervised the premiere of his *Arabella* in Dresden. Clemens Krauss had prepared the production, conducting it with numerous rubatos, pauses, ritards and tempo changes. At the rehearsal Strauss impatiently swept everything clean. "*Nein, kein ritardando,*" or "*Keine fermate,*" or "*Einfach. Im Takt.*" He once told an orchestra, rehearsing the slow movement of a Beethoven symphony, "Gentlemen, please, not so much emotion. Beethoven wasn't nearly as emotional as our conductors."

He substituted clarity and rhythm for a big emotional sweep, and he went about it with restrained gestures and the tiniest of beats. George Szell says that he was very much interested in precision, "and he had a very small clickety, precise beat with always another little upbeat inside his wrist." Strauss himself had quite a few things to say about his beat: "The shorter the movements of the arm, and the more confined to the wrist, the more precise the execution." He even had some heretical remarks to make. "The left hand has nothing to do with conducting. Its proper place is in the waistcoat pocket, from which it should emerge to restrain, or to make some minor gesture— for which in any case a scarcely perceptible glance should suffice." There followed some technical talk:

In fifty years of practice, I have discovered how unimportant it is to beat each quarter note or eighth note. What is decisive is that the upbeat, which contains the whole of the tempo that follows, should be rhythmically exact and that the downbeat should be extremely precise. The second half of the bar is immaterial. I frequently conduct it like an *alla breve* [i.e., in twos]. Always conduct in periods, never bars. . . . Second-rate conductors are frequently inclined to pay too much attention to the elaborations of rhythmic detail, thus overlooking the proper shaping of a phrase as a whole. . . . Any modification of tempo made necessary by the character of the piece should be carried out imperceptibly, so that the unity of tempo remains intact.

These words were written by a conductor of vast experience. Strauss's first attempt at conducting was with the Meiningen Orchestra, and the piece was his own Suite for Winds. Bülow did not give him any rehearsal time, and Strauss conducted his work "in a state of slight coma. I can only remember today that I made no blunders." From Meiningen he went to Munich, where from 1886 to 1889 he was third conductor of the opera. The next few years saw him at Weimar, and in 1894 he succeeded Bülow as conductor of the Berlin Philharmonic. Munich once again; then guest appearances all over the world, generally in his own music; some Bayreuth; a long stay (1898 to 1918) at the Berlin Opera; co-director with Franz Schalk of the Vienna Staatsoper from 1919 to 1924; many guest appearances in Europe and America.

All this time, of course, he was steadily composing: first his remarkable sequence of symphonic poems, then the later concentration on opera. He was also arousing great admiration for his business acumen. Strauss, to put it bluntly, loved money, and his wife loved money even more than he did. The fortunate Strauss was in a position to put a high price on his services, and everybody was talking about his ability to become rich as a composer. As early as 1909 the Cleveland *Plain Dealer* ran a long article on his fees and royalties, figured out that Strauss's income was at least $60,000 a year, "and in five years he hopes to double that figure." Stories about Strauss's greed made the rounds, and whether or not they were true, all Europe enjoyed them. Strauss (so went one story) goes to Dresden for a *Salome* rehearsal. On his return to Berlin he is met at the station by his son. "Papa, how much did you get for conducting the rehearsal?" Strauss is greatly moved; weeps tears of joy; enfolds the boy in his arms. "Now I know you are a true son of mine." When, during his first tour of the United States, he conducted several concerts in Wanamaker's department store at a stupendous fee, a great fuss was raised. Pious musicians threw up their hands. Strauss ignored them. It is better to earn money honestly, he said, than to complain to those who do so.

This side of Strauss's nature is emphasized here because it does explain several things about his approach to his art, which was an eminently practical one. Those close to him admitted that he could be more interested in his fee than in the artistic results. If the music or the surroundings stimulated him, he would throw himself into his conducting. Otherwise it could sound bored and mechanical. Never was his work anything but precise and musicianly, but often it was devoid of life. Gregor Piatigorsky, who once played the Haydn Cello Concerto under his baton, says that Strauss cut the introduction and kept sneaking looks at his watch. Toward the end of his career as a conductor, Strauss's fundamental indifference was obvious to all. He would explain a passage and try it out once or twice. If it went well, fine; if it went poorly, he would shrug his shoulders. "When I was young, I had to take the blame if others made a mistake. Nowadays, if *I* make a mistake, it's all *their* fault." The conclusion is inescapable that Strauss was cynical about his work as a conductor, and some of his *Ten Golden Rules for the Album of a Young Conductor,* written about 1922, do indeed show a certain amount of cynicism:

TEN GOLDEN RULES

For the Album of a Young Conductor

1. Remember that you are making music not to amuse yourself, but to delight your audience.
2. You should not perspire when conducting: only the audience should get warm.
3. Conduct *Salome* and *Elektra* as if they were by Mendelssohn: Fairy Music.
4. Never look encouragingly at the brass, except with a brief glance to give an important cue.
5. But never let the horns and woodwinds out of your sight. If you can hear them at all they are still too strong.
6. If you think that the brass is not blowing hard enough, tone it down another shade or two.
7. It is not enough that you yourself should hear every word the soloist sings. You should know it by heart anyway. The audience must be able to follow without effort. If they do not understand the words they will go to sleep.
8. Always accompany a singer in such a way that he can sing without effort.
9. When you think you have reached the limits of prestissimo, double the pace.*
10. If you follow these rules carefully you will, with your fine gifts and your great accomplishments, always be the darling of your listeners.

---

* Today (1948) I should like to amend this as follows: Go twice as slowly (addressed to conductors of Mozart).

All this is very witty and displays a flair for paradox; and, of course, there is underlying truth in every one of the remarks. But it nevertheless is flippant. It could also be maintained that Strauss's fast tempos stemmed from cynicism or boredom. His tempos were fast from the beginning and became faster as he grew older, to the point where Friedelind Wagner and others describe them as inexplicable. At Bayreuth he conducted the first act of *Parsifal* in one hour, thirty-five minutes, as against Muck's one hour, fifty-four minutes and Toscanini's two hours, two minutes. At the memorial concert for Siegfried Wagner he polished off the Beethoven Ninth in forty-five minutes sharp, "without as much as a damp collar or a drop

CAPITOL RECORDS

Richard Strauss, who started conducting as a protégé of Hans von Bülow and was active on the podium throughout most of his career.

Strauss may well have been the most restrained of all the important conductors. He used a tiny baton, and his beat was delivered in tiny arcs.

CARICATURE BY HANS BÖHLER

of perspiration," one onlooker noted. (Most performances of the Ninth run a little over an hour.) His recording of the Beethoven Seventh, made in the middle 1920s with the Berlin State Opera Orchestra, is amazing. There is almost never a ritard or a change of expression or nuance. The slow introduction is almost as fast as the following vivace; and the last movement, with a big cut in it, is finished in four minutes, twenty-five seconds. (It should run between seven and eight minutes.) His recording of the *Magic Flute* Overture is also taken at a terrific clip. The only thing that explains such conducting is the suggestion that Strauss considered those sessions merely a paying assignment, to be finished as soon as possible. Karl Böhm insists that Strauss in the concert hall was nothing like Strauss on records. But the records leave a bad impression. They are disgraceful, and certainly no testimony to Strauss's probity.

He was especially famous as a Mozart conductor, but even here his recording of the G minor Symphony cannot possibly do him justice. He races through the music with no force, no charm, no inflection, with a metronomic rigidity. Nor can the lack of nuance be blamed on the recording, which is electrical and not acoustic. At about the same time, Erich Kleiber and the same Berlin State Opera Orchestra recorded Mozart's E flat Symphony, and there is no comparison between the respective conductors. Kleiber's performance has much more quality, much more personality, many interesting ideas.

Strauss at his best must have had much more to say than comes through these records. No conductor could have reached his eminence without having had a great deal to offer. His major contribution was probably a corrective to romantic excess. He soon broke away from the Nikisch school, and even the Bülow-Wagner tradition in which he had grown up. Strauss inveighed against the then universal practice of taking ritards before second subjects. Instead he pleaded for a long, continuous line, asking for proportion and balance. He was, as an opera composer, all but rabid on the necessity of adjusting the orchestra so that every word from the stage, every melody from the singers, should clearly come through. And, above all, he avoided sentimentality. Leo Wurmser, a musician who worked with Strauss, says that the big tunes and lyric passages in his own operas, "which under other conductors often sound cheap and sentimental, rarely did so when he conducted. I believe this was mainly due to his taking them at exactly the right tempo, but his unemotional behavior at the desk may have had something to do with it."

In any case, it seems doubtful if Strauss ever had the big vision: the passion and fervent belief, the sheer dedication to art—the one-sidedness, if you will—that is the mark of the great interpreter. But he did scrap many of the mannerisms that had characterized the work of the romantic conductors. Unfortunately he also scrapped some of their best points. What remained was the product of a cool, sharp intelligence, and a musical approach that, like Muck's, led directly into the modern style.

A few words should be said about some of Strauss's more important interpreters. First there was Franz Wüllner of Munich, Dresden and Cologne, who was conducting Strauss music as early as 1885 and later led the first performance of *Till Eulenspiegel* and *Don Quixote*. In Dresden there was Ernst von Schuch, who had come to that city in 1872 and was the director of the opera house from 1882 to 1914. Schuch conducted the world premieres of Strauss's *Feuersnot* (1901), *Salome* (1905), *Elektra* (1909) and *Der Rosenkavalier* (1911). Strauss was on the whole pleased with his work and referred to him as "the conscientious Schuch." Famous for his elegant performances of French and Italian operas, and as a discreet accompanist, Schuch (says Strauss, somewhat maliciously) "had perfected this praiseworthy art to such a degree that under him even Wagner's operas sounded a little undistinguished." During rehearsals of *Elektra* Strauss was constantly nagging at Schuch, trying to get him to liven up the orchestra. So much did Strauss get on his nerves that the angry Schuch conducted the dress rehearsal with sheer fury, and Strauss had to tell him to hold back. "You see!" cried Schuch triumphantly. And, says Strauss, "the first performance had perfect balance." Elsewhere Strauss takes another poke at Schuch. "Cuts were Schuch's specialty. He never, I believe, conducted an opera without cuts, and was particularly proud when he could leave out a whole act of a modern opera." After the premiere of *Der Rosenkavalier*, Schuch promptly proceeded to make "the most dreadful cuts," and those were copied by directors of other theatres. Strauss had to fight for years to correct the situation. Schuch, despite Strauss's digs, was a refined, skillful conductor who made Dresden one of the finest opera houses in the world.

Franz Schalk, who shared the directorship of the Vienna Staatsoper with Strauss in the early 1920s, and was sole director from 1924 to 1931, was a conductor somewhat along Schuch's line: smooth, elegant, with a formidable musical culture. He conducted the world premiere of *Die Frau ohne Schatten* in 1919. Schalk never concerned himself too much with the dramatic elements of opera. Lotte Lehmann, who says he looked like "an incredibly fine courtier," did not think him a very good administrator. He could not cope with the infighting prevalent in any big opera house, and the intrigues that forced him out hastened his death. Schalk left some recordings made with the Vienna Philharmonic, and his interpretations of such scores as the Beethoven Sixth and Eighth Symphonies are notable for their natural flow, refinement and lyricism.

Chronologically the last of the important Strauss associates was Clemens Krauss, who conducted the premieres of *Arabella* (1933), *Friedenstag* (1938), *Capriccio* (1942; he also wrote the libretto) and *Der Liebe der Danae* (produced in 1952, three years after Strauss's death). Known primarily as a Strauss specialist, Krauss was a fine musician completely comfortable in all kinds of music. He also was an admirable pianist who often accompanied his wife, the soprano Viorica Ursuleac, in recital. Strauss had great respect for him, and Krauss's many recordings are ample testimony to a major gift.

· XXII ·

Felix Weingartner

ANOTHER OF THE transitional conductors between the romanticisms of the nineteenth century and the austerities of the twentieth was Felix Weingartner, one of the major figures of his time. As a student of Liszt—Weingartner was an exceptionally fine pianist—he had an opportunity to participate in romanticism undefiled. But within a few years he was attacking romanticism defiled. Weingartner never attacked Liszt, but he did have it in for Bülow, the (to him) archfiend representing everything that was mannered and unmusical in conducting. As early as 1887, only three years after his professional debut, Weingartner broke with Bülow and his school. The specific issue was *Carmen,* an opera that, according to Weingartner, Bülow conducted in a slow and dragging manner. Bülow told the world that he was so conducting the opera because he intended that way to convey the dignity of the Spaniards. When Weingartner conducted *Carmen* in Hamburg, his ideas were so different from Bülow's that the critics and public were in an uproar. Who was this young radical who dared to disagree so violently with the conceptions of *Der Meister,* the great Hans von Bülow? The upshot was that Weingartner was relieved of the opera. He was furious, as much for artistic as for personal reasons. Could Bülow, Weingartner later wrote, "really not see from this much-discussed affair that he was blaming me for his own fault, since it was not I—who restored the unequivocal directions of Bizet—who was the arbitrary one, but he who had disregarded them?" (Weingartner never suffered from a lack of confidence in his own knowledge.) In his autobiography Weingartner graphically describes the Wagner-Bülow type of temporubato conducting so prevalent at the time:

They sought to make the clearest passages obscure by hunting out insignificant details. Now an inner part of minor importance would be given a significance that by no means belonged to it. Now an accent that should have been lightly stressed came out sforzato. Often a so-called "breath-pause" would be inserted, particularly in the case of a crescendo immediately followed by a piano, as if the music were sprinkled with fermatas. These little tricks were helped out by continual alterations and dislocations of tempo. Where a gradual animation or a gentle and delicate slowing-up is required—often, however, without even that pretext—a violent, spasmodic accelerando or ritenuto was made.

This was never Weingartner's way, and it was his loathing of the Bülow school that helped materially speed acceptance of the new style. The age was ready for it. There were murmurings all over against romantic excess. The spirit of the times seemed to be demanding a more stringent interpretive approach, and Weingartner was one of the first to show how it could be done without becoming sterile. Throughout his long career he was a conductor of taste and sobriety, unmannered and unidiosyncratic, nearly always faithful to the score, making music with honesty and nobility. Something of a classicist (he was one of the first modern conductors who approached Mozart with an attempt to approximate eighteenth-century style), he aimed for clear lines, formal balance, firm rhythms. Musicians who worked under him thought he achieved more through inspiration than through pure technique. Carl Flesch, for one, believed that Weingartner's success depended upon whether or not he could bend an orchestra entirely to his will. "Thus his art rested primarily on psychic foundations, whereas his pure craftsmanship, both in his baton technique and in rehearsing the orchestra, was on a comparatively primitive level." But Flesch's contempt for conductors, fine musician though he himself may have been, was notorious, and other musicians were more generous to Weingartner, especially when it came to judging him on his symphonic work. In opera there always were qualifications. The consensus was that his operatic conducting lacked drama, even though Weingartner spent a good part of his life in the theatre. About his symphonic conducting there was no serious disagreement. He was rightly considered one of the giants.

Born in Dalmatia of a Viennese father and a German mother, he studied piano and composition in Leipzig, attended Liszt's class at

Weimar and, turning to the baton, made his debut with *Il Trovatore* at Graz. A restless man, he never stayed long in one place. His apprenticeship was served at Geneva, Danzig, Hamburg and Mannheim. In 1891 he went to the Berlin Opera; then to Munich. When Mahler resigned from the Vienna Opera, Weingartner succeeded him, but only for three seasons. Later years saw him at the Volksoper in Vienna, as guest conductor with major orchestras in Europe and the United States, as director of the Vienna Philharmonic from 1919 to 1927, back at the Vienna Staatsoper in 1935–36.

Like so many conductors, he started out as a choreographic figure on the podium, all motion and gesture. Once, in 1896, when he conducted the Beethoven Ninth in Berlin, he lost control, and the *Musical Courier* said that he "acted and struck himself with stick, hands, legs and feet like a madman." The critic goes on to compare Weingartner disparagingly with Theodore Thomas ("the simplest and one of the most effective conductors in the world") and Nikisch ("a very volcano of suppressed and controlled nervous energy . . . and yet how outwardly quiet and artistically reposeful he is on the conductor's stand"). Weingartner was active in Paris as a guest conductor—he was a Berlioz specialist—and when Debussy saw him, the German conductor reminded him of "a new knife." Weingartner's gestures, said Debussy, "have a kind of angular grace; then suddenly the imperious movement of his arms seems to compel the trombones to bellow and to drive the cymbals to frenzy. It is most impressive and verges on the miraculous." Debussy, who never could resist a good phrase, said that Weingartner conducted the *Pastoral* Symphony with the care of a conscientious gardener. To the French writer Colette we owe a neat picture of the young Weingartner. She was writing a musical column in *Gil Blas* in 1903:

Tall, clean-shaven, and with that colorless complexion, suddenly turning crimson, of an enlightened Jesuit, Weingartner conducts with gestures that are magnificent or ridiculous. His coattails jump up with the ataxic jerks of his arms or fly around to the rhythm of his hammering fists. In opening the floodgates of music, this German works himself up to a state of epilepsy.

But that phase did not last long. Soon Weingartner became famous in orchestral circles for the sobriety of his gestures, the economy of

COLUMBIA RECORDS

Felix Weingartner, who broke away from the exaggerations of the Wagner school of conducting and tried to get back to the printed note. He was one of the major forces in the development of the modern style.

his stick. A little-known description of Weingartner in his early American years was written by H. T. Parker after a concert of the Boston Symphony in January 1906:

A tall, spare, erect, pale man, aquiline of face, high of forehead, supple of body—impersonal almost of appearance until he begins his work. A serious man, a cultivated man, you are sure a man of the world of intellect as well, and the better musician because he is all three. He begins, and the very rap for attention seems a transforming spark. For an instant the vivid incisiveness of his beat is dazzling. It seems to sting his men like a fine lash. The clearness of it is lucidity itself. The precision of it leaves not an inch for error. Then it vanishes, almost, in the fascination of the left hand. With that Weingartner curves a melody, shades a rhythm, stimulates, stills, calls, seemingly, a particular instrument into being . . .

Weingartner was a complicated man, all things to all men. To some who knew him well, he was sweet and innocent, and many referred to him as Parsifal—not always in a complimentary sense; the implication was that he was a pure, simple fool. Extremely handsome, he was called "The Greek God," and women came flocking around him. He did not reject them. Five times was he married. This is the roster: Marie Juilerat; Baroness Fedora von Dreifus; Lucille Marcel, a singer; Roxo Bertha Kalisch, a Viennese poet and singer; and Carmen Studer, one of his conducting pupils. He could be considerate and he could also be tactless. He was a compulsive pamphlet and letter writer who deluged newspapers constantly about everything. As his name was Felix Weingartner, his letters were published. He also was constantly in the courts over one thing or another; his life seemed an endless litigation. Edwin Evans, the British critic, thought that Weingartner had some mild form of persecution mania. Early on he became a convert to astrology, which he called a long-neglected science. In 1891 he had the hour at which he signed his Berlin Opera contract investigated by "an experienced astrologer," and was horrified to learn that the stars were in unfavorable aspect to his horoscope. In his autobiography he darkly says, "The stars did not lie." The tragedy of his life was his failure to establish himself as a great composer. Weingartner regarded himself as an unrecognized genius but, alas, the world did not regard him so. He composed operas, symphonies, chamber music. All had performances and all were promptly forgotten.

His years at the Vienna Opera were strenuous. He entered on a lawsuit, for the Berlin Opera claimed that he had broken his contract to go to Vienna. Then he was accused of being an anti-Semite (a charge that he had to fight a good part of his career). As an opera manager he was the antithesis of his predecessor, Mahler. Shortly after taking command, he conducted *Die Walküre* with substantial cuts, and the press rose in wrath. Weingartner, always relishing an opportunity to exercise his prose, wrote a long letter, defending his position, to the *Neue freie Presse,* in which he said that for decades he had been studying Wagner and had

reached the conclusion that many pages of the *Ring des Nibelungen, Tannhäuser* and even the short *Fliegende Holländer* are too long, not only in actual time but also in organic structure, dramatic necessities and (in the two first-named works) unity of style. I consider judicious cutting an artistic duty that greatly enhances the esthetic pleasure to be obtained.

Weingartner, in this letter, also had some tart remarks to make about "enervating tradition" (presumably aimed at Mahler; and how Mahler would have laughed!). Then he made a defiant statement, throwing the gauntlet right back in the faces of the critics: "I hereby announce that I intend to introduce into several of the Wagner operas the cuts that seem to be demanded by artistic necessity. Nor shall I be turned from my purpose by any kind of opposition." Then, finally, some casuistry: "Permit me to add that I hold 'Wagner' and 'Wagnerian' to be not in the slightest degree related, but on the contrary as diametrically opposed in their conceptions and ideas. I revere Wagner so highly that I consider it an honor to acknowledge myself an enthusiastic anti-Wagnerian."

Perhaps in an effort to show who was the boss, Weingartner as one of his first acts shelved a production of *Fidelio* that Mahler had been ready to give. Weingartner wanted no part of Mahler or his tradition. One of the results was that all Mahler-engaged musicians and singers felt themselves under suspicion. Many left, including some Viennese favorites, and there was an enormous turnover. That did not help make Weingartner popular. In an effort to correct the situation, Weingartner brought in many new singers. Most of them proved incompetent. Roller, who had created some of the great productions of the Mahler administration, became antagonized. Soon Weingartner could do no good as far as Vienna was concerned. Among other things, he was accused of favoritism toward particular singers, especially Lucille Marcel, *née* Wasself. There may have been some truth in the accusation; she became his third wife. Things got to such a point that when some scenery during a *Meistersinger* rehearsal toppled and broke Weingartner's leg, the critic Julius Korngold suggested that even the scenery of the opera house felt impelled to rebel against the conductor. When Weingartner left, with no regrets on either side, he was succeeded by the operatic businessman, Hans Gregor. The Vienna Opera had had its fill of musicians at its head.

When he stuck to the things he knew best, Weingartner was impeccable. He was the conductor of the golden mean: never too slow, never too fast, never too soft, never too loud. "No slow tempo," he once wrote, "should be so slow that the melody of the piece is *not yet* recognizable, and so fast that the melody is *no longer* recognizable." Orchestra players used to say of him that of all conductors he was almost the only one whose tempo never varied between rehearsal and performance. One might add that his performances varied very little through the years. There must be well over a decade between his two recordings of Mozart's E flat Symphony, but the tempos, phrasings and conception are virtually the same. In Weingartner's conducting were no romanticisms, no exploitation of the ego. Instead there were, in Bruno Walter's words, "fiery tempo, naturalness and simplicity." All these can be heard in Weingartner's long and distinguished series of recordings, a series that started in 1913 with a segment of the first movement of Tchaikovsky's *Pathétique* on a single-sided American Columbia disc. His standard was remarkably high. Never is there a lapse in taste, an ugly phrase, anything not motivated by the most graceful musicianship and aristocracy of conception. To many he remains the most rounded and satisfactory of all conductors in his chosen repertoire.

The Italians and Toscanini

THROUGHOUT MOST of the nineteenth century, Italy, which had originated so much of importance in the history of conducting, contributed not a single conductor of importance to the international scene. There were conductors in the country, some of them good, but for the most part they were exponents only of an operatic culture and tradition. Very few symphony orchestras existed in Italy during the century, and even in the major opera houses the standard of performance was low. Italian conductors seldom left Italy; and when they did go as guest conductors to the major capitals of Europe, it was only to take charge of Italian opera.

Angelo Mariani was the first of the great Italian conductors as we understand the term today. He made his debut in Trento in 1844, and by 1846 was at La Scala, conducting a great deal of Verdi and arousing the composer's interest. Later, after appearances in several European cities, he made Genoa his headquarters. Verdi and he became close friends, and Mariani was to the Italian composer what Richter was to Wagner. Indeed, Verdi took advantage of his friend, using him for menial errands and the like. Around 1870 the friendship broke up. It may have been more than coincidence that the rupture was followed by Mariani's espousal of Wagner. He conducted the Italian premieres of *Lohengrin* and *Tannhäuser* in 1871 and 1872 respectively. Mariani seems to have been a vain, temperamental, virtuoso type of conductor who did not hesitate to alter everything that came his way, changing expression marks, rhythms, tempos and even notes. All was aimed at greater orchestral effectiveness. Verdi deeply resented the liberties Mariani took in *Don Carlo* and *La Forza del Destino*. In a letter to Giulio Ricordi, Verdi complained: "We all agree about his ability, but this is not the question of an individual, no matter how great he may be, but of art. I do not allow either singers or conductors to *create*, which is, as I said, a principle that leads to ruin." And Verdi went on to cite chapter and verse, pointing out how Mariani's emendations had literally changed the character of *Don Carlo*.

Verdi himself occasionally picked up the baton for special occasions. Wherever he conducted he made a great impression, and he probably could have been the Italian counterpart of Wagner had he so desired. Other ranking Italian conductors of the nineteenth and early twentieth centuries were Franco Faccio, the Verdi specialist who conducted the world premiere of *Otello* in 1887; Luigi Mancinelli, active in Bologna, London, New York and Buenos Aires; Leopoldo Mugnone, the Puccini conductor; Arturo Vigna, who came to the Metropolitan Opera during 1903–1907; and Cleofonte Campanini, who came to the United States as a conductor for Hammerstein's Manhattan Opera House and then settled in Chicago, where he was active in opera from 1910 until his death in 1919. All of these conductors devoted themselves almost exclusively to one facet of the repertoire, opera; and one facet of the facet, Italian opera. (That remains true. Such later conductors as Tullio Serafin, Bernardino Molinari, Victor de Sabata, Vittorio Gui and Carlo Giulini are considered primarily exponents of Italian opera.)

And then came Arturo Toscanini.

Toscanini was the pivotal conductor of his period: the strongest influence, the one who marks the final transition from the Wagner style to twentieth-century objectivity. He became the greatest single force on contemporary conducting. "Whatever you may think about his interpretation of a specific work," George Szell has written, "that he changed the whole concept of conducting and that he rectified many, many arbitrary procedures of a generation of conductors before him, is now authentic history. That at the same time he has served as a not too useful model for a generation of conductors who were so fascinated that they were unable to follow him with some sort of discrimination is equally true." Elsewhere Szell points out the major characteristic of Toscanini: that he "wiped out the arbitrariness of the postromantic interpreters. He did away with the meretricious tricks and the thick encrustation of the interpretive nuances that had been piling up for decades."

Arturo Toscanini at the turn of the century. Already he was known as a fiery, temperamental genius who always had to have things his own way.

Toscanini with Fritz Reiner in the middle 1920's. The automobile belonged to Reiner, who, incidentally, was a precisionist as a conductor almost in Toscanini's class. Toscanini at that time was director of La Scala.

The point is that Toscanini followed the progression of such as Muck, Strauss and Weingartner to become a highly objective conductor and the greatest of all the literalists. His literalism manifested itself in many ways, and it was something that went far beyond merely observing in a faithful manner the printed notes and the composers' expression markings. It was a total revulsion against the Austro-German tradition, against the Wagnerian concept of fluctuation of tempo. Even more: Toscanini represented a musical objectivity as intense in its way as the subjectivity of Wagner, Bülow and Mahler. Where they kept putting themselves into the music, using the score as a vehicle for self-expression, Toscanini was equally determined to keep himself out of the score.

He had read a great deal about stylistic problems, and he had come to the conclusion that there was no conclusion. He said that it was futile to try to achieve an "authentic" style. Instruments had changed, pitch had changed, concepts had changed, and Beethoven would hardly recognize a twentieth-century performance of his music. Thus the only thing—*the only thing*—a musician has is the notes, and those he must observe as honestly and scrupulously as possible. And not only must he observe the notes, but he must keep a steady rhythmic flow, avoiding the heaving and hauling that characterized the rhythms and tempos that in a previous age had been used in the name of "expression." Conductors like Furtwängler who (according to Toscanini) were constantly overinterpreting in the name of "style" aroused his scorn and derision. No. Here are the notes. To interpret them a conductor has to rely on musicianship, taste, and instinct for what the composer wanted. "The tradition," Toscanini stormed, "is to be found only in one place—in the music!" Thus Toscanini's comment about the *Eroica* Symphony, which he uttered in 1926: "Some say this is Napoleon, some Hitler, some Mussolini. For me it is simply allegro con brio." Several years later, Willem Mengelberg deigned to give Toscanini advice on conducting. Toscanini, who had a low opinion of him to begin with, was enraged. "Talk, talk, talk, that was Mengelberg," he later said. "Once he came to me and told me at great length the proper German way to conduct the *Coriolanus* Overture. He had got it, he said quite seriously, from a conductor who supposedly had got it straight from Beethoven. Bah! I told him I got it straight from Beethoven himself, from the score."

Most conductors with this point of view would normally develop into dispassionate, super-objective time beaters. And, indeed, Toscanini was accused of being exactly that in his early years, just as Josef Hofmann was being called a cold pianist because he refused to bend the rhythm and distort the shape the way pianists of the Liszt school used to do. Giulio Ricordi kept attacking Toscanini in the *Gazzetta Musicale,* charging him with rigidity of execution, mathematical accuracy and lack of poetry. Ricordi said that Toscanini's conducting of *Falstaff* resembled that of a "mastadonic mechanical piano." Later on, Ricordi changed his mind, as did virtually everybody else. Once he had conquered the world, Toscanini for decades seemed immune to criticism. He was considered a miracle, a force of nature. "What is the secret of Toscanini?" the London *Times* wanted to know in 1926. "That he is the greatest of conductors, most of us are agreed." A French musician swore that Toscanini's looks were not on the musicians but on the sound itself. "He *looks* at the sound." There was a *mystique* about this potent figure, and not until the last years of his life did a new school of criticism dare to question it.

The fact that Toscanini did not develop into a sterile technician was a tribute to a patrician musical mind. Literalist though he was, he also knew that music must sing and expand; and despite his own tenets he was perfectly capable of modifying a score, or getting his own personality into his interpretations. Discussing a certain passage with the American conductor Milton Katims, the Old Man (so he was called in those years) reached for a metronome. "Here, this must be absolutely rhythmically precise." He started the metronome and played the passage on the piano. After a few bars, Toscanini was ahead. He uttered his famous "Bah!" He shut off the metronome. "One is not a machine. Music must breathe." And Toscanini did everything in his power to make music breathe, even to the point of altering the instrumentation if that were needed. A literalist he may have been, but not a blind purist. His phrases were long and aristocratic, his climaxes stupendous, his handling of melodic elements gracious and lyric. Above all, the feature that marked his conducting was intensity. There was a tensile quality that no other conductor could match, and even light music suddenly sounded sinewy and powerful when Toscanini conducted. His tempos were supposed to be fast, and sometimes they were. But often they merely *sounded* fast because everything was so perfectly regulated. Instrumentalists know this. A perfectly adjusted scale or run, at a moderate tempo, sounds faster than a scrambled scale or run that in reality may be half again as fast.

In dispensing with the Wagner-Bülow-Nikisch approach to conducting, in discarding the entire romantic style and going straight to the score, in insisting that everything be played exactly as written, in abolishing excess tempo fluctuation, in demanding that orchestras play in tune (most orchestras, even great ones, were careless about intonation even after the turn of the century), Toscanini vitalized interpretation and performance practice. He even did away with the favorite expressive device of the romantics, the string portamento, or slide. Listen to almost any pre-1920 orchestral recording, and there will be a slide between the two important melodic notes of a slow phrase. Even so fine a conductor as Weingartner was not immune, and in his 1913 recording of the *Pathétique* excerpt, something like this can be heard from the violins:

where the space between the A and the D is filled with a long, deliberate swoop. The mannerism (at least, today it is considered a mannerism; then it was standard performance practice) can be heard in all early recordings—in those of Beecham, Stransky, Nikisch, Stock, everybody. Obviously the device was used automatically by violinists in orchestras, and the purpose was to emphasize the key note of the phrase. But not Toscanini's violinists, and his first recordings, in 1921, are devoid of the portamento.

So pure was Toscanini's approach, so heroically did he dispense with the "tradition" of generations, and so forceful was his ability to put his ideas across (no conductor in history before Toscanini demanded and got such unearthly precision and such a wide range of dynamics from an orchestra) that his interpretations came as something new and revolutionary. The standard analogy compared him with a restorer cleaning great paintings that had never really been seen in their original colors by modern viewers. Ernest Newman heard Toscanini conduct *Tristan und Isolde* in Bayreuth in 1931. Now, Newman was the world's greatest Wagner authority and, of course, he had the opera by heart. "I thought," Newman wrote, "I knew that work from end to end and from outside to inside; but I was amazed to find, here and there, a passage coming on me like a dagger stroke." Newman looked up the passages in the score. "Then I found that all, or practically all, he had done was to play the notes just as Wagner directs them to be played." Toscanini always had the ability to balance musical lines so that every relationship was heard, and this kind of fluoroscopic conducting was something he had to a greater degree than anybody else.

The story about Toscanini's impromptu debut in South America is too well known to bear repetition. The correct date, supplied by Walter Toscanini, is June 30, 1886. (It is an interesting coincidence that Mancinelli's debut almost exactly paralleled Toscanini's. Like Toscanini, Mancinelli was a cellist in an orchestra and was suddenly called to the podium in an emergency. The opera was the same— *Aida*.) For almost seventy years after his debut in Rio de Janeiro Toscanini was active as a conductor. At twenty-one he was well launched on his career, though for a long time he was not very well known outside of Italy except by reputation. The first mention of his name in an American publication seems to have been in the Detroit *Song Journal* of February 1, 1896. A correspondent sent a report from Turin: "What a wonderful *chef d'orchestre* Toscanini is! . . . How sure, how calm he is; the best leader in Italy, and the only one in Italy capable of conducting Wagner's music in such a grand manner. And, think of it, he conducts everything from memory!"

In his own country, Toscanini rapidly became the big man, conducting the Italian premieres of *Pelléas et Mélisande*, *Euryanthe*, *Eugene Onegin*, *Götterdämmerung*, *Siegfried* and the world premieres of *Pagliacci* in 1892 and *La Bohème* in 1896. Puccini had wanted Nikisch but had to settle for Toscanini, then director of the Teatro Regio in Turin. Soon Puccini was convinced that he had the right man. "Extraordinary! Highly intelligent!" For years the two men had an uneasy on-again, off-again friendship.

Around the turn of the century, Toscanini began to conduct the symphonic repertoire. But opera remained his chief occupation. At La Scala, where he took over in 1895, Toscanini was admired by many, and also attacked by some for his "rigidity" and his despotism. His departure was characteristic. At the last night of the 1902–1903 season Giovanni Zenatello was singing the tenor lead in *Un Ballo in*

Maschera, and the audience yelled for an encore of an aria. Toscanini refused, and the audience would not let the opera continue. So Toscanini walked out after the second act and remained away for four years. Wherever he went, he had to have complete authority.

In 1908 he came to the Metropolitan Opera with its new general manager, Giulio Gatti-Casazza, and remained for seven seasons. It did not take Toscanini long to make an impact. He arrived with an enormous reputation, made an impression that fully lived up to his reputation, and the Boston *Transcript* wrote about "this modest man" who "is the most heroic figure in grand opera throughout the world. His supremacy is indisputable." Immediately a legend began to be built. At first the papers said that he could conduct sixty operas without a score. Soon this figure was expanded to 150, then 160. Stories were written about his memory, and Wolf-Ferrari was quoted as saying, "It seems strange, somehow, to think that he knows my opera [*Le Donne Curiose*] by heart when I myself don't." Through his seven seasons at the Metropolitan Opera, Toscanini conducted twenty-nine operas; and, unlike most Italian conductors, he was overwhelming in Wagner and French operas. He also conducted some concerts, including a famous evening in 1913 when Beethoven's Ninth Symphony was the featured work.

His rupture with the Metropolitan Opera has never been fully explained. Gatti-Casazza in his memoirs is reticent, saying merely that he, Gatti, did his utmost to retain the great conductor. Walter Toscanini says that his father was dissatisfied with rehearsal conditions and penny-pinching economies. The New York *Times* of September 30, 1915, said that the Metropolitan Opera was prepared to make every concession, "but they reasonably expected him to adapt himself—principal lever though he might be—to the occasional necessities of a great operating machine." *Musical America* went more thoroughly into the case:

Some say, frankly, that while they admire his genius and consider him perhaps the greatest opera conductor in the world today, they would not particularly miss him, for the reason that his great talent and mastery of stage effect were offset by his frightful irritability and his habit of perpetually abusing the artists, the chorus and the orchestra during rehearsals, and never losing an opportunity of hurling invective at poor Gatti-Casazza, whenever he saw him, whether on the stage or in the wings. The result, they said, was that by the end of the season half the company was in a state of nervous collapse.

In any event, Toscanini left the house in one of his typical rages, and he never returned. Nor was he reconciled with Gatti-Casazza until many years had passed. Later the Metropolitan Opera made every effort to lure him back. But Toscanini was one who never forgot or forgave. "I will conduct on the ashes of the Metropolitan," he snarled.

During World War I Toscanini, who was in Italy, conducted relatively little. He returned to La Scala in 1921 and soon got into trouble with the Fascist government. In 1926 he walked out of La Scala when ordered to conduct *Giovinezza*, the Fascist anthem. Because the world premiere of *Turandot* was in the offing, Mussolini bent to Toscanini's wishes. That year, 1926, was also the one in which Toscanini first conducted the New York Philharmonic; and the following year he was co-conductor with Mengelberg. With the merger in 1928 of the New York Philharmonic and the New York Symphony, Toscanini was named principal conductor. Those members of the new orchestra who had never played under Toscanini were petrified with fright at the prospect. Winthrop Sargeant, later a prominent music critic, went from the violin section of the New York Symphony to the Philharmonic, and has written some amusing recollections of the event. The newcomers would point out Toscanini's scowling picture on the Carnegie Hall billboards to their children and warn them if they were not good, Toscanini would get them. When Toscanini finally arrived, the musicians did unprecedented things, such as taking their parts home and practicing them. Toscanini, says Sargent, had the ability above all other conductors to make every performance and rehearsal "a continuous psychology of crisis." Toscanini was merely being Toscanini. "Each movement of a symphony became an emergency which demanded every ounce of energy and concentration if it was not to end in an overwhelming catastrophe. Each performance was played as though our very lives depended on its perfection. . . . Beyond all technique there was a residue of mysterious personal power that lay outside ordinary comprehension."

In the meantime, Toscanini was breaking with his own country. Anti-fascist, anti-Nazi, he once remarked that in life he was a democrat, in music an aristocrat. He refused to conduct in Italy after 1931 and at Bayreuth after 1933. He left Salzburg when the Nazis took over, saying, among other things, that he would not associate himself with Furtwängler and the others who had worked for Hitler.

At the end of the 1935–36 season he left the New York Philharmonic, and apparently the career of the sixty-nine-year-old conductor was over. But in 1937 he returned to the United States as head of the NBC Symphony Orchestra, the group specifically created for him by the National Broadcasting Company. Among the by-products of his programming with that orchestra were the inclusion of concert versions of several of the operas with which he was so long associated, and which two generations of Americans had not heard him conduct—*La Bohème, Fidelio, La Traviata, Otello, Falstaff, Aïda*. A long series of phonograph recordings was another by-product.

It was during those NBC years that the Toscanini legend grew to proportions that dwarfed anything that had gone before. The Old Man was wonderful newspaper copy, though he never sought publicity and, indeed, shunned it. He seems to have been genuinely modest—knowing his own worth, of course, but interested only in his search for musical perfection. Everything else was secondary, as it always had been. He lived only for music, the only thing he really knew. As Adrian Boult has said, "He had nothing else to think of but music. I never heard him talk of anything else. Bruno Walter could discuss the latest play or novel, but not Toscanini."

At his rehearsals he continued to operate as before, maintaining his psychology of crisis. His battle cry, says Samuel Antek, one of the string players in the NBC Symphony, was *"Cantare! Sostenere!"* Sing! Sustain! "No conductor could create such a feeling of ecstasy," Antek says. Toscanini's relatively simple, classic beat, controlled and disciplined, pulled music from the players. (His baton, it can be learned from the August 1941 issue of *Music Trades,* was 18⅝ inches long, with a heavy shaft, a cork grip 4½ inches long and about ⁵⁄₁₆ inches in diameter.) His baton movements were generally between shoulder and waist, and his most characteristic pose was one with legs apart, body swaying a little, left hand over his heart in heavy vibration during lyric passages (former string players have a tendency to do this). When the music was dramatic and strongly rhythmic, Toscanini's beat became shorter (the mark of a good conductor; the wider a beat, the slower the response from an orchestra).

Toscanini leading the NBC Symphony, his face a characteristic scowl of concentration. No conductor had ever achieved such control and intensity.

At Bayreuth, 1930. Toscanini refused to conduct there during the Hitler era.

RCA VICTOR

Toscanini always conducted from memory. His eyesight was too poor for a score to be of any use to him during a performance. But he could see, and correct, the slightest bow movement of a bass some thirty feet away. He worked like a demon and expected everybody else to do the same. If things did not go his way he went into a tantrum, one of his famous tantrums. His rages were legendary. "It was among the most horrifying sounds I have ever heard," Antek says, "and seemed to come from his entrails. He would almost double up, his mouth opened wide, his face red, as if on the verge of an apoplectic fit. Then a raucous blast of unbelievable volume would blare forth." Unknown to Toscanini, the Victor engineers kept an open microphone on many of his rehearsals, and struck off acetate recordings of the more interesting ones for a fortunate few. On some of these discs Toscanini can be heard in full eruption, and the sounds are positively Vesuvian. The discs also give an idea of his demands, of his insistence on clarity, of the number of times he could repeat a phrase to get a tiny point—an oboe staccato, say—to his satisfaction.

To Toscanini there were no short cuts. Nor was there any such thing as evasion. Saul Goodman, the timpanist of the New York Philharmonic, points out that Toscanini's insistence on hearing every note, and every note in exact time and tune, led to higher standards of orchestral playing throughout the world. Every score contains certain awkward things that players had always glided over, either because conductors did not notice the evasion or were sympathetic with the players' plight. Not Toscanini. His musicians had to play the notes as written. At first there were great howls from instrumentalists, who had to devise new fingerings and new ways of blowing. But eventually, under Toscanini, the unplayable became playable.

When things did not go the way his vision wanted them to go, Toscanini suffered, really suffered. A sloppy phrase, a careless note, an awkward entrance—these were enough to ruin his disposition for a week. Such mistakes did not happen very often in a Toscanini orchestra. Players under his baton took special pains, partly from actual fear, partly from pride. Good musicians will invariably make an extra effort when faced with a conductor for whom they have respect. Toscanini may have been disliked, and even hated, by some of his players, but they played for him as they played for no other conductor. Always at a Toscanini concert the audience could be sure of the whiplash attacks and releases, the incredibly perfect ensemble, the horizontal rather than vertical approach to music (that is, to Toscanini, counterpoint—the balance of line against line—was more important than harmony), the clarity, the force, the tensile rhythms that were Toscanini's special contribution.

Toward the end of his career he began to encounter criticism. A new generation of critics was active, and they were looking for more from a conductor than Toscanini could supply. His repertoire came under heavy attack, nor was his musical philosophy immune. Toscanini conducted very few contemporary works; and those he did conduct were mostly ephemera. Nobody queried Toscanini's amazing ability to get results from an orchestra; but, some critics asked, was the result worthwhile? Virgil Thomson, one of the doubters, wondered:

When he conducts any work . . . he knows the score and gives it as careful, as polished a reading as if his whole life depended on that single work. . . . His culture may be elementary, but his ear is true. He makes music out of anything. And the music that he makes is the plainest, the most straightforward music now available in public performance. There is little of historical evocation in it and even less of deliberate emotional appeal. It is purely arbitrary, just ordered sound and little else. There even isn't much Toscanini in it. For in spite of his high temperament, this musician is strangely lacking in personality. That is why, I believe, he has based his interpretative routine on as literal as possible an adherence to the musical texts. . . . He will not loom large, I imagine, in the history books of the future because he has mostly remained on the side lines of the creative struggle. . . . His involvement with the formation of our century's musical style, with the encouragement of the contemporary expression in music, with the living composers, in short, whose work will one day constitute the story of music in our time, has been less than that of any of today's orchestral great.

Thomson, as a composer and one of the leaders of the then avant-garde, was of course bothered by Toscanini's lack of involvement with contemporary music. But certainly Toscanini's record in that respect was not any worse than that of some of his contemporaries—Bruno Walter, Felix Weingartner, or Sir Thomas Beecham, for instance. Few conductors on reaching old age interest themselves in new music, and that applies even to such conductors as Otto Klemperer, who in the middle 1920s was associated with the avant-garde. As a young man, Toscanini had fought the good fight, taking up the cause of Wagner, Puccini and Debussy. In any case, conductors can, *pace* Thomson, live in the history books for other things than being propagandists for modern music; and Thomson's statement that Toscanini had little influence on the century's musical style is nothing more than wishful thinking. The fact is that Toscanini, who had no pupils as such and few protégés—his most promising one, Guido Cantelli, died in an airplane crash at the age of thirty-six—was the greatest influence on conducting in his time, and did more to crystallize a kind of literalism adopted by all musicians than anybody else. As such, Toscanini does indeed have a place in the history books. Almost every young conductor tried to imitate him, refusing to use a score in public, trying to achieve the Toscanini kind of linear independence, adopting a literal approach, avoiding romanticism. The world seemed full of little Toscaninis, all of whom were trying vainly to achieve the impossible. What often resulted was literalism carried to absurdity; movement without vision; music in which technique was more important than communication. None of this was Toscanini's wish, but that was what happened. A few of the younger conductors were able to survive, but not many. To a large extent, the 1960s are still in the Toscanini dominance; his influence remains strongly felt.

The Old Man's last concert was heartbreaking. It took place on April 4, 1954. About a week previously, on his eighty-seventh birthday, he had sent a letter of resignation to NBC. During the broadcast, Toscanini—he of the infallible memory—had perhaps the only mental blackout of his life. Radio listeners heard the Bacchanale from *Tannhäuser* slow up and threaten to disintegrate. There was a pause, and, shockingly, the strains of the Brahms First filled the air. What had happened was that Toscanini virtually stopped beating time, standing with a vacant look on his face. Frank Miller, the first cellist, tried to give the cues. In the control room there was panic; and Cantelli, it is said, told the engineers to cut Toscanini off and put on the Brahms recording. Within some thirty seconds or so, Toscanini recovered, and the Bacchanale went back on the air. The broadcast over, Toscanini went back to his dressing room and, in effect, passed into history. He died three years later.

· XXIV ·

Willem Mengelberg

ALTHOUGH TOSCANINI was the conductor who beyond all others of his time influenced the coming generation, it does not necessarily mean that he had a marked influence on the conductors of his own generation. Their style, stemming largely from traditions of the nineteenth century, had already been formed. As one looks back upon the period of Toscanini's great days, which would be the first half of the twentieth century, it was a golden age, and the chances are overwhelming that never again will there be anything like it. Nikisch, Muck and Mahler were active. There were, in addition to Toscanini, a group of conductors whose very names ring bells—men like Weingartner, Walter, Furtwängler, Beecham, Stokowski, Reiner, Ansermet, Kleiber, Monteux, Klemperer, Koussevitzky, Ormandy, Szell.

Some of these were the antithesis of Toscanini. Three of these important conductors—Mengelberg, Wilhelm Furtwängler and Bruno Walter—were frankly romantic and represented the romantic rather than the modern tradition. Of these three, Willem Mengelberg was the greatest virtuoso, a sort of Horowitz of the orchestra, a conductor of high emotionalism and infinite vigor. A short, rather plump man, Mengelberg was called The Napoleon of the Orchestra. Considering Mengelberg's arbitrary ideas about music and his habit of constantly retouching, it comes as no surprise to learn that the strongest influence on his thinking came from Mahler, whom he met in 1902. Completely Mahlerian was Mengelberg's statement to the BBC Orchestra, as quoted by Bernard Shore, the English violist and writer:

Beethoven, like many other composers, made changements in his scores, even after publication, and then he also vos deaf. So vy not the conductor also, who often knows mooch better than the composer? I vos de best pupil of Schidler, who vos the best pupil of Beethoven, zo I know vat Beethoven meant. [Mengelberg was pulling the orchestra's leg. By "Schidler," he meant Schindler, who died in 1864. Mengelberg was born in 1871.] Zo, in dis verk of Strauss, I haf been great friend of Richard Strauss since I vos a boy, and I know joost what he wants, and ve will make some changements also!

Mengelberg should not be judged too harshly in this attitude, no more than Wagner, Mahler—or, indeed, almost every musician of the post-romantic period. It was expected, even in Mengelberg's day, that the performer help the composer, short of actual violence. When Busoni was reproached for rewriting parts of Franck's Prelude, Chorale and Fugue, he answered quite simply, and to him logically, that Franck did not always know how to obtain the effects he wanted. It should be repeated over and over again, at the risk of being tedious, that fidelity to the printed note is a recent invention; and we can no more condemn a nineteenth-century musician for following the dictates of his age than we can condemn an early Italian artist for not knowing the laws of perspective.

German-trained, Mengelberg conducted at Lucerne for five years and then, in 1895, returned to his native Holland as director of the Amsterdam Concertgebouw. He took a provincial group and turned it into one of the half-dozen glories of the orchestral world. He conducted the Concertgebouw orchestra for forty-one years, until 1941. During the war, Mengelberg collaborated with the Nazis, and in 1945 the Netherlands Honors Council barred him from participation in the musical life of the country. His defense was his art. "My art is public property. I am not supposed to withhold it from anyone. I have no interest in politics." But the fact remained that he had taken a position in the German Culture Cabinet in 1941 and conducted in Germany throughout the war.

He was a conductor of extraordinary skill and drive, one who reveled in the big-sounding, complicated scores of Mahler and Strauss. The latter dedicated *Ein Heldenleben* to him, and it was commonly held that no conductor got such excitement, brilliance and drama from the score. Mengelberg left a recording that bears ample witness to such a statement. He belonged to the Wagnerian school as a stylist. A true romantic, he would slow down between contrasting passages,

Willem Mengelberg, one of the virtuoso conductors of the early twentieth century. He took the provincial Amsterdam Concertgebouw Orchestra and made it one of the most brilliant and responsive ensembles in Europe.

use rubato effects, and leave little to the imagination. As late as 1930 he would let his strings use a portamento for heightened emotional effect, allowing them to slide into notes in the adagio of the Ninth Symphony. This old-fashioned effect, and his tempo changes, bothered many musicians and critics. But his sense of drama and his enormous canvas drove the public wild. As Lawrence Gilman said, "His lapses try one sorely, but his virtues are magnificent."

Mengelberg was quite active in the United States, arriving in 1905 and making constant appearances thereafter. In 1919 he was approached by the Boston Symphony as a successor to Muck. Boston and Mengelberg could not get together on money. "I was always under the impression that America was a very rich country," he told a reporter, "but to judge by the offers that have been made, one would not think so." Later he conducted the New York Philharmonic, and in 1927–28 became co-conductor with Toscanini. Two mighty temperaments clashed, and Mengelberg was the loser. Winthrop Sargeant says that Mengelberg had made the orchestra a perfectly disciplined one. Toscanini, however, did not think so, and started to re-create it, discarding all of Mengelberg's cherished notions. Toscanini greeted mistakes (Sargeant says) not with theoretical explanations but with towering rages, during which he broke batons and knocked over music stands. Mengelberg represented "on the one side the man of principle and tradition battling for a system of musical morality that he believed to be greater than himself. On the other side, a relentless, autocratic genius swept everything before him, demanding absolute subservience not to law and order, but to standards dictated purely by his own instinctive taste." The members of the orchestra knew who was going to be the victor, and poor Mengelberg's rehearsals degenerated into a state of anarchy. Mengelberg stuck to his guns, but he had lost his power and therefore his authority. He tried gamely to stick it out, took the abuse for several seasons, and then went home, not to return.

One other thing about Mengelberg: of all conductors who ever lived, he was the most compulsive talker. Carl Flesch once timed Mengelberg at a rehearsal. The conductor talked for one and a half hours and made music only for three-quarters of an hour. Bernard Shore has described the first time he played under the Dutch conductor, then a veteran. Mengelberg came forth and began by reminiscing about the wonderful experiences he had had all over the world, conducting orchestras everywhere. "And," he said, "you will see there is nothing I do not know. So give me now the A, Mr. Oboe." Whereupon it took the orchestra twenty-five minutes to tune up to Mengelberg's satisfaction. It was a positive ceremony. First the violins took the A from the oboe, then the rest of the string choirs in order, then the rest of the orchestra, again choir by choir, ending with the tuba. When the entire orchestra had the A, then the violins could tune their other strings. The oboe officiated like a high priest and had "to stand and turn in the direction of the department concerned, for the benefit of those far away, while Mengelberg, sitting like a Buddha on the podium, criticized the slightest deviation in pitch." Eventually the orchestra got the tuning down to five or six minutes. (Some conductors are especially sensitive about tuning. Sir Henry Wood, in the early days of the Queen's Hall Orchestra, had a tuning machine built—a silver harmonium with a reed blown by a bellows in a small wind chest tuned at exactly 435.5 vibrations per second at 59° Fahrenheit. He insisted on every single player filing past it, backstage, to tune up.)

Mengelberg's reputation fast dissipated after his death. That often happens to virtuosos, and Mengelberg was unfortunate enough to die in a period that looked down at his two greatest assets—virtuosity and romanticism. Posterity has been unkind to him; he deserves more. His music making may have been mannered by present standards, but it always had life, drive, excitement, exuberance, its own kind of conviction. As a colorist he was excelled by none, not even Koussevitzky or Stokowski. The little man was an authentic force, one of the great individualists, and one of the authentic masters of the orchestra.

Wilhelm Furtwängler

WHERE MENGELBERG'S EFFECTS were primarily external, those of Wilhelm Furtwängler were all internal. Mengelberg's audiences would react as though they were in an arena, while Furtwängler's reacted as though they were in church. Many considered Furtwängler the greatest conductor of his time, the only real rival to Toscanini. It is hard to think of a twentieth-century conductor—indeed, it is hard to think of any conductor, Nikisch included—who made Furtwängler's kind of mystical impact on an audience. He represented the essence of the German idealistic (philosophical idealism, not ethical) approach to music; and he was regarded as a spokesman for something holy and sublime. When he conducted, he seemed often to be under hypnosis, conscious of neither the audience nor the orchestra, wrapped in sound and his inner vision. He gave the impression of operating under forces that moved him, marionette-like; and through him was distilled organized tone bent to an emotional end. Some critics and writers have tried to suggest he was an intellectual. He really wasn't. Yehudi Menuhin, his fervent admirer, comes close to the point when he calls Furtwängler "an inspired mystic in the medieval German tradition . . . with the certainty and assurance of one who has seen visions and followed them."

Primarily he was a Wagnerian offshoot, a subjectivist, a conductor more interested in phrase than in the bar line, more interested in content than execution, constantly employing the very kind of tempo fluctuations Wagner and his school so carefully described. That is one reason why so many of his recordings fail to do him justice. He was the kind of interpreter who, with his peculiar kind of force, raptus and psychic transmission, could do things in the concert hall that sounded exactly right, but which can sound arbitrary and mannered on records. In the concert hall his absorption was a psychological cement binding things together, and there his ideas were in turn lyric, dramatic, colossal, inevitable. Thus, when he conducted the last movement of the Schumann Symphony in B flat, he started with a slow, long buildup, growing faster and faster. Nobody today would dare start the section that slowly; nor would anybody today dare imitate Furtwängler's subsequent ritards and tempo changes in the same movement. Heard on records (a broadcast of the Schumann First with the Vienna Philharmonic is preserved) this kind of interpretation can be perplexing to one brought up on the Toscanini approach. But when Furtwängler stood on the podium, very few criticized him. His performances impressed listeners as logical and beautiful when experienced in the Presence. And, as those interpretations were so personal, they evoked personal reactions. Different listeners heard him different ways. To Hindemith the main thing was that "Furtwängler possessed the great secret of proportion. . . . He understood how to interpret phrases, themes, sections, movements, entire symphonies and programs as artistic unities." To Fritz Sedlak, concertmaster of the Vienna Philharmonic, the secret was that Furtwängler was "a master of transitions, and worked with us—and with himself—again and again to unite tempo changes within a movement with the smoothness that prevented the dissolution of the movement's structure through exaggerated ritardandi and accelerandi." To the cellist Enrico Mainardi the secret was Furtwängler's search for the spiritual basis of a composition, *der innere Plan*. To the conductor Igor Markevitch, the greatest gift of Furtwängler was "to create an atmosphere in which he communicated a love of music."

An intuitive musician, Furtwängler could not have cared less for technique or superficial polish. A musician asked him what the role of the left hand was in conducting. Furtwängler thought it over and said, "After over twenty years of conducting, I must say I have never thought of it." It was his musical vision that counted, not the baton. He once wrote:

The technical difficulties in my early years as a conductor existed for the very reason that my need for expression—that is, my strong determination to see realized outwardly what I had heard within myself—was so very strong. As a matter of fact, it was so strong that I simply skipped over

the technical difficulties, as it were. You might say I was a natural conductor. Later I had to learn all of the technique.

But orchestral musicians all over the world would have taken issue
with Furtwängler's statement that he had learned all of the technique.
Furtwängler's beat was a phenomenon unduplicated before or since:
a horror, a nightmare, to musicians. On the podium he lost himself.
He would gesticulate, shout, sing, make faces, spit, stamp. Or he
would close his eyes and make vague motions. Until orchestras worked
with him and got used to that curious, quivering, trembling baton
they could be in a complete mess. Henry Holst, the Berlin Philharmonic concertmaster from 1923 to 1931, says that at times the orchestra had the feeling he did not know what to do with his baton. When
something went wrong, Furtwängler would shout for the musicians to
follow his beat. "But alas," Holst wrote, "that would not always be
a help!" A member of the London Philharmonic said in all seriousness
that Furtwängler never really brought down his stick until after the
thirteenth preliminary wiggle. Often cited as a prime instance of his
baton unintelligibility was his indecisive, shaking upbeat at the opening of the *Egmont* Overture. The orchestra had to sense when the
oscillations would come to rest and they could start playing. In the
Berlin Philharmonic there was a standard joke: Q.: How do you
know when to come in on the opening bars of the Beethoven Ninth?
A.: We walk twice around our chairs, count ten and then start playing. Or, Q.: How do you know when to come in with such a mysterious downbeat? A.: When we lose patience. As often as not Furtwängler would lean back, his giraffe-like neck slanted toward the balcony,
and use an under-the-table beat. Musicians had to watch his face
rather than his baton. Furtwängler was fully conscious of the difficulties his beat gave musicians. It did not bother him. "Standardized
technique creates in turn standardized art," he would say. He was
convinced that the great secret of conducting

lies entirely in the preparation of the beat, not in the beat itself—in the
brief, often tiny movement of the downbeat, before the point of unified
sound is reached in the orchestra. The manner in which the downbeat,
these preparations, are shaped determines the quality of the sound with
the most absolute exactness. Even the most experienced conductor is

forever astounded by the unbelievable precision with which a well-coordinated orchestra reflects his most minute gestures.

Furtwängler, in his *Vermächtnis*—his artistic testament—went into this at great length. His argument can be summarized as follows: Rhythm is determined through relatively simple gestures. Yet why does any orchestra sound entirely different with another conductor? Why did every orchestra sound so changed under the simple beat of Nikisch? "There are orchestra leaders under whom the smallest village band plays as if it were the Vienna Philharmonic, and there are those under whom even the Vienna Philharmonic sounds like a village band." The phenomenon of unified sound that a conductor like Nikisch achieved was not an accident; it was caused by the way Nikisch "beat into" the sound. He relied on things other than a standard beat. "There is nowadays a conducting technique that is taught in books and is practiced everywhere—a standardized technique, as it were, that produces a standardized orchestral sound. It is the technique of routine whose aim is simply precision." But this leads to mechanical conducting in which the main concentration is on rhythm. Rhythm-orientation, however, does not help a conductor in shaping melodic content. "Here we have the entire problem of orchestra conducting in essence: How do I, the conductor, who can only wave my baton through the air, get the orchestra to render a singing phrase in its proper nature—as song?" In other words, how are mechanical precision (meter) and the freedom of song to be reconciled?

Song (continues Furtwängler) does not mean only those relatively easy passages where the music streams forth in broad, easily perceptible melodies. It also means the much more subtle thing that Wagner called the *melos*. For this *melos* a sharp downbeat has its disadvantages. It reduces the expression, the living flow of the music. The rhythm is established but not the music, the *melos*. In any case, it is not the downbeat itself, or the sharpness and accuracy with which this downbeat is given, that determines precision. What is more important is the *preparation* with which the conductor gives the downbeat. And so, if it is the preparation that most strongly influences orchestral sound,

could not one imagine a style of conducting which would renounce the final points of every beat, the pointing signals that might be likened to

s

Wilhelm Furtwängler, who carried the old romantic tradition to the middle of the twentieth century.

A rehearsal with the Berlin Philharmonic in 1948. Furtwängler may have had the most unorthodox beat of any conductor within memory.

telegraphy, and make use only of the beat, or the preparation as such? I might mention here that this is not mere theory, but that I myself have tried to practice this method for many years. This is the reason why many spectators, accustomed to the usual technique taught at conservatories, do not understand my gestures. They call them unclear. . . .

In any case, Furtwängler derided technique as an end in itself. All of his writings stress the fact that anybody can develop a clear, up-and-down baton technique. Once he stopped an orchestra during rehearsal and said, "You think I can't give you an orthodox beat?" He did so, and took the orchestra along for a few measures. Then he stopped. "But it has no quality." As he put it in 1937:

Anybody who thinks today that it is possible to impart and develop the "technique" of a singer, instrumental player or conductor in the absence of close and constant association with the art itself, in the face of which technique can only be a means, is very much mistaken. Problems of "technique" are exerting a hypnotic influence on us nowadays, and considerable progress has been made in the examination of its foundations —especially by means of the modern biological approach. No matter whether it is a question of skiing or of playing the piano, we are in a position today to achieve considerably better results in a short period of time than we were a few decades ago. The trouble is that, unlike skiers, artists have not become better but worse as far as the decisive point, i.e., the capacity for direct artistic expression, is concerned, in the process. . . . The result of it all is that art is being deprived more and more of its essence and of its soul, which, to everybody's surprise, seems increasingly superfluous the greater its technical perfection. . . . What I dislike and what worries me profoundly is the chasm that has opened up between our knowledge of the technique and that of the "spiritual" aspects of music.

Nikisch was the chief influence on Furtwängler's conducting. Like his predecessor, Furtwängler had the uncanny ability to mesmerize audiences and orchestras. Like Nikisch, he took a free, romantic view toward music. Like Nikisch, he could lift up an orchestra and make it play as it had never played before. But Furtwängler's conducting was no copy of Nikisch's. It was marked by a feeling of space, by a bigness and nobility of concept. It could be mannered and erratic; it could vary from concert to concert; its tempo fluctuations could make a listener dizzy. But his conducting was always dedicated to the service of the composer as he saw it; and what he saw was not music in terms of historical accuracy (for he was a poor historian, and his musical culture was as low as his musical instincts were high) but in terms of expressive content. He was at his best in music from Mozart and Haydn through the late romantics. Modern music meant nothing to him, and pre-Mozart music he conducted as though it were Mahler. His approach to Bach was intensely personal and would not be admitted today. There is in existence an off-the-air recording of Bach's Fifth *Brandenburg* Concerto, in which he conducts and plays the piano. It is safe to say that his performance of the first-movement cadenza would have uncurled Bach's wig, so shockingly unstylistic it is, with great masses of pedal, immense ritards, all kinds of romanticisms. Furtwängler was criticized for this, and he shook his shoulders. "Too many people think that if they are not bored with the music of Bach it has not been played with the right style." But this is no real answer, and the fact remains that temperamentally and intellectually Furtwängler was unsuited to Bach. But when it came to Beethoven, Brahms, Wagner or Bruckner, he was unsurpassable in his best moments. One of the unforgettable things about his conducting was his ability to voice a chord, to make it ring with color and clarity (Nikisch must have been his model here), to float suspended and shimmering in the air. Another was his ability to phrase with an endless line without letting the rhythm sag. His was not a style that could be imitated, especially by musicians of the new generation. Furtwängler's ideas, even in his own lifetime, were becoming anachronistic. He was a subjectivist in an objective, Toscanini-dominated age of conducting.

One of the aspects of his conducting, noted by the musicians of all orchestras he headed, was that he tried to divide the responsibility of interpretation between himself and the orchestra. Considering Furtwängler's baton style, the orchestra would have had to have a great deal of initiative. As Henry Holst put it, "A rehearsal with Furtwängler was always a very exciting experience, partly because he demanded the utmost concentration from his players, and partly because his beat lacked that 'flick of decisiveness' that will help enforce precision over an ensemble. That kind of precision he did not like at all: he wanted the precision that grew out of the orchestra, from the players' own initiative, as in chamber music." Musicians who worked with him say he was never very articulate, that he could not explain what he wanted and had to rely on their instinct. Gregor Piatigorsky tells a charming story of Furtwängler pleading with the orchestra. "Gentlemen, this phrase must be—it must—it must—you know what I mean—please try it again—please." At intermission, well satisfied with himself, he proudly told Piatigorsky, "You see how important it is for a conductor to convey his wishes clearly?" Yet under his baton a miracle of ensemble generally occurred, especially with an orchestra that was accustomed to his beat.

Furtwängler was one of the rare conductors who came to the orchestra without having been a child-prodigy instrumentalist (though his piano playing was good enough in music that did not require virtuoso equipment). He had never played in an orchestra at all and was slow to mature. As a young man, the tall, gangling, skinny musician with the prominent Adam's apple and a neck long to the point of distortion, was shy and did not impress anybody as a forceful musical mind. He studied in Munich (where he was an assistant to Mottl) and conducted in Zurich, Strasbourg and Lübeck without making much headway. Suddenly something happened, something similar to what happened to the American chess genius Bobby Fischer when he started to overwhelm the opposition. Asked about it, Fischer merely said, "I got good." It was at Mannheim in 1915 that Furtwängler got good, and when he conducted at Berlin and Vienna shortly after that, he was hailed as the greatest of his years. (A long time later, Furtwängler was asked the secret of his success. "I had a successful career," he said, "because I was awkward and shy. My colleagues did not consider me dangerous. When they finally realized that I was indeed a danger, it was too late.") In 1922, at the age of thirty-six, he succeeded Nikisch at the Berlin Philharmonic and the Leipzig Gewandhaus. His career from that point was largely concerned with orchestral music, though he did conduct some opera (including Wagner at Bayreuth) and was as adept in that as in anything else, as witness his great *Tristan und Isolde* recording, and also the postwar *Ring* cycle, which can be heard on private recordings. During the 1920s Furtwängler toured with the Berlin Philharmonic and made guest appearances throughout Europe and the United States. He was in New York for three seasons but was overshadowed by Mengelberg and Toscanini. Then came the specter of Hitler and Nazism.

Apparently Furtwängler, a naïve man, actually believed he could remain divorced from Nazi politics. He was torn many ways, and ended up the loser in all. It is a matter of record that he was no anti-Semite. Shortly after the Reichstag fire he invited Schnabel and Huberman, both Jews, to be his first soloists with the Berlin Philharmonic for the next season. (Both refused.) He liked and respected the Jewish musicians in his orchestra, and his prestige was such that they were left unmolested for a long time. As director of the Berlin State Opera he decided to stage Hindemith's *Mathis der Maler* for the 1934–35 season, even though he knew that the composer was considered a "decadent" by the Nazis. The authorities forbade the performance, whereupon Furtwängler wrote an article about Hindemith and his importance. When Hermann Goering put an end to the Hindemith opera, Furtwängler resigned from all his Berlin activities (and Erich Kleiber resigned along with him). Furtwängler was replaced by a more compliant musician, Clemens Krauss.

The New York Philharmonic, looking for a successor to Toscanini, invited Furtwängler as permanent conductor in 1936. This announcement caused a storm in New York, with its large Jewish population. Furtwängler withdrew, saying that he could not conduct in New York "until the public recognizes that politics and music are apart." During the war he remained in Germany, an unhappy, vague, pathetic man. Strauss, Clemens Krauss, Karajan, Heinz Tietjen and some others were amoralists, able to accommodate to any regime as long as they could do their work. Furtwängler, more sensitive, hated what he saw, and yet was too much attached to Germany to leave. He told other musicians that his art would not be understood outside of Germany, and remarked to the conductor Heinz Unger that he needed his German audiences and orchestral players as much as they needed him. Henry Pleasants, the American writer on music, had a few words to say about this attitude:

This assumption that non-Germans can never truly respond to the most intimate communication of German music—or project it, either, as executive musicians—was not unique with Furtwängler. As a native American, resident for twenty years in German-speaking Central Europe, I was made aware of it in just about every conversation I ever had with a German musician, including Furtwängler. I resented it at first as benighted snobbery; but in time I came rather to agree with it. And I still do, even to the extent of believing that Germans who have lived for very long abroad lose something of their musical birthright. German music flourishes in a German environment.

Friedelind Wagner, the granddaughter of the composer, wrote a sympathetic estimate in 1944. Furtwängler's tragedy, she said, "was and is the fact that inside Germany he is branded and despised as an anti-Nazi, while beyond Germany's borders he is being condemned as a Nazi. If we have to sit in judgment over him, then let us either make allowances or condemn his character, which is weak. He never managed to make a decision in his life and go through with it."

Rehabilitated in 1947, Furtwängler made guest appearances everywhere but in the United States, where several tentative announcements of his return created tremendous opposition. To add to his troubles, he became deaf, a fact not generally known (Siemens, the German electronics company, actually wired his podium for sound). During a concert in Vienna in 1953 he collapsed on the podium. He died a year later.

Vincent Sheean, an intelligent and sensitive reporter with more than a layman's knowledge of music, has given us an interesting portrait of Furtwängler. He saw the conductor in Vienna, shortly after his rehabilitation. The two made small talk and Sheean asked him where the canal was, near the opera house, which Brahms had mentioned so many times. Furtwängler said that there never was a canal. Sheean objected, saying that Brahms was constantly describing it. "Well," said Furtwängler, "I first came here over thirty years ago, and there wasn't any canal then, and there never has been any canal." Sheean continues:

There was something so unutterably final and German (however wrong-headed) about the statement that it was useless to dispute the point, which mattered very little anyhow. I found out of course that the canal had been filled before Furtwängler arrived. Because he had never seen it, there *could* not have been a canal. This dogmatism of mind, along with his ramrod appearance and his imperturbable self-confidence, I suppose, gave Furtwängler that ultra-Teutonic external semblance and manner of address which Americans and other Westerners tend to dislike. He *looked* like a Nazi, poor man, and acted like one too in private interviews, though we all know he went to great lengths to save his Jewish musicians and to preserve the values of German music through those nightmare years. I think he was almost pathologically aware of his own stiffness, his lack of grace or charm or human warmth. . . .

Like Weingartner, Furtwängler wanted very much to be recognized as a composer. He felt composition to be his true mission in life. His principal composition teacher had been the German composer-conductor Max von Schillings. At first, Furtwängler conducted a great deal of his own music. His First Symphony was a fiasco in Breslau. None of his compositions took hold, though his Second Symphony received some performances after he became famous as a conductor. That work, and his Piano Concerto, are conventional, large-scale post-romantic works without an iota of originality in them. The music abounds in reminiscences of Wagner, Mahler, Bruckner, Sibelius, Brahms and Reger. No; it is not as a composer that Furtwängler will live. He will live as the conductor who made a concert such an intense emotional experience for himself and his audience. Furtwängler once said, "The conductor has one arch-enemy to fight— routine." It is safe to say that never in his life did Furtwängler give a routine performance.

· XXVI ·

Bruno Walter

BRUNO WALTER, too, who lived to the age of eighty-five, was a romantic in an anti-romantic age. Even more: he was a nineteenth-century moralist and mystic, the preserver of a vanished tradition. His was a tradition of the Germany of the period from about 1875 on, a period in which the creative mind was enhaloed. The creator was considered endowed with something close to divinity; he was touched by God; and in the word *Meister* was inherent something very close to *Herr* as used by a German in addressing God. Bruno Walter, who believed this with all his might, was, above all conductors, a moral force and in his way the conscience of music. He was always think-ing and talking about the spiritual aspects of music: about soul, about beauty, about re-creative inspiration, about music as a force close to divinity. Music was a religion; the musician was its high priest.

These convictions ran counter to the esthetic of the middle twen-tieth century, and some of the younger conductors and critics tended to look upon Walter as something of a relic washed up from distant climes. Today most musical historians and estheticians take a matter-of-fact view toward the great men of music and their creations. Con-temporary estheticians are much concerned with the meaning of meaning in music, and many, indeed, wonder if it has any meaning at all. Some contemporary composers flatly deny that their music has emotional values and insist that their works are not to be "interpreted." They are merely to be played, keeping as close as possible to the notes and directions, with the interpreter keeping himself divorced from any emotional entanglement. The "great man" attitude toward the mighty composers of the past has all but vanished. Beethoven has been psy-choanalyzed. The love affairs of the composers have been clinically discussed. Far from being touched by divinity (so runs much present thinking) the great men were all too human. They ate and drank (sometimes to excess), were petty as well as noble, dishonest as well as honest. And their music? Today's thinking is anti-sentimental and anti-romantic, and the majority of interpreters do not base their conceptions on what the composer felt, for they do not know what he felt. All they have to go on is the printed note. They agree with Toscanini about the *Eroica*: "For me it is simply allegro con brio."

To Walter this was nonsense. If a conductor's personality, he once wrote, "is unable to fulfill the spiritual demands of the works he performs, his interpretations will remain unsatisfactory, although their musical execution may be exemplary." He lived according to his own strictures, believing in spiritual values (". . . music, born of cosmic origin . . . which bears resounding witness to [man's] divinely creative and ruling character") and sought to transcend the printed note. His aim was to present a music "informed by a universal spiritual presence," and his music making was a rite. "Music's immediate and affective impact shows how closely cognate are music and the soul of man. How could it be otherwise, seeing that the vast, transcendental realm of the soul harbors the spring from which music flows?"

It naturally followed that Walter was completely out of sympathy with most modern trends. His repertory did not extend beyond Mahler and Strauss. He made an effort to understand the atonal school but gave up in revulsion. "Had the shrines at which I had prayed and sacrificed all my life really fallen into decay? . . . Yes, it does indeed look as if materialism and intellectualism have taken hold of the present generation and allotted to the arts a lower place in the life of society than the exalted sphere in which they hitherto have reigned." He found atonalism running against music's "natural laws" and would have nothing to do with it. He summed up his feelings in stately, old-fashioned prose:

Though the muses seem exhausted today; though a cold autumn of the soul has called a temporary halt to flowering and fruit-bearing; though the talents and efforts of the present generation are essentially directed to the material and technical; though the spiritual climate of our epoch has perilously changed just as the terrestrial has; my confidence tells me that the genius of mankind shall survive this period of illness once it has re-

COLUMBIA RECORDS

Bruno Walter, who believed in music as a moral force. His conducting was governed by idealistic concepts.

Walter, as a Mahler protégé, was especially famous as an exponent of Mahler's music.

mobilized the spiritual and moral powers that are nourished by those lofty springs.

But it would be a mistake to look on Walter merely as some kind of gifted musical theosophist. He was a superbly equipped musician and one of the great conductors of history. As an interpreter he represented dignity, nobility, compassion. He was a romantic, but took a course midway between the thesis of Toscanini and the antithesis of Furtwängler. Walter's musical approach was warm and completely unegocentric, and he was much closer to Weingartner than to Furtwängler. The Wagnerian ebb and flow of tempo was alien to Walter's viewpoint, and his rhythms and tempos were invariably smooth-flowing and inevitable-sounding, undistorted by rubato. He made music lovingly, and since he himself loved music so much he was able to transmit that feeling to his audiences. A Walter concert always gave a feeling of comfort. "When he accompanies me," Lotte Lehmann said, "I have the feeling of the utmost well-being and security. The end of his baton is like a cradle in which he rocks me." There never was a strained moment, never a trace of hysteria or neuroticism. All was informed by a deep, confident musical culture and an insistence on making music sing—sing not with Toscanini's coiled-spring intensity but with a relaxed, comforting, easy continuity. Precision as such was never a fixation with him, though with his formidable background and technical resource he could be as good a craftsman as any of his colleagues. "By concentrating on precision," he wrote, "one arrives at technique; but by concentrating on technique one does not arrive at precision." Walter could be as epigrammatic as the next man.

In certain kinds of music, notably that of the great German and Austrian composers, he achieved complete identification. For many years his Mozart interpretations were considered the criterion (though there were those who felt closer to Beecham's way with Mozart), and to the day of his death his supremacy as a conductor of Mahler and Bruckner was never seriously contested. To these composers, and to Beethoven, Schubert, Brahms, he brought a genial, unhurried, fluid approach. Tempos, never pushed, always sounded eminently correct, and the architecture of the music had a grand, spacious design. His conducting, of course, reflected the background in which he had been brought up—a background in which Brahms,

Mahler and Bruckner were living figures, in which Schumann had not been long dead and in which Beethoven was still being talked about as though he were alive.

He was born Bruno Schlesinger, took to the piano as a baby, and at the age of nine was in the Stern Conservatory in Berlin. "Throughout my life there has been a singing within me." At first he wanted to be a pianist, but changed his mind when he heard Bülow conduct in 1889. Four years later he was a coach at the Cologne Opera and made his debut in 1894 in Lortzing's *Der Waffenschmied*. He was not yet eighteen, and he had all the confidence of a brilliant young man. "I felt no uncertainty whatever and was not worried. . . . My hand automatically knew what to do; it had the ability to hold the orchestra together and keep the soloists and the chorus in harmony with it. . . . The general aftereffect of my first performance was the encouraging feeling of having stood in the place for which I had been destined." The same year, 1894, he went on to Hamburg, where he worked as a vocal coach, rehearsal pianist and general factotum under Mahler. It was about that time that he changed his name to Walter; he was thinking of Walther von Stolzing in *Die Meistersinger*. His next assignment was Breslau; then Riga; then Berlin in 1900, with the State Opera. There his colleagues included Muck and Strauss. At the age of twenty-four, Walter was assigned a *Ring* cycle in Berlin. He was still a *Wunderkind*.

Mahler called him to Vienna in 1901 and he stayed there until 1912. Walter's association with Mahler was the most overwhelming artistic experience of his life. After Mahler left in 1907, to be succeeded by Weingartner, the Vienna Opera was never the same; but Walter, who found he could work with the new director, stayed on. He could not work with Weingartner's successor, though. Walter liked Hans Gregor personally, but not his ideas about staging. Thus he left for Munich. Felix Mottl had died, and Walter took his place. He remained in Munich from 1912 to 1922. All during these years Walter had also been guest conducting in Europe, in strong demand for opera and symphony (he conducted the world premieres of Mahler's Ninth Symphony and *Das Lied von der Erde*). He also busied himself with chamber music, making many appearances with Arnold Rosé and the Rosé Quartet. Rosé was the famed concertmaster of the Vienna Philharmonic.

After Munich there were the Bruno Walter Concerts with the

Berlin Philharmonic, appearances in the United States, and the Municipal Opera in Berlin. Those were exciting days in the German capital. Young Turks like Hindemith and Kurt Weill were writing a new kind of music. Theatrical life was flourishing. Max Reinhardt was at the height of his career; the State Theatre was attracting international attention under Leopold Jessner, its avant-garde director; so was the Volksbühne under Karlheinz Martin. Furtwängler, Klemperer and Kleiber were active as conductors, and the greatly respected Leo Blech was conducting at the State Opera. (Blech was the kind of conductor who had memorized every opera in the repertoire and could play all of them from memory on the piano. Singers loved to work with him despite his unlovely habit of sending little notes to their dressing rooms during intermission, pointing out mistakes.) But with Hitler taking power, Walter had to leave Berlin. He went to the Staatsoper in Vienna. Came the Anschluss, forcing Walter to Paris; and then the war sent him in flight to the United States, where he became a permanent resident. He was active at the Metropolitan Opera and the New York Philharmonic, of which he was musical adviser from 1947 to 1949. He could have been the principal conductor of the Philharmonic but refused, with a characteristic pronouncement to the effect that he was too old to take full responsibility.

In one of his essays on conducting—he wrote quite a bit on the subject—Walter said that there are three phases to any conductor's life. At first everything is easy and natural; then there is a period of doubt and insecurity; and finally comes maturity. He pointed out that the really good conductor could control tone, having in his ear "a distinct, inner sound-image, or rather, sound-ideal." Inferior conductors take from an orchestra whatever sound they can get, while the good ones impose their ideal of sound on an orchestra. Upon this "depends, in actual fact, the success of every musical performance." Walter said that just as there is such a thing as a good piano hand, so there is a specifically manual talent for conducting. Even the most gifted and highly sensitive musical mind "cannot make up for a lack of material correctness and technical precision in a performance—the clumsiness of the hand will prevent the work from making the right impression."

Walter also was a strong believer in human relations, and he scorned the dictatorial approach of so many conductors. He looked on his men as colleagues and, like Furtwängler, expected them to have their own ideas:

If individual taste or personal emotional participation are ruthlessly suppressed, the result will be a sort of emotional impoverishment of the performance. The conductor should strive to encourage every sign of emotional participation in the orchestra; he should explore and employ to the fullest degree the capacities of his collaborators; he should excite their interests, advance their musical talents; in short, he should exert a beneficial influence on them. In this way the orchestra will not be a subjugated, that is, artistically inhibited, mass of people . . . and the conductor will have at his disposal an instrument from which his soul pours forth.

In a way this represented a chamber music ideal, and it was one reason why Walter and Mozart were so linked through the years. Walter came to Mozart relatively late. Like many musicians with a nineteenth-century orientation, he at first regarded Mozart as a rococo master. But unlike so many musicians of his day, Walter changed his concept. "I finally discovered behind a seemingly graceful playfulness the dramatist's inexorable seriousness and wealth of characterization. I recognized in Mozart the Shakespeare of the opera. . . . My task in Mozart performances had become clear to me: every characteristic and truthful detail must be given vigorous dramatic expression without impairment of the vocal and orchestral beauty. This beauty permits no exaggeration in dynamics and tempos, in gesturing and action, in forms and colors on the stage." So far, Walter was much in line with modern thought about Mozart. But in performing his beloved composer, Walter never tried to get an eighteenth-century feeling. He used a big orchestra, he was not concerned about ornamentation or musicological niceties, about romantic versus classic dynamics. All, apparently, that Walter knew or cared to know about Mozart is that a work like the G minor Symphony is one of the most ineffably beautiful conceptions of the human brain. It was not the passion of the G minor Symphony that Walter looked for; it was its beauty. When he conducted it, he leaned heavily into the theme (using more strings than today's scholarship dictates) and emphasized the singing quality of the music. This in itself was done with extreme sensitivity and refinement but, as usual in Walter's interpretations, there was a kind of transfiguration in which an idealized, tragic Mozart emerged. In conception it may have been somewhat old-fashioned and unscholarly; but its conviction and beauty were unassailable. And with a relaxation of the literalism prevalent today it may be that future decades will drift back to the conception of a Walter, a conception that relies as much on instinct as it does on mechanics. Or, as he himself put it, "My concern was for a higher clarity than that of sound: to wit, the clarity of musical meaning."

XXVII

Sir Thomas Beecham

SIR THOMAS BEECHAM never met anybody halfway, and nobody ever met Sir Thomas halfway. Some called him nothing more than a dilettante, some said he was the equal of any living conductor. Certainly he put his mark on twentieth-century conducting. But he did it differently from anybody else. He was musically different, personally different, sociologically different, intellectually different. Where many conductors are solemn, weighty men, often lost outside of music, Beecham was sophisticated, cultured, irrepressible, urbane, witty on a Shavian level (Shaw himself once said about him, with some amazement, "Beecham is the most adult conductor I have ever met"). Where most conductors come up the slow, hard way, Beecham, thanks to the enormous wealth of his father (Beecham's Little Liver Pills), could purchase an orchestra for himself and learn as he went along. Where most conductors are specialists—in German music, or French music, or whatever—Beecham was as universal an interpreter as it is possible to become—through the post-romantic school, anyway. He may have had the widest repertoire of any twentieth-century conductor. Short, plump, courtly, bearded, with manners as abrupt (and, often, bad) as can be expected of a titled millionaire. Beecham was like the King in *Princess Ida*—a peppery potentate. Or, to quote another Gilbert and Sullivan line, he was a big, bad Bart. His acid opinions ranged impartially over music, musicians, food, wine, socialism, literature, cigars and women; and in all of those subjects he was a real, not a self-appointed, authority. Ethel Smyth, the British composer, called him a poet, savant, lecturer, adventurer, financier and six musicians rolled into one. Among conductors he was the Renaissance Man.

And no conductor in English history came near the fame, prestige, popularity and controversial quality of Sir Thomas Beecham. His was virtually a household name all over the world. Those who knew nothing about his stature as a musician nevertheless knew about him as a personality. He was constantly in the newspapers, whether for an alienation of affections suit, or for his personal antics, or for telling a city or a country off, or for his wit, or for his judgments on the cultural state of various localities. "The English people are not educated enough to appreciate opera. They are the most commonplace, uncultured race in Europe." That made the headlines in 1916. He called Seattle an esthetic dustbin and its critics liars; he described Belfast audiences as intellectual thugs; he said that London was nothing but a mob, and that Britain was a race of barbarians, a country not fit to live in. He told an audience in Nottingham that they looked as though they had lived on grass for three years.

He was equally tart about his colleagues. Toscanini was "a glorified Italian bandmaster." Bruno Walter? "Malodorous." Koussevitzky? "I doubt if he can read a score at all." Richter? "A mere time beater." Weingartner? "A very fine musical culture, but he became slower and slower." He told Neville Cardus, the English critic, that Bronislaw Huberman was "a very fine artist, penetrating, as you say. But as a violinist, he has a certain defect." "And what is that?" "He can't play the violin." Later, Huberman played the Beethoven D major with Beecham. "Very good, very good indeed. I am quite taken aback, quite astonished." The man just liked to hear himself talk, and was not above pulling the leg of the credulous.

In musical circles, stories about Beecham were gleefully recounted in green rooms the world over. One of the most famous concerned Sir Thomas' turning up in the pit and leaning over to ask the concertmaster a question. "We are performing *Figaro* tonight, are we not?" "Oh, no, Sir Thomas. It is *Seraglio*." "My dear fellow, you amaze me." Whereupon he closed the *Figaro* score he had brought and conducted *Seraglio* from memory. Or there was his comment to an errant player during rehearsal: "We do not expect you to follow us all the time, but if you would have the goodness to keep in touch with us occasionally . . ." Or, during another rehearsal: "At Figure 19, cymbals, a grand smash of your delightful instruments to help in the general welter of sound, if you please."

Everybody seemed to have his favorite Beecham story. At a rehearsal of Holbrooke's opera *Dylan*, Beecham called the electrician. "Mr. Fairbairn," he said, "at the precise moment when your very formidable castle walls, contrary to the laws of gravity, rise into the air to allow vast buckets of rice to be poured on the stage in semblance of deluge and flood, may I suggest that it would be appropriate to have a blackout from our friend 'Arry?" Beecham, the grand seigneur, really did speak like that. It was he who asked a trombonist: "Are you producing as much sound as possible from that quaint and antique drainage system which you are applying to your face?" It was Beecham who, during a rehearsal of *Die Meistersinger*, asked the tenor if he had ever made love.

"Yes, Sir Thomas."

"Do you consider yours a suitable way of making love to Eva?"

"Well," said the tenor, "there are different ways of making love."

"Observing your grave, deliberate motions," said Sir Thomas, "I was reminded of that estimable quadruped, the hedgehog."

He told a soprano that her voice reminded him of a cart coming downhill with the brake on. Once, at the Metropolitan Opera, he stopped the chorus and gazed upon it with admiration. "Gad," he said, "just like the Salvation Army." To a cold, undemonstrative audience that refused to applaud, he wheeled around, stared the people down and said: "Let us pray."

He had not only wit and a precise, infallible command of the King's English. He was a very great conductor who meant much to the musical life of the century. It was in England that he was especially important. Until Beecham came along, the orchestral scene and repertoire, dominated by Hans Richter, were Germanic. Beecham, with his restless mind and intellectual curiosity, pried open a different kind of symphonic and operatic repertoire. In the words of Neville Cardus, Beecham "led us out of the German captivity; he mediterraneanized our music." Beecham's very first concert, with his newly formed Beecham Orchestra in 1909, was typical. It contained the Berlioz *Roman Carnival* Overture, Vaughan Williams' *In the Fen Country*, Delius' *Sea Drift* and Berlioz' *Te Deum*. His programs were constantly exploring music by the new British, French and Russian composers. He was equally adventurous in opera, bringing to England such works as *Elektra*, *Werther*, *Feuersnot*, *Tiefland*, *Hamlet* and other rarities.

All of this music, plus the standard repertoire, he conducted in a

Sir Thomas Beecham: man of wit, urbanity, eccentricity, money, bad manners, charm, intellect, culture and also (at right) an exponent of the good life.

COLUMBIA RECORDS

CAPITOL RECORDS

Sir John Barbirolli, the most important English conductor after Beecham's death.

most unusual manner. The man had no baton technique to speak of. Cardus once saw him get his baton entangled in the back of his coat. One of his players said that Beecham broke every rule, and that nobody else in the world could get away with it as he did. On the podium his hands and body would be moving in all directions at once. Olin Downes, music critic of the New York *Times,* wrote a bemused description in 1941:

He may run all around the conductor's stand, or lean over, his toes perilously near its edge, in favoring a group or the players of a solo passage, with his exclusive attention. He may crouch or most ungracefully crook a knee, or stoop down and rise like a large and ungraceful bird flapping its wings in the air. He may indicate a sforzando in the manner of a man hurling a brick or a bomb at a foe, or beat the measure freely with one arm while holding the baton in a clenched fist, invisible to the orchestra . . .

He also generally conducted from memory, once in a while with disastrous results. He himself used to tell, with great glee, of a concert he gave with Alfred Cortot as piano soloist. Cortot's memory was notoriously unreliable, and he had a grievous lapse in the finale of the concerto. Both Cortot and Beecham maneuvered, but were unable to come together. "We started with the Beethoven, and I kept up with Cortot through the Grieg, Schumann, Bach and Tchaikovsky, and then he hit on one I didn't know, so I stopped dead." A charming bit of persiflage, this, but it does contain a kernel of truth. Beecham was proud of his memory, even arrogant about it, and loftily would dispense with a score even if he needed one.

Yet he managed to achieve amazing results from orchestras; and Beecham, with his compulsion to conduct, would take any group that came along. In 1941 he conducted several programs with the New York City Symphony, a low-powered group under the aegis of the Works Progress Administration. Virgil Thomson was bowled over and wrote that the concert proved to him the dictum that there are no bad orchestras, only bad conductors. "No orchestra has played better this season in New York City, by any imaginable standards, than Mayor La Guardia's WPA boys have played for Sir Thomas. . . . Such lyric grace in the interpretation of Handel, and such majestic proportions in the reading of Mozart are not available, to my knowledge, in the work of any living conductor."

Beecham, despite his podium gyrations and antics, had more than enough technique to do what he wanted. He had the prime, mysterious secret of great conducting, and the rhythms he heard in his inner ear, the balances of phrasings, the shape of a phrase, the curvature of a line—all these were transmitted from his body and from his mind to the players in a kind of quantum jump.

His interpretations were never cut-and-dried. Indeed, performances of the same work could vary greatly from concert to concert. There was a large element of improvisation—in the best sense of the word— in Beecham's conducting. There always was the feeling that something different, something unexpected, would happen; and Beecham saw to it that nobody was disappointed. He gave considerable leeway to his first-desk men. Leon Goossens, the oboist of the Royal Philharmonic, has said that every time Beecham lifted his baton he would discover or suggest something different, "so that every time we played a score we had something new, never tiring. . . . He'd leave a tremendous amount to the first-desk men. That's how he got that feeling of spontaneity in those lovely things of Bizet and Delius." One can hear this in many of his recordings—that of *Schéhérazade*, say, where he let some of his solo players get away with an unusual amount of rubato. Their zest for the unexpected opportunity comes right through the vinyl. One can imagine Sir Thomas beating time with a big grin on his face as his frequently frustrated first-desk men, the door swung wide, rushed to take advantage of the chance.

In a way, Beecham can be regarded as the spoiled child of a rich man, except that unlike most spoiled children he went on to make something of himself. Tommy Beecham was a brilliant youngster. His extraordinary memory was noted as a child; it is said that he memorized *Macbeth* at the age of eight. The boy read, and digested, everything in sight, proved to be a facile pianist, and interested himself in every kind of intellectual pursuit. He went on to Oxford but never took a degree. On the whole, his musical training was sketchy. After some desultory study with Charles Wood, Frederic Austin and a few others, he got a job with the Imperial Grand Opera Company, an organization that had ideas as grandiose as its name, but also an organization that shortly departed life having made as little impact as when it had entered. In 1905 Beecham engaged forty members of the Queen's Hall Orchestra for his first London concert. It was not a very good concert, and he knew it. The following year he picked up a floundering group of sixty musicians and founded the Thomas Beecham Orchestral Concerts, calling his group the New Symphony Orchestra. It was there that he started learning his craft. But even then his programs were adventurous and unconventional, with music by D'Indy, Lalo, Smetana and Delius.

The Beecham Symphony Orchestra was founded in 1909 and made a big impression on London, though not always a favorable one. Beecham still had a good deal to learn. His performances were ragged, noisy and irresponsible. A few vintage recordings of the Beecham Symphony Orchestra are in existence. They are frightful. Neither conductor nor orchestra were up to the basic musical and technical demands. In the meantime, Sir Joseph Beecham was pouring some $1.5 million into his son's musical efforts. Beecham money sponsored a season of opera at Covent Garden in 1910 (and the human mind has not yet conceived a way to spend money faster than sponsoring a season of opera). The repertoire consisted of *Elektra, A Village Romeo and Juliet* (Delius), *Hansel und Gretel, The Wreckers* (Ethel Smyth), *L'Enfant Prodigue* (Debussy), *Tristan und Isolde, Carmen* and *Ivanhoe* (Sullivan). No wonder the enterprise lost a fortune. But the Beechams *had* a fortune. The performances were not well received. Beecham, in those years, had ideas about opera that were more concerned with the orchestra than with the voice. As the curtain went up on the opening night of *Elektra,* Beecham was heard telling the orchestra, "The singers think they're going to be heard, and I'm going to make jolly well certain that they are not!" There were subsequent Covent Garden seasons, all run without vocal stars with but one exception. A season of Russian operas featured Chaliapin. Of the first thirty-four operas staged by Beecham, thirty were failures. Beecham was undisturbed. Later he said, nonchalantly, "I lacked the experience to gauge the capacities or incapacities of my artists, and frequently mounted operas more for the purpose of hearing the music myself than for giving pleasure to the public." By the time he was through with his operatic ventures, he had produced a hundred and twenty, sixty of which were either new to England or revived after long neglect.

When Sir Joseph died in 1916, Thomas came into a great deal of money and lived up to it. He ran his orchestra to suit himself, turning up late for rehearsals, canceling them at his whim, paying generous salaries. He became a celebrity and a man about town. During World War I he conducted promenade concerts at Albert Hall, avoiding German music, and he also sponsored several seasons of opera with British singers. For these services he was knighted. After the war he organized the Sir Thomas Beecham Opera Company, Ltd. Its two seasons put him into near-bankruptcy. For years he was in and out of the courts. During most of the 1920s he was active as a guest conductor, and in 1932 he was instrumental in the formation of the London Philharmonic. By that time he was conceded to be one of the major conductors in the world, but his pronouncements, especially on political matters, did not make him popular. When he said that Hitler and Mussolini were great comedians, without whom life would be dull, many did not find this at all amusing. He took the London Philharmonic on tour in Germany in 1936 and, at the request of the Nazis, dropped a Jewish work, Mendelssohn's *Scotch* Symphony, from his programs. That too did not add to his popularity. When the war came, he left England for the United States, to the distress of many of his countrymen. In the United States he conducted every orchestra in sight, from great organizations and the Metropolitan Opera to provincial ensembles. Returning to England in 1944, he created the Royal Philharmonic, which he brought to the United States for a tour six years later. Many of his last years were spent on tour.

As a musician he was typical of the best in the English school, a school that is eclectic, with an orientation to the German style modified to the British national temper. English musicians tend to be urbane, civilized, seldom passionate, with a fine sense of lyricism and feeling for proportion. Beecham was no exception. In his conducting was a strong streak of classicism, in that no matter how strenuous or colorful the attack, the music never sounded swollen or outsized. Beecham had a Mendelssohnian sense of tempo, and was sensitive to the allegation that his pacings were fast. "Through the whole of my career I have been looked upon as the protagonist of rapid tempi, in spite of the provable fact that in the majority of cases I have actually taken more time over performances than many of my contemporaries who have escaped entirely a similar charge." The truth is, Beecham said, that "the average ear confuses strong accent and the frequent use of rubato with tempo itself."

He held himself under emotional control at all times. That does not mean his interpretations were namby-pamby. "The grand line and flexibility," he told one of his associate conductors, "the grand line's the only thing the public understands, and flexibility is the only thing which makes music." Beecham's line seemed endless; and, as for flexibility, he was never afraid to tinker with rhythms, phrases and even actual notes for greater expressive effect. He was not a purist and was constantly tussling with musicologists. "A musicologist is a person who can read music but can't hear it." His ideas about early music were extremely free, and his orchestration of Handel's *Messiah,* done with the aid of Eugene Goossens, caused an explosion in musicological circles and a great tut-tutting elsewhere. Beecham hotly defended his approach. "If Handel and many other composers were left to the purists, with their parsimonious handfuls of strings and oboes, you would never hear any of them. The thing to remember is that no man knows how these works were performed originally. [Beecham underrated the musicologists.] I have thought about the problem for sixty years, much longer than the gentlemen who write strange monographs on the subject."

Admittedly a romantic, he insisted that Delius was the last of the great composers. "No composer has written as much as a hundred bars of worthwhile music since 1925." He would not conduct *Wozzeck* because, though an "ingenious" score, it was to him "entirely uncivilized and uncharming. I am not interested in music, or in any work of art, that fails to stimulate enjoyment of life and, what is more, pride of life." A man like Beecham, who represented elegance and the good life and an Edwardian set of Tory standards, could never bring himself to understand musical atonalism and expressionism. In all other music his conducting was natural and unforced, always in taste, always in proportion, always full of tensile strength that was no less strong for being unknotted. He and Bruno Walter were considered the two great Mozart conductors of the age. But the two men could not have been farther apart in conception. Walter was concerned with the *Innigkeit* and spiritual values of the music. Beecham was more interested in its abstract patterns, in the grace and fluidity of the writing, in the elegance and proportion of the musical architecture. He used a large orchestra for his Mozart; there was nothing rococo

about his approach. But it was a Mozart that never sounded heavy or
sentimental, and there are many who feel that we shall never experience the likes of it again.

Although Sir Thomas was the first British-born conductor to sweep
the world, he had, of course, been preceded by several fine British
orchestral technicians. Chief among those was Sir Henry Wood, the
prodigiously hard-working leader of the famous Proms concerts from
1895 until his death in 1944. Wood, fiery and tempestuous, broke
the deputy system once and for all. A half-century previously, Costa
had "broken" it too, but only for his own orchestras. Musicians in
London at the turn of the century free-lanced, and it was not uncommon for a conductor to be faced with fifty new players at a rehearsal
or even at the performance itself. The standard joke related the story
of a conductor who, through four rehearsals, saw a constant, bewilder-
ing succession of new faces. But through all this sat the same first
clarinet, solid, dependable, understanding. At the end of the fourth
rehearsal the conductor went up to the clarinetist and thanked him.
"At least, you will understand what I am doing at the concert tomor-
row." The clarinetist looked at the conductor. "But I won't be here.
I shall send a deputy."

In 1904 Wood issued an ultimatum: no more deputies. The result
was that almost half of his men resigned and formed the London
Symphony Orchestra. Another result was that Wood was able to
build a superior orchestra for himself, and to maintain it. He was a
fine conductor with an enormous repertoire, and introduced to England much music by Strauss, Debussy, Scriabin, Schoenberg and
Sibelius. The Grand Old Man of English Music, he was called, and
he had a systematic mind that reduced everything to essentials. New
and nervous members of his orchestra would be told: "Don't worry.
You may be reading at sight in public, but you can't possibly go wrong
with *that* stick in front of you." Wood did some conducting outside
of England, and he made many records, but his reputation was primarily local.

A list of other admired British conductors would include Sir Ham-
ilton Harty, for many years head of the Hallé Orchestra and an
authority on Berlioz; Albert Coates, who conducted all over Europe
and America, who was active in Russia and who introduced many
important Russian scores to the West; Sir Eugene Goossens, the
composer-conductor, part of the avant-garde of the 1920s and 1930s,

and a brilliantly talented man. Sir Adrian Boult, whose career extended past Beecham's, was (and is) a sane, intelligent, polished interpreter, and the same can be said of Sir Malcolm Sargent.

Sir John Barbirolli shared the latter part of Beecham's life as the only other British conductor accepted on the international circuit. Barbirolli's reputation suffered for a while as a result of his first important assignment. He succeeded Toscanini as head of the New York Philharmonic in 1937, and the thirty-seven-year-old conductor, though clearly talented, was not yet ready for so demanding a position. Even then, however, a great deal of vigor and ebullience marked his work. In 1943, after leaving New York, he took command of the Hallé Orchestra, which had not had a permanent conductor since Harty's retirement in 1933. Barbirolli made the Hallé one of Europe's best orchestras. He grew along with it, becoming a conductor admired for his clear, well-proportioned, healthy and natural-sounding interpretations.

XXVIII

Serge Koussevitzky

RUSSIA WAS THE LAST of the European countries to develop musically. For centuries Russia was outside the mainstream of Western
thought and culture, and it was not until the nineteenth century,
with the emergence of Glinka, the Five and Tchaikovsky, that the
world suddenly woke up to the mighty Russian musical potential.
Not only composers suddenly emerged. Anton Rubinstein stormed
from the steppes, second as a pianist only to Franz Liszt. A brilliant
school of violin playing established itself toward the end of the
century. A handful of Russian singers, headed by Feodor Chaliapin,
conquered the West.

But conductors were slower coming, and they still are. Even today
the important Russian-born conductors—Eugene Mravinsky, Kiril
Kondrashin, Igor Markevitch, Jascha Horenstein—have scarcely made
much of an international impact, though they are respected figures.
And in the last half of the nineteenth century there was only one
important conductor in Russia, and he was not Russian-born. Eduard
Nápravnik came from Bohemia. He had studied in Prague and, in
1861, gone to Russia as conductor of Prince N. Yussopov's private
orchestra. Nápravnik remained in Russia, becoming a citizen and
specializing in opera. He reorganized the theatres, modeling them
along Western lines. By the end of his career he had conducted over
4,000 operatic performances, including the world premiere of virtually every important Russian opera. He also did some symphonic
work. A small, thin man with sharp, squinting eyes and a square-
shaped head, his right shoulder lifted like a hunchback's, he looked,
as the conductor Nikolai Malko has said, "like a dying lion, but still
a lion." His performances stressed shape and discipline, and Tchai-

kovsky called him dry. But Tchaikovsky, like everybody else, acknowl-
edged that he was a superb craftsman.

After Nápravník came Vassily Safonoff, who studied at the St.
Petersburg Conservatory, was one of Russia's ranking pianists, and
conducted orchestral concerts in Moscow. Safonoff was a colorful
figure—a big, stout man of immense exuberance, lusty (he had eight
children), dynamic. Apparently he was the kind of conductor—there
are many such—who makes an extraordinary initial impression but
who cannot hold on to it. When he came to New York in 1904 he
created a sensation, and from 1906 to 1909 was conductor of the
Philharmonic. Naturally, Russian music was his specialty, and nobody
argued about his authority there. *Harper's Magazine* noted that if the
Philharmonic should choose to announce a series of concerts devoted
only to a single work—the Tchaikovsky *Pathétique* as conducted by
Safonoff—it could count on sold-out houses. In non-Russian music,
he seems to have been less satisfactory. The *Musical Courier* summed
up his three seasons: "Safonoff came to New York with a reputation
as a Tchaikovsky expert and he leaves our city with his original honors
intact, but no fresh ones added to his credit."

Safonoff was followed to New York by Modest Altschuler, who
formed the Russian Symphony Orchestra in 1904 and kept it alive
until 1919. The idea of the orchestra, as Altschuler described it, was
"to make propaganda for Russian music." It was not a very good
orchestra, nor was Altschuler a very good conductor, but he did make
propaganda by introducing to New York many examples of the new
Russian school.

It is not generally known that Rachmaninoff could have become as
great a conductor as he was a pianist. In his early years his efforts
were bent toward composition, but he loved the baton and, in addition
to conducting his own music, he occasionally turned to other composers. As late as 1933 the composer-pianist Nikolai Medtner recalled
a concert Rachmaninoff had conducted in 1904:

I shall never forget Rachmaninoff's reading of Tchaikovsky's Fifth Symphony. Before he conducted it we knew it only in the version of Nikisch
and his imitators. True, Nikisch had saved this symphony from a complete
fiasco (as conducted by the composer), but then his pathetic slowing of
the tempo became the law for performing Tchaikovsky, enforced by conductors who had followed him blindly. Suddenly, under Rachmaninoff,

all this imitative tradition fell away from the composition and we heard it as if for the first time; especially astonishing was the cataclysmic impetuosity of the finale, an antithesis to the pathos of Nikisch that had always harmed this movement.

Even more unexpected . . . was the impression of Mozart's G minor Symphony, which had long been labeled dull—a thing in rococo style. I shall never forget this symphony as conducted by Rachmaninoff; it suddenly came toward us, pulsating with life and urgency.

After leaving Russia for good in 1917, Rachmaninoff was offered several American orchestras, including the Boston Symphony, but decided to stick to composition and his piano. He conducted no public concerts thereafter. But around 1940 he led the Philadelphia Orchestra in a recording of his Third Symphony, and it is a remarkable performance—sharp, with superbly articulated rhythms characteristic of his work at the piano, full of authority, strength and aristocracy. The world lost a major conductor when Rachmaninoff turned elsewhere.

The most important of all Russian conductors, and still the greatest, was Serge Koussevitzky, who came to full flower in the United States as conductor of the Boston Symphony. For twenty-five years it was his life. Unlike the majority of ranking conductors, Koussevitzky did not conduct opera at all, and he made surprisingly few guest appearances. Nor did he encourage the appearance of guest conductors with his Boston Symphony. He was quite frank about it. "I prefer that we may not have one like Toscanini, or Beecham, or Walter, but that [Richard] Burgin, our own concertmaster, conduct. For he goes in my way. I feel that my orchestra remains its same artistic discipline." (This is a verbatim quotation. Koussevitzky's English never was idiomatic.)

He may have had a Franco-Russian orientation, and he may have mangled the English language, but no conductor of his time meant more to the musical development of America. For Koussevitzky was as intensely interested in the new as in the old, and he sponsored virtually every important American composer of the day—Copland, Piston, Schuman, Barber, Harris, Hanson and many others. Contemporary European composers, especially French and Russian, got as much attention, and Koussevitzky introduced to America significant scores by Prokofieff, Shostakovitch, Milhaud, Stravinsky, Roussel and Ravel.

Koussevitzky was an authentic force. He was a conductor of high emotional fervor whose performances had drama, color, the big line, the big gesture. Definitely not the intellectual type, Koussevitzky would stand before his orchestra with pleading gestures, with shaking hands, shoulders and body in that peculiar, quivering beat of his, a huge blood vessel pulsating redly in his perspiring forehead. Like Toscanini, he was always pleading for his men to sing. "There is no music without singing." He had the knack of creating a diaphanous mist of sound, a sheer aristocracy of pure sound; and in scores that were his specialties—*Daphnis and Chloe, La Mer,* the last three Tchaikovsky symphonies, the Strauss tone poems—there was a sensuous approach unparalleled by any orchestra in the world. In Beethoven and Brahms he was more reserved and seldom took liberties, although—being Serge Koussevitzky—he still brought to those scores a nuanced, emotional kind of interpretation that distressed purists of the German school.

Some of his colleagues looked down on him, saying that he was an inferior baton technician and an even worse score reader. But the fact remained that Koussevitzky had extraordinary personality, projection and rapport. When he conducted music close to him, his work negated criticism. Many thought that under his baton the Boston Symphony Orchestra was the greatest in the world, superior even to so virtuoso a group as the Philadelphia Orchestra under Stokowski.

A self-made conductor, Koussevitzky started out as a double-bass player. When he tried to enter the Moscow Conservatory at the age of fourteen, he discovered that the only open scholarships were for horn, trombone or double bass. He opted for the bass and soon made himself the premier European soloist on that unwieldy instrument. He gave solo recitals, or would play cello concertos on the double bass. In 1905 he married the daughter of a wealthy tea merchant, and that enabled him to go to Germany, where he gave recitals and carefully studied the conducting of Nikisch. He always had wanted to conduct, and in 1908 he engaged the Berlin Philharmonic for a concert. It was well received. The critic of the *Musical Courier* was much taken: "This was his first public appearance in this capacity, and incredible though it seems, he led with all the assurance, cer-

RCA VICTOR

Serge Koussevitzky, the first and greatest conductor of the Russian school. His most important work was done in Boston.

Eduard Nápravnik, Czech-born musician who went to Russia and became the most important conductor in that country.

MUSIC LIBRARY, LINCOLN CENTER

tainty and circumspection of a conductor of long experience." Soon Koussevitzky was being called the Russian Nikisch.

Even at that time Koussevitzky's dynamism and electricity were apparent, but he, more than anybody else, knew how much he had to learn. He was a natural musician in that he exuded music, had good rhythm and a superior ear. But there were certain weaknesses, and they were present his entire life. From the very beginning he needed the assistance of a pianist, for he himself could not play the instrument and was at best an indifferent score reader. "Having learned a score by heart," Arthur Lourié has written, "he made some pianist play it in accordance with the plan which he himself intended to adopt in conducting this composition. Whilst the pianist was playing, Koussevitzky conducted, and he had the work repeated until he had mastered the technique of the gestures." Fred Gaisberg, the recording director of His Master's Voice, once went to Koussevitzky's home in Paris. "The windows were open, and through them came the thunder of a piano. I looked in, and there was Prokofieff at the piano playing one of his latest works, and Koussevitzky at a music stand following with a baton. That was his way of mastering the work."

In a way, Koussevitzky and Beecham were similar. Both were, at the beginning, inspired dilettantes; both had the money to buy orchestras upon which to learn; both took a long time to develop. On his return to Russia in 1909, Koussevitzky not only organized his own symphony orchestra (almost at the same time that Beecham was organizing his) but even established a publishing house, Editions Russes de Musique. Among the composers he signed were Rachmaninoff, Prokofieff, Stravinsky, Medtner and Scriabin. The last-named was of particular importance, for Koussevitzky became the champion of the little mystic. Koussevitzky took his orchestra on tour, including those famous trips on a chartered steamer for 1,200 miles along the Volga. Debussy, who went to Russia in 1913, wrote excitedly about "the unique Koussevitzky" and his orchestra, "which is absolutely distinguished by exact discipline and a devotion to music rare enough in enlightened centers of our old Europe"; and Debussy further wrote admiringly of Koussevitzky's "burning will to serve music."

Koussevitzky survived the 1917 Revolution and was even offered the State Symphony Orchestra, which he conducted until 1920. Then he left for Paris. There, in 1921, he founded the Concerts Koussevitzky and introduced, among other things, Ravel's orchestration of the Mussorgsky *Pictures at an Exhibition*, Honegger's *Pacific 231* and music by Prokofieff and Stravinsky. In 1924 he was called to the Boston Symphony to replace Pierre Monteux. His very first program showed how things were going to be: it contained Vivaldi's Concerto Grosso in D minor, the Brahms *Haydn* Variations, the Berlioz *Roman Carnival* Overture, Scriabin's *Poem of Ecstasy* and Honegger's *Pacific 231*. Quite evident was the Franco-Russian imprint that was to persist for the next quarter of a century.

It took a great deal of time before Koussevitzky and the Boston Symphony learned to get along together. In his first seasons the conductor was discouraged. He felt that he was in over his head, and he made many mistakes. The virtuoso players of the orchestra considered him a sadistic bluffer and were not below trying to undermine him. Eventually they bent to his imperious will. Moses Smith, who followed Koussevitzky's career from the beginning (and wrote a biography that Koussevitzky tried to suppress), says that the Boston Symphony worked grudgingly with Koussevitzky, neither liking nor respecting him:

Out of a motive of sheer self-protection, the men, non-union musicians who would find it difficult and expensive to get jobs elsewhere, made the best of their situation. If Koussevitzky's cues were inadequate or incorrect, they learned to understand his wishes in spite of his mistakes. If his upbeat was uncertain, they learned to watch one another. They worked out a set of signals to insure their playing together. The orchestra, which followed its leader when he knew how to express his intentions, played like a superb conductorless ensemble when he didn't. Thus arose, for a purely negative reason, that wonderful *esprit de corps* which enables the Boston Symphony Orchestra to play like a fine chamber music group.

By 1930, Smith says, orchestra and conductor understood each other. "The orchestra learned to interpret his wishes, not his signs." The men also learned to respect his mania for perfection, and for trying to get to the expressive core of a work once the technical core had been mastered. Howard Hanson has described some of Koussevitzky's "dogged detail" at rehearsals:

I have heard him rehearsing the opening of the Overture to *The Flying Dutchman* dozens of times, not because the horns could not play the notes, but because the notes as played did not yet convey their emotional and dramatic portent. I have heard him rehearse passages in Elgar's familiar *Pomp and Circumstance* repeatedly until the low trumpets sounded brilliant. Every student of orchestration knows that low trumpet tones *cannot* sound brilliant, but at the end of that rehearsal they *did* sound brilliant.

Koussevitzky developed into one of the most colorful figures in the American musical scene—Koussevitzky with his cape, his indescribable accent, his frequent malapropisms, his Dostoevskian rages, his feuds and reconciliations. He also developed into a smooth diplomat. Indeed, in this activity he had no peer. He could promise and then break his promise without causing great hurt. Those concerned would shrug their shoulders. "Oh, well, he's only an emotional Russian." He hated to say no to a composer and would lavishly promise performances. A composer once got up enough nerve to reprimand Koussevitzky for his failure to play a score. "You promised. You have a terrible weakness for making promises." "Yes, my dear," answered Koussevitzky, "but thank God I have the strength not to keep them." Koussevitzky did nothing without rationalizing it. Charles O'Connell, the RCA Victor executive who worked with him, said that Koussevitzky "can be the imperious patrician, the suave diplomat, the accommodating colleague, the daring young man or the venerable patriarch—as circumstances and occasions indicate."

Among the legacies left by Koussevitzky was the Berkshire Music Festival, which had been organized in Tanglewood, Massachusetts, by Henry Hadley in 1934. Koussevitzky took it over in 1936 and created a music school there in 1940. Both festival and school throve. The festival became the most prestigious in America, and from the school, especially from Koussevitzky's conducting class, came some of America's brightest young men, headed by Leonard Bernstein.

In his day Koussevitzky was one of the big three of American conductors, the others being Toscanini and Stokowski. Of the three, Koussevitzky was by far the most important to the cause of American music, for in him the composer had a spokesman and an exponent. In addition, Koussevitzky's taste was catholic enough to include the most significant works of the modern European school, with the exception of twelve-tone music (but nobody at that time paid much attention to the dodecaphonic school; that was to be a postwar phenomenon). A glamorous, egocentric figure, Koussevitzky managed to make every

concert an experience, partly through his own overwhelming personality, partly through the great orchestra he had built. Music in Boston
revolved around him. He was the star and he hated to share the spotlight. Not only did the Boston Symphony have very few guest conductors during Koussevitzky's tenure; it also had fewer soloists than
any comparable orchestra the world over. Those years in Boston from
1924 to 1949 did represent what the Russians used to call a cult of
personality. But what a personality!

XXIX

Leopold Stokowski

Toscanini, Koussevitzky and Stokowski: the conducting heroes of the American musical scene in the decades from the mid-twenties to the late forties, when all were simultaneously active. Toscanini was the objectivist, the elemental, the conductor of supreme clarity and cataclysmic force. Koussevitzky was the colorist, the sensualist, the self-appointed spokesman for the modern American and European schools. And Stokowski? He was the virtuoso, the publicist, the musical man about town, the egoist, the showman supreme. Toscanini loathed publicity. Koussevitzky enjoyed it. Stokowski could not live without it. At the very beginning of his career he bounced into the newspaper columns and he has never left them.

Born and trained in England, he came to America as an organist and had virtually no experience in front of an orchestra (apparently he had conducted only twice in Europe, both times with pickup orchestras) when Herman Thumann, music critic of the Cincinnati *Enquirer,* had a stroke of genius. He recommended the unknown, twenty-five-year-old Stokowski to the board of the Cincinnati Symphony as musical director. Stokowski was accepted, and lost no time turning the orchestra, and the musical life of the city, inside out. He brought a new concept of conducting, a new kind of glamour, a new set of instrumental standards. He remained in Cincinnati for three years, from 1909 to 1912. When the Philadelphia Orchestra was looking for a replacement for Karl Pohlig in 1912, Stokowski's name inevitably came up, and an unpleasant hassle followed. The details have never been fully disclosed, but the orchestra claimed that Stokowski had broken his contract to accept the Philadelphia assignment. He eventually got his release. A letter from the board of the orchestra to Stokowski stiffly said that ". . . your recent behavior and repeated aspersions upon members of the Board of Directors of the Association, and your unfounded reflections upon the musical public of Cincinnati have destroyed your usefulness to the Cincinnati Orchestra Association." Stokowski loudly cried that he had not been fired. "It is impossible to dismiss a man who has repeatedly and publicly asked to be relieved." The Cleveland *Leader* of April 28, 1912, had some strong words to say:

Thus ends for Cincinnati, at least, the drum and cymbal career of Leopold Stokowski—née Stokovski—who brilliantly and quickly rose from an inconsequential position in the East to the leadership of one of America's greatest orchestras; who made Beethoven dance on his ears; who made Brahms a puling, sickly sentimentalist; who calcined Strauss in more clashing and fighting colors than Strauss ever knew; and who Stokowski-ized each composer whom he took into his directorial hands; who clenched his shaking fists, threshed the air with his arms and distorted his body to secure innocuous and unconvincing effects; and who in violation of all professional ethics caused his pictures to be published far and wide above columns of fulsome matter which had Stokowski for its subject.

Thus came Stokowski to Philadelphia, flying in on a cloud of controversy. Already he was known as a glamour-boy type, interested more in effect than in substance. How would Philadelphia react to this? Stokowski apparently decided to take it very easy during his first years, and he impressed everybody with his sobriety. One critic wrote, rather amazed after having read the Cincinnati reports, "There was no exaggeration, no profusion of manner or gesture that would betoken the possession of vanity or desire to 'shine.'" The only eccentric thing about Stokowski during those years was his repertoire. In 1916 he conducted the American premiere of Mahler's Eighth Symphony, that enormous choral work, and soon his programs were peppered with Hindemith, Schoenberg, Cowell, Varèse, Eichheim, Stravinsky (including the first American performance of *Le Sacre du Printemps*), Berg (the first American performance of *Wozzeck*), Shostakovich and Vaughan Williams. But soon he started moving under full acceleration. His famous series of Bach transcriptions for full orchestra began to appear (thus making much more current than it had been in Cincinnati the infinitive "to Stokowski-ize"). He busied himself mak-

Leopold Stokowski in 1905.
At that time he was the or-
ganist of St. Bartholomew's
Church in New York City.

Stokowski at the head of the
American Symphony Or-
chestra in the middle 1960's.
He was still as magnetic as
ever.

ing records and motion pictures. He was constantly experimenting with the seating arrangement of the orchestra, and his players never knew what to expect. Sometimes the first oboe or third horn would be sitting in the concertmaster's seat. Sometimes the position of concertmaster was in constant rotation, with a trembling and miserable violinist who formerly had enjoyed the anonymity of the last chair getting a reluctant crack at being the leader. When not experimenting with seating for (he said) the sake of a homogeneous sound, he was spending a good deal of time lecturing his audiences in that indescribable accent of his. It was an accent with a vague sort of international flavor, and apparently Stokowski could turn it off and on at will. A reporter once asked the Philadelphia Orchestra manager where Stokowski got his accent. "God alone knows!" These lectures to audiences included long harangues on their duty to modern music; or perhaps Stokowski would be scolding them about coming late, or leaving early, or for coughing, or for making noise. It did not take too many years before the Stokowski concerts in Philadelphia were covered by newspapers as a matter of routine news, like police courts, baseball games or local disasters.

Stokowski began to experiment with lighting effects. He would have the hall darkened, with a spotlight on his aureoled head and his beautiful hands. A different kind of spotlight cast the shadows of his hands, and even of his autocratic Roman profile, on the ceiling. All this, Stokowski gravely told the press, was necessary because that way the players could follow his facial expressions. He paid a great deal of attention to his clothes, and a fashion report from the New York *Post* hailed Stokowski's tailor as a great artist, as great as Stokowski himself. Stokowski's marriages and amours were front-page news. On returning from Europe in 1938, where he had been traveling with Greta Garbo, Stokowski told the press: "I am not interested in publicity."

For years there was speculation about Stokowski's birth. In Philadelphia there was a rumor that he was a descendant of Wagner. Stokowski neither denied nor confirmed it. The one thing he did deny, vociferously, was that he had been born in 1882. He insisted the year was 1887. In 1955 he was actually cut off a radio broadcast during a contretemps about his birth date. The announcer began by saying: "Leopold Stokowski was born in 1882—" when the listening audience heard an anguished shout. "No, no, no, *no, no.* That is not true! I was born in 1887!" The announcer continued: "He was born of a Polish father and an Irish mother—" when he was interrupted by another yell. "My mother was not Irish! Where did you get that stuff?" Then Stokowski went into action. As reported in the news-papers:

There followed a scuffling noise (Stokowski vs. The Script), a cry of "Cut the broadcast!" and then the saving sound of music, issuing not from the Miami Symphony Orchestra [which Stokowski had been scheduled to conduct during this broadcast] but from a phonograph, which the station foresightedly keeps ready for such emergencies. Rushing to their morning papers to find out what had happened, tantalized radio fans were some-what disappointed. Stokie, they learned, had not flattened Prosser [John Prosser, the announcer] or vice versa. After thrusting what remained of the script into the conductor's hands, Mr. Prosser had gasped, "Here, take it all," and retired, a shaken man.

Finally the New York *Times* decided to solve the mystery and partly did so, in its issue of September 25, 1959. "The records of the district of Marylebone, Middlesex County, London, show the former [i.e., the earlier date] to be correct. He was born the son of Kopernik Stokowski, a Pole described by some writers as a cabinetmaker, and by others as a diplomat, and Annie Moore Stokowski on April 18, 1882."

He was constantly retouching scores ("You must realize that Bee-thoven and Brahms did not understand instruments"), constantly experimenting with swollen orchestral effects, and it cannot be said that he had the respect of the profession. His Bach transcriptions were considered monstrosities by most musicians, who in addition were outraged over his free hand with the orchestration of sacred masterpieces. Intellectuals simply laughed at him. Stokowski early in his career had lost the respect of the intellectuals by his sheer genius for looking a platitude as square in the face as the history of human thought can show. One sample: "We are going to South America on a musical mission of good will and friendship to our sister republics. Al-though they speak Spanish and Portuguese in South America, they will understand the universal language of music." Walter Damrosch could not have done better. Intellectuals gagged. His book, *Music for All of Us,* starts out with much the same bold observation: "Music is a uni-

versal language—it speaks for everyone—is the birthright of all of us."
(As a matter of fact, music is *not* a universal language.) Stokowski
continues his book with such profound observations as "The sounds
of the ocean have an immense range of rhythm and dynamics. . . .
There are millions who find solace in music—it opens for them the
sun-bathed gates of inspiration . . ." Nor were musicologists happy
about Stokowski's bland disregard of fact in his efforts to be a popu-
larizer. "Bach lived all his life on the edge of starvation." And he
told a Carnegie Hall audience that Bach had been buried in a
pauper's grave. Expressions like "charlatan," "phony," "vulgarian,"
were applied to Stokowski and his work. Virgil Thomson reflected the
intellectual view:

> His ambition to shine and his lack of a sound musical culture have led
> him often into distorted interpretations and into lapses of musical taste
> that have enraged musicians on three continents. . . . His whole per-
> formance is a violation of musical tradition and taste the more surprising
> in that he has always managed to remain high in his profession notwith-
> standing.

But there was another way of looking at the Stokowski phenomenon. Conceding that Stokowski was a showman, conceding that he
tampered with scores more than any conductor since the turn of the
century, conceding that his transcriptions and often his interpretations could be vulgar—conceding all that, the fact remained that Stokowski, in his years with the Philadelphia Orchestra (1912–1936),
created one of the most brilliant groups that had ever existed, a
marvel for its color, precision, power and virtuosity. This necessarily
had to be the accomplishment of a musician with a superior ear for
sound, and the technical expertise to draw it forth. More than any
conductor in the history of music, Stokowski was governed by sound,
pure sound. Sound meant more to him than construction, shape or
logic. In a speech to an audience, Stokowski once said that "Some
people complain that we put more in the music than is supposed to
be there. That's nonsense. It's simply that we get more out of the
music than others do." It was not an entirely accurate observation.
Stokowski got more *sound* out of the music than others did. The other
great conductors could get more *music* out of the music.

Nowhere else in America, until the arrival of Koussevitzky in Boston, could one hear so much important new music as in Philadelphia. At his best—and Stokowski was not *always* tampering with scores— his performances could have vitality, a fine athletic feeling with bracing tempos and a feline grace, taut rhythms and a soaring line. His first recording of the Brahms C minor Symphony is a case in point.

Showman though he was, he saved that aspect for his audiences. At rehearsals he was, for the most part, strictly business, and his players would attest to that fact. "His methods are unique," wrote one. "He is absolutely free of those artistic tantrums often condoned in the name of genius. He has never been known to rip a score or splinter a baton (when he used one). His tirades, when necessary, are soft-spoken, gentlemanly, often epigrammatic and wittily turned." Sto-kowski, fascinated by sound, tried all ways to get results. Says this player:

To get a certain quality in one single high note . . . he made his first trumpeter go to a machine shop with a design for a radically different mouthpiece. Time and again he circumvents the impossible by invention and musical daring. A certain note, an F sharp at the close of Tchaikov-sky's *Pathétique* Symphony, always dissatisfied him because it logically belonged to the violins but was given to the bassoons since G is the lowest note on the violin. Stokowski solved that by simply having his violins continue to play while they slid the G string down to F sharp via the tuning peg.

Of course, this action would be cited by most musicians as simply another example of Stokowski's musical irresponsibility. Yes, they would say, a great technician with a flair for the orchestra. But a serious musician? Never!

After resigning from the Philadelphia Orchestra in 1936, Stokowski continued to conduct parts of subsequent seasons but left the or-chestra for good in 1941, returning only for occasional guest-conduct-ing assignments. But he kept as busy as ever, forming the All-American Youth Orchestra (1940–1942) and taking it on a South American tour. He appeared with the NBC Symphony, the New York Phil-harmonic, the Houston Symphony, the New York City Opera and the Metropolitan Opera (where he had a single assignment, *Turan-dot*). His most recent endeavor has been the creation of the American Symphony Orchestra, which started an annual series in New York in 1962. Stokowski has lived long enough to be considered an old master, and his recent performances have had little of the flamboyance that had characterized his previous work. His interest in the presentation of new music has continued, and in 1965 he conducted the world premiere of Charles Ives's monumental Fourth Symphony. Even in the twilight of his career the octogenarian Stokowski has remained a sight to behold: stiffly erect, his head framed by fluffily arranged snow-white hair, his batonless hands firmly beating time, his clothes impeccable, his behavior still unpredictable, his interpretations more sedate than they used to be but still full of fire, sonority and personality. Personality: perhaps that is the word. Stokowski always had a personality, a blazing magnetism, that made the public idolize him no matter what sour-faced musicians and critics were muttering.

· XXX ·

Otto Klemperer
and the German School

IN OTTO KLEMPERER'S life has been a Job-like succession of misfortunes. A giant of a man, physically as well as musically, he has been rocked by blows that would have demolished a weaker person. Each time, slowly, doggedly, he picked up where he had left off. He is a man of iron will, and that quality is transmitted in his conducting. Never a musician to go in for color or effect, he approaches a score with the attitude of a mountain climber preparing a difficult ascent. There are heights to be scaled, and there are dangers ahead. It is a serious business, not to be taken lightly. All of Klemperer's career has been spent trying to ascend the heights. The lowlands are not for him. It would automatically follow that he is most successful in music of heroic stature. Lighter music can find him heavy-footed and uncomfortable.

He represents the Austro-German tradition, and in his later years has been the sole surviving exponent of the mighty school of German conductors represented by Mahler, Muck and Strauss, and extending through Weingartner, Kleiber, Blech, Furtwängler, Walter and the others. One might also mention Carl Schuricht, who was born five years before Klemperer and was still active in the sixth decade of the twentieth century; but Schuricht's reputation was largely confined to Germany, whereas Klemperer's was international. It was a tradition that had its roots in the nineteenth century, and all German and Austro-Hungarian conductors active at the time had certain things in common no matter how much they may have varied individually. They all were of the German school, a school in which the musical essence is the thing, a school of high seriousness tinged with a meta-physical approach toward music. German musicians take very seri-ously—sometimes even arrogantly—their responsibilities as musical rep-resentatives of the countries that produced the great, unbroken con-tinuity of composers from Bach through Mahler and Strauss. The German school is an intense and one-sided, almost monomaniacal, one. There is no room in it for the wit and banter of a Beecham, the sensuality and emotion of a Koussevitzky, the virtuosity and exhibi-tionism of a Stokowski. Relatively humorless, the German school is apt to be severe and heavy, thorough, contemptuous of frills, dedicated to one thing only—the selfless transmission of a musical message. German conductors, no matter how powerful their personality—and the personality of a Furtwängler, Walter or Klemperer could be meas-ured only in astronomical units—are completely alien to showmanship and flamboyance. They are interested in one thing only—making music as authoritatively, as honestly, as unostentatiously as possible.

Otto Klemperer in his earlier years was typical of that school, and in his last years he has been the archetype. As he grew older, his tempos broadened and his approach became absolutely monolithic. The tre-mendous man (six feet, four inches), crippled by a stroke and other misfortunes, would slowly come from the wings, seat himself and beat time awkwardly with closed fists the size of beer kegs. He would be oblivious of anything but the music, and that was always his way. As Neville Cardus wrote, Klemperer invariably "gives the impression of an aloof artist, independent to the point of appearing indifferent to the audience's reactions. . . . Klemperer is content with truth naked." Or, as William Steinberg has put it, "His attitude toward music is one of the strictest purity, both in opera and concert. Music to him is an absolute expression—intense, cerebral and extremely per-sonal." Or still another view, that of Wieland Wagner: "Classical Greece, Jewish tradition, medieval Christendom, German romanti-cism, the realism of our own time make Klemperer the conductor a unique artistic phenomenon."

His physical troubles started in 1933, during a rehearsal in Leipzig. He leaned back against the rail of the podium and went through it, landing on the base of his skull. His health never afterward was the same, and he suffered from intense headaches. A brain tumor was diagnosed, and the operation left him partially paralyzed and perma-nently marked. He was a forbidding specimen, one side of his face twisted into a permanent scowl, his immense bulk looming over the orchestra. What with his uncontrollable temper and physical strength, he scared orchestras when he went out of control. But he also could have a dry sense of humor, and several stories about him entered the green-room repertoire. "Good," says Klemperer to a player during a rehearsal. The orchestra, astounded, breaks into applause. Klemperer had never before complimented anyone. "It was not *that* good," Klemperer then growls. Or Klemperer is conducting a rehearsal, and the players are anxious to break off. Klemperer appears oblivious to everything but the music. The concertmaster looks meaningfully at his watch. Then he looks again, even more ostentatiously. By now it is far past the hour when the rehearsal is supposed to be over. Finally he all but waves it under Klemperer's nose. "Is it going?" asks Klemperer.

In 1940 there were rumors that Klemperer had had a mental breakdown, and the newspapers carried an unpleasant story to the effect that he had escaped from an asylum and was dangerous. It ensued that Klemperer had indeed been at a rest home. But, explained Klemperer, he had not "escaped" from anything. He had left to go to New York without telling anybody. His explanation was greeted with raised eyebrows in musical circles. Klemperer had a reputation for being erratic, and musicians, especially those who had played under him, were only too anxious to believe that he was capable of anything. When stories about his "insanity" appeared, Klemperer immediately sank whatever money he had into a Carnegie Hall concert, to show the world he was unimpaired mentally and physically.

His troubles were not over. In 1951 he slipped and broke the upper femur of his right leg. That put him out of circulation for a year. A later misfortune occurred in 1959. Klemperer was on the verge of making his Metropolitan Opera debut with *Tristan und Isolde*. In Zurich he fell asleep smoking in bed and was awakened by the smoldering bedclothes. He grabbed the nearest liquid and poured it over the fire and himself. The liquid was spirits of camphor, and Klemperer was horribly burned. His survival was in doubt for months, and he never did conduct at the Metropolitan. Then in 1966, Klemperer, who may be accident-prone, broke his hip in a fall.

Klemperer studied in Frankfurt and Berlin. On Mahler's recommendation ("This young man is destined to become a great conductor") he was appointed conductor of the German Opera House in Prague (1907), went on to opera houses in Hamburg (1910), Strasbourg (1914), Cologne (1917) and Wiesbaden (1924). He also conducted in England and North and South America. In 1927 he was appointed chief conductor of the Kroll Opera in Berlin. There were three opera houses in the city at that time—the Kroll; the Staatsoper, headed by Erich Kleiber; and the Städtische Oper, headed by Walter. The Kroll Opera was new and had been created as a supplement to Kleiber's house. It was intended for special and experimental productions.

Kleiber, that tough, stubborn, difficult disciplinarian, had two years previously conducted the world premiere of Berg's *Wozzeck* after blood, sweat, tears and thirty-four full orchestra rehearsals. He also conducted premieres of music by Stravinsky, Schoenberg, Milhaud, Bartók, Weill and Janáček. A true theatre man, Kleiber once said: "A conductor must live in his house like a lion with its claws deep in its prey." This he did, working without letup. On three consecutive evenings in 1926 he conducted *Salome, Die Meistersinger* and *Der Rosenkavalier*. "When Kleiber comes into this theatre," sighed one Intendant of a German opera house, "there's trouble with a capital T." Kleiber, not a Jew, left Germany in 1935 in protest against the Nazi movement and spent the war years in the United States and South America. Returning to the East Zone of Berlin in 1954, he took over the direction of the Staatsoper but resigned the following year on the grounds that the Communists, like the Nazis, injected propaganda into art. It was a typical Kleiber gesture. After leaving the East Zone he refused to conduct in West Germany because, he said, the West German government had not let him conduct there while he had been in the Soviet sector. "Small-minded and hostile," he called the Bonn government. The following year, defiant to the end, he died in Zurich at the age of sixty-six.

Walter at the Städtische Oper represented a traditional repertoire. But Klemperer, like Kleiber, was attracted to the moderns. He and Kleiber made Berlin the world center of avant-garde operatic activity. Klemperer was especially interested in Janáček and Hindemith, and also conducted stage works by Schoenberg (*Die glückliche Hand* and *Erwartung*), Stravinsky (*Oedipus Rex* and *L'Histoire du Soldat*) and Křenek (*Leben des Orest*). At the same time, he was giving concerts in the Kroll building, introducing numerous works to the German public. The Kroll Opera closed its doors in 1931, largely because of

Otto Klemperer in the early 1960's. He was the dean of conductors and the last active exponent of nineteenth-century traditions.

Herbert von Karajan, whose conducting represents the more recent ideals of literalism and objectivity.

the opposition of the reactionary element. Klemperer then moved to the Staatsoper, but when the Nazis came into power his contract was canceled (he was Jewish) and he had to leave Germany.

During the war he busied himself in the United States, conducting the Los Angeles Philharmonic and the Pittsburgh Symphony. He had a difficult time. In 1947 he returned to Europe and took over the Budapest Opera. He resigned because the government refused to let three of his colleagues—the singers Mikhail Szekely and Alexander Sved, and the conductor Janos Ferencsik—travel abroad. Guest conducting assignments followed.

His second career started in 1951. Walter Legge had founded the Philharmonia Orchestra that year, primarily for the purpose of making records, and Klemperer conducted two concerts with brilliant success. Legge knew that Klemperer was becoming a symbol; that he was selling out in Vienna, London, Berlin, Munich, wherever he appeared; that he was being recognized, and venerated, as virtually the last of the conductors with nineteenth-century roots. Toscanini in 1951 was conducting only radio broadcasts, and Walter and Furtwängler were less and less active. Legge secured the services of Klemperer for the Philharmonia, and his instincts were correct. With his own orchestra, and freed from financial troubles, Klemperer came into second bloom. There were those who did not like his conducting, calling it heavy and ponderous, with impossibly slow tempos. But there were others, and they were the great majority, who all but achieved some sort of religious communion at a Klemperer concert. They found his conducting tremendous in scope, with the kind of austere statement that purifies music. A critic attended a Klemperer concert in 1961 and was struck by the physical as well as the musical characteristics of the man:

In an age of well-tailored virtuoso conductors, he stands out like a Michelangelo sculpture among Dresden figurines. He makes his way slowly to the podium, dragging his mighty body, cane in hand. On the podium is a large chair on which he sits after a curt nod to the audience. He does not use a baton and the score is open before him. Generally he beats time with his fists, a minuscule beat for so tremendous a man. Often no beat is visible at all. . . . His conducting retains its intense drive and vitality. Never has he had much charm. He is always ultra-serious, pursuing his ends in a straight, uncompromising line. In the big pieces of the repertoire there is nobody exactly like him. Nobody can so convey the size and grandeur of Beethoven, Brahms, Mahler, Bruckner. In a way he is a transfigured Kapellmeister—a non-virtuoso conductor who may even have something of the pedant in him, but whose vision and conception happen to be so big that he and his music emerge monument-size.

Other important conductors of the German school during the first half of the century have been Hermann Abendroth, Otto Ackermann, Hans Knappertsbusch, Karl Böhm, Fritz Busch, Eugen Jochum, Josef Krips, Hans Rosbaud, Rudolf Kempe, Wolfgang Sawallisch, Fritz Stiedry, Joseph Keilberth, Hans Schmidt-Isserstedt and Hermann Scherchen. The veteran Robert Heger, highly regarded by Furtwängler and Walter, should also be mentioned. And several foreigners who went on to major careers were German-trained. One of the most important was Ataulfo Argenta, from Spain, a country that had produced only one important conductor—Enrique Arbós. Argenta was on his way toward becoming one of the international stars when he met his death in an automobile accident in 1958, at the age of forty-five.

Böhm's career extends through Graz, Munich, Darmstadt, Hamburg, Dresden and Vienna, where he was head of the Staatsoper. He has been active at the Metropolitan and is perhaps the world's ranking expert on the Strauss operas. Busch, an Aryan anti-Nazi who was in charge of the Dresden Opera, left Germany in 1933 and was the chief conductor of the Glyndebourne Festival from 1934 until his death in 1951. He also was active in the United States, appearing with the short-lived New Opera Company, the New York Philharmonic and the Metropolitan Opera. Busch's Mozart recordings from Glyndebourne (*Figaro, Don Giovanni, Così Fan Tutte*) introduced a generation of music lovers to the delights of that most perfect of opera composers. Scherchen and Rosbaud were specialists in contemporary music. The former was instrumental in the formation of the International Society for Contemporary Music, and the latter was one of the very few to interest himself in serial music. Stravinsky calls Rosbaud "the most scrupulous of musicians and one of the few non-delinquent conductors," meaning that he did his best for the avant-garde. Stravinsky, incidentally, in his *Themes and Episodes,* names Alexander von Zemlinsky as, of all the conductors he has heard, "the one who achieved the most consistently high standards. I remember a *Marriage of Figaro* conducted by him in Prague as the most satisfying operatic experience of my life." Zemlinsky was a Vienna-born conductor and composer whose major position was at the German Opera House in Prague from 1911 to 1927. Later he conducted at the Kroll Opera. He also was the teacher and father-in-law of Arnold Schoenberg.

Hans Knappertsbusch, active in Munich, Vienna, Salzburg and Bayreuth, was famous for his Wagner performances and even more famous for his slow tempos (which he may have inherited from his teacher, Hans Richter). He did not care to travel, and hence had primarily a local reputation. But he had everybody's respect. To many he represented a link to an earlier, mellower, more relaxed style of conducting: honesty, ideals, the pure dedication to music. Knappertsbusch exerted a great deal of quiet influence on German music, and his performances of Brahms and Strauss, in addition to Wagner, were models for many of the younger conductors. Orchestral musicians respected his vast experience and loved his easygoing podium ways. They especially loved his relaxed rehearsals. Orchestral players simply dote on conductors who cut rehearsals short. Knappertsbusch, faced with a piece of music he had known all his life, would say: "You know it and I know it, so why rehearse it?" John Culshaw, the Decca recording director, tells about the time Knappertsbusch was forced into rehearsing a piece. At the public performance the orchestra got all mixed up on the repeats. Some went ahead, some went back. The perspiring Knappertsbusch left the podium with the grumbling comment: "Wouldn't have happened if we hadn't had that —— rehearsal." He had a drawling wit. At the height of the Toscanini furor, when everybody was trying to imitate the Italian and conduct from memory, Knappertsbusch was asked why he invariably had the score before him. "Why not?" he said. "I can read music." He also could be brusque and stubborn, sticking to his beliefs even if they endangered his life. An anti-Nazi, he was removed from the Munich Opera in 1936 because he refused to join the party. He always said what he thought. Culshaw asked Knappertsbusch his opinion of Richard Strauss. "I played cards with him every day for years and he was a pig."

The conductor of the German school who has attracted most attention since World War II has been the fabulously successful, Austrian-born Herbert von Karajan. Karajan, indeed, was flying so high and in so many directions during one period that he seemed to be an airline; he was simultaneously head of the Vienna Staatsoper, of the Berlin Philharmonic, of the Salzburg Festival, one of the chief conductors at La Scala and conductor of the Philharmonia in London. Jokes about Karajan's activity made the rounds. He gets into a cab and the driver asks "Where to?" Answers Karajan: "It doesn't matter. I've got something going everywhere."

This incredible career started as that of a piano prodigy, with a debut at the age of eight. Later Karajan went to the Vienna Conservatory, where his conducting teacher was Schalk. His first post was at Ulm, followed by seven years at Aachen. During the war he conducted at the Berlin Opera. A Nazi party member, he was directly supported by Hermann Goering, who set him in opposition to Furtwängler, Goebbels' man. It was after the war that Karajan's rapid ascent began. There was something about this short, slim, handsome, dynamic, decisive conductor that seemed to make everything come to him. For a few years he was the supreme conductor in Europe. He had the reputation in America of being a virtuoso conductor, and when he brought the Berlin Philharmonic to New York in 1955 the critics braced themselves for a tonal and choreographic onslaught. Instead they saw a conductor whose gestures were quite restrained and who was, if anything, completely objective in his interpretations. Machine-like efficiency characterized his work. There was never any doubt about his command, but there was about the amount of poetry and imagination he had. He proved to be one of the literalists, one who at his best conveyed a great deal of excitement and electricity, and one who at his worst represented a sort of bored, dispassionate perfection. The charge of objectivity has constantly followed Karajan, and a German critic has written that Karajan's brilliance "has the shining translucency of a perfectly formed icicle."

For a while it appeared that Karajan was going to seize all of musical Europe. In anything he did, he had a compulsion to excel, to dominate, to command—whether it was on the podium, behind the wheel of a racing car, the controls of an airplane, or on the ski slopes (he has the reputation of being one of the best amateur skiers in Europe). But controversy follows him wherever he goes, and he has broken off associations almost as fast as he has formed them. He had joined the Vienna Staatsoper in 1956, resigned in 1962, rejoined the company the following year as co-director with Walther Erich Schaefer and—amid great explosions of wrath and an international press coverage—again resigned on May 11, 1964. Karajan proved to be an expensive man to have around, and a hard one to work with. He demanded, à la Mahler, full control over a production—the staging, acting, decor, musical direction, everything. But he was not a very good administrator, it was claimed, and he antagonized people. Ostensibly, the second fight in Vienna came over Karajan's appointment of an Italian prompter. The hassle sounded silly, but it concerned a matter of authority, and even the Parliament was drawn into it, with the Socialist members accusing Karajan of running the opera house as an absolute monarchy. The prompter could not get a union permit, and Karajan insisted that he work nevertheless. When the prompter showed up for a performance, the stagehands struck and the curtain came down. Karajan, in a fury, resigned and swore that he was through. "True art must die when it depends on the whim of a glorified clerk. I will never set foot in Vienna again."

In recent years, mannerisms have crept into Karajan's conducting: artificial-sounding tempos, unusual accents and emphases. But his conducting has an extraordinary degree of finish and, often, power. His theories involve letting the orchestra share the responsibility. "For a concert with my Berlin Philharmonic, I first achieve rehearsal perfection—complete mastery of detail and mechanization. Then I let the men play freely during the actual performance, so that they are making the music as much as I am—sharing the emotion which we all have together." About baton technique he has little to say. "I have no theories about stick technique. A baton, a pencil, it makes no difference. You can tie my wrist to my side and the orchestra will still get the beat. I tell my pupils: 'You must feel the tempos and rhythms, and then the orchestra will feel them.' Diagrams and that, I don't believe in them." This is an observation that goes back to Spontini, who boasted he could conduct with his eyes alone. And it is a fact that rhythm is a mysterious force that goes out in pulses from conductor to orchestra. Inner rhythm—actual and psychic—is more important than rhythm conveyed by arm or body movement. The arm or the body is merely the carrier. Karajan, like all major conductors, has this kind of inner rhythm, as subtle and controlled as that of any conductor. It also can be said that Karajan marks the first break from the nineteenth-century German conducting tradition. He is a cosmopolitan who is interested in other music than that of the Austro-German school; he is entirely twentieth-century in his thinking; he is an eclectic, and of very few previous Austro-German conductors (if any) can that be said. Karajan is not the end of the old school; he is the beginning of the new—and it no longer is a German school.

· XXXI ·

The Modern French School

AFTER THE PERIOD of the Big Three—Pasdeloup, Lamoureux and Colonne—of late nineteenth-century French conducting, there was a hiatus. French conductors were generally admired for their solid musicianship and *expertise,* but very few of them were export products. Like so many Italian conductors, they did not travel well, and their fame was local. That pertains to Chevillard, Pierné, Gaubert, Paul Taffanel (the famous flute player who was the tyrant and scourge of the Opéra), Albert Wolff, François Ruhlmann, Georges Marty, Vincent d'Indy, Henri Rabaud and any number of other conductors. Some of them made brief guest appearances outside of France but hastened back. Some, like Alfred Cortot, turned to an instrument or to composition after promising beginnings on the podium. Cortot, a young Wagnerian and the most brilliant keyboard talent in France, had been an assistant conductor in Bayreuth under Richter and Mottl. In 1902 he founded, in Paris, La Société de Festival Lyrique and made his debut at the age of twenty-four with the French premieres of *Götterdämmerung* and *Tristan und Isolde.* The following year he founded a concert society for choral music, and the year after that was active as a conductor with the Société Nationale, at which he introduced much new music by French composers. Cortot must have been a strenuous figure on the podium, and Debussy poked gentle fun at him:

Cortot is the French conductor who has most successfully appropriated the usual pantomimic technique of the German conductors. He advances on the orchestra, directing at them a threatening baton like a banderillo at a bull fight determined to undermine the confidence of the bull. (The members of the orchestra remain as cool as Icelanders; they have seen displays of this sort before.) Like Weingartner, Cortot leans affectionately over the first violins, murmuring intimate secrets, then swoops around to the trombones, whom he exhorts with a gesture that apparently means: "Courage! Put some go into it! Try to be super-trombones!" Whereupon the obedient trombones conscientiously try to swallow their brass tubes.

Later, Cortot became the most important French pianist. In the latter part of his life he never conducted.

It was not until the appearance of Pierre Monteux that France once again boasted a conductor of international stature, a conductor admired and loved all over the world. The word "loved" is used advisedly. Even among his colleagues—even among orchestral musicians—Monteux seemed to have no enemies. A short (five feet, five inches), stout (185 pounds), mustachioed man of geniality and elegance, Monteux moved sedately through life and music, starting as violinist and violist, picking up the baton at the turn of the century, and continuing without pause until his death in 1964 at the age of eighty-nine. (Toscanini had retired ten days before his eighty-seventh birthday, and only Pablo Casals has conducted at a more advanced age. But Casals has always remained primarily a cellist, despite long flirtations with the podium going as far back as 1920.) About the only things in life that seemed to bother Monteux were base suggestions that his hair was dyed black. He spent much more time explaining the top of his head than he did explaining his musical interpretations. Thus, in an interview in 1955:

As you see, my mustache is white, but my hair is black. Would you put in your paper, to stop rumors, that that is a natural condition? My hair, I assure you, is not dyed. My mother died at 84 and although she had very little hair left, what remained was coal black. Also you might mention that I have all my teeth.

And he told another reporter that anybody was welcome to come with alcohol, with shampoo, with anything, just to wash his hair and prove it was colored as nature had designed.

Monteux led an all-embracing life as a conductor, having been prominent in opera, ballet and symphony. Like so many French conductors, he played the violin in orchestras before becoming a stick wielder. Around 1910 he organized his Concerts Berlioz at the Casino de Paris, and then he became conductor for Diaghileff's Ballets Russes.

While there, he conducted the world premieres of Stravinsky's *Petrouchka, Le Sacre du Printemps* and *Rossignol,* Ravel's *Daphnis et Chloe* and Debussy's *Jeux.* Through the years he also conducted at the Opéra, founded the Société des Concerts Populaires, and appeared throughout Europe and America as a guest. A busy man. In 1917–18 he was at the Metropolitan Opera, from which he went to the Boston Symphony. Monteux walked into a labor battle in Boston. The musicians were on strike, and when it was settled, the concertmaster and thirty musicians had left. Monteux had to build an orchestra virtually from scratch.

He had come to Boston with the reputation of being a specialist in modern music, and he did not disappoint his audiences. Avoiding hackneyed programs, he began to conduct pieces by the newer Americans, Stravinsky, Honegger, Respighi, Vaughan Williams. Monteux left Boston in 1924 and then started a ten-year association with the Amsterdam Concertgebouw Orchestra. He also, in 1929, founded the Orchestre Symphonique de Paris and conducted it until 1938. In the United States his principal activity after Boston was as head of the San Francisco Orchestra, from 1936 to 1952. After 1952 he resumed his career as a guest conductor, including a series of performances at the Metropolitan Opera. In 1961, at the age of eighty-six, he took over the job of musical director of the London Symphony.

Musicians enjoyed working with him. He was authoritative without being despotic. "I don't want to follow you, so you'll have to follow me," he would say. A superlative baton technician, he stood almost motionless on the podium, using a greatly subdivided beat, something like that of an old-fashioned French bandmaster. It was a beat of uncommon clarity, precision and flexibility. Stravinsky has said that of all the conductors he has ever known, Monteux was "the least interested in calisthenic exhibitions for the entertainment of the audience and the most concerned to give clear signals to the orchestra." His repertoire covered most music from Beethoven to the present day, and he was one of the few French conductors who could be entirely convincing in Beethoven and Brahms. In these composers, and in any kind of German music, he was anything but heaven-shaking. Rather he brought out the lyric grace and charm of the music, without sacrificing its strength. His approach was quite different from that of the German conductors, who were slower, more powerful, thicker in sound (Furtwängler always excepted). Monteux always aimed for, and achieved, a transparency of sound. His ear was infallible, and his performances of any music had an airy, springy quality.

In many ways, his was a type of conducting for the connoisseur. Monteux never created the kind of frenzy that Toscanini, Stokowski or Koussevitzky aroused. His work, like Beecham's, rather was eminently civilized, and Virgil Thomson was but echoing the opinions of musicians the world over when he wrote of Monteux' "beautiful mixtures of sound . . . perfect balance and blending . . . Eloquence . . . Translucency." Monteux once compiled a list of rules for conductors—eight "musts" and many "don'ts." All reflect his intense practicality. Don't overconduct. Don't make unnecessary noises or gestures; don't conduct solo instruments in solo passages; don't worry or annoy sections or players by looking intently at them in ticklish passages; don't stop for obviously accidental wrong notes.

In Monteux' musical outlook was little theory or theosophy. He merely translated notes into sound. Toscanini did the same, but where Toscanini's translations were intense and propulsive, Monteux' were elegant, graceful, full of charm and sentiment. (Sentimentality, never.) His conducting was always supple and natural, somewhat fast-moving but with an incessantly flowing line, clarification of detail, and a taste calculated to bring out the poetry of a piece of music without ever becoming mannered or maudlin. The phrase "French taste" has been abused, but if ever it had a meaning in music it applied to Pierre Monteux.

Charles Munch, who followed Monteux as the most important French conductor of his generation, was born in Strasbourg. Unlike most important conductors, he came late to the podium. He followed the usual French pattern of becoming a violinist and playing in orchestras. But unlike most French musicians, he drifted to Germany and was concertmaster of the Leipzig Gewandhaus Orchestra under Furtwängler for many years. Not until 1932, at the age of forty-one, did he start conducting. He has explained this late start by saying it was so much easier for him to make a living as a violinist. Appearances in 1932 with the Straram Orchestra were successful, and Munch soon formed his own orchestra, the Paris Philharmonic. He became musical director of the Paris Conservatoire Orchestra in 1937, visited the United States in 1946 and succeeded Koussevitzky in Boston in 1949.

Munch never has been so protean a figure as his great predecessor, Monteux. He has never conducted opera, for example, and most musicians would agree that his specialty is music of the French school.

LONDON RECORDS

Ernest Ansermet, Swiss born but a conductor whose work is allied to the French school. Many consider him to be the outstanding interpreter of Stravinsky's music. Debussy and Ravel are also among his specialties.

Three successive conductors of the Boston Symphony Orchestra. From left to right: Pierre Monteux, who led the orchestra from 1919 to 1924; Serge Koussevitzky (1924–1949); and the Alsatian Charles Munch (1949–1962).

RCA VICTOR

That he conducts with authority and brilliance. When one speaks of the French school, one thinks of grace and elegance; of logic rather than high emotion; of an emphasis on exterior polish (glittering, top-of-the-keys passagework from pianists; a refined, smooth, mellifluous delivery from violinists); of objectivity and a refusal to dig into the mystical elements of music as so many Germans do; of a kind of detachment; of an emotional identification with things French to a point where most other things are excluded. All of these traits are exhibited in Munch's conducting, as they also are in the work of such admired French conductors as Paul Paray, André Cluytens and Jean Martinon. Munch seems rather impatient in German music, where his tempos tend to be very fast and where the expression can be perfunctory. Munch makes no secret of his feeling. Since leaving the Boston Symphony in 1962 he has remained active as a guest conductor, and his programs are almost exclusively French.

Though born in Switzerland, Ernest Ansermet, through his long association with French music and culture, can be classified as a product of the French school; and this although he studied conducting with Bloch, Nikisch and Weingartner. Originally a mathematician, he taught at a high school in Lausanne from 1906 to 1910. At the same time he pursued musical studies, and in 1910 started conducting in Montreux. His first important assignment was with the Ballets Russes in 1915, and during the years he was there he led the world premieres of, among others, Stravinsky's *Renard* and *Les Noces;* Ravel's *La Valse;* Falla's *Le Tricorne.* His life's work, however, was in Geneva. L'Orchestre de la Suisse Romande had been formed in 1918, and Ansermet became its first conductor. As things turned out, he was its only conductor until 1967, when he retired.

For years Ansermet enjoyed primarily a local reputation. But after World War II a long series of records began to come out, and the world discovered what the experts had known all along—that in Geneva was a conductor who was one of the finest of all interpreters of Stravinsky and of the modern French school. After his return to the United States in 1946—he had visited briefly with the Ballets Russes in 1916—the critical consensus was that he was one of the half-dozen supreme conductors. Everywhere Ansermet's work was hailed for its culture, strength, finesse and probity.

In the 1960s, Ansermet came into the news for reasons other than his conducting. He was widely quoted as a strong opponent of the dodecaphonic school. Ansermet, a logician and something of a philosopher, always had had theories about music and its social impact. During World War I he told an American reporter that the war could be blamed on Wagner. "Wagner laid the train and powder, and Strauss put to it the spark that caused the final explosion. Wagner took music out of the reign of international appreciation and confined it within the narrower compass of a national cult." This remark was made in 1916, and Ansermet may have had occasion to think of it during the rise of Nazism and its associated Wagnerianism.

Anyway, Ansermet, who had started out as a mathematician, "proved" the fallacy of twelve-tone and serial composition in his book, *The Fundamentals of Music in the Human Consciousness* (1961). The former champion of Stravinsky, the conductor who had led the world premieres of the *Symphony of Psalms*, the Mass, the *Capriccio* and *L'Histoire du Soldat* in addition to the ballet premieres, broke with his idol and challenged the idea of tonal disintegration. He accused Schoenberg of robbing music of expression ("What remains is dead theory") and ridiculed the idea that the ever-increasing complexity of contemporary music meant anything in particular. "If significance depended upon structural complexity, many classical works would seem poor indeed." As for Stravinsky, his serial scores speak "as if by proxy; he does not give of himself." It was to Bartók that Ansermet turned, especially Bartók's later works: "among the most beautiful tokens of hope that the music of our time has produced." Ansermet attempted a mathematical proof of his theory. "I have shown that the traditional system of harmony, based on the common intervals of the third, fourth and fifth, is the only logical one." Ansermet's book, however, remains a study more talked-about than read.

Ansermet, like all experienced conductors, has strong feelings about the right of the conductor to touch up the score and otherwise follow his instinct. Composers, he points out—quite accurately—are often willing to give the interpreter more leeway than is generally believed (though Ansermet does not add that this is true only when the composer trusts a particular interpreter). "I once asked Debussy how fast he wanted a passage marked *modéré* to go. He said, 'Well, perhaps this way or perhaps so. You will know.' . . . In the final pages of [Debussy's] *Iberia* there are some glissando passages for trombones that come off better if they are reinforced by horns. So I add the horns. I cannot believe that accuracy is more important than good sense."

· XXXII ·

From Central Europe

EVER SINCE THE DAYS of Stamitz, the Eastern European countries have contributed their share of conductors. From Hungary came Liszt, Seidl, Richter and Nikisch. From Bohemia came Smetana, Nápravník and Mahler. Bedrich Smetana today is remembered primarily as a composer, but he was a brilliant pianist and a conductor who directed orchestras in Sweden and his own country. He was constantly on the podium between 1865 and 1874. Antonin Dvořák, too, was considered a fine conductor, and not only in his own music.

The line in the twentieth century is just as pronounced. Important Hungarian conductors have included Fritz Reiner, George Szell and Eugene Ormandy, with such younger ones as Janos Ferencsik and Istvan Kertesz beginning what obviously are going to be major careers. Antal Dorati and Georg Solti, two other Hungarians, have already achieved them; and many consider Solti the greatest Wagnerian conductor of the post-Furtwängler period. Ferenc Fricsay, who died young, was still another Hungarian: a conductor with immense potential both in opera and symphony.

Bohemia—now part of Czechoslovakia—has contributed Vaclav Talich, Rafael Kubelik and Karel Ancerl to twentieth-century conducting. Talich had a tremendous reputation but did little traveling, though he did take the Czech Philharmonic—which he conducted from 1920 to 1941—on several tours of Europe. Experts who were familiar with his work were unanimous in saying that he was one of the authentically great ones of the century, and his recordings bear out that opinion.

The modern Hungarian group has, however, been of greater international importance. In many respects, Hungarian musical training was German-dominated, and many of the great Hungarian musical figures went off to Austria or Germany to complete their studies. But even if there was an Austro-German orientation, the Hungarians almost invariably have had something of their own to contribute. Their Magyar blood runs warm, and while the better Hungarian musicians have always controlled the *Zigeuner* in them, their temperament generally comes through.

It is interesting to note that the careers of three of the most important of this century's Hungarian conductors have closely been identified with the United States. Ormandy, indeed, is primarily an American product as a conductor, for he started his career in America and made his entire reputation in Minneapolis and Philadelphia. Reiner, after conducting in Budapest and Dresden, came to the United States to be active in Cincinnati, Pittsburgh, the Metropolitan Opera and Chicago. Szell's major post since 1946 has been in Cleveland.

Reiner was conceded to be the greatest of baton technicians and a musician who, in the words of a New York Philharmonic player, "knew everything." Always a precisionist and a perfectionist, he got his results through perfect coordination plus a nature that scared music out of his players. Reiner was not one of the beloved conductors of his time, and would probably have run at the bottom in any kind of popularity poll taken among orchestral musicians. Irascible, impatient, tough, sarcastic, he rode roughshod over orchestras, and many of his musicians called him a sadist. To his colleagues he was a conductor's conductor, much as Leopold Godowsky was a pianist's pianist—a musician of formidable background and knowledge who could do anything with an orchestra. In certain kinds of contemporary music— in all kinds, indeed, except that of the dodecaphonic school, which did not interest him—he had a stupendous ability to clarify the most complicated writing. A score like Bartók's *Miraculous Mandarin* came out with titanic surges of sound and wild (but perfectly controlled) rhythms, and with textures that in their clarity and balances were positively Mozartean. Nikisch had been the creator of his style. "It was he," Reiner said, "who told me that I should never wave my arms in conducting, and that I should use my eyes to give cues." Elsewhere Reiner explained that he tried to achieve the maximum of musical result with a minimum of physical effort. Reiner was proud of his technique, and he tried to pass it to his pupils, of whom Leonard Bernstein was one. That was at the Curtis Institute of Music, where

Reiner taught from 1931 to 1941. "When students have completed a course under my direction," Reiner said, "any one of them can stand up before an orchestra he has never seen before and conduct a new piece at first sight without verbal explanation, by means of only manual technique."

He was a short man who used a big baton in a tiny beat, the tiniest since Richard Strauss. The tip of his baton would move in tiny arcs, and musicians had to give his beat their full attention. Perhaps that is why Reiner performances invariably sounded so alert. At one rehearsal with the New York Philharmonic, the musicians decided to "throw" Reiner in the Mussorgsky-Ravel *Pictures at an Exhibition* after he had passed a few scathing comments on their playing. "We purposely hung back," one of the musicians later told a friend. "Our rhythm started to collapse. Reiner knew what was happening, all right. He compressed his lips, and his beat, which had been tiny to begin with, got absolutely miniscule. We *had* to follow him. It was a sort of bawling-out in reverse."

Reiner's beat, small as it was, had infinite nuance. The tip of his baton cued everybody in and out, held the rhythm, shaped phrases, anticipated all trouble. Orchestral players were constantly amazed. "In some of those complicated modern pieces," one of his players has said, "the tip of his baton would be beating three, the elbows would be beating four, his hips would be beating seven and his left hand would be taking care of all the other rhythms." Musicians respected him and played for him. They had to. In some respects his personality was reminiscent of Toscanini's. Like Toscanini, Reiner was an autocrat and a despot once he stepped before an orchestra. He could be bitter and cutting to his players. He had no leniency toward human failings and frailties; he expected nothing but perfection. Reiner had hooded eyes like a falcon's, and his piercing look was enough to paralyze an errant player.

In his early years Reiner had been criticized as being too much a technician. There was some justice to the charge. But by the time he took over the Chicago Symphony, an ailing organization, and made it a spectacularly responsive ensemble, those days were long past. Stravinsky called the Chicago Symphony under Reiner the most precise and flexible orchestra in the world. It is true that Reiner never was the sort of *gemütlich* conductor that, say, Walter was. His iron technical and emotional control never relaxed, his rhythms never broke ranks, and he never leaned into a melody the way more sentimental conductors did. But that is not to say his interpretations lacked heart. All of his music making had dignity and bigness; melodic material was drawn with surety, elegance and style. Reiner was of the new breed, and even though he had been born in 1888 he was a modernist from the very beginning, able to resist the prevailing romanticisms. He paid immense attention to detail, but he was never swamped by detail. Architectural solidity was always present. Following the Toscanini way, Reiner studied scores with the determination of getting rid of "tradition" and going straight to the music itself. This he did, with a Toscanini-like ability to translate the blueprint of a score into an exact aural equivalent.

There is something of Reiner's approach in George Szell, another anti-romantic, another literalist, another precisionist. Szell is an eminently pragmatic conductor and musical mentality. It is characteristic that where Walter, discussing conducting, would talk about soul and spirit, Szell talks about technique and the problems of style. In a long interview with Paul H. Lang the conductor had a great deal to say about his approach. "I personally like complete homogeneity of sound, phrasing and articulation within each section, and then—when the ensemble is perfect—the proper balance between sections plus complete flexibility—so that in each movement one or more principal voices can be accompanied by the others. To put it simply: the most sensitive ensemble playing." Szell is a fanatic about ensemble. He looks for a chamber music approach and tries to get each of his hundred-odd men to listen carefully to the others while playing. He hears horizontally—that is, polyphonically—and thinks that most conductors have monodic hearing. He has an aural image that takes in the whole score, not merely the melodic elements. "I have been trained to hear in my mind," he told Lang, "the whole texture, and I hear the various parts and voices in their relationship and proportion before I hear the actual sound." Like Toscanini and Reiner, he starts with the assumption that "everything a good composer writes down is expected to be heard, except in obvious cases where a coloristic impression is intended, as for instance the violin figurations in Wagner's *Magic Fire Music.*"

Szell, born in Budapest, was trained in Vienna. A prodigy, he made his debut as a pianist at the age of eleven and conducted his first concert at sixteen. Nikisch and Toscanini were the two major influ-

COLUMBIA RECORDS

George Szell, conductor of the Cleveland Orchestra. He is regarded as one of the finest technicians in the post-Toscanini era of conducting.

Lower left: Eugene Ormandy, for many years conductor of the Philadelphia Orchestra. Many consider it the world's greatest virtuoso orchestra.

Lower right: Fritz Reiner, who ended his career as conductor of the Chicago Symphony Orchestra, was famous for his clarity and control.

COLUMBIA RECORDS

RCA VICTOR

ences on his conducting. Strauss recommended him as conductor on the staff of the Municipal Theatre in Strasbourg in 1917. From there he went to Darmstadt, Düsseldorf, Berlin and Prague. Caught in New York at the outset of World War II, he stayed in the United States, conducting at the Metropolitan Opera from 1942 to 1946. His appointment to the Cleveland Orchestra followed. Szell has devoted most of his time to Cleveland, though he still fills many guest assignments in Europe and for several years had lengthy stays in New York as guest with the Philharmonic.

Cleveland had a good orchestra when Szell arrived, but it was not a group that rated high in the international scale. Szell transformed it. He went to Cleveland dreaming of "a combination of the best elements of American and European orchestral playing. I wanted to combine the American purity and beauty of sound and their virtuosity of execution with the European sense of tradition, warmth of expression and sense of style." Szell, after a few years, began to think he had reached his goal. He was quoted as saying: "In Cleveland we begin to rehearse when most orchestras leave off." Remarks like this do not make Szell very popular with his colleagues; and, indeed, his career has not been unmarked by explosive episodes. He withdrew from the Metropolitan Opera in a huff, under conditions that have never been fully made public. Later he and the New York Philharmonic had a passage at arms. Then there was the San Francisco affair, in which Szell demolished the reputation of a conductor, Enrique Jorda, and cast aspersions on the integrity of a music critic, Alfred Frankenstein. Actions like these have caused friends of Szell to call him his own worst enemy (to which Rudolf Bing of the Metropolitan Opera has said, "Not while I'm alive").

Nobody disputes Szell's pre-eminence as a technician. There are some who call his interpretations pedantic and unimaginative, a charge Szell (naturally) bitterly resents. "It is perfectly legitimate to prefer the hectic, the arhythmic, the untidy, but to my mind great artistry is not disorderliness." But for every musician who calls him pedantic, who feels that his performances are over-rehearsed and too fussily perfect, there are fifty who admire his comprehensive musicianship and his ability to achieve a textured kind of tonal clarity. No other living conductor, they insist, and possibly only Reiner and Toscanini in the history of conducting, can get such beautifully articulated sound from an orchestra. None, they say, conducts Haydn and Mozart with such finesse and elegant proportions, such perfectly chosen tempos, such precise balances. None, they continue, has an equivalent kind of strength in the Austro-German school from Beethoven through Strauss and Mahler.

Eugene Ormandy is an entirely different kind of conductor from that of the Reiner-Szell axis, and in many ways his has been a strange career. For although he has been at the head of the Philadelphia Orchestra—a group commonly held to be the greatest virtuoso orchestra in the world—since 1938, there is a singular reluctance in musical circles to admit him into the ranks of the great conductors. Ormandy is considered an excellent technician with a technicolored approach to music. He has been described as the best of the second-rank conductors, a man who goes in for brilliant external effects and few deep or memorable ones. Stravinsky contemptuously dismisses him as an ideal conductor of Johann Strauss. The feeling seems to be widespread.

It is true that Ormandy's programs do concentrate more on the showpieces of the repertoire than do those of most other conductors. He programs very little Haydn or Mozart (who does, these days, aside from Szell?), approaches Beethoven in a rather gingerly manner, picks up with Brahms and is happiest with the post-romantic and early modern schools—Tchaikovsky, Sibelius, Strauss, Mahler, Ravel, Debussy, Respighi, early Stravinsky. It is a rather limited kind of repertoire. It also is one that he handles with unusual flair and command. But the unfortunate Ormandy has been given a bad name, and even when he finishes a brilliant, clean-cut performance of a Strauss tone poem or Debussy's *Iberia* there are apt to be criticisms of his "shallowness" or "vulgarity" or "distortion"—where, in fact, there is neither shallowness, vulgarity nor distortion at all.

Part of the trouble is ironic: it stems from the rich sounds made by the Philadelphia Orchestra. Many critics and listeners still have a pronounced streak of Puritanism, and instinctively distrust such voluptuous sounds. Can anything so lush also have probity? they ask themselves. Ormandy is not hesitant when he discusses the famous "Philadelphia sound." It is very simple. The Philadelphia sound? "It's me. My conducting is what it is because I was a violinist. Toscanini was always playing the cello when he conducted, Koussevitzky the double bass, Stokowski the organ. The conductors who were pianists nearly always have a sharper, more percussive beat, and it can be heard in their orchestras."

Ormandy started as a violinist, and at the age of five and a half was the youngest student ever admitted into the Budapest Conservatory. In 1921 he came to the United States for a concert tour. It did not materialize, and Ormandy, stranded, played the violin in movie houses. That was where he made his debut as a conductor—at the Capitol Theatre in New York. In 1931 he was called to Minneapolis, and in 1936 to Philadelphia, where he shared two seasons with Stokowski before becoming musical director in 1938. There he inherited a great orchestra and, at the very least, maintained its aural standards. Many claim he improved them. Of all conductors he has one of the most infallible ears and memories, and is one of the fastest studies. In 1935 he was scheduled to record Roy Harris' *When Johnny Comes Marching Home* and did not receive the score until the very morning of the session. It took him an hour to memorize it. He rushed to Northrup Auditorium and conducted a quick rehearsal without a score, correcting errors in the parts as he went along. Harris was present. He checked, and found Ormandy's corrections entirely accurate. It was an impressive feat of pure musicianship; and that, plus his ability to evoke great washes of sound from an orchestra, has kept him at the top for many years. Ormandy does not conduct with the overwhelming personality of a Furtwängler, or with the ferocity and clarity of a Toscanini, or with the immense knowledge and classicism of a Szell. But he has carved out an area for himself, and within it he is secure, a perfect workman and a sensitive interpreter. And it is an area that takes in a great deal more than Strauss waltzes.

The Foreign-Born Contingent
in the United States

THE HISTORY OF MUSIC in the United States was, until the end of World War I, primarily a reflection of German traditions. Most American composers went abroad to study, coming home with diplomas from Leipzig, Cologne or Berlin. Most American orchestras were staffed predominantly by Austro-Germans, with a contingent of Italians backing them up. Most American orchestras, too, were conducted by foreign-born leaders, many of whom had come to the United States during the European revolutions of 1848 and 1849. It was not until the early 1920s that there was a break. Suddenly Americans started to go to Paris, where the big attraction was Nadia Boulanger. The period from 1920 to 1935 saw the emergence of a strong national school of composition, and it seemed that American music and musicians would soon stand on their own feet. But soon came another exodus from Germany and Austria. The rise of Hitler resulted in a general dispersal of non-Aryan musicians or even, in some cases, of Aryan musicians who could not live with Nazi thought. Schoenberg, Milhaud, Hindemith and Křenek were among the composers who settled in the United States. Walter, Kleiber, Klemperer, Busch, Steinberg, Stiedry and Leinsdorf were some of the prominent conductors who left for good, settling in the Western Hemisphere. (A few German musicians went East instead of West. Oskar Fried fled to Russia in 1934 and became a Soviet citizen in 1940.)

All of those eminent figures had little trouble securing important positions. It meant that the Austro-German musical traditions would be perpetuated. It also closed the door, for the time being, on American conducting talent, especially where the major orchestras were concerned. Who would appoint John Smith when a Walter or Klemperer was available? Thus, from the beginnings of orchestral culture in America to the emergence of Leonard Bernstein, one had to look long and far before coming up with a native-born conductor holding an important position.

In Chicago, the German-born Frederick Stock was sole conductor for many years, and the current incumbent—after the Czech-born Kubelik and the Hungarian Reiner—is a Frenchman, Jean Martinon. In San Francisco the important figure for many years was the German-born Alfred Hertz. Later there were Pierre Monteux (French), Enrique Jorda (Spanish) and Josef Krips (Austrian). In Minneapolis, the German-born Emil Oberhoffer founded the orchestra, to be succeeded by the Belgian-born Henri Verbrugghen; and Verbrugghen was followed by the Hungarian Eugene Ormandy, the Greek Dimitri Mitropoulos, the Hungarian Antal Dorati and the Pole Stanislaw Skrowaczewski. In Detroit it used to be the Russian-born Ossip Gabrilovitsch. Then Detroit had, among others, Paul Paray (French) and Sixten Ehrling (Swedish). In Boston were Wilhelm Gericke, Max Fiedler and Karl Muck (all Germans), the Bohemian-born Emil Paur, the Hungarian Nikisch and the Frenchman Henri Rabaud. Los Angeles saw the German-born Klemperer and the Dutch-born Eduard van Beinum, the latter a major conductor who died at the age of fifty-eight before fulfilling his career. (From 1943 to 1956, Alfred Wallenstein was the conductor of the Los Angeles Symphony—the only American to hold a relatively important symphonic post.) In New York the long procession included the German-born Leopold Damrosch, the Hungarian Anton Seidl, the Russian Vassily Safonoff, the Bohemian Mahler, the Bohemian Josef Stransky, and so through Mengelberg, Toscanini, Barbirolli, the Polish Artur Rodzinski and the Greek Mitropoulos. The first two conductors of the Philadelphia Orchestra were Fritz Scheel and Karl Pohlig, both Germans. In St. Louis for many years was the French-born Vladimir Golschmann. Cincinnati saw the Belgian Eugène Ysaye, the Hungarian Reiner, the Englishman Eugene Goossens and, currently, the German-born Max Rudolf. Cleveland, for its first conductor, went to the Russian-born Nikolai Sokoloff. In Pittsburgh, such conductors as Paur, Klemperer and Reiner have been succeeded by the German-born William Steinberg.

Some of these conductors were among the greatest of their time. A few were misfits. Joseph Stransky, for example, succeeded Mahler at the New York Philharmonic with the comment: "I shall get $15,000, just half of what Mahler received, but then I am not Mahler." He certainly wasn't, and he all but ran the orchestra into the ground during his twelve years there. Musicians had no respect for him. Muck told Harold Bauer, "Stransky can do nothing, and the nothing he can do least is accompany."

The majority of those foreign-born conductors, most of whom settled permanently in the United States and became citizens, were much superior to the Stransky run of conductors. They were competent, conscientious musicians who gave much to their community and to America. If they helped form an unbreakable sort of union, to which native-born conductors were not admitted, that was inevitable. America at the time simply did not have competitive talent. In recent years the country has started to produce conductorial talent; but only in recent years. Thus, any form of native orchestral style was, for well over a century, stifled before birth, stifled by an ambience that heavily reflected the great and all-powerful German school.

Typical of the breed were Alfred Hertz and Walter Damrosch, to pick two at random. Hertz, the tremendously bearded, bald, burly, crippled (infantile paralysis) and volcanic behemoth of a German, went to San Francisco after a period at the Metropolitan Opera that extended from 1902 to 1915. A temperamental figure, Hertz often was in the headlines. In New York it was for his brilliant work at the Metropolitan Opera and also for his feuds with singers and colleagues. His quarrels with Arturo Vigna, the Italian conductor, were gleefully reported all over the country. This feud was over the conductor's chair. Hertz liked it forward, Vigna back. One day Hertz arrived for a rehearsal to find the chair nailed to the floor—back. Great was Hertz's rage, and long were the newspaper columns about it.

In San Francisco, Hertz had to contend with an apathetic orchestra and audience, and with a near-bankrupt financial situation. He fought the good fight, programming the best music, acting as educator, firing up the orchestra. When he left in 1930 his career was far from finished. He became a pioneer in radio broadcasting, with the Standard Symphony Hour, which ran from 1932 for about ten years. He also conducted at the San Francisco Opera and at the Hollywood Bowl concerts, which he had inaugurated in 1922. And he was much more receptive to new music than most of his colleagues. As early as 1912 he kept an open mind about Schoenberg. He had heard *Pierrot Lunaire* and refused to join the wolf pack. Schoenberg, said Hertz, was not a *poseur*. "There is a method in his apparent madness, and a definite musical scheme behind it all—only it is a scheme we do not know as yet. I have watched him, and I am certain from the way he makes his corrections that he does know, that it is there in his head. No doubt in time we shall grasp it too."

Walter Damrosch, German-born, was the son of a famous conductor. Leopold Damrosch had worked with Liszt—as violinist, not pianist; he had been the concertmaster of Liszt's orchestra at Weimar —and had become the conductor of the Breslau Philharmonic and Breslau Orchesterverein before coming to the United States in 1871. Three years later he founded the Oratorio Society in New York (it still exists) and also conducted the New York Philharmonic. In 1878 he founded the New York Symphony, which was New York's second orchestra before its amalgamation with the Philharmonic in 1928. He literally worked himself to death. For the 1884–85 season of German opera at the Metropolitan, Leopold Damrosch conducted all performances but the last seven—a sheerly heroic achievement. He would have conducted those seven, too, but caught pneumonia and, in his overworked state, was an easy victim to the then dread disease.

He had two sons, Frank and Walter. Both were musicians. Frank was active as a choral conductor and musical educator. Walter, groomed to take his father's place, helped finish the Metropolitan Opera season (along with Leopold's assistant, John Lund) and also took over the New York Symphony and the Oratorio Society. Handsome, a man who moved in the best circles, Walter Damrosch had a long career. He died at the age of eighty-eight.

He was never taken very seriously by the critics and by his fellow musicians, but he did leave an imprint on American musical life. He kept the New York Symphony alive, against all odds, and even toured Europe with it in 1920. The orchestra was ready to go under in 1914 when Harry Harkness Flagler guaranteed forty or more concerts a year on a regular subscription basis. Flagler even backed the tour of Europe in 1920. Damrosch, in addition to conducting his symphony orchestra, was a frequent conductor at the Metropolitan Opera and even composed two operas that were presented there. Like Hertz, he also was a pioneer in radio work. In 1927 he became musical adviser to the National Broadcasting Company, and two years later started a music-appreciation hour that enjoyed a national hookup. It is estimated that every Friday morning as many as six million impressionable schoolchildren were forced to listen to his broadcast in the name of culture. Many alive still remember his hearty, unctuous salutation: "My dear children . . ." Damrosch conceived the idea of implanting great melodies in his youngsters' heads by writing words to the tunes and having the children sing along. Goodness knows how many potential music lovers were permanently maimed by this idiotic procedure. To this day there are those who cannot listen to the Schubert *Unfinished* without hearing the words: "This is/the symphonee/that Schubert wrote and ne-ver/fi-nished." Or, to the second movement of the Beethoven Fifth: "Sound the trum-pet and drum,/for our he-ro/ has come." Or, especially unforgettable, to the march movement of the Tchaikovsky *Pathétique:* "I want to go to/Par-*iss*/a-and play/with the mi-din-ettes." At least, the jingle sent some children to the dictionary to look up the meaning of "midinette."

The tradition of assigning major American orchestras to foreign-born conductors extends to our own time. The New York Philharmonic, after Toscanini, Barbirolli and a series of guest conductors, settled upon Artur Rodzinski and Dimitri Mitropoulos. Rodzinski had been born in Split, on the Dalmatian coast of what is now Yugoslavia. He was the son of a Polish army officer, and his first conducting assignments were in Poland. He came to the United States in 1926 as an assistant to Stokowski. Then he took over, successively, the Los Angeles Philharmonic, the Cleveland Symphony, the New York Philharmonic and the Chicago Symphony. Controversy seemed to be part of his nature. A respected conductor with a reputation as an orchestra builder—he had trained the NBC Symphony for Toscanini —he was, especially in his later years, in one fight after another. Rodzinski's ideas about the psychology of orchestra players were sound —on paper, anyway—but he did not always adhere to them. "Every violinist," he told a reporter, "is a Mischa or a Sascha who has been built up by his parents to be a Heifetz and sweep the world. In the second fiddle section he has to play tremolo—ta, ta, ta. A soloist never plays tremolo. How do I make them like this ta, ta, ta? By building their self-respect, by calling them to my room, by countless talks. . . . Orchestral work is maybe 75 per cent psychology."

Whereupon Rodzinski's first action with the New York Philharmonic was to discharge fourteen players, including the concertmaster: a piece of psychology that was not highly appreciated by the orchestra. A furious fight ensued, and Rodzinski won. But he did not win four years later, when he resigned after charging interference from the manager of the orchestra, Arthur Judson. Rodzinski went to Chicago, snorting that New York was "nothing more than a great market place where one comes to sell goods." But in Chicago he did not last as long as he had in New York, and was dismissed after one season. He fought over everything—the length of the season, the budget, his contract. After Chicago he made guest-conducting appearances. He was a specialist in the moderns, and in 1935 had conducted the American premiere of Shostakovich's *Lady Macbeth of Mtsensk*. He also introduced music by Berg, Piston and Vaughan Williams.

Dimitri Mitropoulos was even more interested in the moderns, and was one of the few to conduct twelve-tone music in the 1940s. A superb pianist, he had studied in Berlin with Busoni, and later studied conducting with Kleiber. He turned to the baton in 1930, came to the United States in 1936, headed the Minneapolis Symphony from 1937 to 1949, and became conductor of the New York Philharmonic from 1950 to 1956. Later he was guest conductor with the Philharmonic, and had several seasons at the Metropolitan Opera. He died in Milan on November 2, 1960, while rehearsing the Scala Orchestra in Mahler's Third Symphony. Among the works he introduced to the Philharmonic were Berg's *Wozzeck,* Schoenberg's *Erwartung,* Milhaud's *Choëphores,* Busoni's *Arlecchino* and Strauss's *Elektra.* At the Metropolitan Opera he conducted the world premiere of Barber's *Vanessa.*

Mitropoulos made a big impression in his day. It was not that he was a precisionist; indeed, he was anything but. His beat (he used no baton) was jerky, nervous and inexpressive, full of head shakes, shoulder wiggling and body writhings. At the Metropolitan he drove singers wild by his beat, and also by his variability. He could conduct one way at rehearsals, another way at performances. The impression that he did make was for the wide range of his musicianship and his infallible memory. It was a photographic memory. One glance at a score, and it would be committed for good. The more complicated the score, the more he liked it—the scores of Mahler and Strauss,

Erich Leinsdorf, Austrian-born director of the Boston Symphony Orchestra.

William Steinberg, long-time conductor of the Pittsburgh Symphony Orchestra.

the scores of Schoenberg and Berg. He was less convincing in earlier music. His was the type of mind that responded to complexity rather than simplicity.

He was a gentle, sweet man, and that was one of his troubles. "If I were a lion tamer," he once said, "I would not enter a cage of lions reading a book entitled *How to Tame Lions*. In the same way I would not enter a rehearsal not completely prepared." But he *did* enter the lions' cage unprepared: not musically, of course, but temperamentally. He was far too gentle to snarl back at the lions in his cage. As a result, the players had a tendency to take advantage of his good nature. This led to slack discipline. Players would talk about how much they loved him, but they also did what they wanted to do, rather than what he wanted them to do.

Pittsburgh has the German-born William Steinberg, and Boston the Austrian-born Erich Leinsdorf. They have much in common, being precisionists and literalists, representative of the modern anti-romantic approach to music, both possessed of much the same background and tradition. Steinberg, a good violinist at the age of ten, and a pianist at fifteen, came up the classic German way: vocal coach, accompanist, rehearsal pianist, backstage conductor, conductor. His career took him from Prague, Frankfurt, Berlin and Palestine to the United States (at Toscanini's invitation). In the United States he conducted the NBC Symphony, the Buffalo Symphony and, from 1952, the Pittsburgh Symphony. Steinberg is also a steady guest conductor of the New York Philharmonic and with American and European groups, and has appeared at the Metropolitan and San Francisco operas. His conducting is undemonstrative ("The more they dance, the quieter I stand"), sober, objective and well proportioned.

Leinsdorf made an impact at a much earlier age. A graduate of the Vienna Conservatory, he became assistant to Walter and Toscanini at Salzburg. In 1938 he was brought to the Metropolitan Opera to relieve the ailing Artur Bodanzky, who had been head of the German wing since 1915 and was virtual dictator there. Bodanzky died just as the season began in 1939, and the entire German repertoire was thrown into Leinsdorf's lap. He was twenty-seven years old. Leinsdorf stayed with the Metropolitan Opera until 1943, going to the Cleveland Orchestra, the Rochester Philharmonic, the New York City Opera and back to the Metropolitan Opera from 1957 to 1961. In 1962 he was appointed musical director of the Boston Symphony, and promptly proceeded to change its Franco-Russian orientation. Charles Munch had been an inspirational, easygoing type of conductor. Leinsdorf was the reverse: methodical, thorough, demanding. Some of his musicians felt that his approach to a score was too clinical, and one critic wrote that Leinsdorf seemed to regard a score as a series of problems to be solved rather than a series of emotions to be conveyed. But whatever resistance there has been to Leinsdorf's powers as an interpreter, nobody has ever disputed the technical finish of his work and his serious approach to music.

· XXXIV ·

Leonard Bernstein

AND WHERE were the American conductors all this time?

They were building up toward Leonard Bernstein. There were, to be sure, a handful of American conductors in the pre-Bernstein era. Indeed, one can go back to Ureli Corelli Hill, the New York violinist who was a founder and first president of the New York Philharmonic. Hill conducted the orchestra for a while. Frank van der Stucken, by virtue of being born in Texas, could technically be classified as an American conductor, though he really was a Theodore Thomas in reverse. Where Thomas came here as a child from Germany, and was American-trained, van der Stucken was taken to Antwerp as a child and was German-trained; and while he was active for many years in American musical affairs, as conductor of the Cincinnati Symphony and (for a short time) of the New York Philharmonic, he preferred Germany and spent the last twenty years of his life there.

Shortly after the turn of the century the American composer-conductor Henry Hadley received some attention. He conducted in Seattle, San Francisco and New York, did much to promote contemporary music and, in 1934, founded the Berkshire Music Festival. He was a respected figure, but his conducting never made much of an impression. There was Leon Barzin, who came to the United States from Antwerp at the age of two, became first violist of the New York Philharmonic and in 1930 was appointed conductor of the National Orchestral Association. This was a training orchestra of young musicians, and its "graduates" entered the ranks of orchestras all over the United States. There was Alfred Wallenstein, who deserted his companions in the cello section of the New York Philharmonic to concentrate on conducting. He had a radio program for many years, in which he had the courage to present such esoteric items as all of the Mozart piano concertos and untold numbers of Bach cantatas. In 1943 he became conductor of the Los Angeles Philharmonic and remained there until 1956. Still another deserter from an orchestra was Milton Katims, the first violist of the NBC Symphony, who took over the Seattle Symphony in 1954. Howard Mitchell in Washington, D.C., Izler Solomon in Indianapolis and Robert Whitney in Louisville are American-trained conductors. Whitney, thanks to a Rockefeller Foundation grant, has probably conducted more world premieres than any living conductor. More recently, a group of American youngsters is beginning to attract international attention, especially Thomas Schippers and Lorin Maazel.

When Serge Koussevitzky established the Berkshire Music Center in 1940, he gathered unto himself some of the most gifted young musicians in America. Thor Johnson was one; he later became conductor of the Cincinnati Symphony. Walter Hendl was another, and he went away to become musical director of the Dallas Symphony. Lukas Foss (Berlin-born) was another of Koussevitzky's bright young men, and he has become conductor of the Buffalo Symphony in addition to being one of the leaders of the avant-garde.

But none of Koussevitzky's cadets "made it" the way Leonard Bernstein has. Bernstein became famous overnight and has remained famous—a controversial figure, a showman, a romantic, a glamour boy not fully accepted by his peers, disliked by many critics in America and Europe throughout much of his career, yet the most important conductor—by far—that the United States has produced. The only native-born conductor to be musical director of a major American orchestra, he has captured the imagination of the public to a degree unprecedented in history. He has been accepted as the Renaissance Man: conductor, composer of serious music, composer of successful Broadway musicals, pianist, educator, writer, poet, television personality. He symbolizes music to the Americans, and it has been said of him that nobody loves him but the public. This was a remark that had some validity up to the middle 1960s, when he suddenly took Europe by storm, creating a sensation conducting *Falstaff* in Vienna and Mahler in London. Even in New York some of the critics began to discuss his work in respectful terms instead of looking upon him as a perpetual *Wunderkind:* "the Peter Pan of music," as the New York *Times* said in 1960.

In many respects that is what Bernstein has been—a perpetual *Wunderkind.* But from the beginning he had the kind of hypnotism that Nikisch exerted, plus the glamour of the young Stokowski. Unknown until November 14, 1943—he was twenty-five years old then— he stepped before the New York Philharmonic, where he was assistant conductor, and led a concert for the indisposed Bruno Walter. His career from that point took off in some kind of weird, jet-propelled, missile-like ascent. His physical appearance had something to do with making him a public idol. As a young man he described himself as looking like "a well-built dope fiend," and he retained that intense look: part visionary, part oozing with sex, part filled with a suppressed nervousness. Above all, he managed to give the impression of eternal youth, and that was still true when he was almost fifty.

He came in with the television age, and that too contributed to his fame. His educational broadcasts, infinitely more sophisticated and infinitely less condescending than Walter Damrosch's used to be, carried his words and his work to millions of people, all of whom regarded him as omniscient in matters musical. He brought to the television public a potent mixture. On the one hand he was glamorous, romantic-looking, a "long-haired musician" who delved into the mysteries of Beethoven and modern music. On the other hand he was boyish, he used slang, had an urban American background, had gone to college (Harvard, '39), liked jazz. No wonder he achieved an identification with the American psyche. Millions of words were written about him. No greater-publicized figure than Bernstein ever appeared on the American musical scene.

That was one of his problems. Many thought he came up too fast, and for years he had to fight to overcome the suspicion, actual hostility—and jealousy, too—created among many professionals by his fantastic success at so early an age. Too much attention was paid to him; and professionals, who know only too well how a career can be built by publicity, have a tendency to look with suspicion on a big publicity buildup. So do many intellectuals. Bernstein was popular, was written up in mass magazines—*ergo,* there had to be something wrong with him. A man of supreme confidence in himself, Bernstein stepped on toes and made enemies; and there could be no denying that some of his extracurricular activities caused a great deal of un-favorable talk: his lofty pronouncements, the kiss he gave to Jacque-line Kennedy on television, even his flamboyant clothes. He was described as having a pre-Copernican ego, *i.e.*, seeing the whole world revolve around him. Some critics believed he would never grow up. Irving Kolodin, writing in 1964, summed up a prevalent critical feel-ing: "Of the promise he had twenty years ago as a conductor, the judgment from this bench would have to be that it has spread wider but it has not penetrated more deeply. . . . Most of the time . . . one gets the feeling that he gets by on facility, quickness of mind, instinct, and that age-old endowment called *chutzpah.*" *Chutzpah* is a Yiddish word, and it has been applied more than once to Bernstein. It means, roughly, gall, or nerve. A teen-age boy murders his parents and then pleads for clemency on the grounds that he is an orphan. That is *chutzpah.* Kolodin concluded that if Bernstein would only put his mind to it, he could be a conductor of the first rank. "But," wrote Kolodin,

there is equally little doubt that he is not temperamentally constituted to decide on such a function. It doesn't absorb him sufficiently, interest him enough, reward him adequately, to sacrifice other things at which he may be less adept, but which tempt him irresistibly. There comes a time, inevitably, of boredom, in which all sorts of other impulses—theatrical, verbal, creative—come to dominate him.

Kolodin's words were prophetic. In 1966 Bernstein announced that he would leave the New York Philharmonic at the end of the 1968–69 season. He gave as a reason his compulsion to compose. The Phil-harmonic named him "Laureate Conductor" for life.

Bernstein himself has never disabused anybody about the breadth of his desires. Shortly before his appointment to the New York Phil-harmonic in 1958 he proclaimed the diversity of his tastes:

I don't want to give in and settle for some specialty. I don't want to spend the rest of my life, as Toscanini did, studying and restudying, say, fifty pieces of music. It would bore me to death. I want to conduct. I want to play the piano. I want to write music for Broadway and Hollywood. I want to write symphonic music. I want to keep on trying to be, in the full sense of that wonderful word, a musician. I also want to teach. I want to write books and poetry. And I think I can, and still do justice to them all.

COLUMBIA RECORDS

Leonard Bernstein, the first American-born conductor to direct a major American orchestra. With his combination of brilliance and glamour, he has become the most publicized figure in the history of American music.

He has tried. After studying at Harvard and the Curtis Institute of Music (piano with Isabelle Vengerova, conducting with Reiner), he went to Tanglewood and became Koussevitzky's pet at the Berkshire Music Center. Rodzinski engaged him as assistant conductor with the New York Philharmonic for the 1943–44 season. When Bernstein substituted for Walter at that famous concert, it was front-page news. Bernstein was invited back to the Philharmonic as guest conductor several seasons thereafter. In the meantime he composed the successful musical *On the Town*, which was an expanded version of a ballet he had written for Jerome Robbins. From 1945 to 1948 he conducted the New York City Center Orchestra. His three seasons there are fondly remembered as examples of about the most stimulating symphonic concerts New York has ever had. Audiences heard major works of the major twentieth-century composers, plus complete novelties, plus some of the standard repertoire. Bernstein was young and vital; his audiences were young and enthusiastic. There was a special air of excitement at these concerts; the atmosphere crackled like the rhythms in a Stravinsky ballet. Bernstein spoke the language of his young orchestra and his young audience.

After resigning because of a budget cut, Bernstein did much guest conducting. He also composed two other successful Broadway musicals and one that did not last long—*Candide*. The bouncing *Candide* Overture, however, has made its way into the American symphonic repertoire, and is the only Bernstein work to do so. His serious music has not been accepted by other conductors, and is kept alive mainly through Bernstein's own performances. In 1958 Bernstein took over the New York Philharmonic, inheriting a sullen orchestra and a badly disciplined one. Within a season the orchestra began to thrive. There were mutters about the "show-business approach" that Bernstein represented, but there was no disputing its success. Concerts were sold out. The orchestra played with enthusiasm. In Bernstein the players found a considerate conductor with a clean-cut technique and a first-class ear. Some members of the orchestra, especially the older men, mumbled about Toscanini and Mengelberg doing things differently. But Bernstein made the Philharmonic a happy orchestra. An economic situation, to which players are always sensitive, entered into the picture. Bernstein proved to be a good provider. With his advent came longer seasons (culminating in a contract that called for full employment), added revenue from television and records, and other emoluments. As one member of the orchestra said at the time, "It's a positive honeymoon! As long as Lenny treats us good, we'll treat him good." It should be pointed out that as the years progressed, familiarity did not breed contempt. The musicians of the Philharmonic, a temperamental collection of prima donnas who have worked under every great conductor, are all but unanimous in proclaiming Bernstein's gifts. They think he is a superlative technician, they admire his ear and his musicianship, they claim that rhythmically he is the equal of any living conductor. Some of the musicians have less regard for the way Bernstein approaches the eighteenth- and nineteenth-century repertoire; but that, they say, has nothing to do with his natural gifts.

As a young conductor, Bernstein was identified with the moderns, although he never had much sympathy for dodecaphonic music. His performances of the classics through Brahms have never been fully accepted. Where his ideas about Stravinsky, Strauss and Bartók can be brilliant and sure-footed, his ideas about earlier music have impressed many as mannered and wayward. How much his podium mannerisms have colored critical thought is hard to say. Probably a great deal. Bernstein is the most choreographic of all contemporary conductors. He is a specialist in the clenched fist, the hip swivel, the pelvic thrust, the levitation effect that makes him hover in the air in defiance of the laws of gravity, the uppercut, the haymaker. These wild motions juxtaposed against a Beethoven symphony convince many that there is more to the choreography than to the music. But even listening to Bernstein on records, where choreography is not a factor, illustrates a kind of musical approach much different from that of today's predominantly literal conductors.

For Bernstein is essentially a throwback, a romantic. He employs considerable fluctuation of tempo, often slows down for second subjects, underlines melodies, is constantly using a full palette of expressive devices that are generally scorned today. Virgil Thomson believed that Bernstein, a child of the twentieth century, was uncomfortable in a nineteenth-century repertoire and thus had to counterfeit an emotion he did not really feel. And, indeed, there always has been something calculated about Bernstein's romanticisms. Authentic exponents of a romantic tradition—Walter, Furtwängler—almost never broke a musical line. They always kept the shape of a phrase. Bernstein, on the other hand, often does break the line. He also can, in such music as the second movement of Mahler's Second Symphony, wallow in sentimentality. A good part of this excess may have come from his impulse as an educator, as the man who explains music to the multitude. A natural pedagogue and a high-pressure musical salesman, he can be the exponent of the Big Sell as a conductor. Until recently he had a tendency to reduce his audiences to a common denominator; to play down to them, consciously or unconsciously. He seemed to think that unless he made a big thing out of a specific passage, audiences would miss the point. Look (he would in effect say), now comes the second subject of the exposition! I will have to make it clear to you that this is the second subject of the exposition! And so in his eagerness to emphasize the point, he would slow up to make sure everybody understood the difference between first and second subject. Generally the result was uncomfortably obvious and even vulgar. Similarly, in the second movement of the Mahler, Bernstein would seem to be rationalizing somewhat as follows: "I have to make them realize this is Viennese *Gemütlichkeit*. I will do it by slowing up and then phrasing the theme with great tenderness. I will make a *Luftpause* here and a rubato there." The intentions may have been good. But the playing sounded cute, over-expressive, artificial.

In recent years there have been signs of a change. Bernstein took a sabbatical during the 1964–65 season, and when he returned to the Philharmonic it was with a new kind of confidence. The choreography was still present—that is a permanent part of Bernstein—but there also was greater reliance on the taste of the audience, a more direct approach to music, less of the obsessive exhibitionism that had so marred his work. He also began to think more and more about opera conducting. Bernstein had come to opera relatively late in his career. American-trained musicians have little opportunity to gain experience in an opera house—the route of every Austro-German conductor. Bernstein had always been around the theatre, however, and his performances at La Scala, the Metropolitan Opera and the Vienna Staatsoper had whetted his appetite. He always has had a dramatic flair, and it could be that the great part of his career is before him. Bernstein and opera would appear made for each other.

· XXXV ·

Present and Future

AFTER WORLD WAR II nothing much happened except the most convulsive scientific, social and cultural upheaval in history. Naturally music was affected in general, and the symphony orchestra in particular. Completely new attitudes came into being. Culture, which had been a dirty word in the tobacco-chewing, rural-dominated legislatures of the United States, suddenly became a way of life. This may have resulted from competition with Russia. If Russia could send its great musicians and dancers around the world, to its own infinite credit, the United States could do the same. It did. But there was more to it than that. Something was in the air; and legislators, who previously would not have bothered to send in a single marine had all the orchestras of the country been against a wall faced by a firing squad, began to vie with one another to create arts councils and cultural centers. Culture was Cinderella, and the little lady needed a coach-and-four and a nice, new palace in which to live.

Musicians, especially those who played in orchestras, demanded an equivalent change in their economic status. For the first time, the possibility of full employment and a satisfactory wage scale came within their grasp. Not without fighting for it; there were strikes and cancellations of part or all of a season. But an extraordinary amount of money—government, foundation, industrial and private— was being poured into the American symphony orchestra by the middle 1960s, and the musicians were determined to share in the general prosperity. The Big Five of American orchestras (Boston, New York, Philadelphia, Cleveland and Chicago) actually negotiated contracts that called for full employment. In smaller cities, negotiations resulted in longer seasons and a wage scale that gave more than the miserable pittance prevalent until then.

The esthetic side saw as much of an upheaval as the cultural. Composers immersed themselves in a new kind of music that seemed incomprehensible to all but a few other composers. The schism between avant-garde musician and audiences seemed complete. Another upheaval was the dominance of musicological research, which began to color the viewpoints of all performing musicians, especially when it came to early music. By trying to eradicate certain traditions of romantic performance practice, musicology helped cement a general anti-romantic attitude that had been becoming more and more general since the 1920s.

All this, and more, after World War II.

Efforts were made to meet the new problems. But there were those who seemed to think it a waste of time. For suddenly, in the middle 1960s, began to be heard the cry that the orchestra was dying, and such eminent figures as Leonard Bernstein took to print worrying about the future.

At the basis of their argument was the fact that, as far as the repertoire of the symphony orchestra was concerned, music was no longer a living art. The active repertoire began with Bach and continued through Strauss and Mahler, with a tapering-off at Prokofieff and early Stravinsky. Conductors therefore were museum-like custodians of the past. Composers were no longer writing for the symphony orchestra, on the whole. When they did, the public refused to listen. Tonality was dead, and the public had no interest in atonal music. So ran the argument. In any case, electronic music was around the corner, and this medium did away with the orchestra entirely. As David Burrows wrote in the July 1966 *Musical Quarterly*:

. . . only in this century has music found a technology to compete with what had long been taken for granted in the other arts; if so, it does qualify as the cultural *Spätling* [late arrival] that Nietzsche called it. Electronic media have put the composer in the position of the painter and the poet, not only by giving him complete control over the final result, but also by making his tradition continuously and directly available to him in recordings. "Pre-electronic" may one day have the meaning in music that "pre-literate" does now in literature.

The thought had occurred to some who had attended, in the early 1960s, the first concert of electronic music sponsored by the Columbia-Princeton laboratory. When the curtain went up, it revealed some half-dozen loudspeakers on stage in addition to those placed throughout the auditorium. The audiences, after a startled gasp, applauded the speakers. (The speakers did not applaud back.) Throughout the entire evening, not one human being was seen on stage. Science had finally done it: abolished the performer and his nasty little ego. Now the composer (and *his* nasty little ego?) could rule supreme. Every composer from Mozart on had always been complaining about the virtuoso and his ego. The complaints rose to such a crescendo after World War II that today most performers would no sooner change or even modify a composer's score than a theologian would alter the meaning of the Sermon on the Mount. But now, after millennia, electronic music had arrived, and the composer could snap his fingers at the world. He could, literally, create his own tonal universe, assemble the results on tape with appropriate instructions for copying, and *the* one performance, *the* definitive and only performance, unchanging, permanent, could be duplicated anywhere in the world for all time to come.

Electronic music, together with much avant-garde music, are but a reflection of the new set of problems that are changing the lives of everybody, and music along with it. Every generation sees a change in musical philosophy, but never in history has there been the kind of accelerated movement that began with the atomic age following World War II. It is the end result of a process of disintegration that has been going on since 1900: an appropriate date, for 1900 saw the formulation of Max Planck's quantum theory, upon which all modern physics is based. The first decade of the twentieth century saw the breakup of classical physics with the work of Planck and Einstein. The first decade of the twentieth century also saw the breakup of representational art with the abstractions of Kandinsky. The first decade of the twentieth century saw the breakup of tonality with the music of Arnold Schoenberg. All within ten years! Seldom has the *Zeitgeist* functioned so obligingly and so convincingly.

But if life and thought started to undergo traumatic change shortly after 1900, the accelerated movement of the period after World War II is frightening. We are faced with the shards of thought that represent the smashup of centuries of accumulated learning, and nobody as yet knows how to put the shards together again. Very little seems anchored. Why should not theologians discuss the death of God if Heisenberg is right and molecular movement is merely a set of statistical probabilities? What happens to causality? Scientists are busy questioning, and even disproving, assumptions that had been held basic since Euclid. Existentialism has taken hold of a sizable segment of postwar philosophical thought and has even become a quasi-popular philosophy. Outer space is being explored, and the planets are within our reach: the planets, when the basic problems of humanity are as far from salvation as ever, when modern weaponry can mean the end of the world, when the threat of the population explosion is a prophecy of still another kind of end. It is an age of psychic unrest, and creators reflect it in their several ways.

Musicians of the avant-garde reflect it by composing a kind of music that is pointillistic, atonal, athematic, rhythmically complicated, resembling nothing so much as atoms in a cloud chamber. Musicians even call upon modern mathematical thought to support their compositions. Thus Yannis Xenakis in 1957 composed a work named *Pithoprakta,* and he explains it by citing "discontinuity . . . dense clouds of sound-atoms. . . . Use is made of the law of large numbers: the normal curve of Gauss, of Maxwell, of Poisson, of continual probabilities, etc., with the criteria of Pearson, Fisher, etc." Connoisseurs of the new argot dote on those etceteras.

The new music has led to a split between composer and audience. Today there is much talk about the "crisis in composition," meaning that the avant-garde produces music that only a tiny percentage of the public wants to hear. A more or less straight line has been broken, and this total rupture between composer and public is new in the musical scheme of things. In previous generations, roughly to the beginning of this century, there was no problem. The avant-garde, starting with Mozart (who was considered quite a dangerous radical in some quarters), always saw its music played. Audiences expected new music. In the eighteenth century, indeed, brand-new music was the only music in the repertoire. Audiences wanted to hear the very latest; and if they were disturbed by Mozart or the young Beethoven, there always were more comforting composers like Salieri or the great Paisiello to satisfy them. In the nineteenth century, new music never had to wait very long for a hearing. If anything, it was old music that had to wait. When Mendelssohn decided to give a series of programs devoted to Bach, Handel, Mozart and Beethoven, he did so with much preparation and apology, calling them "Historical Concerts." Berlioz, Liszt, Schumann and Wagner may have been controversial figures, to be damned by such important conservative critics as Chorley and Hanslick; but their music was played, discussed, argued about, constantly analyzed in the newspapers and magazines. And, again as in the eighteenth century, there always was a bulwark of new music that was less controversial. It was supplied by such composers as Raff, Rubinstein, Parry, Gade: all part of the then active repertoire, all big men in their day.

Today there are few big men, in the sense that the previous avant-garde composers were. Of the manifestations since World War II—serialism, full atonality, aleatory, Dada, third-stream jazz—the public will have none of them, even from Stravinsky. Electronic music is attracting many young composers, but, again, not the public. Many musicians themselves are baffled. The new music is immensely hard to play, demanding new ideas about rhythm, color and, even, basic instrumental technique. Its notation frequently is meaningful only to a relatively few specialists, and it displays an unheard-of complexity. It is so difficult, poses so many problems, scares so many performers, that some composers of the avant-garde have been pleading for a return to common sense, saying that matters have gotten out of hand.

Orchestral musicians on the whole like this music as little as the public does. The conductors of the older generation find it meaningless; the conductors of the younger generation avoid it for other reasons: active dislike, in some cases; fear that their orchestras are not equipped to play it; fear that their audiences will be alienated. Avant-garde music thus has had to be conducted by young, dedicated men, none of whom is an international podium star: men like Pierre Boulez, Gunther Schuller, Robert Craft, Bruno Bartoletti and Lukas Foss. (Two exceptions were Hermann Scherchen and Hans Rosbaud, both nineteenth-century men who managed to accommodate to the new thought of the twentieth.) The problems of conducting, rehearsing and playing avant-garde music are of such fantastic complexity that only full-time specialists can handle it. The New York Philharmonic discovered that during its avant-garde series in 1963. Its players could not play the music; and more, they fought it, laughed at it, resented it. Perhaps the next generation will see musicians who are able to play this music. At the Berkshire Music Festival, the student orchestra conducted by Schuller can play avant-garde material with much more authority, technique and style than their opposite numbers in the Boston Symphony. When the new supply of musicians enters the symphony orchestra the problem may be solved. Until then, there will exist a breakdown in musical communication between the avant-garde creator and his audience. Right now there is a sort of backlash, in which the public actively resents the new music and goes out of its way to avoid it. It is all very well to say that all creators of the avant-garde have had to fight and wait until their work was accepted. This is true. But the cultural lag until the twentieth century never extended much beyond twenty years or so. In its present phase it has run over a half century, if such a pivotal score as *Pierrot Lunaire* is taken into account. And, considering avant-garde music after World War II, never in music has there been the kind of universal loathing that has been created. Which leads to some hard questions. Is this lack of rapport and communication necessarily the public's fault? Has the composer failed in his function? Or has the language of music itself been exhausted?

It is an interesting speculation whether or not the general retreat from the new music has caused a different post-World War II phenomenon, the baroque revival. Up to 1948 baroque music was something for the history books. But, thanks to the long-playing record, baroque music suddenly became a potent force. Vivaldi, Corelli, Zelenka, Fasch, Schütz, Geminiani—their music became the rage. They stepped from the pages of the history books, bowing and saying hello, very much alive. There was something in the ordered and logical patterns of much of their music, something in their objective approach, with which modern intellectual life could, and did, identify. But who was going to play their music? Certainly not Furtwängler or Toscanini. And that is where musicology stepped in, to correct the abuses of romanticism and show a new generation how this music should be performed.

To the romantic interpreter of the nineteenth century, life and music were relatively simple. The romantic period had created the concept of the Virtuoso-as-Hero. With the arrival of Paganini and Liszt, and the great singers of the 1830s, and the emergence of Wagner and his Bayreuth school of conductors, a performance style for the entire century was formed. It was a style in which strict textual fidelity did not exist, any more than it had existed in previous centuries. It goes without saying that romantic performers were completely at home in romantic music. When it came to earlier music, they were not troubled by the kind of questions that so agitate today's performers. They merely used their own romantic conventions in the earlier music. Their instinct and intuition were their sole guide.

Today those practices are frowned upon. It is felt that instinct and intuition are not enough; that a specific set of tools is needed in addition. In any age dominated by science, the prevailing attitude is objective, and it is an attitude that involves enormous respect for the findings of the specialist. Music is not exempt, and it is part of the *Zeitgeist* that the findings of musicology have, in recent years, done so much to shape musical thought. Musicology has supplied the tools.

Musicology, one of the newest of the scholarly disciplines, has been conditioning all performers and critics to a greater or lesser degree since World War II. For the past fifty years, musicologists have been attempting to codify musical thought and performance practice of the past, and in the last twenty years a tremendous amount of material has been published. Instead of superimposing artificial, arbitrary and obviously incorrect notions upon early music, said the musicologists, why not try as closely as possible to duplicate the actual practices of the seventeenth and eighteenth centuries? To do so, certain questions had to be answered. How big was Bach's orchestra? Mozart's? How were the instruments distributed? Exactly how are the ornaments to be played and the figured basses to be realized? How is a trill executed? How did the execution of the ornaments vary from period to period and country to country? Just how corrupt were the editions of early music commonly used by performers? (Very corrupt, it often turned out.) What was pitch 250 years ago? Tempo?

Conductors with their roots in the nineteenth century—Walter, Beecham, Furtwängler, Toscanini—never worried much about those problems. Nor did younger conductors, for their training was in a romantic tradition. In any case, the problems were largely immaterial. Aside from a few pieces by Bach and Handel (who was known almost exclusively by one work, his *Messiah*), and some ten symphonies by Haydn and Mozart (who composed 145 between them), the repertoire up to the end of World War II was an overwhelmingly nineteenth-century one, Stravinsky, Bartók, Shostakovich and Prokofieff notwithstanding. Then came the LP disc, and for some inexplicable reason there arose an unprecedented demand for baroque music. The law of supply and demand immediately went into effect, and with it the emergence of a new kind of podium specialist—a conductor who devoted himself almost exclusively to pre-Beethoven music, often working closely with musicologists, anxious to present early music with maximum authenticity. Such conductors as Karl Münchinger, Karl Richter, Mogens Wøldike, Frederic Waldman, Antonio Janigro, Safford Cape, Rudolf Baumgartner, Thurston Dart, Noah Greenberg, Karl Haas, Denis Stevens, Newell Jenkins and August Wenzinger came into prominence after World War II as scholar-conductors who knew much more about performance practice in early music than any of the international stars.

Europe and the United States were inundated by the baroque. But there was a curious by-product. Popular as it is—many record companies have been kept alive specializing in it—baroque music has made very little impression on the international symphony orchestra, which, by and large, plays much the same music it did fifty years ago. Therefore, small orchestras had to be created to take care of early music; their big brothers could not be less interested. In addition, small performing groups sprang up. A close study of the New York recital scene shows a formidable number of concerts devoted to baroque and Renaissance music. Some are well publicized and fill the major concert halls; many are intimate affairs played by little-publicized musicians in the smaller halls. This interest in the baroque is one of the phenomena of the postwar period, and it is not the antithesis of the other phenomenon—the international serial language of the avant-garde—that one might imagine. Like serial music, the preponderance of baroque music is objective, dealing more with workmanship than with striking ideas, bearing its own built-in academism.

One other striking aspect of the period following World War II should be mentioned, and it involves the newer conductors. Two of them are Oriental—Zubin Mehta, from India, and Seiji Ozawa, from Japan—and they are the first two in history to impress one as altogether major talents. But take a look at some of the other prominent young conductors: Lorin Maazel (United States), Bernard Haitink (Holland), Colin Davis (England), Istvan Kertesz (Hungary), Claudio Abbado (Italy). Each of these is a candidate for greatness, and it is interesting to note that there is not a German or Austrian on the list.

BOSTON SYMPHONY ORCHESTRA
SAM FALK

Four conductors who will play a prominent part in the next generation. Upper left, Seiji Ozawa, born in Japan, a musician with temperament and powerful projection. Upper right, Lorin Maazel, an American who represents a neo-Toscanini kind of clarity and objectivity. Lower left, Zubin Mehta, born in India, a conductor with pronounced virtuoso inclinations. Lower right, Colin Davis, born in England, whose conducting is marked by taste, strength and an eclectic approach characteristic of English musicians. Each is an individualist, but they have in common the middle-twentieth-century tendency to avoid romantic exaggeration.

PHILIPS RECORDS

Can it be that the great Austro-German tradition of conducting is in the process of being broken up? For some two hundred years it has been the most potent force in the history of conducting, but Wolfgang Sawallisch and Herbert von Karajan seem to be the last major conductors of that school, and they can no longer be considered young conductors.

What we have, all over the world in every aspect of music, is something that can be described as The New Eclecticism. A few exceptions to the contrary, it is hard to tell the difference between a young American and a young English or Hungarian conductor, just as it is getting harder and harder to distinguish national styles in piano playing or composition. Even symphony orchestras are beginning to sound alike, no matter where their point of origin.

The chances are that—barring a universal disaster—future years will see less and less of a national school of conducting or, indeed, of any kind of nationalistic music making. Slowly the one-world idea is becoming more than mere idea. Intellectual life today has become highly international. Ideas are disseminated with, quite literally, the speed of light, and there has been since World War II a kind of cross-pollination that is making provincialism and nationalism a thing of the past. Even physical bodies are transported so quickly and efficiently that there has been a smoothing-out in human contact. It has come to the point where regional accents have all but been eliminated, even in Russia, where once-forbidden ideas are now openly discussed, and where there are active schools of ultra-modern music and painting. A sort of musical *lingua franca* will be the end result. As human beings, musicians, of course, will respond individually to the various stimuli they encounter and absorb; but the stimuli are beginning to be much the same everywhere, thanks to radio, television, Telstar, the jet plane, the tape recorder and LP records, the breakdown of social classes and the generally higher educational background. Interpreters of music will continue to be individuals in that they *are* individuals; but they also will be representatives of international rather than local thought. While none of us will live to see the Schiller-Beethoven ideal—*Alle Menschen werden Brüder*—it is inevitable in the progress of music, just as it is inevitable in the progress of mankind.

Index

[*This index lists all persons mentioned in the text. Wherever possible, dates and places of birth and death are given, for conductors only.*]